HOW TO MAKE THE UNIVERSE RIGHT

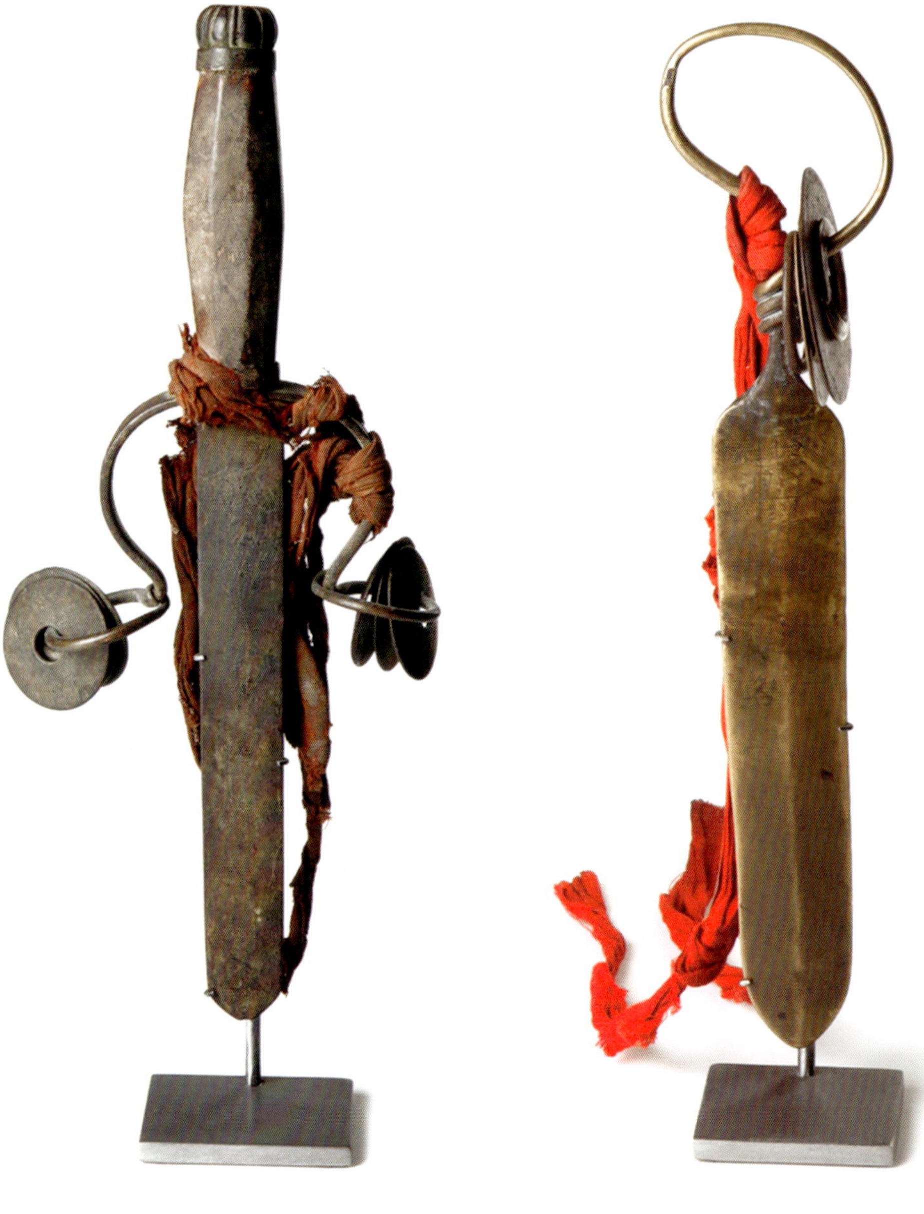

HOW TO MAKE THE UNIVERSE RIGHT

The Art of the Shaman from Vietnam and Southern China

Trian Nguyen

The Catalogue of an Exhibition
Curated by Barry Kitnick, Dan Mills,
and Trian Nguyen

Art, Design & Architecture Museum
University of California, Santa Barbara

Published by the Art, Design & Architecture Museum, UC Santa Barbara, Santa Barbara, CA 93106-7130, in conjunction with the exhibition *How to Make the Universe Right: The Art of the Shaman from Vietnam and Southern China.*

Exhibition dates: January 17–May 1, 2015

Library of Congress Cataloging-in-Publication Data
Nguyen, Trian, author.
How to make the universe right : the art of the shaman from Vietnam and southern China / Trian Nguyen ; [includes] the catalogue of an exhibition curated by Barry Kitnick, Dan Mills, and Trian Nguyen.
pages cm
Published in conjunction with an exhibition held January 17-May 1, 2015 at the Art, Design & Architecture Museum, University of California, Santa Barbara.
Includes bibliographical references.
Summary: "Exhibition catalogue featuring the collection of Barry and Jill Kitnick of Vietnamese shamanic art and artifacts, with a monographic essay on the material by Asian art scholar Trian Nguyen"-- Provided by publisher.
ISBN 978-0-942006-12-4 (pbk. : alk. paper) --
ISBN 978-0-942006-16-2 (e-book)
1. Art, Vietnamese--Exhibitions. 2. Art, Chinese--Exhibitions. 3. Ceremonial objects--Vietnam--Exhibitions. 4. Ceremonial objects--China, Southwest--Exhibitions. 5. Shamanism--Vietnam--Exhibitions. 6. Shamanism--China, Southwest--Exhibitions. 7. Minorities--Vietnam--Religion--Exhibitions. 8. Minorities--China, Southwest--Religion--Exhibitions. I. University of California, Santa Barbara. Art, Design & Architecture Museum, issuing body. II. Title.
N7314.N463 2015
709.597'07479491--dc23
2014041419

EDITED BY
Thomas Frick

DESIGNED BY
Studio Sigler, Santa Barbara, CA

TYPESET IN
Minion and Gotham

PRINTED & BOUND BY
Haagen Printing | Typecraft Inc., Santa Barbara, CA

A NOTE ABOUT NAMES, TERMS, AND THEIR TRANSLITERATION

The ethnic minorities discussed in this catalogue migrated from China to the mountainous regions of Vietnam. Though they adopted the local language for daily communication, they used written Chinese for religious and literary purposes. In this book one will find Chinese and Vietnamese terms along with romanized transliterations and English translations. Pinyin is the current system for transcribing the Mandarin pronunciations of Chinese characters into the Roman alphabet. Scholarly writings published before the early 1980s used the Wade-Giles system. For example, Celestial Master Zhang is written with three Chinese (C) characters as 張 天 師. The Yao (Y) sound the characters as Tsiang T'in Sai (based on a Wade-Giles romanization). Zhang Tienshi is the Pinyin (P) version. Finally, in modern Vietnamese (V) the name is Trương Thiên Sư. Some deities have only one consistent English translation, such as the Jade Emperor (玉 皇, C; Nyut Hung, Y; Yuhuang, P; Ngọc Hoàng, V). Others have various English renditions. For example, 拾 殿 冥 王, (C) (Tsiep Tin Ming Hung, Y; Shi Dien Ming Wang, P; Thập Điện Minh Vương, V) can be translated in many different ways: The Ten Kings of the Underworld, or Hell, or Purgatory, or Hades; the Ten Courts of Hell; the Ten Yama Kings; and the Lords of the Ten Tribunals of Hades. For consistency, only one English translation is used.

ILLUSTRATION CREDITS
Checklist numbers follow the order of illustrations in the text. Following each checklist item the Kitnick Collection number will be found in parentheses.
Photography for Kitnick numbers 1–325 is by Scott McClane.
Photography for Kitnick numbers 0001–0230 and altar on p.10 is by Chris Owen.
Field photos on pp. 41, 51, and 135 are courtesy of 54 Traditions, Hanoi, Vietnam.

FRONT COVER
The High Constable (detail), dated 1899
Handmade mulberry paper, pigments, rice paper attachments, bamboo sticks, string, 45¼ x 17 in.
Red Yao, Vietnam

BACK COVER
Ritual robe, c. late 19th–early 20th century
Handmade textile, embroidery, 45½ x 29 ¼ in.
Tày, Vietnam

PAGE ii (left)
Ritual sword with rattle, c. late 19th–early 20th century
Metal, wood, textile, 16¼ in.
Yao, China or Vietnam

PAGE ii (right)
Ritual sword with rattle, c. late 19th century
Bronze, red textile, 10⅝ in.
Hmong, China or Vietnam

CONTENTS

FOREWORD

HOW TO MAKE THE UNIVERSE RIGHT presents an extraordinary group of painted scrolls and ceremonial objects used by shamans of the Yao, Tày, Sán Dìu, Cao Làn, Nùng, Sán Chảy, and other ethnic minority peoples. Originally from the southwestern and southern provinces of China, these groups migrated to Vietnam during the Qing dynasty (1644–1912) and settled in the mountainous regions of the north. Each brought along its own tradition of shamanism, which includes the use of scroll paintings, musical instruments, clothing, and other ritual articles. These remarkable objects, and the complex systems of shamanic spiritual life in which they are used, are the focus of the exhibition and catalogue *How to Make the Universe Right.*

A shaman is a person who serves as an intermediary between the physical and spiritual worlds. This ability is used to cure illnesses, foretell and even change the future, and interact with spiritual forces in myriad ways. In order to become a shaman, one must go through rigorous education, training, and culturally specific initiation rites. For the Yao, this includes learning the precepts and pantheon of Daoism. Other groups represented in the exhibition incorporate a synthesis of Daoism, Buddhism, aspects of Hinduism, Confucian ancestral worship, animism, and local folk beliefs into their practice.

An exhibition of sacred objects from these groups and on this scale is unprecedented in the United States, and will further the understanding of these little-known cultures in the West. The predominant portion of the exhibition consists of more than ninety scroll paintings in a wide variety of artistic styles. They depict—and by believers are thought to be inhabited by—deities, animals, and mythic creatures. Many of the other types of ritual objects and clothing featured are depicted in the paintings. For example, similar garments are worn, and scepters and musical instruments are held by the deities.

The scrolls, ceremonial costumes, masks, instruments, and associated ritual items represent an unbroken link to the past of Asian mountain cultures, whose roots go back thousands of years. Shamans throughout the centuries have inspired their peoples' vital spiritual life, binding them together and helping them "make the universe right" by rectifying wrongs, communicating with ancestors, and dealing with the unfriendly forces of nature.

This exhibition and book are the results of the collecting that Barry Kitnick has accomplished since 2002 during many trips to Vietnam and China, as well as in Europe, New York, San Francisco, Honolulu, and even a few antique shops in out-of-the-way locations. His sympathetic, knowledgeable, and sophisticated eye has led him to build a uniquely comprehensive and extraordinarily rich collection of shamanistic art and artifacts. We are grateful to Barry and Jill Kitnick for sharing these objects with our publics, and especially for making them available to the diasporic Vietnamese and Chinese communities in our regions. We are also grateful to Professor Trian Nguyen, whose extensive research is the basis for this catalogue. With their combined efforts we are able to present for the first time this fascinating material, complex in its subject matter and symbolism but fresh and exciting in its visual and aesthetic qualities.

Additional thanks go to the two teams who made the exhibition possible. At the Bates College Museum of Art, we thank William Low, curator; Anthony Shostak, education curator; Ayse Ikizler '15, research assistant, and Anne Odom, academic administrative assistant. We are also deeply grateful for the funding provided by a grant from the E. Rhodes and Leona B. Carpenter Foundation, anonymous donors, and the Departments of Art & Visual Culture and Asian Studies. At the Art, Design & Architecture Museum, we thank the vision of Mehmet Dogu, principal designer, and the work of Thuy Tran, assistant curator. In addition, Susan Lucke, registrar, and Michaela Upp, assistant to the director, provided invaluable support. We are grateful as well to our editor, Thomas Frick, and designer, Leslie Lewis Sigler, for their assistance in producing this book.

Dan Mills, Director
Bates College Museum of Art

Bruce Robertson, Acting Director
Art, Design & Architecture Museum
UC Santa Barbara

PREFACE AND ACKNOWLEDGMENTS

THE DEVELOPMENT OF THIS EXHIBITION and the writing of this catalogue have provided me with an opportunity to study the ceremonial paintings and the ritual objects of the Yao, Cao Làn–Sán Chỉ, Sán Dìu, Tày, and Nùng peoples of northern Vietnam in the Barry and Jill Kitnick Collection. Though I am familiar with traditional folk paintings and popular woodblock prints from Đông Hồ village in Bắc Ninh province and Hàng Trống Street in Hanoi, this has been a new line of research for me in the study of religious art.

In the late 1990s and the fall of 2005, I visited several ethnic communities in Sapa district, Lào Cai province, and also toured the Bắc Hà open market, where there are large gatherings of the Yao, Tày, Nùng, and Hmong. While I had visited the Vietnam Museum of Ethnology and Vietnam Museum of Fine Arts in Hanoi in the summer of 2006, and been captivated by the sheer beauty of their collections of artifacts and costumes of ethnic minorities, I never imagined that one day I would be writing a catalogue detailing their cultural and spiritual presence in and outside of the art world.

Earlier scholarship and collection catalogues were of great value to my investigations. First and foremost, Jacques Lemoine's pioneering work *Yao Ceremonial Paintings* (1980) offers an excellent description of all major and minor Daoist deities employed by the Yao shaman priests in their ritual services and ceremonies. Jess G. Pourret's study *The Yao: The Mien and Mun Yao in China, North Vietnam, Laos, and Thailand* (2002) presents many different perspectives on the Yao.

However, neither of these writings touches upon ceremonial paintings and ritual items from the other ethnic minorities of the region. Phan Ngọc Khuê's *Taoist Paintings of North Vietnam* (2008) was very helpful in this regard, because it not only provides historical and religious background but also describes and analyzes major ceremonial paintings. Three major catalogues supplemented his work: *Ancient and Traditional Paintings of Vietnam* (1995), *Ceremonial Paintings of Northern Ethnic Minorities in Vietnam* (2006), and Phạm Đức Sĩ's collection *Vietnamese Ceremonial Paintings* (2009).

My understanding of these ceremonial paintings and ritual objects in relation to the roles of shaman priests and priestesses was greatly enhanced by the published works of Vietnamese anthropologists, ethnologists, and cultural specialists. Phan Ngọc Khuê's *The Ceremony of Hanging the Lamps of the Yao in Lô Giang, Lạng Sơn* (2003) and Lý Hành Sơn's *The Main Ceremonies and Rituals in the Life of the Yao People in Ba Bể, Bắc Kạn* (2003) offer a deep look into the ritual ceremonies of the Yao people. Nguyễn Thị Yên's *The Tày Shaman Then* contains the best field research on Tày shamanism and its high priests. Triệu Thị Mai's *The Journey of Searching the Shaman's Pựt Spirits* (2008) provides greater comprehension of the roles of shaman priestesses. Other important and well-researched works that I am indebted to are listed in the bibliography.

Additionally, I would like to express my gratitude to the following people for their support. First and foremost is Barry Kitnick, who gave me my first look at the entire collection and supported me throughout the creation of this catalogue. The photographs of Scott McClane and Chris Owen are crucial elements of this project, as they provide the visual evidence that underpins the entire book. Dan Mills, Bates College Museum Director, spent countless hours meeting with me almost every week, from mid-spring to the early winter of 2013, in planning this unique exhibition and making suggestions on the early drafts of the catalogue. Likewise, I am grateful to Thomas Frick, who spent much of the summer of 2014 editing the final version of the manuscript, from general concepts to minute details. The images in this catalogue, considered as separate musical notes, became alive, harmonized, and unified with the written text through Leslie Lewis Sigler's wonderful design; thus I am very grateful to her. I also am thankful to Mr. Phan Ngọc Khuê and several colleagues at the Vietnam Museum of Ethnology and Vietnam National Museum of Fine Arts in Hanoi for granting me the opportunity to see the cultural materials in question and offering invaluable insight into the arts of ethnic minorities. I spent many hours with Mr. Khuê at his house discussing the collections. Li-ping Miao and Xing Fan, two of my colleagues in the Chinese language program at Bates, helped me decipher some of the difficult inscriptions in the paintings. Michelle Pham and Do Thuy My, two of my student assistants, aided me in some early work. Ayse Irem Ikizler assisted in the proofreading of the catalogue. My thanks to Chris Schiff of the Bates Ladd Library for ordering books on the Yao. Nevertheless, I bear responsibility for any mistakes that remain in the book.

The research and writing of *How to Make the Universe Right* would not have been possible without the generosity of an anonymous supporter from California, two separate Bates Faculty Development grants (allowing me to travel to the Harvard libraries and to Vietnam), and a summer research apprenticeship, which helped a student involved with the development of the project. Finally, I am especially thankful to H-Trang, Thế-Yên, and Thế-Việt for their understanding, patience, and support throughout the writing of this book—traveling, research, and other chores—which occupied me for a while. Thank you all.

Trian Nguyen

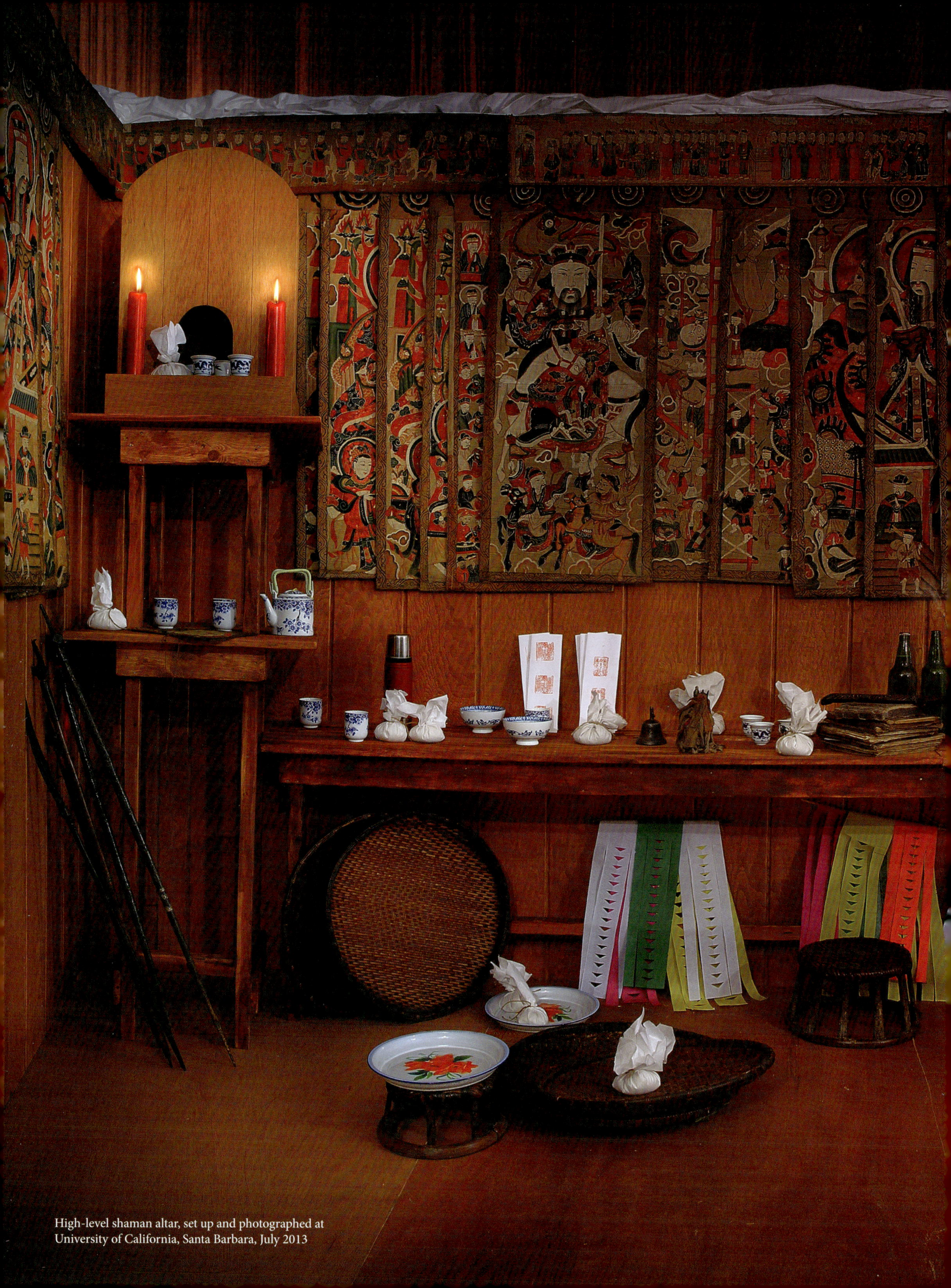

High-level shaman altar, set up and photographed at University of California, Santa Barbara, July 2013

INTRODUCTION

How to Make the Universe Right: The Art of the Shaman from Vietnam and Southern China presents an extraordinary group of shamanic painting scrolls and an extensive array of ceremonial objects of the Yao, Tày, Nùng, Sán Chay, Sán Dìu, and other small populations of northern Vietnam and southern China. These related ethnic minority peoples originally lived in the mountains of southwestern and southern provinces in China. For political reasons, they migrated to Vietnam over time and settled in the mountainous regions of the north.[1] Each group brought with it a particular tradition of shamanism, which includes the use of scroll paintings, musical instruments, clothing, and associated accessories. These remarkable objects and the complex system of shamanic spiritual life for which they are used—central to the Yao, Tày, Sán Dìu, and other groups—are the focus of *How to Make the Universe Right.*

A shaman is a person who serves as an intermediary between the physical and spiritual, the natural and supernatural worlds. This ability is used to cure illnesses, foretell and even change the future, interact with spiritual forces, and perform various kinds of rituals and ceremonies, ranging from welcoming a newborn baby to wedding celebrations and funeral rites. In order to become a shaman, one must go through rigorous education and training, or receive a calling through visionary dreams, along with culturally specific initiation rites. For the Yao, this training includes the ability to read and write Chinese and the study of Daoism. For other ethnic groups represented in this catalogue, the shamans incorporate an amalgamation of Daoism, Buddhism, aspects of Hinduism, Confucian ancestral worship, animism, and other naturalistic spiritual beliefs into their practices.

The sacred objects and portable religious icons used by shamans provide many vital clues as to how they communicate directly with the spirits of unseen worlds in order to exorcize evil demons and bring prosperity to families. Considered by shamans to be empowered with spiritual forces, and unique and beautiful in their own way, these painted scrolls, ceremonial objects, and costumes are inherited from generation to generation, highlighting the importance of the spiritual path among village communities. They embody the extraordinary richness of artistic traditions and the religious heritage of cultures that, for many reasons, are gradually disappearing.

To understand shamanist practice, it is worthwhile giving a brief account of their ethnic and religious backgrounds. For centuries the Yao, Tày, Nùng, Sán Chay, and Sán Dìu peoples, dwelling in the mountainous regions of northern Vietnam, have engaged in ceremonial religious practices using painted scrolls, masks, musical instruments, and other handcrafted items. These artifacts, full of symbols and spiritual intent, are also beautiful art objects, as evident in the collection of Barry and Jill Kitnick featured in this catalogue. Comprising more than five hundred important items, the Kitnick Collection includes scroll sets, ceremonial robes, and ritual instruments. The breadth and depth of the collection provides an exciting opportunity to explore details of Yao ceremonies and traditions and to gain a clearer understanding of the Yao people, along with related ethnic groups who share some of their religious beliefs and ritual practices.

These ethnic groups all originally lived in China, but at various periods migrated to remote mountainous regions of northern Vietnam. During the Ming (1368–1644) and Qing (1644–1912) dynasties, the Yao, consisting of seven subgroups,[2] settled in more than seventeen Vietnamese provinces. Currently the Yao population numbers nearly three-quarters of a million people,[3] the ninth largest of fifty-four ethnic groups in Vietnam. Although related, the subgroups, especially the women, wear different costumes, but their major religious belief—Daoism—and its initiation rituals, paintings, ceremonial instruments, and cultural roots are basically unified.

The Tày are the second largest ethnic group, with a population of approximately 1.5 million. The Tày culture and language are closely related to the Nùng, thus it is convenient to discuss them together. The Tày have been present in the northeastern region of Vietnam for more than two millennia, with many Tày subgroups having been integrated into Vietnamese culture.[4] The Nùng also have a long history of settlement in the northern regions of Vietnam, and have had a close relationship with the Vietnamese people as well.[5] In a recent survey, the Nùng population was approximately 850,000.[6]

Unlike the Yao, whose religion is primarily based on Daoism, Tày and Nùng beliefs are a mixture of Buddhism, Daoism, Confucianism, and animism. In particular, they honor the Buddhist bodhisattva Guanyin, the Goddess of Mercy, commonly known as Avalokiteśvara, who holds a special place among them, and most Tày and Nùng families have an altar venerating this compassionate deity. Some scholars remark that they also incorporate their own indigenous beliefs, employing a mixture of all of these in their shamanic practice. For example, they honor the Flower Deities who bestow children, the Midwife Deity who protects newly born children, and the Mother Goddesses who oversee rivers, forests, soil, and plants.[7] In their shamanist rituals, they often combine Buddhist sutras, Daoist texts, and their indigenous literature and manuscripts.[8] They also believe that their property, domestic animals, land, soil, and forest are monitored and ruled by the local God of the Earth, who protects and provides them with livelihood.[9]

The Sán Chay are composed of two subgroups, known as the Cao Làn and Sán Chỉ. Their ancestors were from the border region of China, moved to Vietnam about four hundred years ago, and settled in the neighboring Vietnamese provinces.[10] Their population, about 150,000, is the smallest among the ethnic peoples represented in this collection.[11] Their religious beliefs have been strongly influenced by Buddhism and Daoism, mixed with popular Chinese divinities. For example, the basic set of the three painting scrolls entitled *The Three Pure Ones and Three Merciful Ones* (三 清 三 慈) typically represents an amalgamation of Daoist and Buddhist divinities (Figs. 1–3). This set combines the three supreme Daoist deities—the Supreme, Grand, and Jade Pure Ones (三 清) with the Buddhas of the Three Periods—the Past, the Present, and the Future—also known as the Three Jewels (三 寶), referring to the Buddha, the Dharma, and the Sangha.[12] Other popular Buddhist deities are also illustrated in the scrolls, such as the Bodhisattva Samantabhadra, who is associated with great vows and action, and rides an elephant (Fig. 1); the Bodhisattva Mañjuśrī, a personal manifestation of transcendent wisdom, riding a lion; and the famous Indian Buddhist monk Maudgalyāyana, who ventured to the underworld to save his mother from being tortured in the realms of hell (Fig. 2). The well-known Chinese Buddhist monk Xuanzang rides on horseback and is vividly depicted on his long journey to India in search of the Buddhist sutras (Fig. 3). Xuanzang is

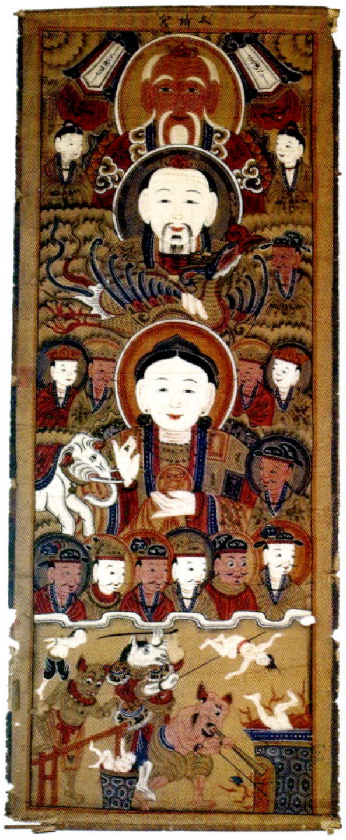

Fig. 1

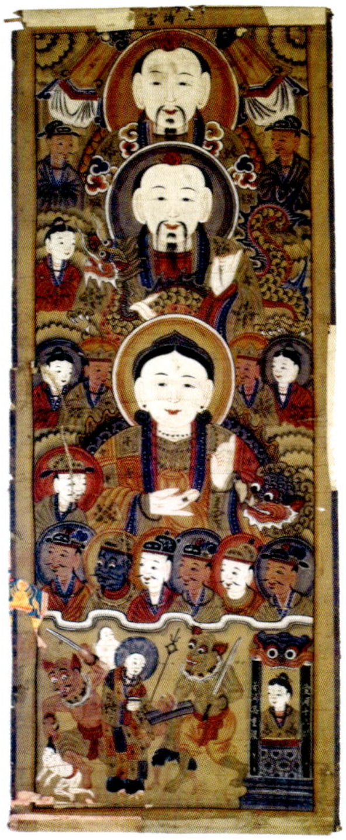

Fig. 2

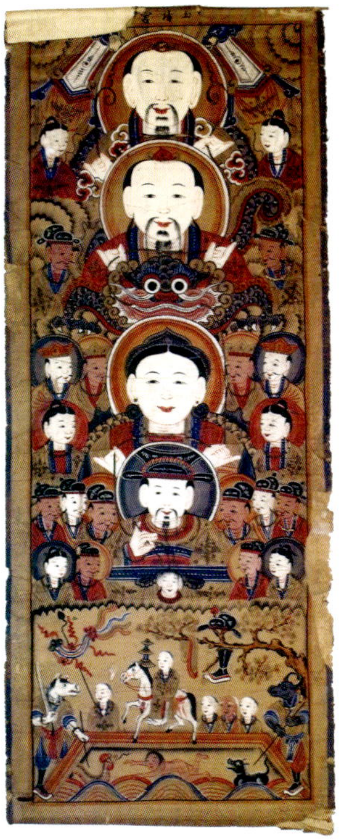

Fig. 3

worshipped as an important deity among the Tày and Nùng shaman priests (and priestesses, who are called *pụt*), known as the disciples who intercede with the Buddha to carry out spiritual missions.

The Sán Dìu are another distant subgroup of the mountainous Yao, known in Chinese characters as 山 瑶. Originally they lived in southern China and are thought to have migrated to northern Vietnam from Guangdong at the end of the Ming and the early Qing dynasties. Their population is estimated to be 147,000.[13] Vĩnh Phúc province has the largest number of Sán Dìu residents in Vietnam, 37,000, or 25% of the population (2009). They speak an archaic variant of Cantonese with some Iu Mien (one of the main languages spoken by the Yao in Southern China, Vietnam, Laos, and Thailand). Unlike the major Yao people, the Sán Dìu believe in an amalgam of religions, mainly Daoism mixed with major elements of Buddhism, Hinduism, animism, and ancestral worship.[14]

As we have seen, the religious beliefs of the Yao and the other ethnic minority groups discussed here combine many elements. Of these, Daoism plays the most prominent role, guiding ritual practices for important life events such as weddings and funerals, and praying for the dead. For the Yao in particular, Daoist deities are central to many religious practices in the lives of individuals, families, clans, and communities. The rituals and ceremonies performed by the high shaman priests of the Yao and other ethnic peoples involve placating various heavenly deities and spirits of the natural world, honoring ancestors, and determining propitious times to engage in significant actions, for which they have received years of spiritual training from master practitioners. Among these peoples there is no conflict or factionalism regarding their religions and belief systems. In fact, they have no organized church or religious leaders, no Daoist shrines or Buddhist temples. All ritual cer-

Fig. 1
Palace of the Grand Pure One, c. early to mid-20th century
Cao Làn–Sán Chi (Sán Chay), Vietnam

Fig. 2
Palace of the Supreme Pure One, c. early to mid-20th century
Cao Làn–Sán Chi (Sán Chay), Vietnam

Fig. 3
Palace of the Jade Pure One, c. early to mid-20th century
Cao Làn–Sán Chi (Sán Chay), Vietnam

emonies and religious services take place in homes or at makeshift altars temporarily constructed for special events. The deities and ritual texts of these two great religions provide the shaman priests with the spiritual power to communicate with ancestors, deal with unfriendly natural forces, and treat diseases. As a result of this complex mingling of influences, analysis of the religious subjects of this collection, especially of the scroll paintings, presents an intellectual challenge, due to the wide range of deities, mythical figures, and legendary characters represented.

Long ago these ethnic groups learned to read and write Chinese characters, which enabled them to use classic texts and ritual manuals, both Daoist and Buddhist. Chinese, considered to be a sacred language, was also used to compose the memorials and petitions that were sent to the Jade Emperor and other high gods during rituals and ceremonies. An ability to use classical Chinese was regarded as a required asset in order to become a shaman priest or priestess. Like the Vietnamese people, these minority groups also used Chinese characters to create their own writing, known as Nôm script (㝐 喃), to represent their native words. This script was used for popular literature as well as for prayer texts and ritual manuals, which are written in a poetic form of verse and prose, used mainly by Tày and Nùng priests and priestesses. The Yao high shaman priests, on the other hand, use ritual manuals written in classical Chinese. For the Yao people, the Nôm script is only employed in popular literature, myths, epic poetry, love songs, and other secular writing.[15]

However, during the last two decades the majority of young people, aged fifteen to twenty-five, have not been able to read and write in Chinese and Nôm and do not want to study these classical scripts.[16] A simple reason is that most of the younger generation come from families whose members no longer follow the traditional path of becoming a high priest, and are not trained in Chinese. As a result, the older books and ritual texts have no purpose and are discarded. In addition, the current Vietnamese government policy in public schools requires students to study modern Vietnamese, which uses the Roman alphabet.[17] Finally, Protestant missionaries have aggressively penetrated these groups of people in several regions and attempted to convert them to Christianity. Once converted, they discard their traditions and ritual items.[18] Thus, in many ways, not knowing the Chinese language, the basis of their shamanic practices, has caused some of the traditional culture to fade away. However, since the Vietnamese government has recently been more open with its policy of religious tolerance, Yao religious shamanic practice has gradually revived. Also, with the help of the Ford Foundation, many old books written in Chinese have been collected and preserved, and a new movement of learning the Chinese written language and Nôm script has slowly begun in Lào Cai province.[19]

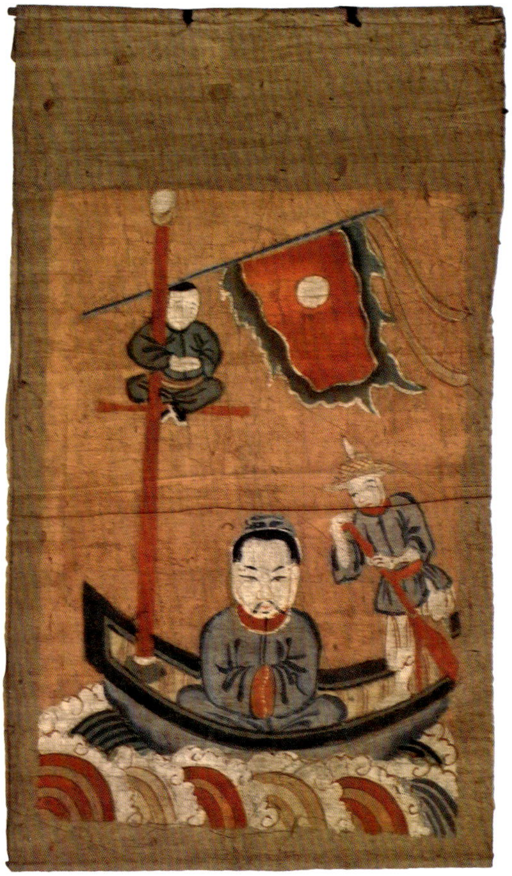

Fig. 4

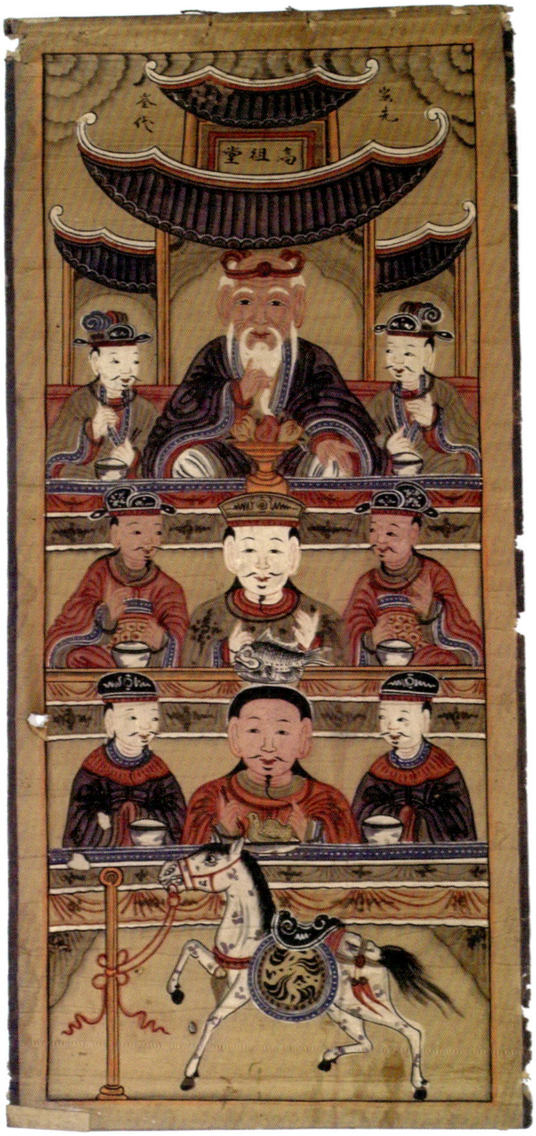

Fig. 5

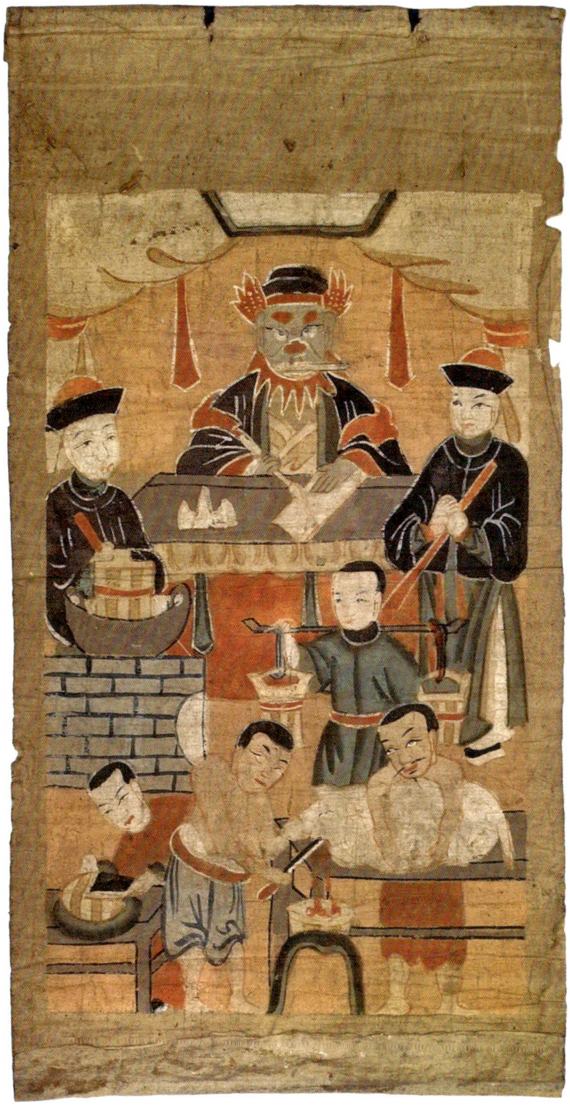

Fig. 6

Fig. 4
Pan Hu's Five Banners of Knights, c. late 19th–early 20th century
Red Yao, China

Fig. 5
The Family Forebears, c. early to mid-20th century
Cao Làn–Sán Chi (Sán Chay), Vietnam

Fig. 6
Enforcers of Fasting and Charity, c. late 19th–early 20th century
Red Yao, China

Painting Sets, Scroll Formats, and Thematic Subjects

The Kitnick Collection includes a variety of complete and incomplete painting sets as well as individual paintings. The majority of painted scroll sets range in number of included images from the essential basic set of three, to a medium-sized grouping of ten (as in a set of the Ten Kings of the Underworld, discussed in that chapter) or twelve (see the chapter on the Twelve Guardian Deities), to the largest set, which can comprise more than twenty-seven pieces. These include the fixed set of seventeen (or sometimes eighteen) pieces, plus two or four paintings of the Four Heavenly Messengers (discussed in that chapter), one or two long horizontal scrolls (see "Finding the Way to Heaven"), and other small-sized paintings, such as the Ancestors (Fig. 5),[20] the Enforcers of Fasting and Charity (Fig. 6),[21] and Pan Hu's Five Banners of Knights (Fig. 4).[22] Although produced by different ethnic groups residing in various regions, the religious themes and subject matter are often similar. There are more than one hundred thirty painted scrolls in the collection depicting not only an assortment of Daoist deities, who figure prominently in Yao myths and legends, but also a range of buddhas, bodhisattvas, and other figures important in Buddhism, along with some popular Hindu deities.

Vertical Handscrolls

There are two types of scrolls represented in the collection, following the traditional Chinese formats: the vertical handscroll and the long horizontal handscroll. The vertical scroll, also known as a hanging scroll, is a depiction of religious deities or legendary figures. This type, hung on the walls or on the main altar during ceremonies, usually comes in fixed sets either commissioned by the owner or inherited within the family.

The basic set of three paintings, known as the Administration, is the minimum requirement for a newly ordained Yao man when he is initiated into the religious path. This set introduces the most important Daoist deities for a young Yao man to be familiar with and honor during his life. It includes the High Constable, the God of the Sea, and the Ancestors (see the chapter on the three basic scrolls). When viewing the three basic scrolls, a Yao man would proudly reflect on his official recognition as a full-fledged member of the Yao community, with the right to participate in all social activities and be united with his ancestors after death.

The larger set of paintings also belongs to the vertical handscroll type. It usually consists of thirteen or fourteen scrolls plus the basic set of three paintings, making a full set of seventeen (or sometimes eighteen or more scrolls; see the chapter on the full set of scrolls). This set is acquired by an adult Yao man who is fully ordained as a high shaman Daoist priest. At this stage he is able to perform all the important religious rituals. In the set all of the supreme Daoist deities are depicted either on separate hanging scrolls or grouped within the same scroll. Two important ideas underlie the complete training of a high shaman. First, he has an established family and is married to a dutiful wife, with whom he shares the family responsibilities. Second, under the influence of Chinese Buddhism, it is believed that if a person commits severe crimes or deadly sins on earth, his soul will be taken to the underworld after death and judged by the Ten Kings of the Underworld. But if a Yao man has been initiated, and has observed moral and ethical principles, he can pass through this judgment and be reincarnated into a better life. His initiation also means that as a Yao shaman priest he can perform services for the dead, which is the foremost ritual in the Yao community. In short, the complete set of painted scrolls is required for a high Yao shaman priest. Wherever they are unrolled and set up, the scrolls become a holy shrine allowing the shaman priest to conduct ceremonies.

In the full set of Yao hanging scrolls, scenes of the Ten Kings of the Underworld are painted onto a single scroll (Figs. 7, 105). For the Tày, whose religious belief system is heavily influenced by Buddhism, the artist depicts the Ten Kings of the Underworld in ten scrolls, one king per painting. With ten scrolls devoted to scenes of hell, the Tày kings are vividly and graphically portrayed; some scenes also refer to three popular episodes from the famous epic novel *Journey to the West*, a story that serves an educational purpose. In one, Emperor Huizong of the Tang dynasty journeys through the underworld to witness terrible punishments in hell; in another, a husband dares to go to hell to save his wife and preserve family happiness. These episodes emphasize themes such as the righteous king, the principled minister, and the good husband. Moreover, Buddhist morality and basic teachings, such as the concepts of karma, rebirth, and reincarnation, are vividly proclaimed both visually and through inscriptions of verses on each scroll. In the ritual Praying for the Soul of the Dead to be Liberated from Hell and Born into Heaven (or the Pure Land), the entire set of ten painted scrolls is hung around the main room of a house, and the shaman priest imagines them as the real underworld on which he must concentrate while chanting the ritual, thereby entering hell to save the soul of the recently dead. The lower sections of scrolls depicted in Fig. 1 and Fig. 3 illustrate this concept and practice.

The Kitnick collection has a unique twelve-painting set of the Sán Dìu people from Vĩnh Phúc province (see the chapter "The Twelve Guardian Deities"). Similar to the Tày, the Sán Dìu's religious belief is a mixture of Daoism, Buddhism, Hinduism, animism, and ancestral worship. These synthesized elements can be seen in this scroll set of the guardian deities, which include Indra and Brahma (Hinduism); the Buddha's soldiers and Guardian Deities of the Left and the Right (Buddhism); the Heavenly King, Earthly King, King of the Underworld, King of the Water Realm, Lords of the Three Caves, Governor of the Earth Soldiers, the Twelve Divinities, and Celestial Master Li (Daoism); the God of Medicine,

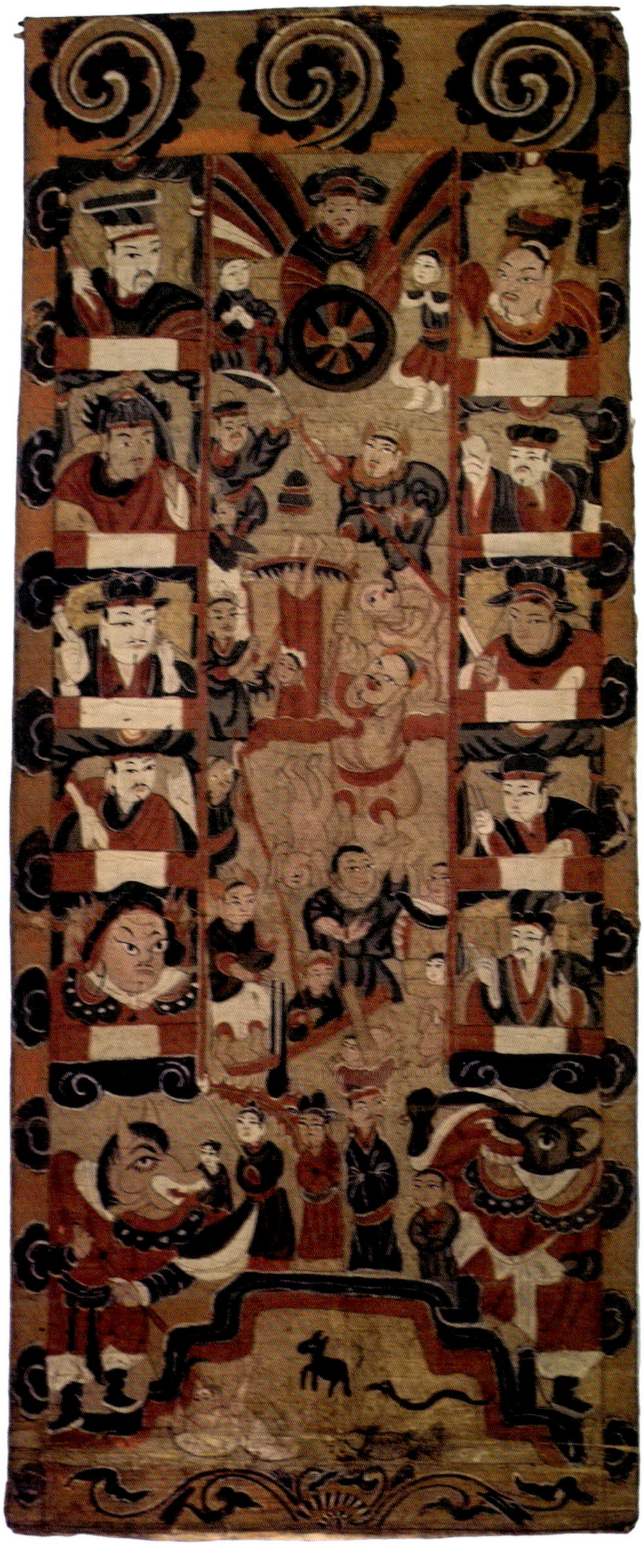

Fig. 7
Ten Kings of the Underworld, 1829–30
Red Yao, China

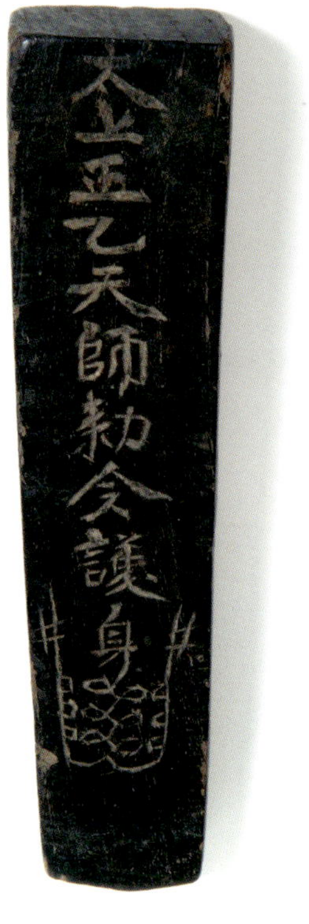

Fig. 8

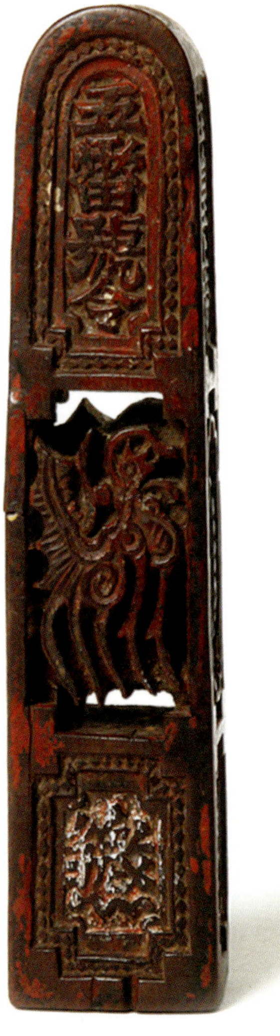

Fig. 9

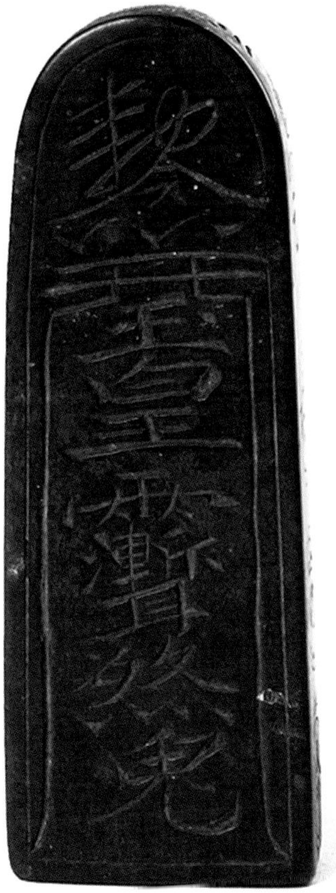

Fig. 10

Fig. 8
Ritual scepter, c. late 19th–early 20th century
Tày, Vietnam

Fig. 9
Ritual scepter, c. late 19th century
Yao, China or Vietnam

Fig. 10
Ritual scepter, c. late 19th century
Tày, Vietnam

and the deity of Chinese writing (Chinese myths and legends). When being ordained, a common practice among shaman priests and priestesses is to receive a certain number of spirit soldiers to help them communicate with the invisible spirit worlds. These spirit soldiers originally belonged to specific divine army divisions and were assigned to a shaman to carry out religious work, as authorized by the Jade Emperor. When granted spirit soldiers, the shaman then acquires the authorized tablets (Figs. 8–10) allowing him to command them during the performance of rituals. Among these soldiers, Daoist deities are dominant because the shaman priests believe they possess more magical authority than deities from other religions.

Distinguished among the painted handscrolls in the collection is a Sán Dìu set of three of the most popular Buddhist bodhisattvas: Avalokiteśvara, Mañjuśrī, and Samantabhadra, known in Vietnamese as Quán Thế Âm (Fig. 12), Văn Thù (Fig. 13), and Phổ Hiền (Fig. 11). It is very rare for these three to be depicted as a set among the Sán Dìu people. The first bodhisattva, Avalokiteśvara, known in Chinese as Guanyin and usually rendered in a female manifestation, is also popular in Yao Daoist scroll paintings. She is always represented with other Daoist deities, such as in the Heavenly Host scroll, where she occupies the central position on the second level of the painting (Fig. 14). The Bodhisattva Samantabhadra is often incorporated in the cohort of such Daoist-Buddhist assemblies (as in Fig. 1), rather than standing alone. As the Tày, Nùng, and Sán Dìu's beliefs are strongly influenced by Buddhism, accordingly in their main family altar they honor a painting of Guanyin, which is flanked by paintings of a tiger and a dragon (Figs. 35, 36). This compassionate deity will ensure the family's safety and prosperity, and the two auspicious animals will ward off evil spirits, preventing calamity.[23] In this set, originally owned by a Sán Dìu family, Guanyin, in the central scroll, is seated on a lotus throne. She holds a Buddhist sutra, her signature attribute, and a nectar vase is placed on her right (Fig. 12). Flanking her on the right is Mañjuśrī, seated

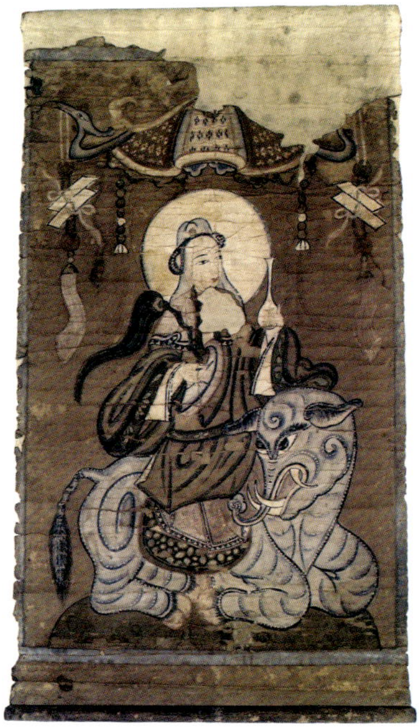

Fig. 11

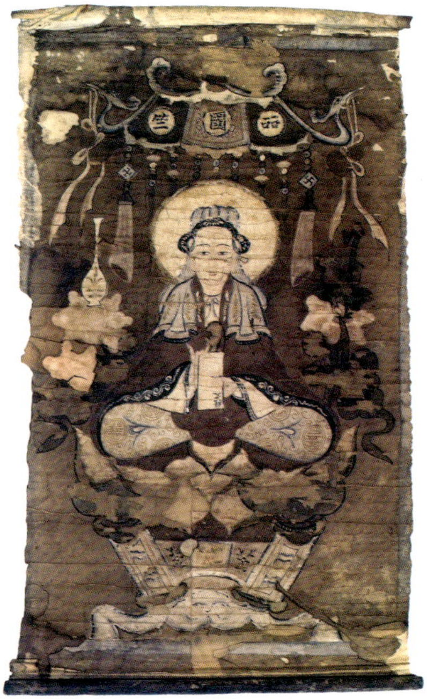

Fig. 12

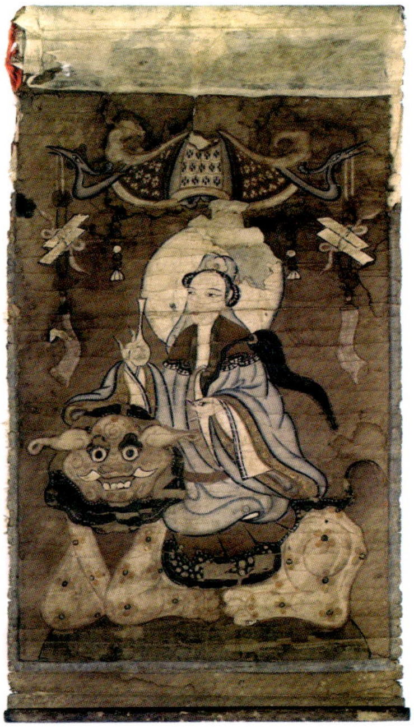

Fig. 13

on a lion (Fig. 13), and to her left is Samantabhadra, seated on a white elephant (Fig. 11). This bodhisattva triad symbolizes compassion, wisdom, and action, the foundations of Buddhism.

The Buddhist trinity is a common topic in painted scrolls. Two different sets in the collection reflect two distinct worldviews. The first set represents the Buddhas of the Three Periods—the Past, the Present, and the Future. The handscroll of the Buddha of the Present is always positioned at the center, easily recognized by a cartouche written in Chinese (當今皇帝壽萬歲萬萬歲), meaning, "Long live the current emperor!" (Fig. 16), implying a prayer from monks and Buddhist communities for the current ruler. The Buddha of the Present sits on a white lotus, wearing a monk's robe and attended by four Daoist immortals. On the left is the Buddha of the Past, attended by two Buddhist deities: the Bodhisattva Samantabhadra standing by his white elephant, and the Dharma guardian behind him (Fig. 15). On the right, a pair of Daoist immortals attends the Buddha of the Future, with the Bodhisattva Mañjuśrī standing next to his blue lion and the Dharma guardian (Fig. 17). Accompanying the Buddhist subjects in this set are the eight Daoist immortals, identifiable by their robes and attributes (holding a fly-whisk or bowl of sacred water).

Another set of three paintings (Figs. 56–58) portrays the Buddhas of the Three Periods in the top register, with small images of the popular Bodhisattva Mañjuśrī on the extreme right (Fig. 58) and Bodhisattva Samantabhadra on the extreme left (Fig. 56). The four levels below are crowded with Daoist deities, including the Governor of Water, Governor of the Sky, Lords of the Three Realms (water, earth, and underworld), Taisui (God of the Year), heavenly masters and marshals riding on horses, the Lords of the Six Directions, and many more. Clearly the set acts as an assembly of many Buddhist and Daoist deities. The images of the Buddhas have recognizably female features including oval faces, with long, curly black hair wrapping around their heads; phoenixlike eyes; long, thin curly eyebrows; and earrings. In contrast, the majority of the Daoist deities are rendered less distinctively and lack fixed iconographical features. These female features indicate that the works were painted for the *pụt* and *then* shaman priestesses, common among the Nùng and Tày peoples, not high Yao Daoist shaman priests.

A type of miniature painting is represented by four portable scroll sets depicting the Buddhist and Daoist deities. They are from the Tày and Sán Chảy, though they can also be found among other ethnic groups. These paintings are primarily used during the ritual of praying for the dead, but are also employed in the ordination ceremony. The first set consists of the Buddhas of the Three Periods flanked by two popular bodhisattvas, Avalokiteśvara and Mahasthamaprapta (Fig. 18). All are depicted in a stylized manner without specific iconographical features. The second set consists of the Pure Land triad—the Buddha Amitābha, along with Avalokiteśvara and Mahasthamaprapta—which is the focus of worship in Pure Land Buddhism while praying for personal salvation and rebirth in Amitābha's Western Paradise, along with the Three Pure Ones, the Jade Emperor, the Lord of the Underworld, the Jade Girl, and the Golden Boy (Figs. 20, 21). The third and the fourth sets together portray the Ten Kings of the Underworld (see Fig. 19). Each figure was painted on paper, pasted onto thick cardboard, then affixed to a bamboo stick. These small images function as a portable altar for memorial services at burial sites, since the pointed bamboo sticks can easily be fixed in the ground. If used indoors, the set is arranged in a single line, with each scroll anchored in a bowl of sand or rice.

By reviewing all the vertical handscrolls from large to small, both sets and individual paintings, it is clear that this format is used to depict religious deities. If principal deities are present, each dominates the whole space (as with bodhisattvas in Figs. 11–13, or the two Daoist Celestial Masters in Figs. 22, 23), or the lower two-thirds of the image is accompanied by two attendants (as with the Three Pure Ones [Figs. 39, 40, 99–101], the Jade Emperor [Fig. 98], the Master of the Saints [Fig. 102], and Tai Wai [Figs. 95, 109]). Other midlevel deities share the space within the pictorial structure. The scrolls of the Ancestors/Heavenly Hosts, the Three Pure Ones, the Three Merciful Ones, and the Family Forebears are always thronged with major and minor deities. A

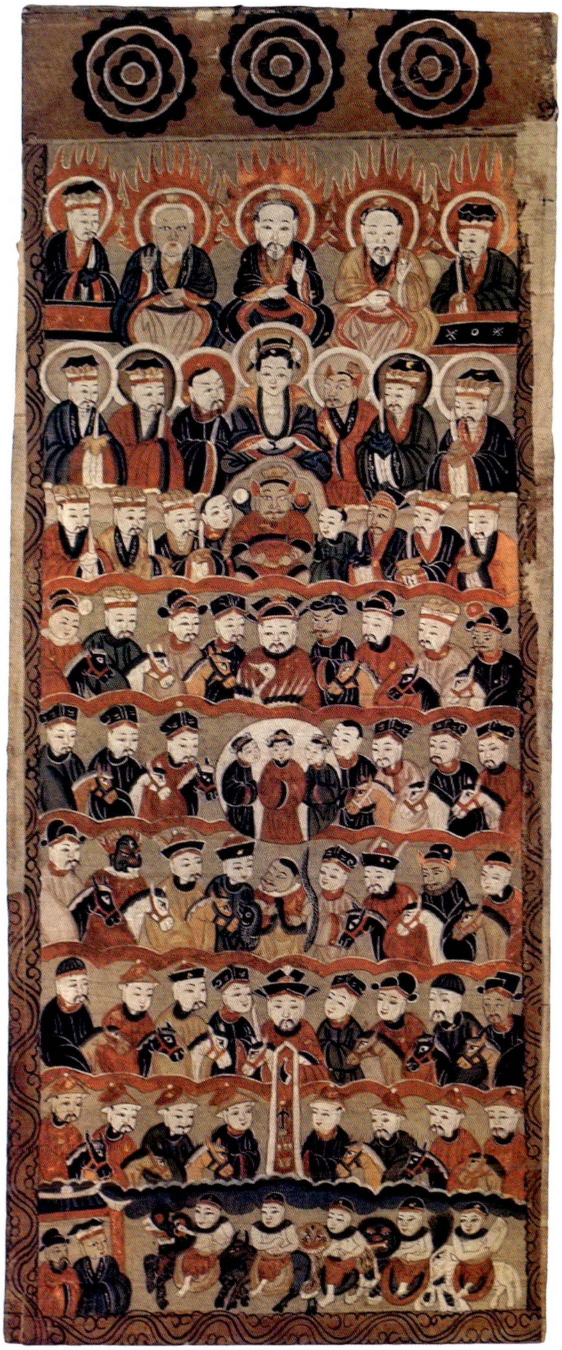

Fig. 14

Figs. 11, 12, 13:
The three popular bodhisattvas
From left: Samantabhadra (Bồ Tát Phổ Hiền), Avalokiteśvara (Bồ Tát Quán Thế Âm), Mañjuśrī (Bồ Tát Văn Thù),
c. late 19th–early 20th century
Sán Dìu, Vietnam.

Fig. 14
The Ancestors/Heavenly Host, 1819
Red Yao, China

significant number of the scrolls also include animals. Generally, all of the deities are highly regarded objects of devotional worship, and their scrolls are hung vertically on the wall behind the main altar during rituals. The hanging-scroll format dominates the collection of paintings. The Kitnick Collection also contains many individual scrolls that were separated from their sets, too many to discuss even briefly in this introductory essay.

In Yao Daoist rituals the placement of each scroll depends upon the importance of the figure it depicts, the most important deity occupying the center spot and lesser figures hierarchically fanned out on either side. In this manner the scrolls depicting the Three Pure Ones are placed in the center, with the Master of the Saints scroll to the left and the Jade Emperor scroll to the right, and so on. However, the shaman priests often do not always strictly follow that order, instead approximating it as they hang large scrolls layer upon layer, with small scrolls on top, the configuration contingent on the space in the house where the makeshift altar is set up.[24]

Long Horizontal and Vertical Handscrolls

The second major type of painting in the collection is the long, narrow handscroll, found in both vertical and horizontal pictorial formats. These long handscrolls have a similar purpose: to pray for the dead and guide their spirits toward heaven. However, long handscrolls from different ethnic groups reflect great pictorial diversity in the wide range of deities they represent.

The Yao painting known as *Dragon Bridge of the Great Dao* (Figs. 24, 137–140) is the oldest type of the long handcrolls in the Kitnick Collection (and probably in general). Since the Yao were the last group to migrate to northern Vietnam and thus preserved the Daoist tradition for the longest time, this scroll is without a single element of Buddhist influence. The Yao long scroll is a continuous form that reads from left to right, in which the viewer becomes a traveler moving through time and space. The majority of Daoist deities are represented in the scroll, along with the local God of the Earth. The most distinctive feature is the image of the souls of the recently deceased, a man or couple, being carried in sedan chairs on the way toward heaven. It also truly reflects the traditional Yao costumes, musical instruments, and their primary spiritual belief system.

Another type of scroll in the collection is vertical in format, reading from bottom to top. One example, called *Guiding the Soul* (Fig. 142), combines the members of Daoist pantheon with elements of Chinese folk belief. The scroll is also inscribed with Chinese characters identifying the names of deities, their dwelling places, and the passages that the soul must overcome to ultimately arrive at Daoist heaven. The Tày scroll *Praying for Salvation for the Dead* (Fig. 141a-q) prominently features members of Daoist pantheon and underscores concepts of the afterlife, the long journey of departed souls, and their judgment in the underworld before they are united with their ancestors in heaven. This remarkably long scroll presents the pictorial journey, the first part in horizontal format and the second part in vertical format (see “Finding the Way to Heaven”).

Finally, the Sán Dìu always include Buddhist figures—Buddhas, bodhisattvas, and other guardian

Figs. 15, 16, 17
The Three Jewels, also known as the Buddhas of the Three Periods. From left: the Dharma, the Buddha, and the Sangha, or the Buddha of the Past, the Present, and the Future, c. early to mid-20th century
Sán Dìu, Vietnam

Fig. 18
Buddhas and bodhisattvas, portable scrolls,
c. mid-20th century
Cao Làn–Sán Chi (Sán Chay), Vietnam

Fig. 19
Five Kings of the Underworld, portable scrolls,
c. mid-20th century
Cao Làn–Sán Chi (Sán Chay), Vietnam

Fig. 20
Buddhist and Daoist deities, portable scrolls,
c. early–mid-20th century
Tày, Vietnam

Fig. 21
Buddhist and Daoist deities, portable scrolls,
c. early–mid-20th century
Tày, Vietnam

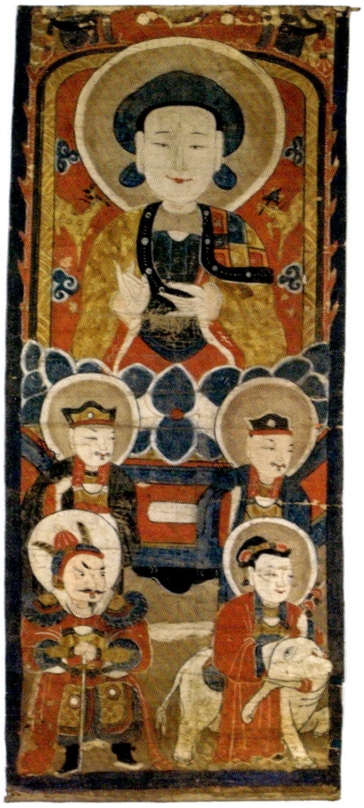

Fig. 15

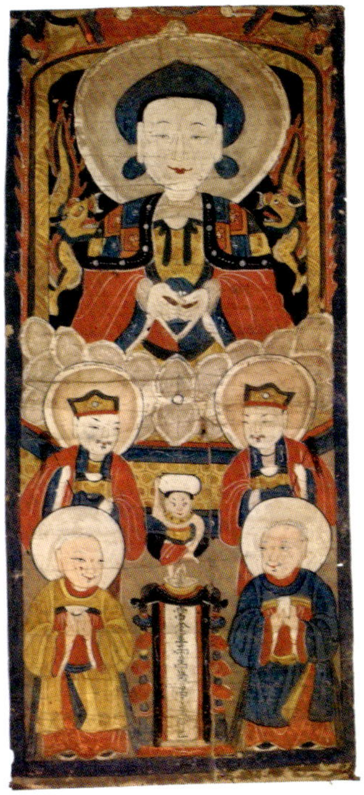

Fig. 16

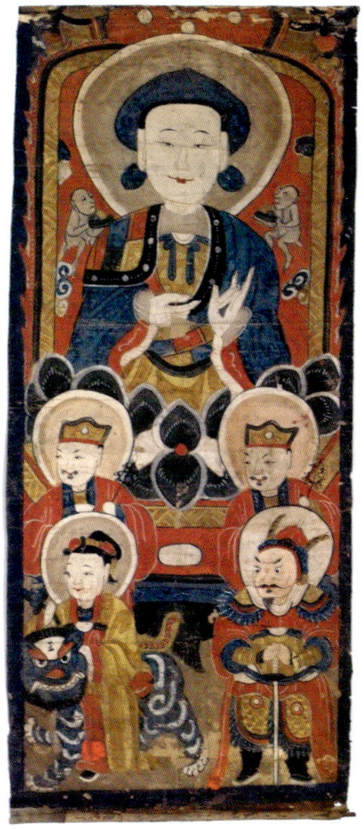

Fig. 17

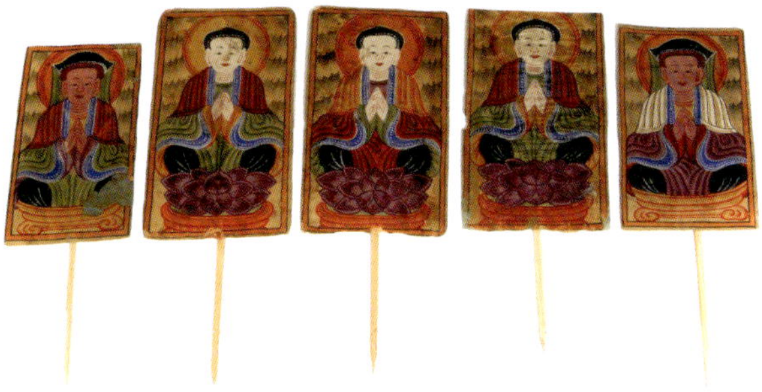

Fig. 18

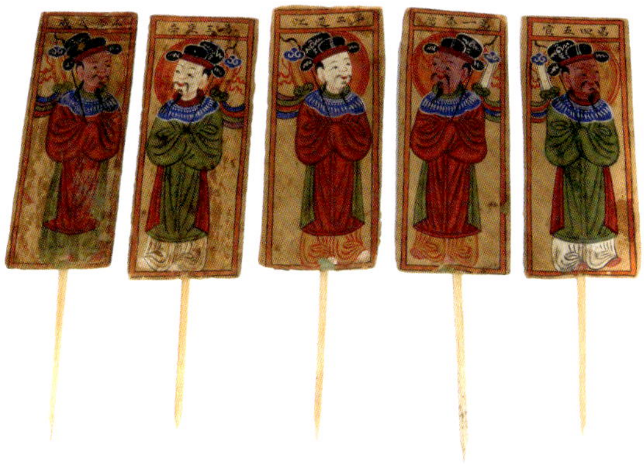

Fig. 19

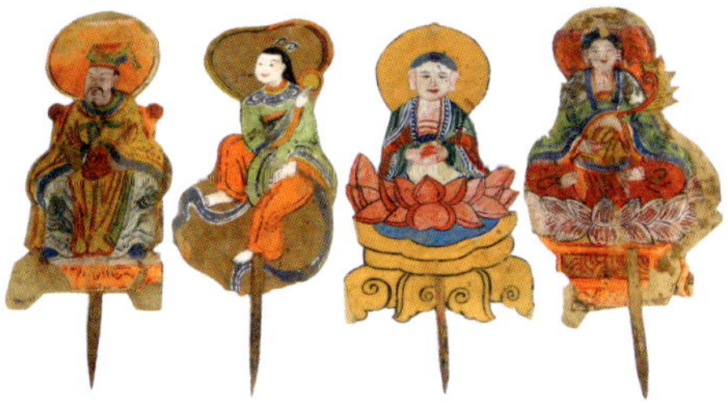

Fig. 20

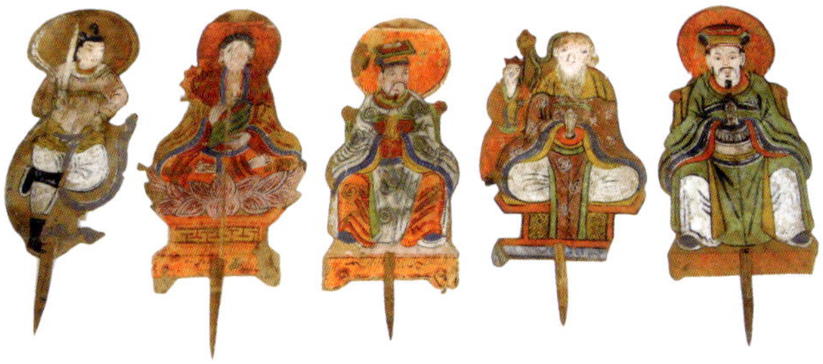

Fig. 21

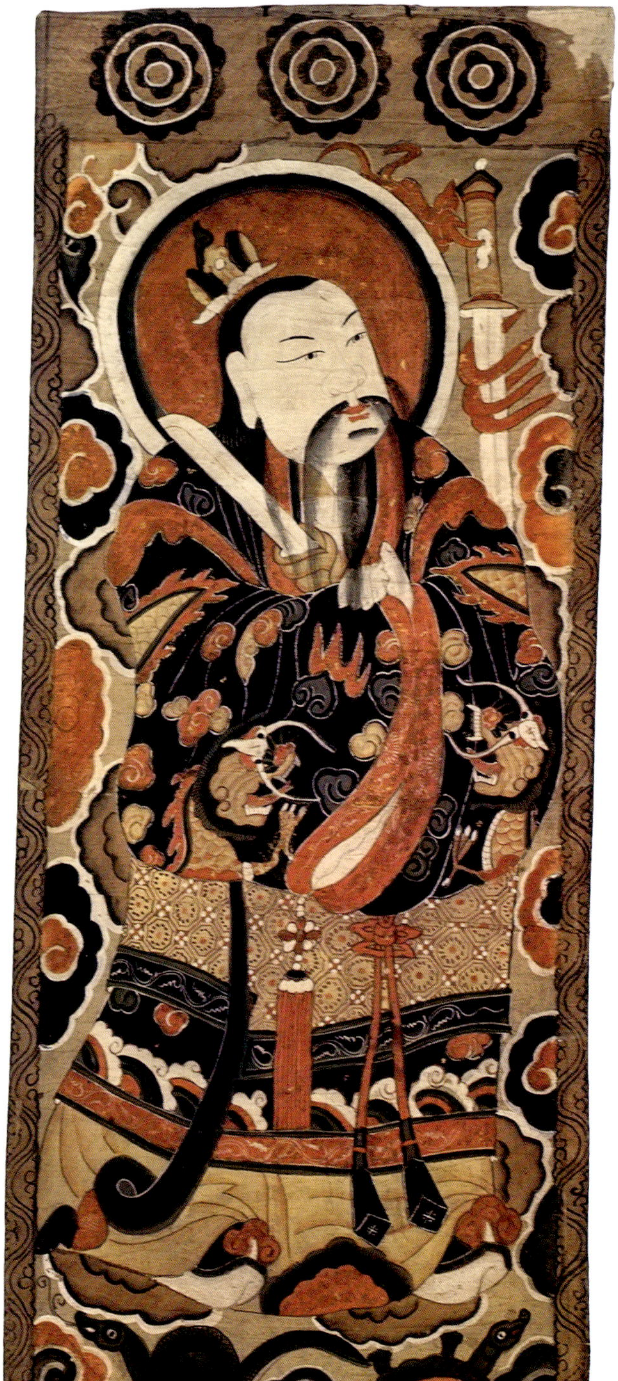

Fig. 22

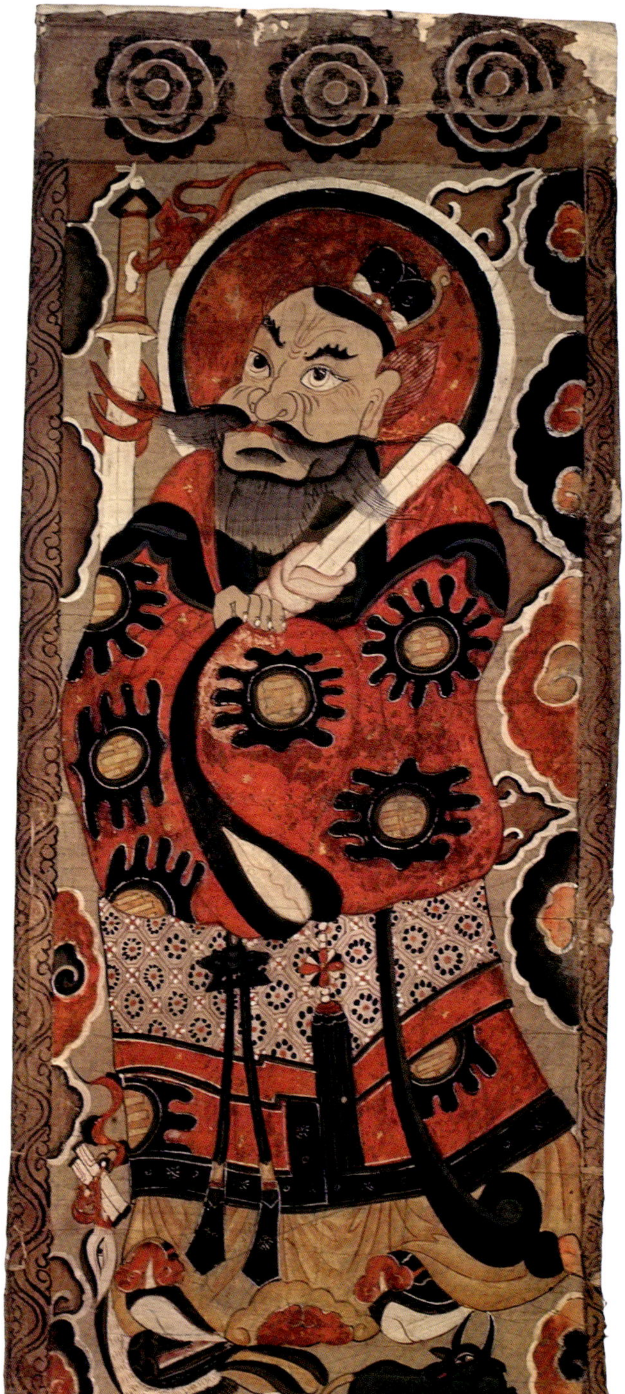

Fig. 23

Figs. 22, 23
Two Celestial Masters of Daoism
From left: Master Li, Master Zhang, 1819
Red Yao, China

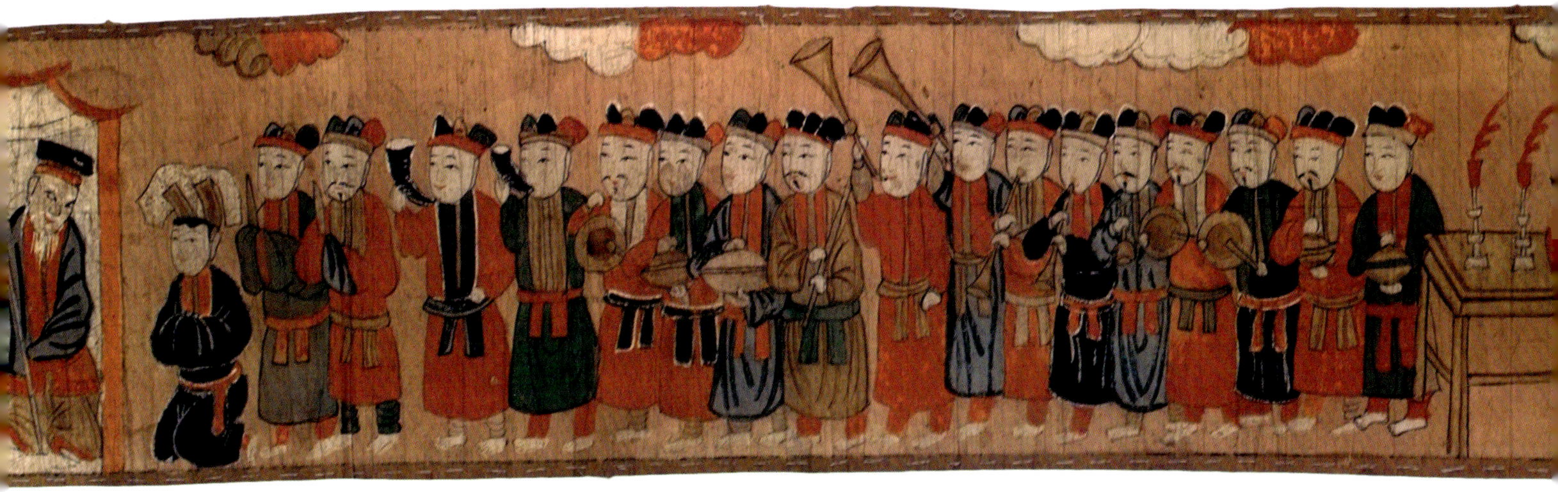

Fig. 24

deities—along with Daoist deities in their paintings, as seen in the two long scrolls *Respectfully Welcoming the Saints* and *Respectfully Welcoming the Buddhas* (see chapter on long scrolls).

Long scrolls such as these are displayed differently for various events. During Hanging Lamp Rituals (see "The Shaman Priest and Priestess"), the long horizontal scroll is placed at the top of the full set of paintings.[25] It is connected to a long piece of white cloth, emblematically representing heaven. On special occasions, as anthropologist Jacques Lemoine observes, "the long scroll is suspended horizontally from the lintel of the front door of the house to the middle of the room, thus forming a symbolic bridge coming down to Earth from the Heavens."[26]

Robes, Crowns, and Other Ritual Accessories

Other items in the collection include an extensive array of ornate robes and other items including ordination crowns, embroidered turbans, headbands and streamers, ceremonial belts, silk skirts, and embroidered leggings. There are also numerous wood and paper masks and a large number of ceremonial hats, embroidered headbands, and headdresses that accompany the robes during ritual ceremonies. Ritual instruments, such as iron swords, sacred daggers with rattles, wooden seals, chops, spears, Chinese feng shui compasses and diagrams, used together (Figs. 27, 28), wooden court tablets, wooden stamps, and wooden statues, along with other religious paraphernalia and small decorative architectural pieces, are also included. In addition, the collection contains various types of musical instruments: hand drums, water buffalo horns, handbells, large and small Chinese cymbals, and a two-stringed instrument.

It is important to note that, in addition to its quality and depth, the collection's prominence is unlikely to be surpassed, for a variety of reasons. From 1954 to 1990, these types of cultural artifacts were targets of negative propaganda by the Communist government. Shamanic practices, along with ritual paintings and other items, were considered superstitious, backward thinking, contrary to the teachings of modern science. Consequently, government officials confiscated and destroyed a vast number of religious artifacts.[27] In addition, many items were lost during the Vietnam War, and the resulting general poverty over the past fifty years drastically reduced the number of skilled craftspeople available to produce such items. Moreover, government policy requiring minority populations to adopt Vietnamese as their primary written language curtailed the number of people able to read and write Chinese. This in turn has affected the younger generation of artists, who,

Fig. 24
The Dragon Bridge of the Great Dao (part 1 of 4),
c. late 19th–early 20th century
Red Yao, China

while possessing talent and artistic training, cannot read or produce ritual manuals for ceremonial use. Finally, Yao tradition itself has played a part in the extinction of these objects. If sacred paintings are no longer used in specific rituals to assure their potency and to provide prosperity for the family, they are desacralized and destroyed. In families where a Yao priest in possession of numerous artifacts dies without an heir, surviving family members normally burn all paintings and ritual tools, to ensure that the priest's spirit soldiers and assistants from other worlds will not subsequently haunt or harm his family members.

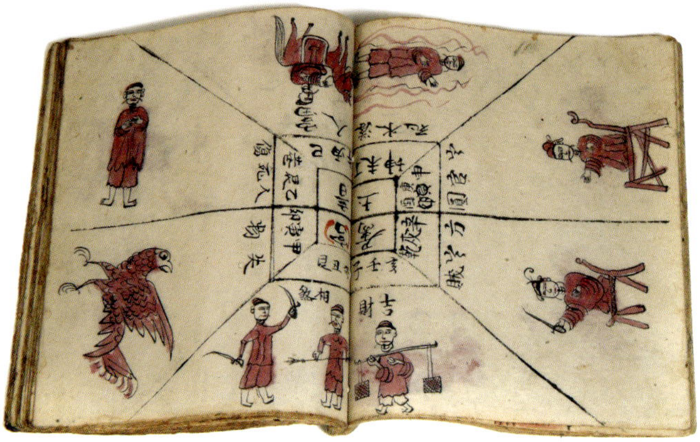

Fig. 25

Shaman Books

Rounding out the collection, and providing many vital clues to the purpose of the objects, are manuals (written in Chinese or Nôm characters) and illustrated manuscripts. These ritual books are an integral part of being a shaman. Generally, shaman books are exclusively Daoist (Fig. 30) or Buddhist, or occasionally a hybrid of the two (Fig. 29). The majority of the books, made of mulberry paper (commonly known as "rice paper" among the Chinese and Vietnamese), are illustrated, exhibiting the same range of quality as can be found in the scrolls, from sophisticated to crude, and ranging in date from the mid-nineteenth to the mid-twentieth century.

The books, varying in size from as few as twenty pages to more than one hundred, function as repositories of general information; other texts, written on small scrolls of paper, serve as reminders of ceremonies to be held. The information may relate to funeral rites, the summoning back of souls, or the propitiation of spirits during planting and harvesting.[28] Some books contain the ceremonies used to pay respect to various deities in a prescribed fashion. Others concern subjects such as astrology, medical practices, history, songs, law and etiquette, children's tales, divination, hunting practices, formulas for talismans and spells, and feng shui (Figs. 25, 31, 32).[29] A fully ordained shaman might have a fairly large library of handmade books, which are tailored to the traditions of the specific group, so that no two books, even those addressing the same ceremonies, are alike.

Inscriptions

Inscriptions play a valuable role in providing essential information for many painting sets and ritual pieces in the collection. For the most part, the inscriptions found on scrolls, masks, robes, crowns, seals, and ritual instruments are handwritten in classical Chinese, though some later objects are inscribed in Vietnamese. These can provide indispensable information: the date, place of creation, name of the painter, name of the commissioner, price paid, number of paintings or masks in the set, names of deities, the reason for commissioning the work, how long it took to complete, and prayers and wishes.

An inscription commonly takes one of three forms. First, it can be a long caption inscribed directly on the front of a scroll (Fig. 95) providing many types of

Fig. 25
Feng shui manual, dated 1908
Cao Làn–Sán Chỉ (Sán Chay), Vietnam

Fig. 26
Guiding the Soul, c. early–mid-20th century
Tày, Vietnam

Fig. 27
Feng shui compass with lid, c. late 19th–early 20th century
Cao Làn–Sán Chỉ (Sán Chay), Vietnam

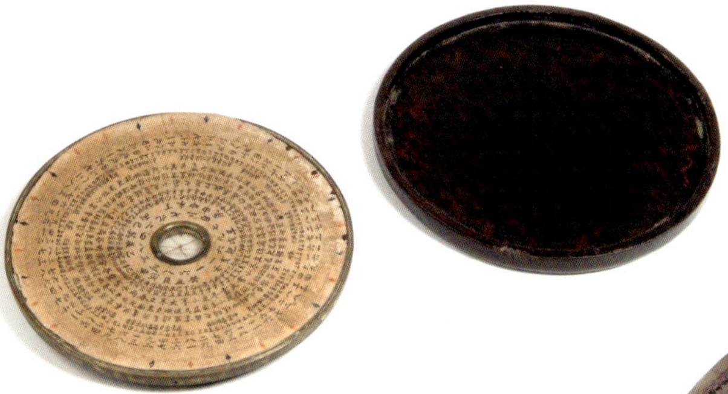

Fig. 27

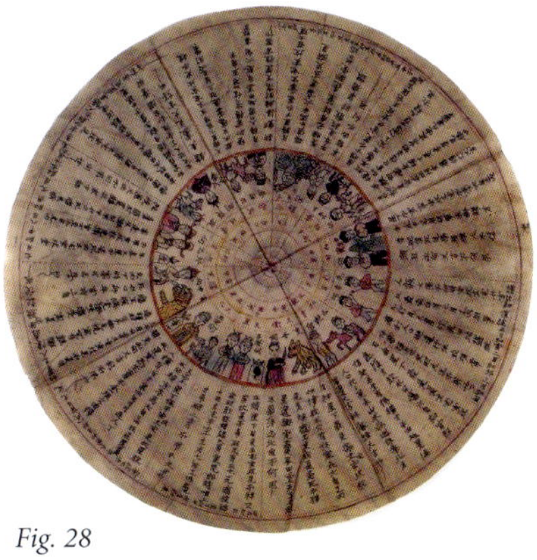

Fig. 28

Fig. 26

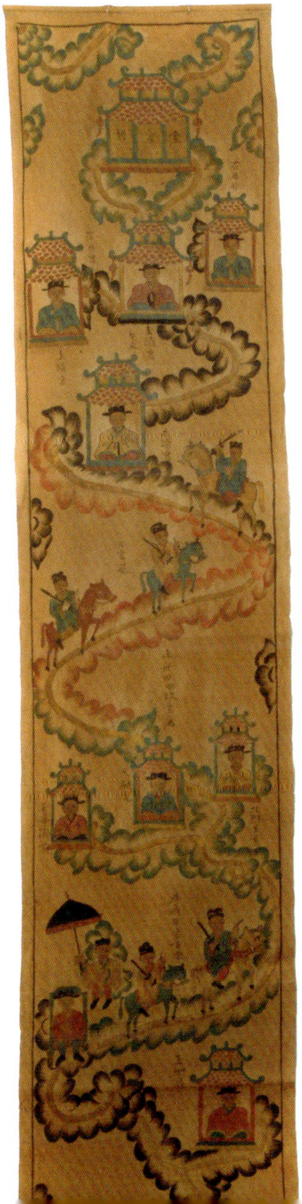

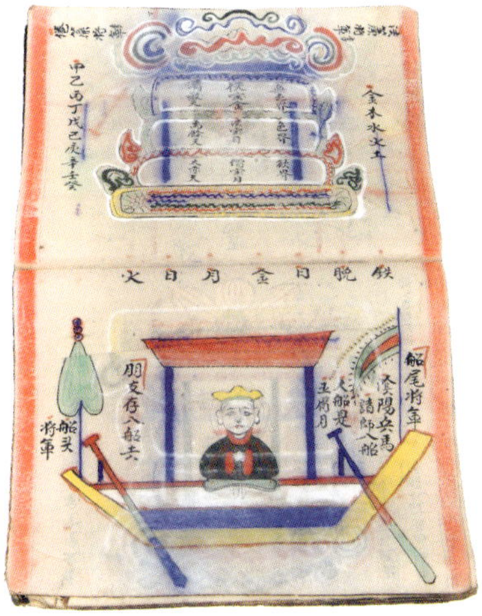

Fig. 29

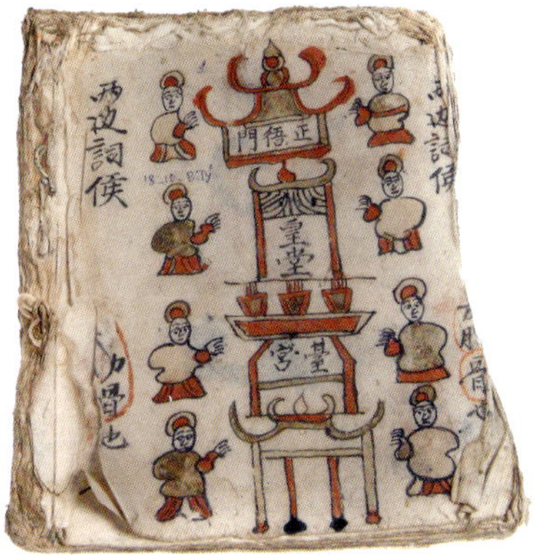

Fig. 30

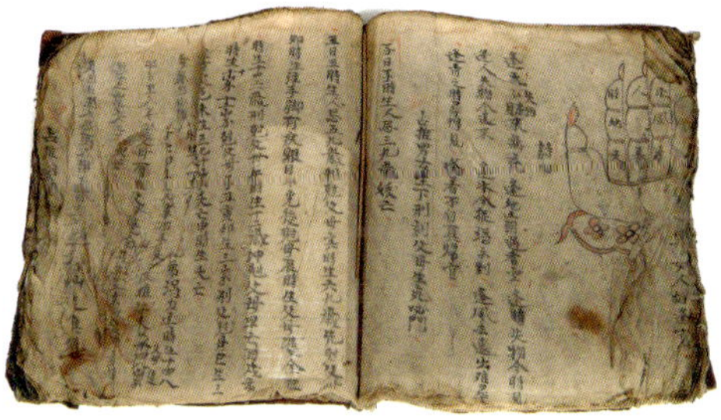

Fig. 31

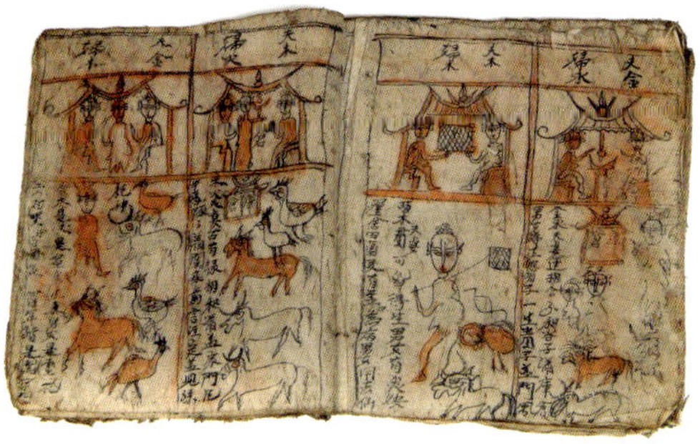

Fig. 32

Fig. 28
Feng shui diagram, c. mid-20th century
Cao Làn–Sán Chi (Sán Chay), Vietnam

Fig. 29
Buddhist-Daoist manual, dated 1910
Tày, Vietnam

Fig. 30
Manual of Daoist ritual and astrology, dated 1936
Yao, China or Vietnam

Fig. 31
Book, c. late 19th century
Cao Làn–Sán Chi (Sán Chay), Vietnam

Fig. 32
Astrology manual, dated 1952 and 1956
Tày, Vietnam

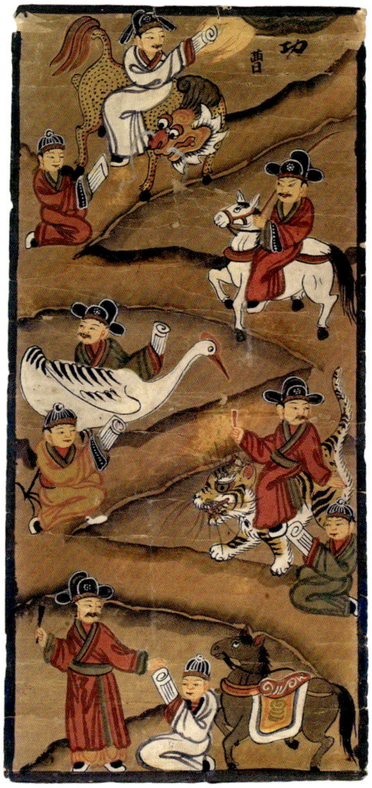

Fig. 33

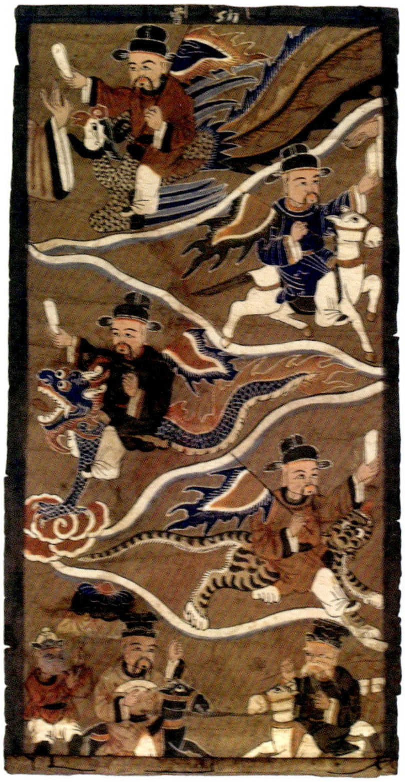

Fig. 34

information. More typically, however, the inscription is short and includes only the names of the deities, names of places, and perhaps short phrases written by the artist or later by the owner, as seen on the Four Heavenly Messengers scrolls (Figs. 33, 34, 128, 129, 131, 133, 134), the two Daoist sacred animal scrolls (Figs. 35, 36), or on the scrolls depicting the Ten Kings of the Underworld (Figs. 146–155). Second, the inscription can be written on a long piece of thin rice paper and then glued to the painting (Figs. 38, 39, 96). This form, though found on the five painting scrolls in the collection, is also uncommon. It is usually a prayer to Daoist deities asking for special favors, added on special occasions such as praying for the recovery of a person who is ill. Finally, the inscription might be written on the back of the painting. If it is long, it usually includes the name of the owner, date of commission, name of the artist, the price, and special prayers. There are several examples in the collection, including the Jade Pure One scroll (Fig. 40, inscription in Fig. 41) from the set of eighteen paintings, and the Heavenly Host (Fig. 42, detail of inscription in Fig. 43) within another set. Though there is no fixed rule determining which painting in a set would be written on, there would undoubtedly be some cogent reason; for example, that it was the central piece of the set when it was commissioned. If the inscription is short, it usually includes only the name of the

Fig. 33
Four Heavenly Messengers, c. early to mid-20th century
Tày, Vietnam

Fig. 34
Four Heavenly Messengers, c. early to mid-20th century
Thanh-y Yao, Vietnam

Fig. 35
Roaring Tiger, c. late 19th–early 20th century
Tày, Vietnam

Fig. 36
Humming Dragon, c. late 19th–early 20th century
Tày, Vietnam

Fig. 37
Four Heavenly Messengers, c. late 19th–early 20th century
Tày, Vietnam

Fig. 38
The Grand Pure One, 1829–30
Red Yao, China

Fig. 39
The Jade Pure One, 1939
Red Yao, China/Vietnam

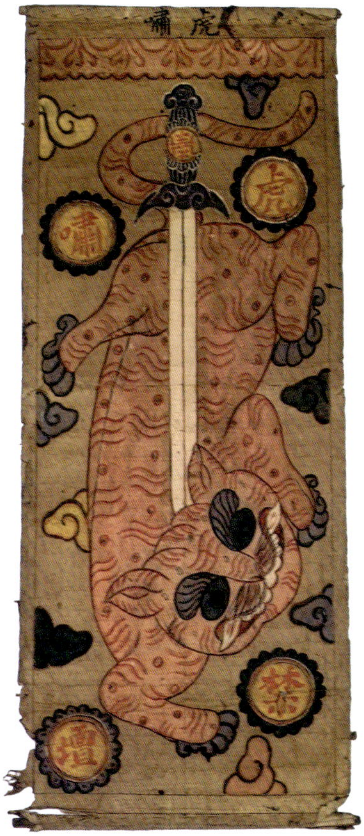

Fig. 35

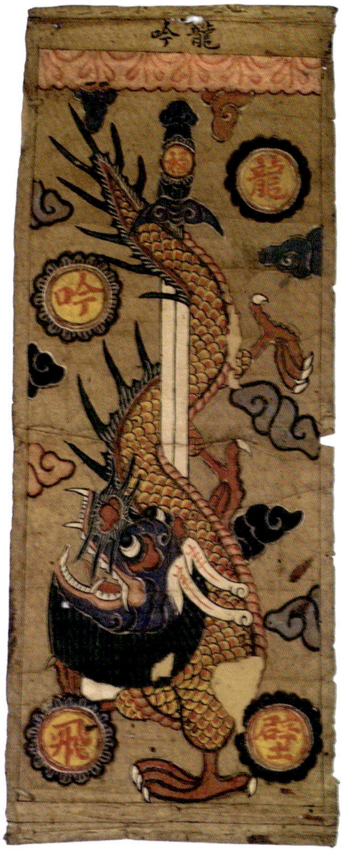

Fig. 36

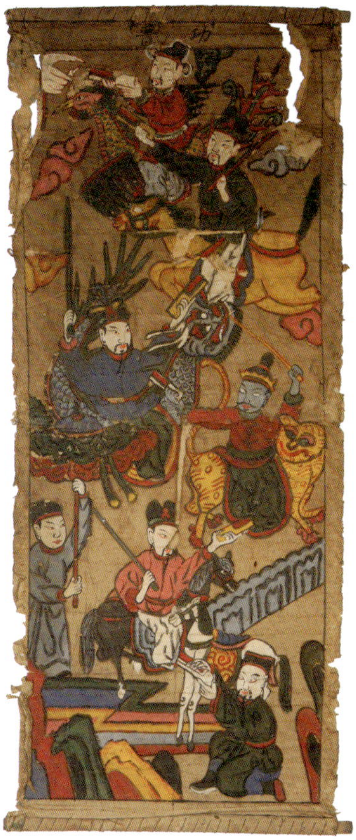

Fig. 37

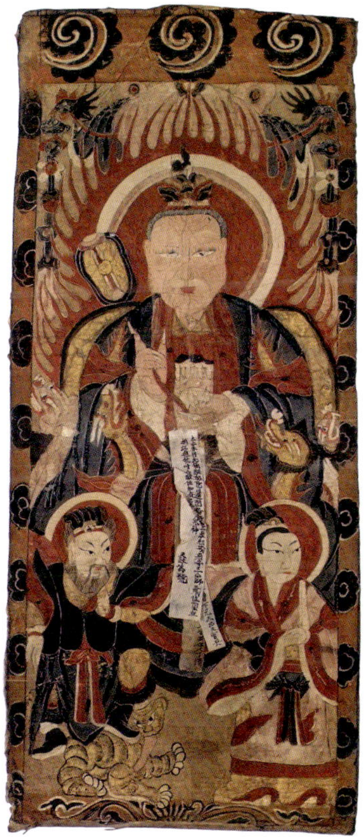

Fig. 38

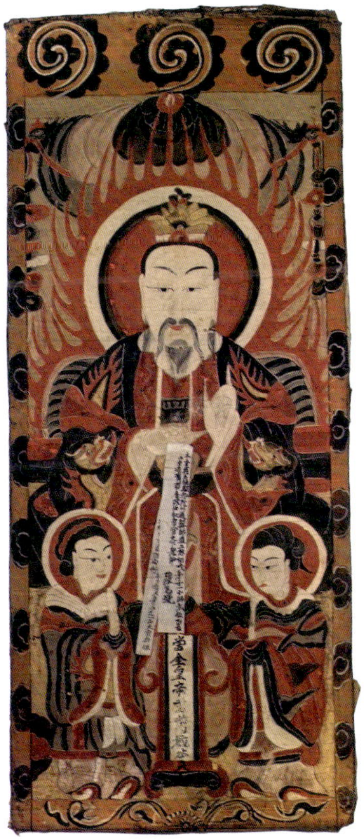

Fig. 39

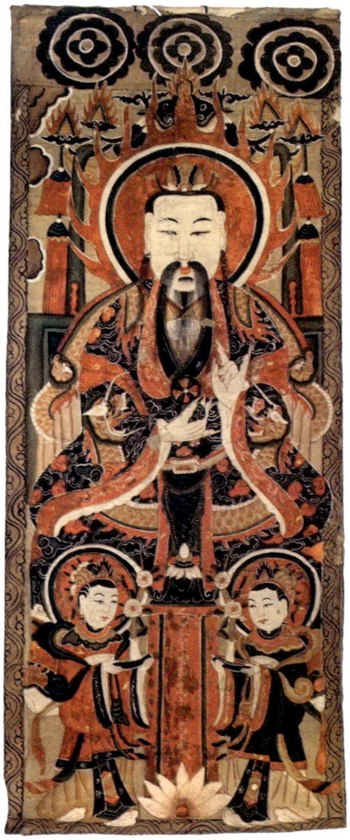

Fig. 40

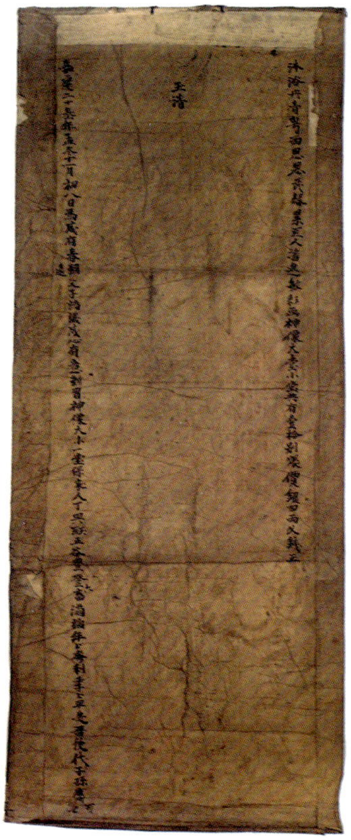

Fig. 41

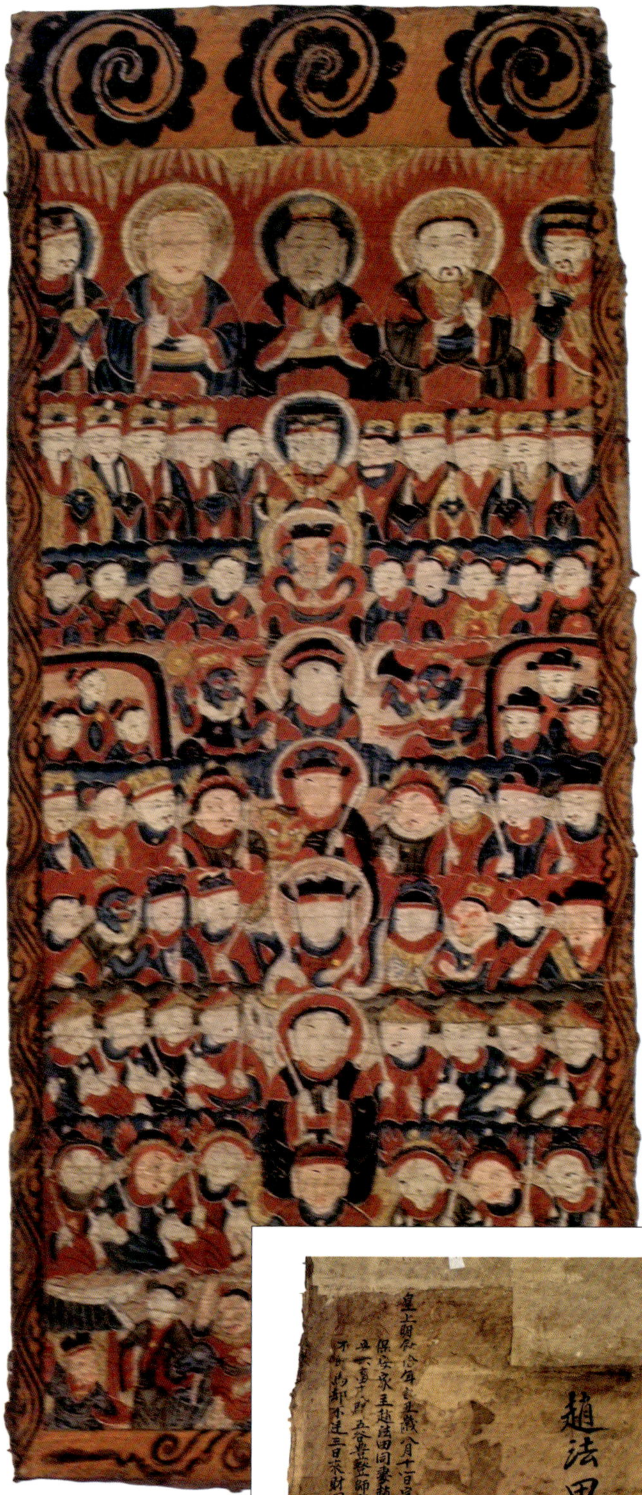

Fig. 42

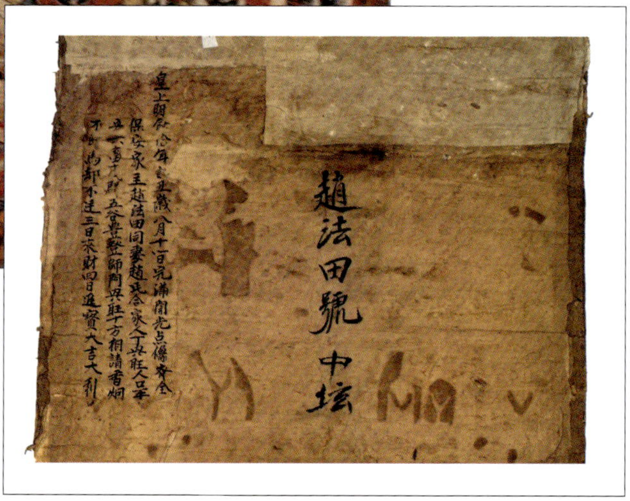

Fig. 43

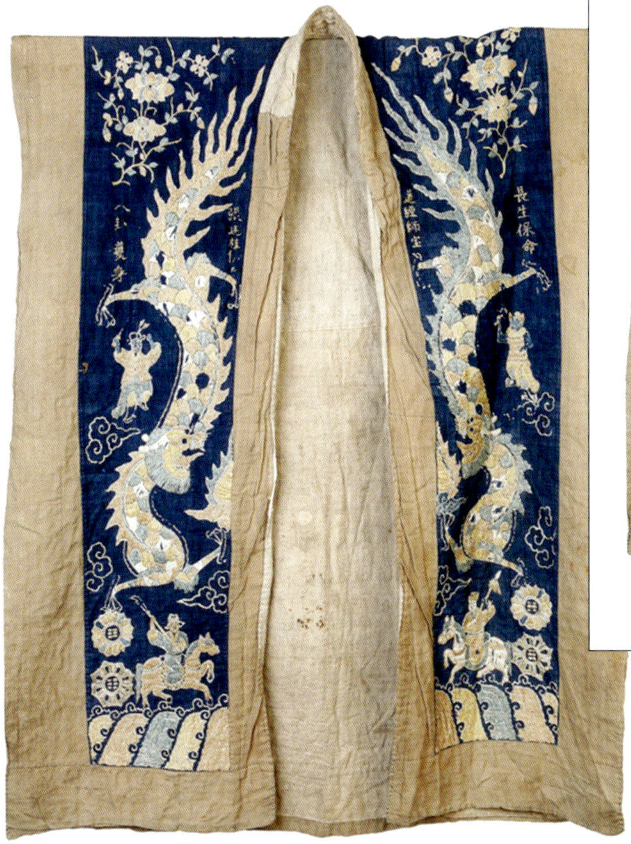

Fig. 44

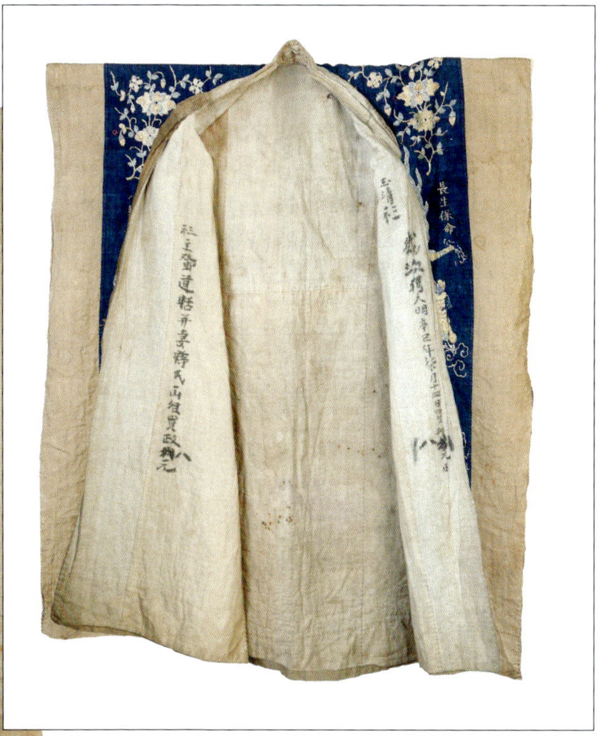

Fig. 45

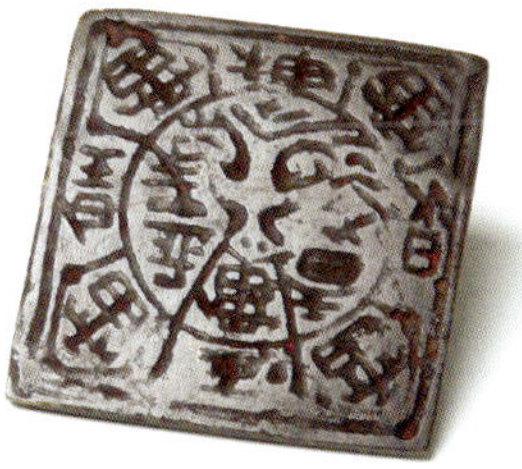

Fig. 47

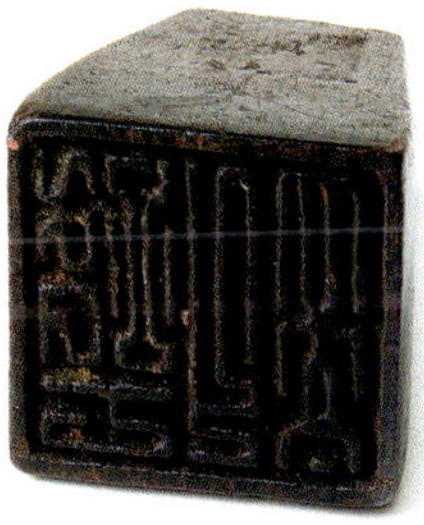

Fig. 46

Fig. 48

Fig. 40
The Jade Pure One, dated 1819
Red Yao, China

Fig. 41
Rear of Fig. 40

Fig. 42
Ancestors/Heavenly Host, dated 1829–30
Red Yao, China

Fig. 43
Rear of Fig. 42

Figs. 44-45
Ceremonial Robe with inscription inside, c. late 19th century
Tày or Nùng, Vietnam

Fig. 46
Seal, c. late 19th century
Tight Trouser (Quần Chẹt) Yao, Vietnam

Fig. 47
Seal (Five Thunder Gods stamp), c. late 19th century or earlier
Tày, Vietnam

Fig. 48
Seal, c. late 19th–early 20th century
Nùng, Vietnam

owner, his religious name, the name of the deity, and occasionally the order of the scrolls marked by the shaman, as seen in the set of twelve guardian deities (Figs. 116-126, one missing). A similar type of short inscription—name of owner, deity, commission date, and artist—is found on the back of each of the set of twenty-seven paper masks (see Figs. 50-53, 196, 197).

For dragon robes, crowns, hats, capes, and banners, the inscriptions are embroidered. The front side of the robe may have only a few inscriptions, while the back has a plethora, which might include the names of the Three Pure Ones, the sun, the moon, the Great Net Heaven, the twenty-eight lunar mansion deities, the five Daoist sacred mountains, and notable Chinese characters associated with good fortune, blessing, and longevity. There is one rare case of a handwritten inscription on the linen lining of a dragon robe (Figs. 44, 45). It was most likely added later by a new owner while replacing the linen. For crowns, the inscription is usually short, typically just a few Chinese characters to identify the deities or provide brief teachings (Figs. 165–167). Inscriptions engraved on seals and scepters are also frequently short phrases denoting the authority bestowed by the Jade Emperor on the shaman priests.

Handwritten inscriptions of Chinese characters on scrolls are usually easy to read. However, some are clumsily or incorrectly written, making it difficult to discover the intended meaning. And some inscriptions, like those embroidered on dragon robes and crowns, are in small Chinese characters, often rendering them illegible. Chinese characters engraved on seals are carved in the ancient style of Chinese calligraphy known as "seal script" (Figs. 46–48) or convey Daoist spells, talismans, or formulas called *fu* (符), which emphasize their magical powers (Figs. 49, 186).

With the passing of the older generation of Yao, who were trained in Chinese, coupled with Vietnamese becoming the enforced language of their country, some objects have been labeled in Vietnamese. For example, an itinerant art dealer, who was hoping to acquire and eventually replace a shaman's complete set of paintings, wrote the following on the back of an old and worn-out Four Heavenly Messengers scroll (Fig. 37): "Hey Quý! Help me to paint a picture exactly like the original one. You must paint it beautifully so I can exchange it with the shaman's original painting set. He gives one of the original paintings to test your skill. Thus, please try hard to paint it fast.This being done, I can exchange the new set with the old set." The shaman, in time, did part with the set.[30]

Fig. 49

Fig. 49
Seal, c. late 19th–early 20th century
Yao, China or Vietnam

Figs. 50, 51, 52, 53
Four paper masks from a set of twenty-seven, dated 1936
Yao (Mun), Vietnam

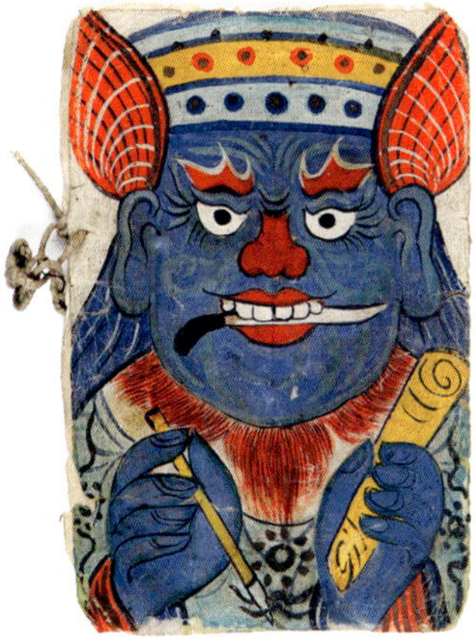

Fig. 50

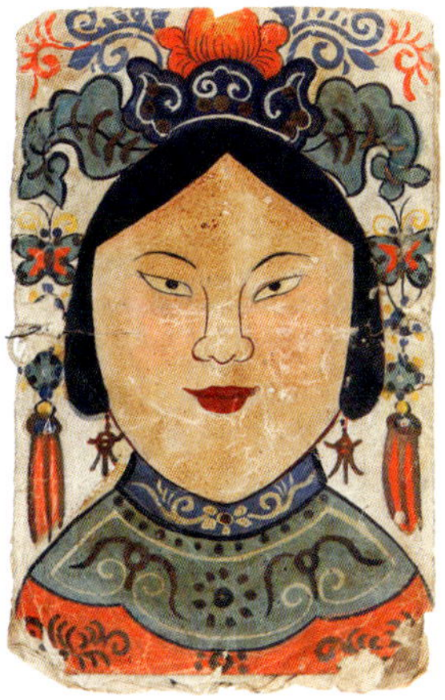

Fig. 51

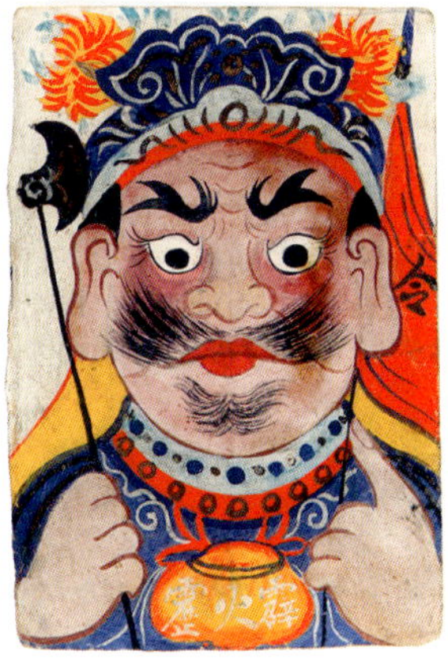

Fig. 52

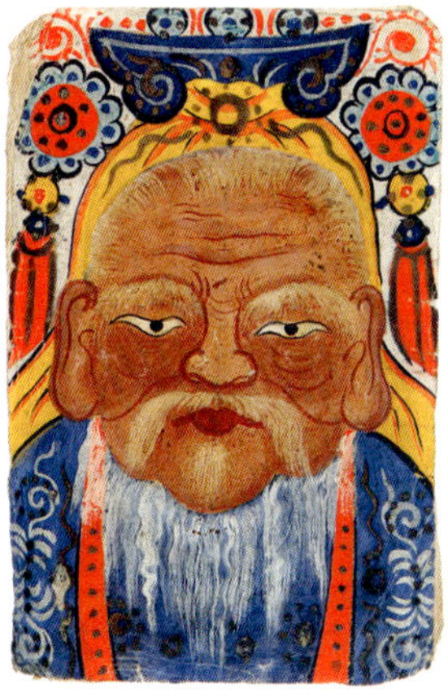

Fig. 53

Dating, Artists, and Artistic Styles

Inscriptions reveal that the dates of painted scrolls in the collection span almost two hundred years, from the mid-Qing dynasty (1644–1912) in China to the early period of the Vietnamese Nguyễn dynasty (1802–1945), and even as recently as the 1970s and 1980s.

The oldest items in the collection belong to a full set of eighteen scrolls (see "A Full Set of Eighteen Paintings") commissioned by the Feng family, a father and son, with the inscription indicating 1819 as the fixed date. However, a second full set (see Figs. 7, 42, 43) has mixed dates, as a few scrolls were replaced in later periods. The main inscription, on the back of the Administration/Heavenly Host scroll (Fig. 43), is dated 1829-30, yet the Supreme Pure One scroll is dated 1845, and the Jade Emperor scroll is dated 1939. From details about eras that are part of the dating we can tell that the set was originally painted by a Yao shaman priest, and then passed down within the family for at least three or four generations. On special occasions, such as when a male member of the family received a higher ordination, any worn-out paintings were replaced with new scrolls. However, it is rare to find an inscription with dating on a set of the three basic scrolls required for a young Yao man being initiated into the spiritual path of the Dao.

Paper masks were rarely dated, but the Kitnick Collection has a complete set of twenty-seven, dated May 1936 and also signed by a painter named Mỹ Đình.

According to researcher Phan Ngọc Khuê, many of the full sets of scrolls were originally brought from China, but because the majority of Yao communities in northern Vietnam live in isolated mountainous regions that are a great distance from their ancestral communities in China, Yao shaman priests hire local artists to paint their scrolls. These painters could be Yao, Tày, Nùng, or Vietnamese, as indicated by the artistic styles, paper types, inks, and particularly the artists' names, and they would model their work on Chinese Daoist paintings. Khuê encountered a well-known shaman family in Cao Bằng province whose family members have been making Daoist ritual paintings for four generations. They have a large collection of Chinese Yao Daoist paintings that they use as prototypes.[31] Trained as an artist himself, Khuê remarked that the Chinese artists, using fine brushes along with high-quality ink and paint on good paper, produced paintings with a smooth surface. Vietnamese artists, on the other hand, used powdered ink or watercolors, making the painting surface rather wavy.[32] However, the basic set of three paintings done in Vietnam, dated 1899 (Figs. 95–97), is of extraordinary quality, and can be regarded as a masterpiece in this collection. In general, paintings done in either China or Vietnam follow established iconographies in depicting deities, featuring symmetrically balanced compositions and harmonious colors. More recent sets, on the other hand, painted by amateur Vietnamese artists in the later decades of the twentieth century, are very awkward and do not even follow the standard features attributed to the deities. For instance, the small painted set of the Ten Kings of the Underworld (see Fig. 19) was modeled after Vietnamese mandarin court officials, rather than the traditional Kings of the Underworld seen in other finely painted scroll sets. In scrolls painted from templates the human figures generally lack facial expressions and individualization.

Conclusion

The Barry and Jill Kitnick Collection constitutes a rich and important group of objects representing the cultural heritage of the Yao, Tày, Nùng, Sán Chay, and Sán Dìu peoples. This group of more than five hundred artifacts is an unprecedented collection outside Vietnam, giving people in the United States a rich view of almost unknown cultures. These religious artifacts can provide scholars, researchers, and all those interested in these ethnic groups with an exciting opportunity to study the details of their ceremonies and traditions, and to gain a clearer understanding of their religious practices and traditional ways of life. Together with ritual manuals and illustrated manuscripts detailing their ceremonial practices, these objects bring us closer to the ways in which shamans communicate with the beings of unseen worlds, exorcize evil spirits, and bring prosperity. The Kitnick Collection additionally preserves the artistic traditions and religious heritages of cultures that for many reasons are gradually disappearing. These sacred objects, many of which can be regarded as masterpieces, represent the extraordinary artistic range and richness of ritual life in the mountainous regions of northern Vietnam.

Fig. 54
Celestial Marshals Ma and Deng, c. late 19th century
Cao Làn–Sán Chi (Sán Chay), Vietnam

Fig. 55
Celestial Master Li, c. late 19th century
Cao Làn–Sán Chi (Sán Chay), Vietnam

Fig. 56
The Dharma Jewel, c. late 19th century
Cao Làn–Sán Chi (Sán Chay), Vietnam

Fig. 57
The Buddha Jewel, c. late 19th century
Cao Làn–Sán Chi (Sán Chay), Vietnam

Fig. 58
The Sangha Jewel, c. late 19th century
Cao Làn–Sán Chi (Sán Chay), Vietnam

Fig. 59
Celestial Master Zhang, c. late 19th century
Cao Làn–Sán Chi (Sán Chay), Vietnam

Fig. 60
Celestial Marshals Zhao and Zhang, c. late 19th century
Cao Làn–Sán Chi (Sán Chay), Vietnam

Fig. 61
Four Heavenly Messengers, c. late 19th century
Cao Làn–Sán Chi (Sán Chay), Vietnam

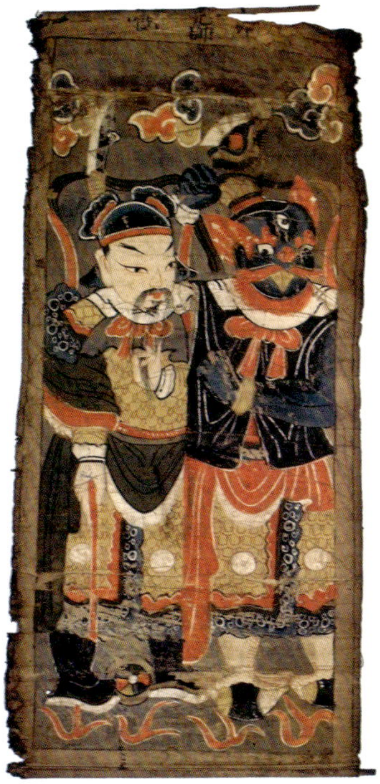

Fig. 54

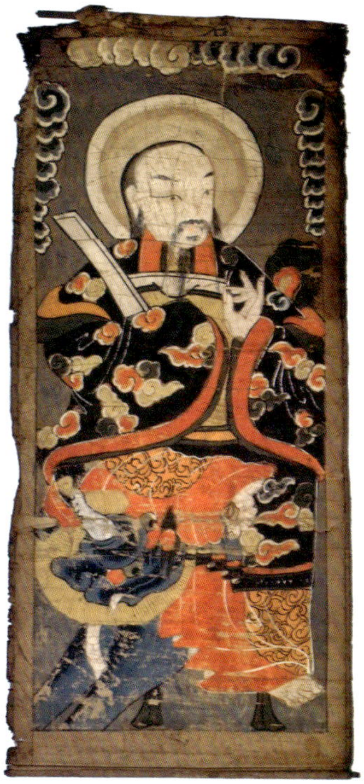

Fig. 55

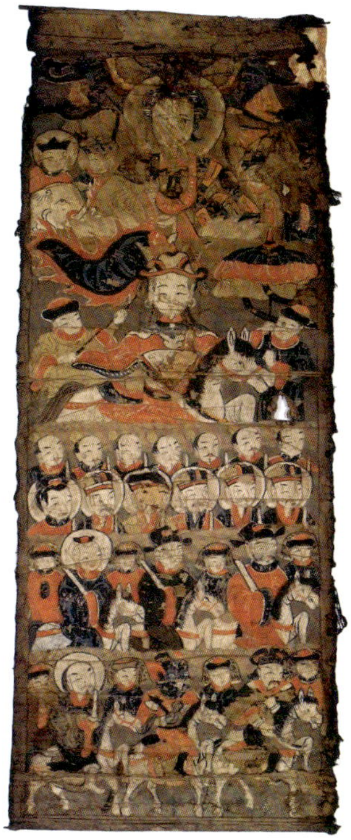

Fig. 56

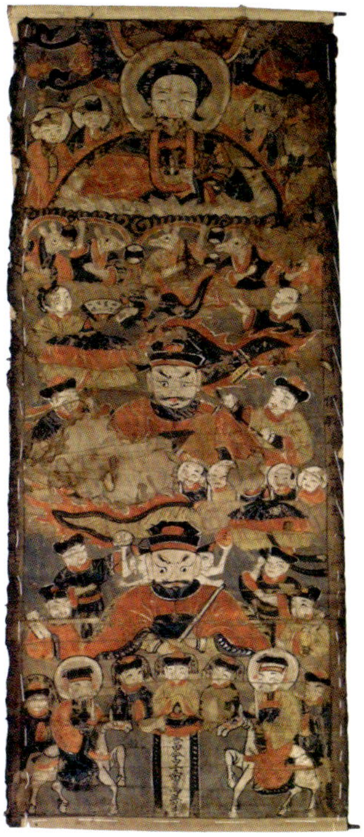

Fig. 57

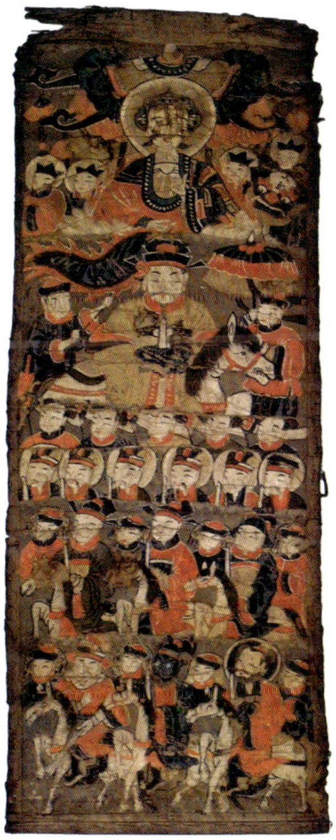

Fig. 58

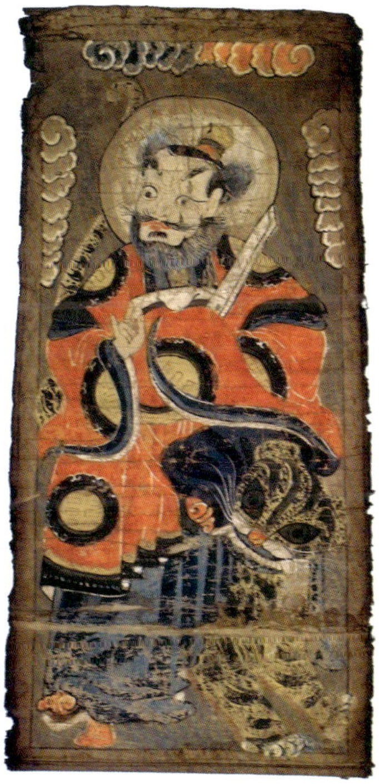

Fig. 59

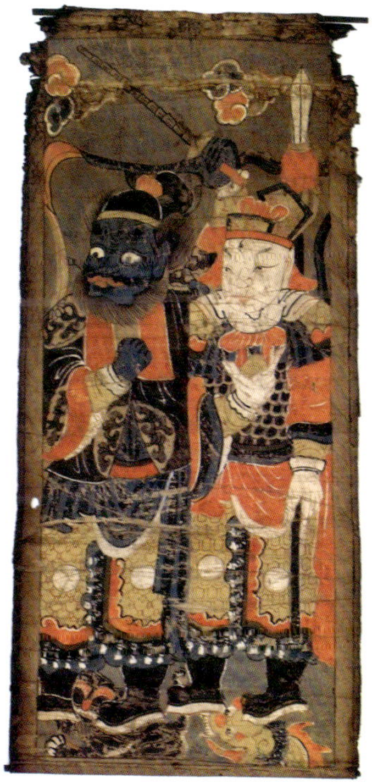

Fig. 60

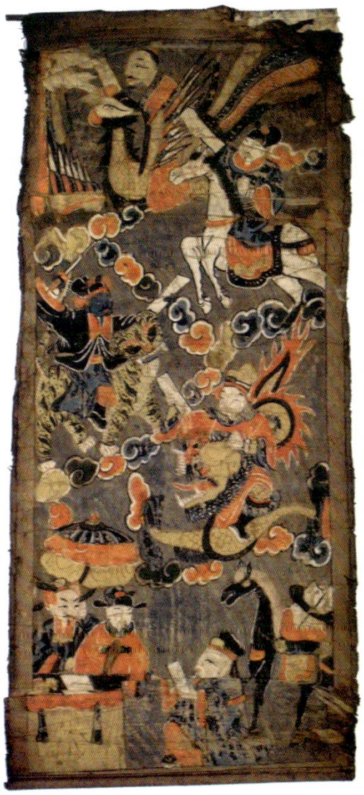

Fig. 61

NOTES

1. Based on several studies, Chinese and Vietnamese scholars conclude that the Yao ethnic people started migrating to northern Vietnam at the end of the Chinese Song dynasty (963–1279). However, the main immigration took place during the Ming (1368–1644) and the Qing (1644–1912) dynasties. For a summary of these studies, the reasons why the Yao migrated to Vietnam, different Yao subgroups, and their population and settlements, see Trần Hữu Sơn, *Sách Cổ Của Người Dao* [The Traditional Books of the Yao], vol. 1 (Hanoi: Nxb Văn Hóa Dân Tộc, 2011), pp. 23–59.

2. Vietnamese scholars and anthropologists generally agree that there are seven subgroups of the Yao in Vietnam, based on features of the female costumes. They are the Red Yao, the Coin Yao, the Tight Trouser Yao, the Lô Gang Yao, the White Trouser Yao, the Indigo-Clad Yao, and the Long-Dressed Yao. See Vũ Quốc Khanh, ed., *The Yao People in Vietnam* (Hanoi: VNA Publishing House, 2006).

3. According to the Institute of Anthropology in *The Yao People in Vietnam*, the Yao population in 2003 was 685,432. In 1999, according to the Vietnamese national census bureau, the Yao population was 630,528, as quoted in Chu Thái Sơn and Võ Mai Phương, *Người Dao* [Yao People] (Hồ Chí Minh City: Youth Publishing House, 2005), p. 98. Thus within only four years, the Yao population increased by 54,904 people.

4. For a good reference on Tày history and culture, see Vũ Khánh, *The Tày in Vietnam* (Hanoi: Vietnam News Agency Publishing House, 2009), pp. 10–22; 125–170. For the population and geographical location of the Nùng, see Chu Thái Sơn & Hoàng Hoa Toàn. *Người Nùng* [The Nùng People]. Ho Chi Minh City: Youth Publishing House, 2006, p. 127.

5. For a full discussion of the Nùng, see Chu Thái Sơn and Hoàng Hoa Toàn, pp. 11–23.

6. Ibid., 11–19.

7. Hoàng Bé, Hoàng Hữu Bình, et al., *Các Dân Tộc Tày Nùng ở Việt Nam* [The Tày and Nùng Nationalities in Vietnam] (Hanoi: Institute of Ethnography, 1992), pp. 238–239.

8. Concerning Tày ritual manuscripts transmitted through oral tradition and then written down in Nôm script, but still remembered by heart when performed by female shamans called *then*, see Triệu Thị Mai, *Hành trình đi tìm vía của pựt Ngạn* [The Journey of Searching the Shaman's Spirits] (Hanoi: Nxb Từ Điển Bách Khoa, 2008). Note that Ngạn is one of the three subgroups of the Tày people living in Cao Bằng province, northern Vietnam. See also Nguyễn Thị Yên, *Then Tày* [The Tày Shaman *Then*] (Hanoi: Social Sciences Publishing House, 2006). Yên's book is the most comprehensive study of Tày shaman culture and religion. A large part of her book (p. 309 to p. 646) transcribes the whole text of the Tày shamanist ritual in the Tày native language, which is then translated into modern Vietnamese. The manuscript is the main ritual text used during the three-day ordination ceremony of a Tày community in Cao Bằng province.

9. Chu Thái Sơn and Hoàng Hoa Toàn, pp. 88–89.

10. Some Vietnamese scholars divide the Sán Chay into two subgroups thus: Cao Làn–Sán Chỉ. However, the Vietnam Institute of Ethnology officially calls this ethnic group the Sán Chay. I follow this classification, though within the Kitnick Collection some items are from the Cao Làn subgroup and some from the Sán Chỉ subgroup. For a further discussion on Sán Chay, see Trần Bình, Ngọc Bích, et al., ed., *Fifty-Four Ethnic Groups in Vietnam* (Hanoi: VNA Publishing House, 2011), pp. 197–200; see also Phan Ngọc Khuê, *Taoist Painting of North Vietnam* (Hanoi: Vietnam Fine Arts Publishing House, 2008), pp. 69–70 (hereafter, *Taoist Painting*).

11. According to the 1999 survey data by the Vietnamese government census bureau, the population of the Cao Làn–Sán Chỉ is only 147, 315, scattered over nine provinces in northern Vietnam. See Chu Thái Sơn and Hoàng Hoa Toàn, p. 127.

12. For some other examples and a short explanation of the religious paintings of the Sán Chay, see Phan Ngọc Khuê, *Taoist Painting*, plate 49, pp. 152–153. For another set of three paintings on the same subject, see Phạm Đức Sĩ, *Vietnamese Ceremonial Paintings: Pham Duc Si's Collection 2001–2009* (Hanoi: Icon Communication, 2009), p. 13 (note that the three paintings in this catalogue are wrongly captioned).

13. According to the Vietnamese government census bureau in the 1998 survey, the Sán Dìu population in Vietnam was

126,237, living in seven provinces in northern Vietnam. See Chu Thái Sơn and Võ Mai Phương, p. 102. However, in the 2009 survey, the population was up to 147,000. See *The 2000 Vietnam Population and Housing Census: Complete Results* (Hanoi: Census Publication House, 2010), pp. 134–225.

14. For a brief discussion of the Sán Dìu religious belief system, see Phan Ngọc Khuê, *Taoist Painting*, pp. 70–71.

15. For example, Trần Hữu Sơn has translated about forty stories, myths, and love songs of the Yao, written in the Nôm script. See Trần Hữu Sơn, vol. 2.

16. According to the 1993 survey by Lào Cai provincial government officials, 80% of the young people from age fifteen to twenty-five could not read classical Chinese; 65% of those from forty to fifty could not read and write. Only 8% of those above fifty years old could read and write. The survey also asked the young generation about their desire to learn Chinese in order to read traditional texts; only about 4% answered yes, whereas the rest said that they did not want to study the written languages—Chinese and Nôm—used by their forebears. See Trần Hữu Sơn, "Sách cổ của người Dao ở Lào Cai—Di sản văn hóa có giá trị [The Traditional Books of the Yao: The Valuable Cultural Heritage], in *The Culture and Social Development of the Yao: The Present and the Future. Proceedings of the International Symposium, Thai Nguyen, December 1995* (Hanoi: Social Sciences Publishing House, 1998), pp. 173–174 (hereafter, *The Culture and Social Development of the Yao*).

17. See Chu Thái Sơn and Hoàng Hoa Toàn, pp. 21–22.

18. In his early study of Yao Daoist painting, Jacques Lemoine looked at the case of the Yao from Laos who migrated to Thailand at the end of the Vietnam War, and already noticed this situation in the refugee camps in Thailand. See "Yao Taoist Paintings," in *Arts of Asia* (Jan.–Feb., 1981), pp. 61–71. In Vietnam, in recent decades, there are similar scenarios.

19. Trần Hữu Sơn, pp. 88–94.

20. The painting of the Ancestors depicts the deceased immediate ancestral members of the Yao high shaman priests who commissioned the whole painting set of seventeen or eighteen pieces (or more). The Ancestors paintings contain the portrait images of the commissioner's family clan members, starting from the deceased parents, grandparents, etc., up to at least seven generations. The portrait images are always identified by captions next to their heads with their true names. For a further discussion on this subject, see Jacques Lemoine, *Yao Ceremonial Paintings* (Bangkok: White Lotus, 1982), pp. 131–134; Phan Ngọc Khuê, *Taoist Painting*, pp. 120–121. See also Jess G. Pourret, *The Yao: The Mien and Mun Yao in China, North Vietnam, Laos and Thailand* (Chicago: Art Media Resources, 2002), plate 590L, p. 225, for a good illustration.

21. The Enforcers of Fasting and Charity are two small-sized paintings depicting the Lady Overseer of the Fast; Yao priests, the postulants, and their wives refrain from all meat prior to and during the ordination ceremony. The paintings also depict the killing of sacrificial pigs and chickens as an offering to the deities at the conclusion of the ceremony and subsequently as part of the feast for participants. For a full discussion of this topic, see Lemoine, *Yao Ceremonial Paintings*, pp. 142–146. See also Phan Ngọc Khuê, *Taoist Painting*, pp. 128. In his book Khuê refers to the painting as the Kitchen Official.

22. The painting scroll of Pan Hung's Five Banners of Knights depicts the Yao journey as they crossed the sea on a boat through turbulent water. The Yao ran into trouble, thus Pan Hung, the Yao's ancestor, came to their rescue. There are many different variations of pictures depicting this theme. Some are simple, with few figures, and others are full of action. For a full discussion of this topic with many illustrated examples, see Lemoine, *Yao Ceremonial Paintings*, pp. 147–151. See also Phan Ngọc Khuê, *Taoist Painting*, pp. 127. Khuê calls the painting the Five Banners of Horsemen, or Boat of Officials.

23. Lã Văn Lô and Hà Văn Thư, *Văn hóa Tày Nùng* [Tày and Nùng Cultures] (Hanoi: Nxb Văn Hóa, 1984), pp. 32–33.

24. See J. G. Pourret, plates 79, 80 (p. 51) and plate 596 (p. 214), for good examples of how different painting scrolls are arranged in makeshift religious chapels.

25. Ibid.

26. Jacques Lemoine, *Yao Ceremonial Paintings*, p. 135.

NOTES CONTINUED

27. Phan Ngọc Khuê, "Tranh thờ của dân tộc Dao ở Bắc Bộ Việt Nam [The Religious Paintings of the Yao in Northern Vietnam]," in *The Culture and Social Development of the Yao*, pp. 136–137 (hereafter, "The Religious Paintings of the Yao").

28. Pourret, pp. 251–252

29. Ibid.

30. Here is the original Vietnamese handwriting: "*[Q]quí ơi mày vẽ hộ anh 1 tờ chanh đúng như gốc phải vẽ thật đẹp thì anh mới đổi được bộ cũ của ông thầy tạo ông thầy gửi vẽ thử cho ông ấy xem mày cố gắng vẽ càng nhanh ctốt cho anh mang đi đổi. anh Thanh.*" Note that although this person writes in Vietnamese, his sentences are without any punctuation, and a few words are misspelled.

31. Phan Ngọc Khuê, "The Religious Paintings of the Yao," p. 144.

32. Ibid.

Fig. 62
Belt, c. early 20th century
Tight Trouser (Quần Chẹt) Yao, Vietnam

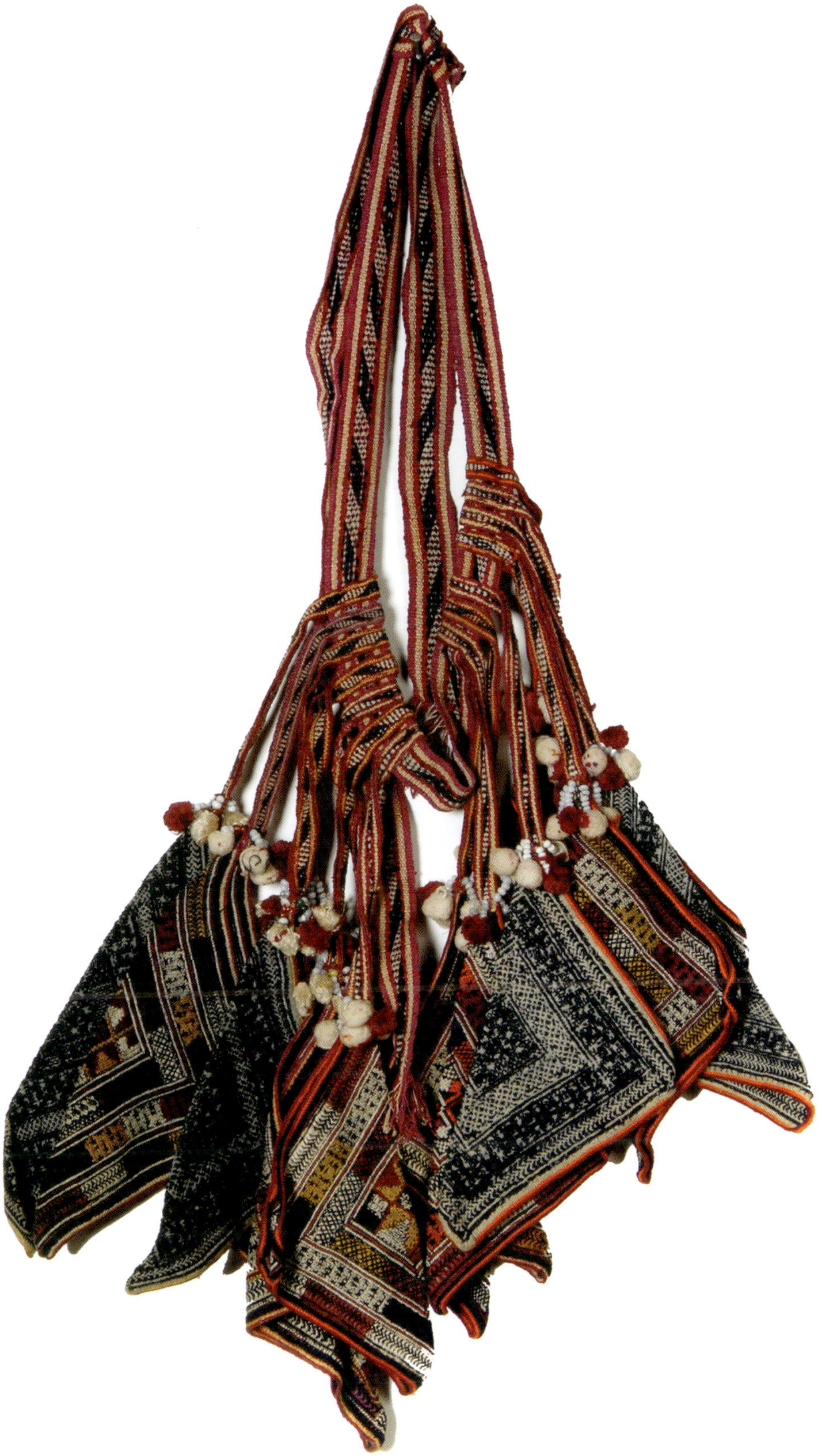

Fig. 62

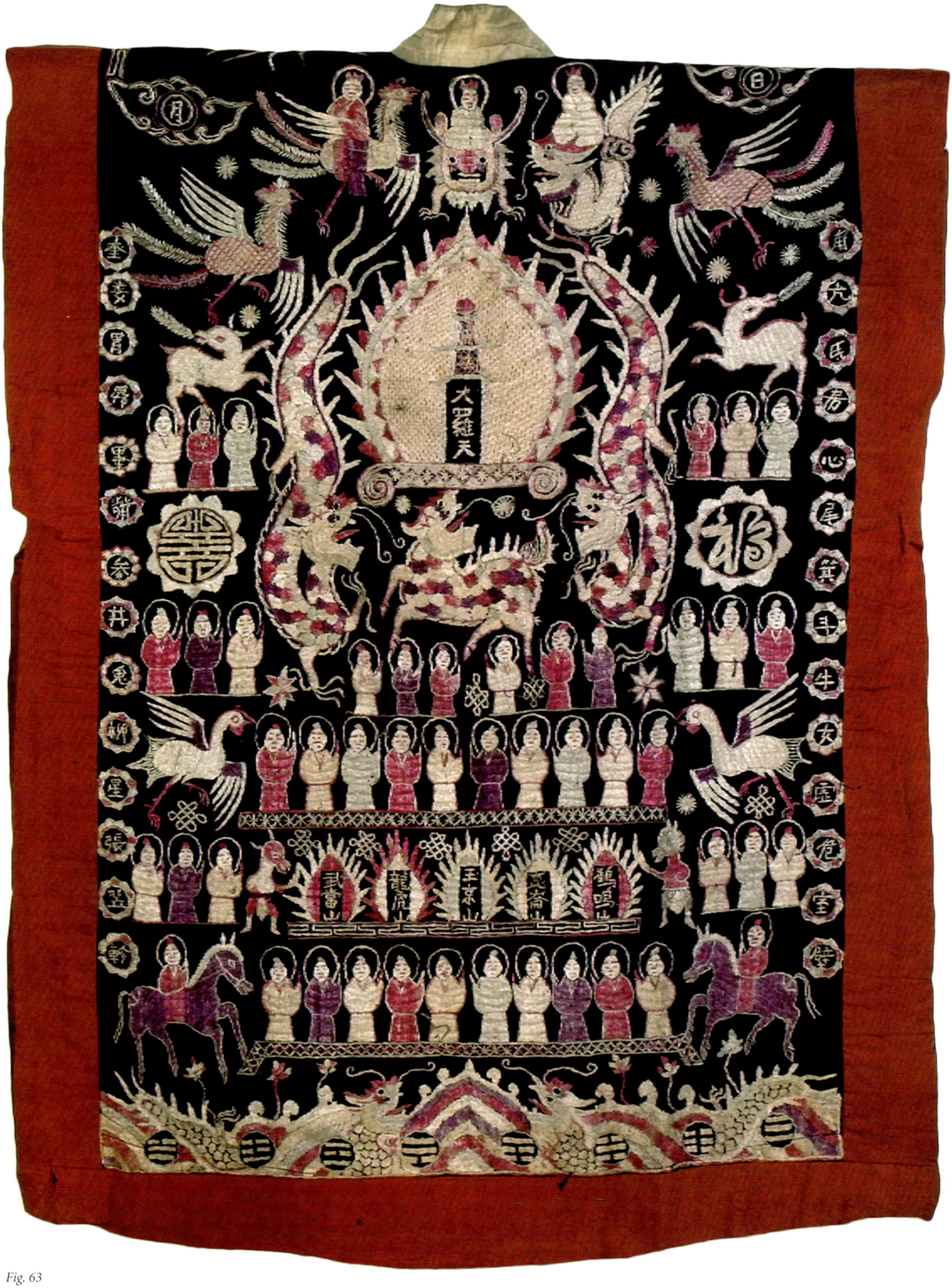

Fig. 63

THE SHAMAN PRIEST AND PRIESTESS:
Their Heavenly Mission and the Ordination Rituals

In Vietnam, for more than a thousand years, natural disasters, drought, diseases, and other catastrophic factors have threatened the livelihoods of ethnic people dwelling in remote mountainous regions. These people believe in unseen worlds, nature spirits, and heavenly deities who protect them on earth and provide them with an eternal life in heaven. They accept that when a person is sick, his soul leaves the body and wanders. If the soul doesn't return to its body, the person will die. High shaman priests, who possess magical power and spiritual ability, can call the lost soul back, making it regain its vital energy.[1] Shaman priests can also guide the souls of the dead out of hell, so they can go to heaven and be united with their ancestors.[2] Without an understanding of the causes of disease, with no knowledge of science, without access to advanced medicine, these isolated and primitive people rely on the spiritual abilities, religious knowledge, and magical powers of the high shamans.

Shaman priests are considered the backbone of the social and religious fabric in these ethnic communities. They are the most educated, can read and write Chinese, and own collections of books that include Daoist texts, Buddhist sutras, ritual manuals, volumes on Chinese medicine, feng shui, astrology, even historical epics, and popular myths and legends.[3] Shaman priests have years of training in practicing magic, and are authorized by deities such as the Jade Emperor to ward off the evil forces that can bring misfortune to community members. They have the ability to communicate with the unseen world and, during high ordination, they receive spirit soldiers to assist them during their shamanic career. They have special altars in their homes where they cultivate their magic and train the spirit soldiers, creating a mystical atmosphere around themselves.[4]

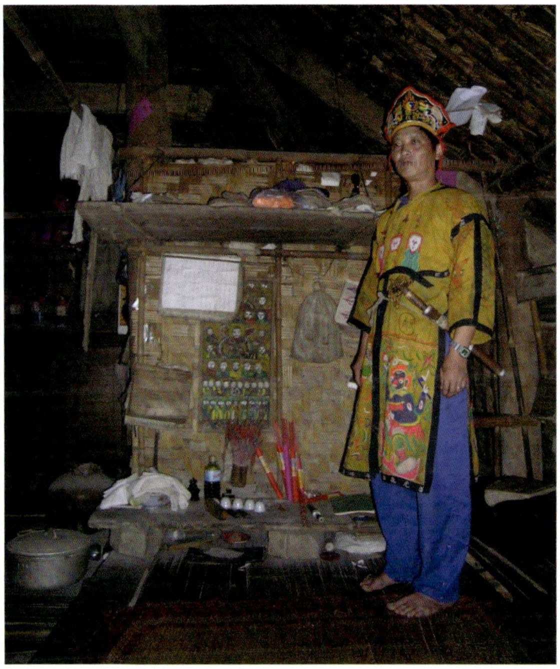

A Sán Chay shaman with family altar, Thái Nguyên province, Vietnam, 2006.

Fig. 63
Ritual robe, c. early 20th century
Sán Chay, Vietnam

Cultural anthropologists and ethnologists generally agree that there are four major kinds of shamans among the different ethnic groups living in the mountainous regions of northern Vietnam. The rituals they practice have a wide variety of sources, including Daoism, Buddhism, Confucianism, Hinduism, animism, and elements of popular myths and legends. The four major types of shaman are known in Vietnamese as *thầy tào, thầy mo, then*, and *pụt*.[5] *Thầy* in Vietnamese is an honorific term referring to a spiritual teacher or religious master (師 in Chinese). *Tào* is the local pronunciation of the Chinese word *Tao*, or *Dao* (written in Chinese as 道).[6] Thus, a *thầy tào* is a Daoist master who specializes in religious rituals, and of the four types, the *thầy tào* is the highest ranking. Relying on centuries of Chinese cultural and religious influence from before the migrations to Vietnam, he must be able to compose memorials and petitions in classical Chinese and utilize ritual manuals, both Daoist texts and Buddhist sutras. Long ago, Chinese was the only written language system used in Vietnam. Much later the Nôm script was developed, based on Chinese characters. Strictly speaking, the shaman is a Daoist master; yet in a society where all major Asian religions harmoniously coexist and there is no established religious institution, the *thầy tào* also incorporates Buddhist texts and ritual instruments, and honors a number of deities that originally derive from Buddhism. A shaman is in charge of all significant ceremonies, including funeral rites, memorial services, and praying for the well-being of others. A shaman can perform a ritual alone, or with the help of other shamans in groups of three, seven, or twelve. Large ceremonies are accompanied by and enhanced with music. To that end, shaman priests form an orchestra, with several major musical instruments.[7] As a ritual master, the high priest shows his skill in reading texts written in Chinese, as Phan Ngọc Khuê observed: "While performing rituals the *thầy tào*, in his role as master of ceremonies, has to open his ritual book and strictly follow line after line, even though he knows it by heart. None of the participants understand the language, which is foreign to them, but because they have heard the ritual so often, they have become accustomed to the recitation of the *thầy tào* and 'like its rhythm.'"[8] A *thầy tào* possesses many paintings, ceremonial tools, musical instruments, books, and other ritual paraphernalia. Among the four types of shamans, he is the only one who can wear the dragon robe, decorated with Daoist symbols, and the ritual hat made of human hair. In general, the term *thầy tào* can be used for any ordained and respected shaman within all the ethnic groups.

Thầy mo is the second-highest type of shaman priest, popular among the Yao, Sán Chay, and Sán Dìu peoples. The term *thầy mo* is probably derived from the Chinese characters 道 公 (*daogong*) or 師 公 (*shigong*). He is a master of exorcist rituals, specializing in treating and curing the sick. Regarded as a miraculous healer and worker, the *thầy mo* employs spells, talismans, and amulets. He has an ability to communicate with and summon invisible spirits, and to make connections between the world of human beings and the spirits. When a family, clan, or even a whole community celebrates important events, such as naming a newly born baby, lauding a one-month-old baby, welcoming a newlywed bride into a bridegroom's house, or doing something considered critical, such as cutting down a very old tree, they invite the *thầy mo* to make offerings and pray for safety and a happy ending.[9] He often works alone but occasionally serves as assistant to the *thầy tào*. Though he cannot read or write classical Chinese, he knows all the rituals by heart and can perform many of them without texts. He owns fewer musical instruments, dons a one-color robe, and wears a simple crown. [10]

Though not the highest ranking priest, the *thầy mo* is regarded as a crucial member of family and society. As Phan Ngọc Khuê has commented: "It is a common wish among the Shan You Sán Dìu families to have their adult sons ordained and embrace the profession of *shigong thầy cúng*, 'master-healer exorcist.'"[11] This is because it is believed that if a family has an exorcist or a healing master, he can make offerings to divinities, communicate with spirits, and ward off evil forces, factors that aide him in protecting family and clan members.[12] As a healer, he honors the Medicine God (Fig. 64). As an exorcist, he venerates many mighty guardian deities who possess the power to subdue evil and uphold the good.

The third kind of shaman, known as *then,* only exists among the Tày and the Nùng peoples. They are regarded as the representative agents from heaven carrying out noble work on earth,[13] and are believed to be the mediums between human beings and heavenly deities. Their functions include praying for rain during the drought period, presiding over important rituals, such as appeals to the Fertility Deity—the Flower Lady—for a young married couple who has not had children after a few years of marriage, and praying for the well-being of a newborn baby.[14] They also preside over rituals such as weddings, funerals, and opening a new house.[15] Furthermore, they are able to perform apotropaic rites, saving people from bad luck.

Their musical instruments are the two-string *tính* lute, rattling bells, and small bronze cymbals.[16] The *tính* lute produces a sweet, warm tone and is always played in ritual ceremonies and traditional dances. The bells (Fig. 68) are made of bronze, copper, or iron, are connected by chains, and hang from the fingers or toes during rituals. The *then* priestess shakes them to make a special sound representing a divine horse on its way toward heaven.[17] Occasionally, a *then* also holds a folded fan and plays small handbells.[18]

Finally, *pụt* or *pựt* is the term for a female shaman among the Tày and Nùng. *Pụt* is the local pronunciation of a word rooted in the Sanskrit term *budh*—to awaken, to become aware, to know and understand—referring to the Buddha (佛). The term is probably influenced by the Vietnamese term Bụt, also referring to the Buddha. Thus a *pụt*, in the context of Tày and

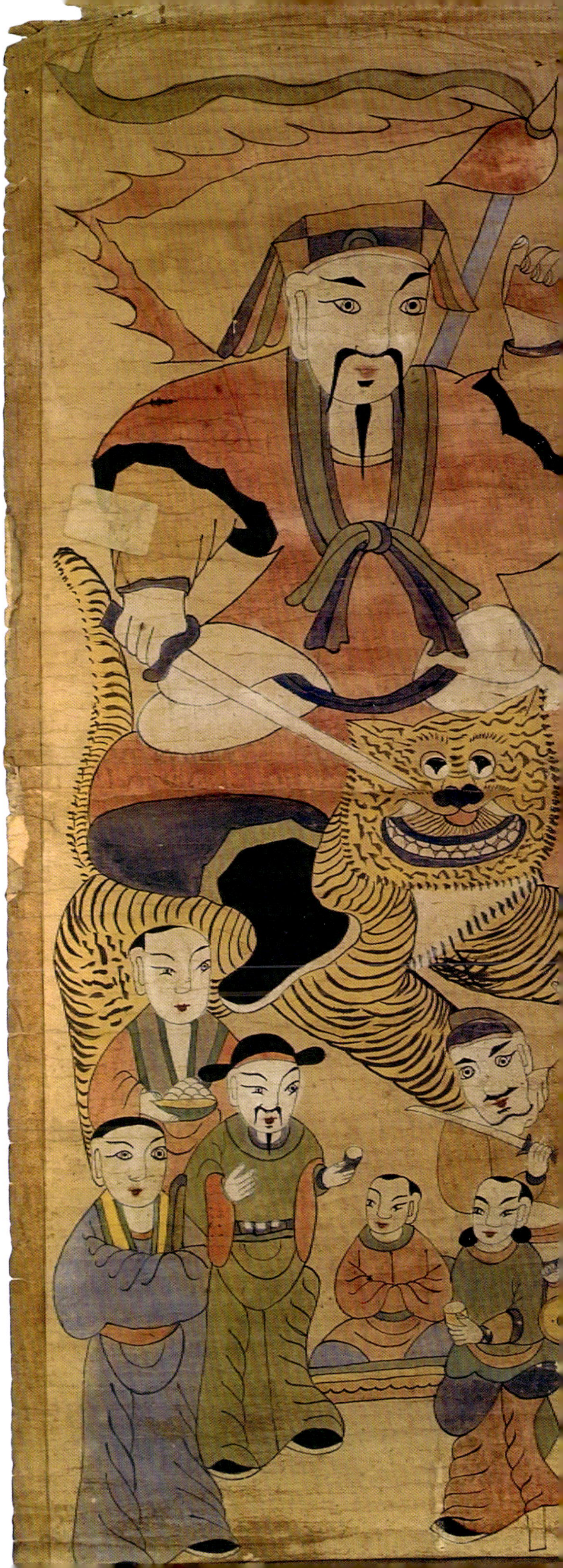

Fig. 64
The God of Medicine, c. early 20th century
Sán Dìu, Vietnam

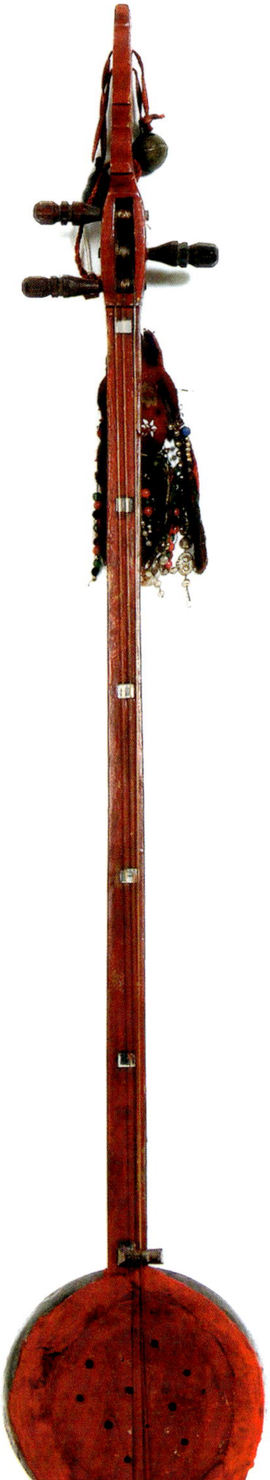

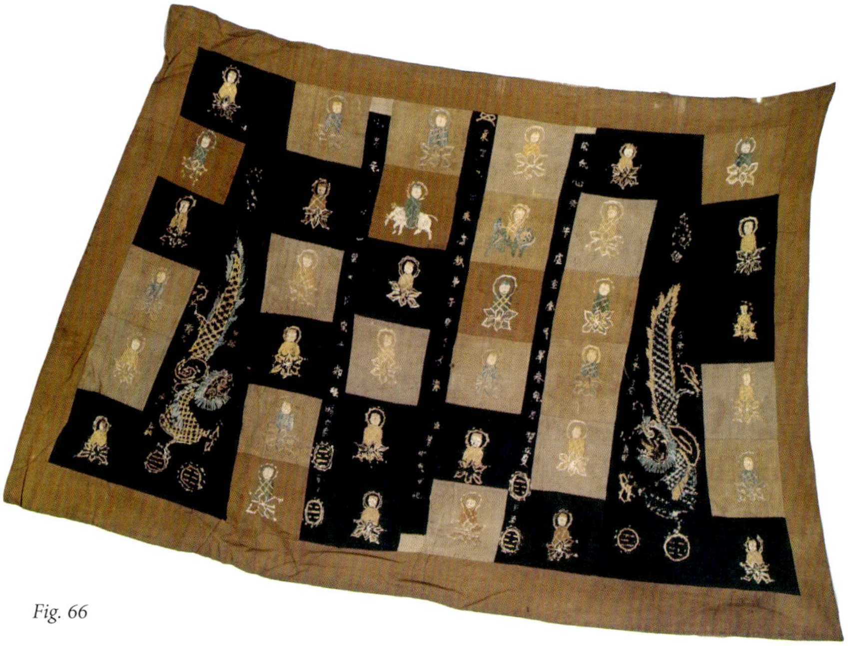

Fig. 66

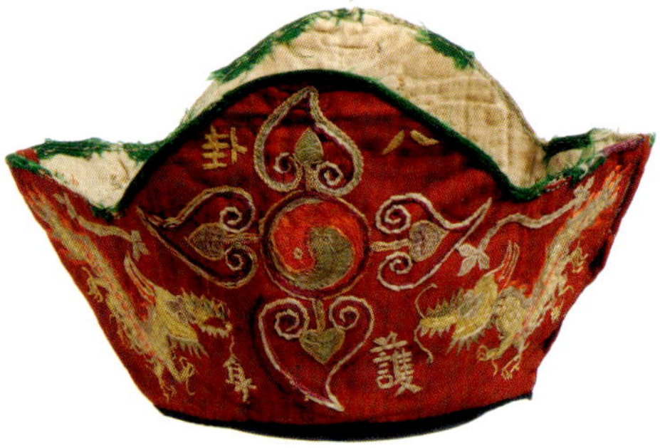

Fig. 67

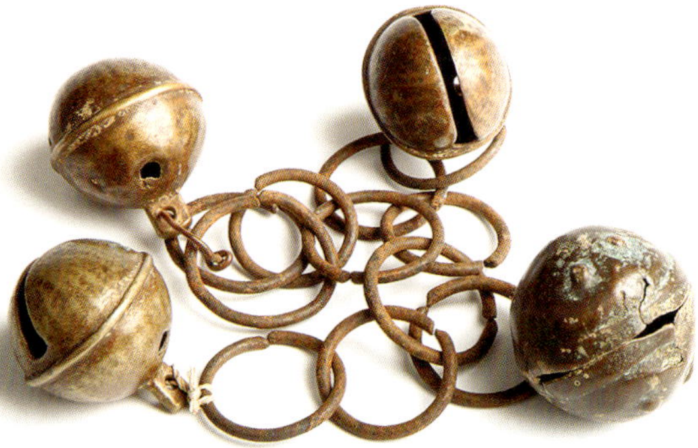

Fig. 68

Fig. 65

Fig. 65
Lute *(đàn tính)*, c. early 20th century
Tày, Vietnam

Fig. 66
Formal robe, c. early–mid-20th century
Cao Làn–Sán Chi (Sán Chay), Vietnam

Fig. 67
Ritual hat, c. early–mid-20th century
Nùng, Vietnam

Fig. 68
Small spherical bells, c. early 20th century
Tày, Vietnam

Nùng religions, is a priestess who is believed to be possessed by a Buddhist spirit, or Buddha's essence, when she is in a trance and performing rituals based on Buddhist texts. In the Tày and Nùng culture, a *pụt* usually performs jointly with a *thầy tào* in common rituals such as praying for well-being, good health, happiness, and longevity, or at a housewarming.[19] In her fieldwork among the Ngạn, a Tày subgroup living in Cao Bằng province, Nguyễn Thị Yên specified three important rituals that must be presided over by a *pụt* priestess: welcoming a new bride into the groom's house during the wedding, celebrating the birth of the first child in a family by honoring the Flower Goddess, and guiding the soul of the newly dead to be united with their ancestors in heaven.[20] It is believed that if the children of dead parents cannot afford to pay for the rituals to ensure their being reborn into heaven, their souls will come to haunt the children. Therefore, the children try their best to organize religious prayers for their dead parents, even if they are poor.[21]

The shaman priestesses' religious rituals are in poetic form. Usually the verbal forms were passed down orally from teachers to students to be learned by heart, but they were also recorded in written form. The liturgical texts are recited in the local dialect with a lively melody, accompanied by a two-stringed lute (Fig. 65) and punctuated with the rattling of small spherical bells (Fig. 68). Since the *pụt* priestesses perform rituals influenced by Buddhist texts, they wear a formal Buddhist robe (Fig. 66), a ritual Buddhist hat (Fig. 67), a crown with banners, and use a square sitting mat made of cloth.[22] The number of streamers or ribbons attached to the crown indicates their rank (Figs. 69–74). The lowest grade is indicated by five ribbons, then the grades increase with seven, nine, eleven, thirteen, up to the highest rank of fifteen ribbons.[23] Customarily, every three or six years a shaman priestess can be promoted to a higher rank; this involves an elaborate ritual with the participation of at least one high-ranking male ritual master *thầy tào* and a few high shaman priestesses.[24]

Pụt and *then* are practiced in singing and chanting rituals, and have the ability to pray for the well-being of family members, particularly during New Year celebrations, or when someone gets sick. They are asked to choose auspicious dates for engagements and weddings, check horoscopes to determine compatibility, and, finally, to select auspicious sites for burials and building new houses.[25] They can offer apotropaic rituals to prevent bad luck and communicate with heavenly deities through singing.[26] Many of their ritual texts are vernacular ballads describing the long journey of the shaman's spirit in its quest to heal the sick or to save the souls of the dead.[27] The long scroll of the Tày (Fig. 141a-q) illustrates the ritual roles of *then* and *pụt* shamans in services guiding the souls of the dead in their journey from the earthly world to heaven. However, *then* and *pụt* cannot perform certain complex and important rituals, which are reserved for the high shaman priest, the *thầy tào*.[28]

The shamans of these four ranks strongly influence the religious lives of the common people. They are the most educated members of the ethnic communities of remote regions and are regarded as having special abilities, bestowed upon them by the Jade Emperor, to take care of people on earth.[29] They fulfill religious needs while also playing important cultural roles: many of them are skilled musicians who can play ritual music, chant, sing, and dance.[30] Among these four hierarchical groups, the high Daoist masters (*thầy tào*) are the teachers who are able to ordain others.

Becoming a Shaman Priest or Priestess

In general, there are two kinds of people who follow the religious path to become a shaman. First, it is often a family or clan tradition, a professional trade passed down from the old to the young, as in this description from Kristofer Schipper: "The mastership rests in part on ownership of the manuscripts for liturgical use: books for reciting, rituals, collections of formularies, sacred formulas, talismans, and diagrams, passed on from generation to generation within families."[31]

In every generation there is at least one person who undertakes an apprenticeship with the guidance of

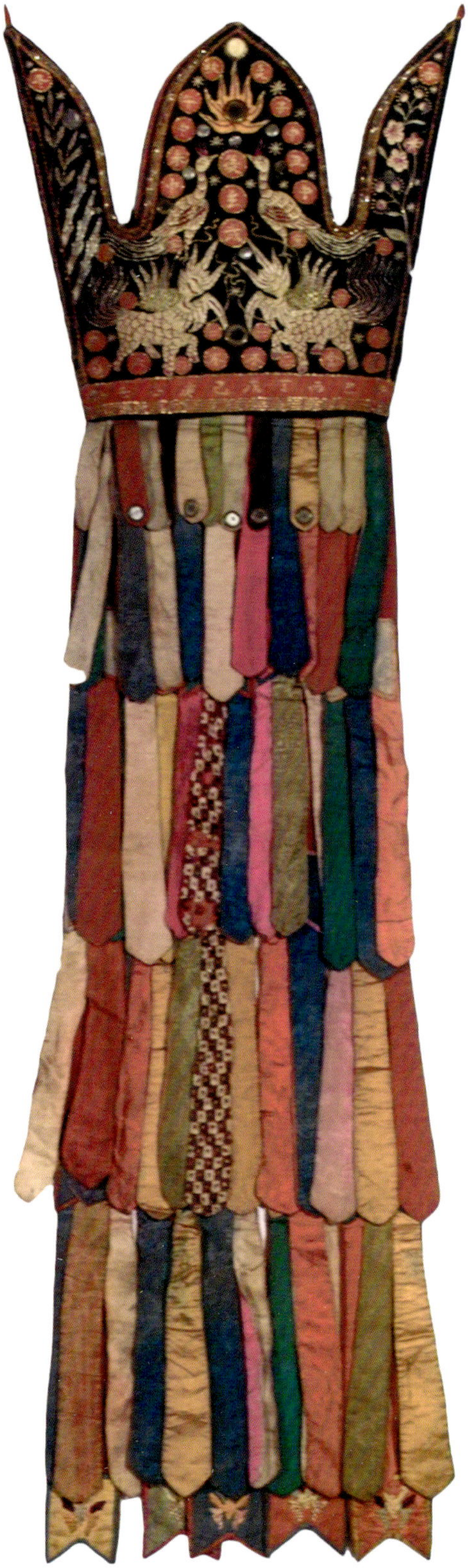

Fig. 69

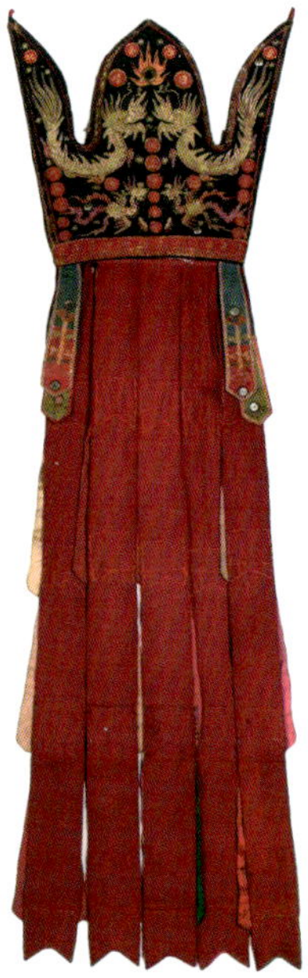

Fig. 70

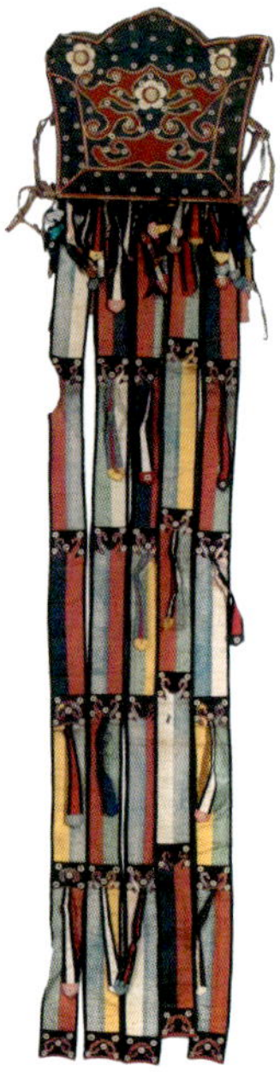

Fig. 71

his grandfather or father. Many stories recount that when young, the offspring of high shaman priests would follow their grandfathers or fathers to the ceremonies. The children perform small tasks, play musical instruments, sing songs, and dance. At home they learn Chinese from their father or grandfather, copy liturgical manuscripts, study magical diagrams and symbolic writings, and practice special dance movements as well as ritual recitations. They must learn the Daoist liturgical rituals and the precise rhythms and melodies for both solo recitations and group chanting. When they are in their late twenties or older, frequently after establishing a family, they can receive ordination to become a high priest.[32]

The second type is a religious calling. Such people are thought to have a special spiritual capacity, as if preordained by the Jade Emperor to carry out his earthly missions. They are considered to be born with a deeply spiritual soul in a mundane body, which is regarded as a vessel, a means to carry out the spiritual work of the high deities in their communities. Many *then* and *pụt* priestesses are in this category. Many stories also narrate that if, when growing up, such persons did not follow their reli-

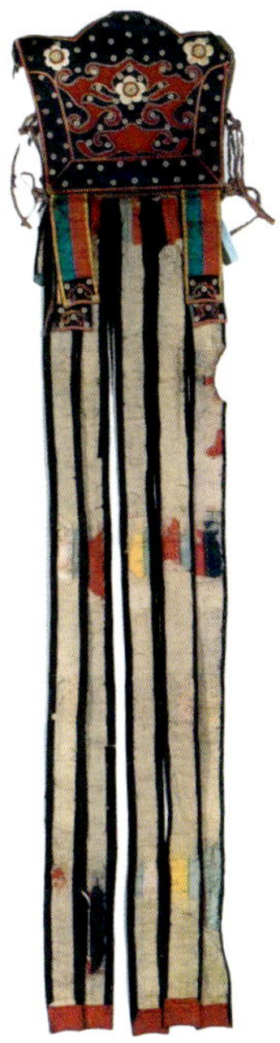

Fig. 72

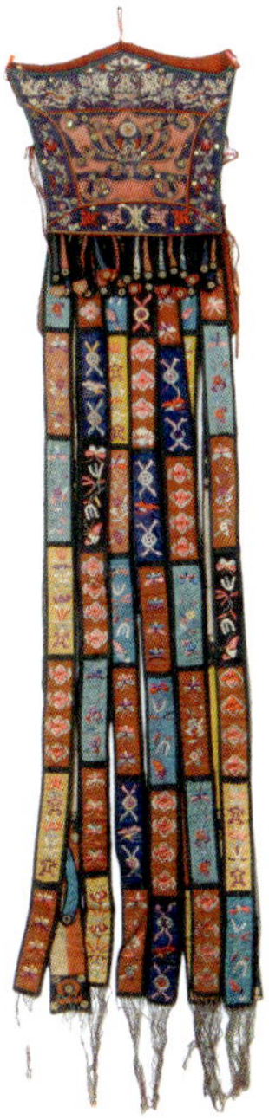

Fig. 73

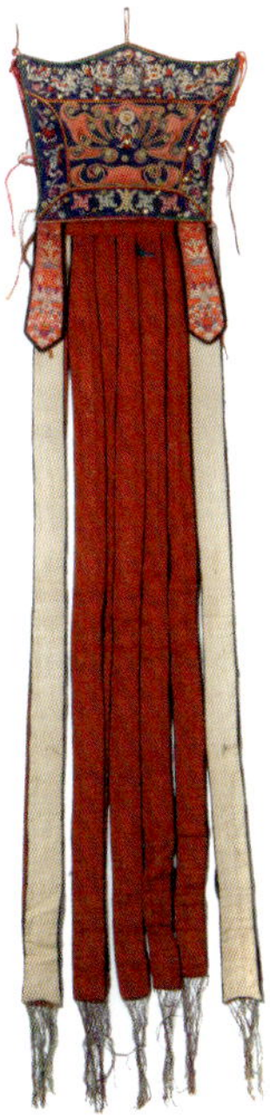

Fig. 74

gious calling, they got sick or acted strangely. For instance, they would climb high trees and stay there without wanting to come down, immerse themselves in a lake or river for many hours, even during the winter, or run away from their family. Such people are attracted to shaman priests and declare that they want to become their followers.[33] It is somehow easy for them to remember the rituals by heart after hearing them only a few times, as if they knew them from a past life and were now merely recalling them. Once these people find a master to follow, their strange behaviors, or "psychological problems," suddenly disappear, allowing them to become normal again.[34]

Among the ethnic groups considered here, the Yao have the most complex and elaborately organized ordination ceremony. As such, it can provide a framework for understanding the other ethnic groups discussed. Thus, the significance and the meaning of the Hanging Lamp Rituals and other procedures are discussed next, in order to provide information about the art and material culture of both the Yao and other groups.

The Yao Hanging Lamp Ritual

The Yao believe that a man must undergo an initiation ceremony to become a mature and recognized person within the society. Afterward, the postulant receives a religious name, which is certified by the Three Pure Ones and other Daoist deities during the ritual. He also accepts a certificate that constitutes a "passport" to heaven after his death, an important document that keeps his soul from being taken to the underworld, judged, and punished by the Ten Kings of that domain. After the

Figs. 69, 70
Ritual headdress (rear and front), c. late 19th–early 20th century
Tày, Vietnam

Figs. 71, 72
Ritual headdress (rear and front), c. early 20th century
Tày, Vietnam

Figs. 73, 74
Ritual headdress with banners (rear and front), c. early 20th century
Tày, Vietnam

ceremony he is recognized as a full member of Yao society and acknowledged as a true descendant of Pan Wang, the first ancestor of the Yao people, and as a divine being who protects his descendants. It is believed that only after the initiation ritual will his ancestors receive and welcome him into heaven after his death.

A person must be initiated and ordained into the spiritual path to become a shaman and offer such services to others. At the ordination he receives a number of spirit soldiers and magic formulas, which allow him to conduct certain services, along with a certificate that is seen as a license to practice rituals, heal the sick, and achieve social status within the Yao community.[35] Yao ancestors only recognize those who have been initiated and only bless and protect those who have specifically experienced the Three-Lamp Hanging Ritual. The Yao are reliant on the belief that their life will be better, their existence more fortunate, their harvest more abundant, their domestic animals more numerous, and their clan and descendants more prosperous if all male Yao are initiated through Hanging Lamp Rituals.[36]

Only a person who undergoes the Three-Lamp Hanging Ritual is recognized as an adult; otherwise, he must sit with the children during community banquets, even in old age.[37] If a man can't afford to do so, he cannot be properly buried. Therefore, if his children plan to receive the ritual, they must include their father in it. Likewise, in Yao society only a person who has been a part of the Hanging Lamp Ritual is qualified to undertake certain tasks and fill certain positions, including the first rice planting of the season, holding administrative positions, representing the groom's family in welcoming the bride into the house, moving furniture into a new house, and sitting on the upper level during the village banquet.

In Yao society, the shaman priests are believed to have magical powers and the authority to lead spirit soldiers. The Yao believe that the existing wicked and malicious spirits wandering around can harm family members. If a family has no ordained male, the family is not protected from these bad spirit forces. Furthermore, a family needs to possess the right religious tools—such as a sacred buffalo horn and magic seals—to pray to the Jade Emperor for help when needed. If a Yao family has only daughters, the family must adopt a son to carry out the family line. In the case of a Yao man who has already received the initiation ritual and marries a woman whose parents want to adopt him as their son, he must change his surname and undergo the long Daoist ritual process to relinquish his family ancestors. This can cost a large amount of money and even his family's honor. Unless there are special circumstances and strong financial support, no Yao man would want to be adopted into the wife's family clan after receiving the initiation ritual.[38]

There are three levels of ordination. The general name for all of the rituals is 過 燈, or 掛 燈, commonly referred to among the Yao as *Kwa Tang* (*guadeng*). The first one, 過 燈, means that a Yao person "experiences" or "undergoes" (過) the ritual process of lighting lamps or candles (燈). The second, 掛 燈, refers to a Yao man receiving the ritual of the hanging lamp or light (掛). In other words light (燈), whether provided by oil lamps or candles, is the consistently required component of the rituals.

The first is the Three-Lamp Hanging Ritual (掛 三 台 燈, *Gua san dai deng*, or *Kwa fam toi tang* in Mun Yao language), because the new postulant has three lights (usually candles) hung on his body.[39] It is the most important initiation rite for Yao males. Some authors have called this initial ritual *lập tịch* (立 籍, *liji*), meaning that this important passage of life has given the postulant his religious name and recognized him as a full-fledged member of the Yao community and as Pan Wang's descendant.[40] Although not an equivalent, it is similar to the Bar Mitzvah celebration in the Jewish tradition.

The second level of ritual ordination is called the Seven-Star Hanging Light Ceremony (掛 七 星 燈, *Gua qi xing deng*, or *Kwa tsiet fin tang* in Mun Yao). After this ordination, the postulant officially becomes a Daoist shaman priest, after which he is entitled to possess a full set of painting scrolls and receive more spirit soldiers. He is now also able to wear a priest's hat made of human hair and perform all essential ceremonies. Moreover, his wife is also recognized and admitted into the Daoist path. Thereafter she can join her husband in Daoist heaven after death. This path to heaven is clearly depicted in the grand procession of a husband and wife being carried on sedan chairs (Fig. 138).

Sometimes, a special ceremony called 掛 大 羅 燈 (*Gua da la deng*, or *Kwa ta lo tang*), the Great Net Hanging Light Ceremony, is organized. It is a ritual combining the first two degrees of ordination. The Great Net is the central heaven in the Daoist universe, and is surrounded by other celestial elements.[41] The image of the Great Net Heaven is embroidered at the center on the back of several dragon robes in the collection (Figs. 63, 75, 76). The Great Net Heaven (大 羅 天, Đại La Thiên) is believed to be the abode of the heavenly beings, over which the Jade Emperor presides. It is depicted as a three-tiered, oval-shaped pagoda framed with fire rings. This ritual is usually performed for a group of many postulants, in order to share the expense.

The last and highest ordination is the Twelve-Star Hanging Light Ceremony (掛 十 二 星 燈, *Gua shi er xing teng*). This ceremony only survives in the memory of older Yao men, and now rarely takes place among Yao communities in Vietnam or elsewhere.

When Yao men experience initiation ceremonies at different levels (usually the first two), they organize great celebratory events, requiring many kinds of musical instruments and masks that represent different gods. The preparatory work takes from a few months to more than a year: saving money, raising two fat pigs and many chickens, and storing plentiful sweet rice for the special event. At the same time, they must invite high shaman priests a few months in advance, so they will have time to prepare themselves. Once the main priest is invited, the prospective postulants must observe many rules during the ritual period. They are required to eat vegetarian food, as a part of a special diet that is cooked solely by men, and to wear all new clothing. In this manner the ritual becomes a patriarchal process; women are not allowed into the area of the main altar.[42]

During a period spanning three months before and after the actual ceremony takes place, all invited priests must refrain from sexual intercourse with their wives. Postulants also observe many precepts such as not killing, not drinking alcohol, not using bad language, and not arguing. In this way they keep their bodies and minds pure, preserving spiritual energies for the forthcoming event. To get ready, they must also ensure that the ritual books, seals, staffs, garments, and musical instruments are in good order.

These rules, regulations, and proper manners aim to help the shaman priests, postulants, and assistants to prepare both mentally and physically. It is believed that if their minds and bodies are purified and strong, the chief ritual master will be able to transmit magical power and spiritual energy to the postulants. Conversely, it is thought that the heavenly deities, the universal energy, and the most sacred and mystical spirits cannot enter unpurified bodies during the most sacred rituals. To symbolically represent the protection of the heavenly deities and divine guardians, both priests and postulants must wear paper masks during the ritual.

The Three-Lamp Hanging Ritual (掛 三 台 燈)

In this ritual a Yao boy, usually between thirteen and twenty (sometimes younger), must be prepared by his parents for initiation into the spiritual path. According to Yao custom, the male with the most seniority within a family or clan goes first. For example, the father must receive the Three-Lamp Hanging Ritual before his children, and an elder brother should be ordained before a younger brother. However, in order to save on the cost, all male members of a family or clan can be ordained in the same ceremony. Generally, the whole process takes two days and one night, or two nights and one day.

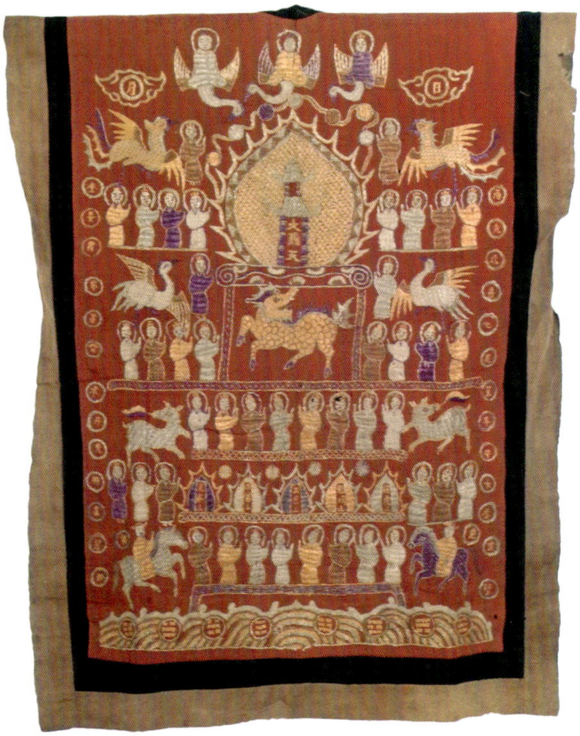

Fig. 75

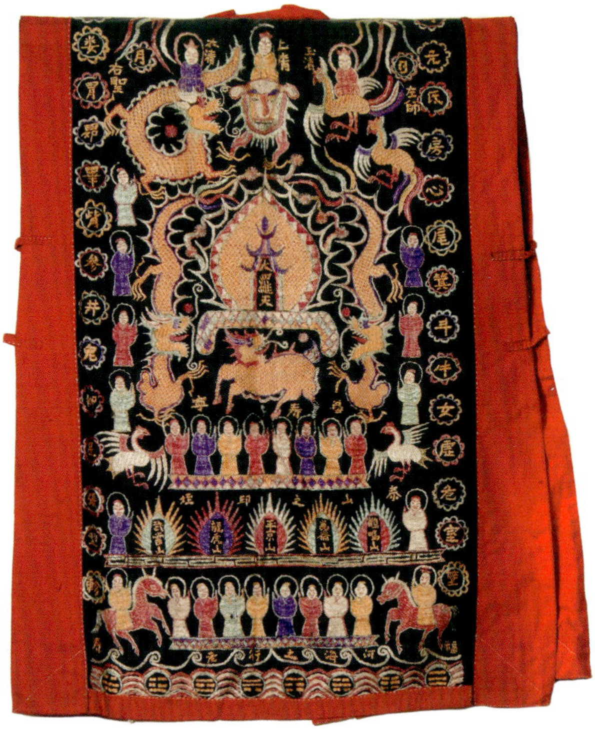

Fig. 76

Fig. 75
Ritual robe, c. early 20th century
Tày, Vietnam

Fig. 76
Ritual robe, c. early 20th century
Cao Làn-San Chi (San Chay), Vietnam

It involves three high priests, three assistant priests, and many additional assistants who have already undergone the initial ritual and have significant experience with it.

Symbolically, the three main shaman priests represent the Three Pure Ones and other assistant priests represent the Celestial Masters and the High Constable Tai Wai[43] (as explained in the chapter on the three basic scrolls). The ceremony includes the six following rites: 1) introduction and the lighting of the lamps; 2) praying, receiving precepts, and taking oaths; 3) transferring the spirit soldiers and other ritual instruments; 4) receiving a religious name; 5) group dancing for celebration; and 6) a concluding ceremony honoring Pan Wang.

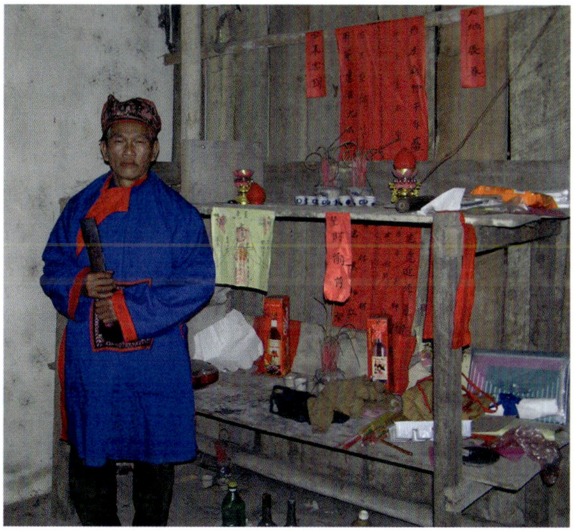

A Nùng shaman with family altar, Vietnam.

1. Rites of Introduction and Lighting the Lamps

The first ritual is the introduction ceremony, during which all of the new postulants line up in front of the main altar. The chief priest introduces them to the Daoist deities by reading their biographies, including their names, birthdays, parents' names, birthplaces, etc. He then reports to the Three Pure Ones, giving his name, religious rank, and duties during the ceremony. Next he introduces the other priests and the assistants in the same manner.

After the introduction ritual, the three priests hold buffalo horns, handbells, and magic swords (or daggers) to conduct a ritual dance and present offerings. Then they put on their formal ritual outfits—the dragon robes—and paper masks. The new postulants also don new green or blue robes, short jackets, and masks. Together, masters and postulants pray to the two Celestial Masters, Zhang and Li, requesting them to protect the sacred platform, to ward off all evil spirits, and to assist them in performing the sacred ritual. In addition, they are given streamers to tie around their heads or necks; the postulants must wear the masks and streamers until the end of the ceremony.[44]

This is followed by the rite of hanging the three lamps. With all the postulants sitting in front of the main altar behind the three priests, the chief priest prays and chants rituals. He then places the first lighted lamp (or candle) on the postulants' heads. The first assistant priest and the father place the second and the third lamp on the postulants' shoulders, creating a three-lamp triad that symbolizes the sun, moon, and stars, the three main sources of eternal light. With the spiritual authority of the chief priest, the new postulants are now initiated into the Daoist way of life, with their paths being illuminated and guided by the eternal forces, the Three Pure Ones, and other celestial deities.

2. Praying, Receiving Precepts, and Taking Oaths

The chief priest then reads the ten prayers, ten vows, ten prohibitions, and ten oaths through which specific religious concepts are formulated. Each postulant repeats them three times.[45] These four sets of prayers, vows, prohibitions, and oaths lay an important foundation upon which the Yao man builds his life. Since these texts have not been printed or mentioned in any Western language, they are translated here:

Ten Prayers[46]

1. May the spirits of the Three Origins (*sanyuan*) lead the Way.
2. May the lion and elephant accompany (me).
3. May the spirits of the Three Origins protect (me).
4. May the six ways glorify.
5. May the five stars illuminate (me).
6. May the six horses be strong.
7. May the domestic animals multiply.
8. May a treasure horse return to heaven.
9. May the good spirits be safe and protected.
10. May the evil spirits be destroyed.

Ten Vows

1. (I) vow to be efficacious.
2. (I) vow to have no doubt.
3. (I) vow the spirits of the Three Origins descend from heaven and aid (me).
4. (I) vow the Four Saints distribute the spirit soldiers.
5. (I) vow the Five Masters protect (me).
6. (I) vow the Six Spirits always be pure.
7. (I) vow the Seven Stars protect (me).
8. (I) vow the Eight Diagrams appear.
9. (I) vow the Nine Mystic Methods be born.
10. (I) vow everything will be perfect.

Ten Prohibitions

1. You are prohibited to kill domestic animals and all living beings.
2. You are prohibited to curse the heaven, earth, sun, and moon.
3. You are prohibited to curse your parents, and your immediate and distant relatives.
4. You are prohibited to be greedy, lust after women, and cheat others.
5. You are prohibited to fear death and desire life.
6. You are prohibited to esteem the rich and look down on the poor.
7. You are prohibited to be adulterous and practice dishonest trade.
8. You are prohibited to disregard your siblings, relatives, and friends.
9. You are prohibited to be afraid of tigers, snakes, heavy rains, and storms; when someone asks you for help, you must be ready to go.
10. You are prohibited to curse saints and sages, but will always honor them.

Ten Oaths

1. If a river, a stream, or a creek is flooded, when someone invites you, can you go? Yes, I can.
2. If there is a heavy rain, a big storm, when someone invites you, can you go? Yes, I can.
3. If there are big insects blocking the road, when someone invites you, can you go? Yes, I can.
4. If someone invites you to go in the middle of the night, can you go? Yes, I can.
5. If someone is very sick, and his relative comes to beg you to save the sick, can you go? Yes, I can.
6. If someone invites you, but you must cross the streams, climb the mountain passes, can you go? Yes, I can.
7. If there are robbers waiting to ambush the route, when someone invites you, can you go? Yes, I can.
8. If someone in a poor family invites you, can you go? Yes, I can.
9. If someone from a far distance, separated by mountains and ocean, invites you, can you go? Yes, I can.
10. If you are engaging in the funeral service, or an initiation ritual, and there is somebody who is very sick and his family invites you to come, can you go? Yes, I can.

These prayers, vows, prohibitions, and oaths constitute the religious and ethical requirements of being both a Daoist shaman and a good man. The first two sets initiate the postulants into Daoism, in that the Daoist system is full of mystical language and symbolic numerology. The ten prohibitions aim to educate Yao men to become better people in society by observing ethical principles. The ten oaths lay the foundation for a young Yao man to be a good shaman, one who observes the principles of being a strong and courageous person, who will always try to help other people without a moment's hesitation and without question. In other words, his future ministry work of fighting demons and healing the sick in order to become a good shaman is definitive, as he pledges an alliance with Daoist deities.

3. The Rite of Transmitting Spirit Soldiers and Bestowing Other Instruments

After the official initiation into the spiritual path by lighting the lamps, taking vows, and making oaths, the postulants concentrate on the images of the Daoist pantheon displayed in front of them. As they are now seated with lit lamps, the high priest begins to bestow spirit soldiers. He holds a white cloth by one end, while the postulants (one by one) hold the other end. The assistant priests place a few handfuls of rice and silver coins on the cloth. The chief shaman then uses a magic staff to lift up the cloth, dividing the rice and coins into two parts, one half for the new postulant and the other half for the priest. He then cuts the cloth into two pieces, letting the coins and rice fall into two bamboo baskets. The coins symbolically represent the power of the spirit soldiers, while the rice represents provisions to feed them. From now on the newly ordained postulants can train their spirit soldiers for protection. However, they must set up small altars in the family home, always burn incense, and make offerings.

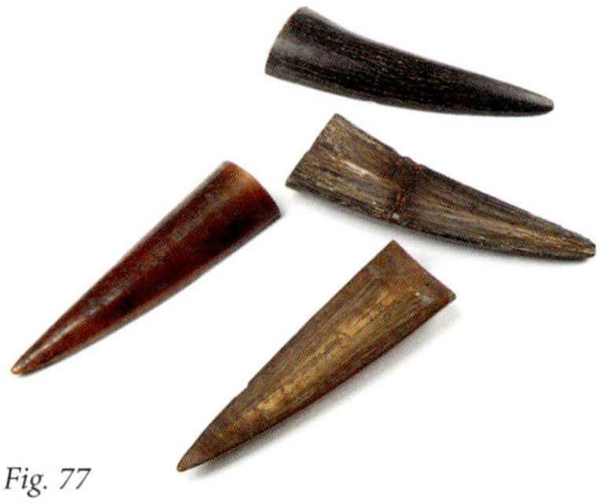

Fig. 77

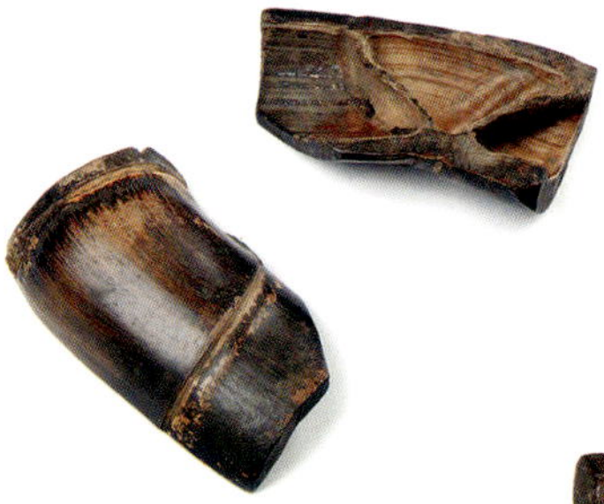

Fig. 78

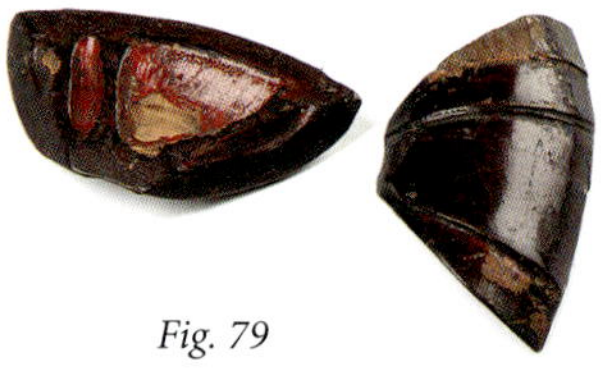

Fig. 79

Next, the chief shaman bestows a buffalo horn, a magic staff, a magic dagger, two yin-yang divination blocks, a crown, paper masks, the fixed set of three paintings along with their bamboo carrying tubes, a magic seal, and more to the postulants. These are symbolic gestures, since the majority of the postulants cannot afford all of these at one time. In special cases, if a postulant's grandfather or father is a high shaman priest, he would either be able to afford many of these ritual items or he would inherit them from his relatives.

4. The Rites of Giving a Religious Name and Transmitting Magic Power

To be officially inducted into the Yao Daoist religious order and become a full-fledged member of Yao society, the new postulants are granted a religious name, *fa bua* (法 洺, *faming*, *pháp danh*).[47] During this important rite, the high priest writes down the religious name for the postulant on a piece of paper and places it on the altar. He then prays to the gods and uses the yin-yang divination blocks (Figs. 77–79) to request a religious name for a new postulant. If they fall to the ground with different sides up, one yin and the other yang, the gods are pleased and the religious name is accepted. If the answer remains negative after a few attempts, the priest must create a new name, trying until the heavenly deities agree. The newly permitted religious name is the postulant's official name, which he must use in the family lineage record and, as Jacques Lemoine noted, "in all religious documents, and all ceremonies including his own funeral."[48] His religious name must be different from those of his family members and clan ancestors, as his *fa bua* will be used for honoring him and on his memorial tablet after his death.

After granting the postulant's religious name, the high priest starts transmitting magical and spiritual power to the new disciple. The chief priest places three grains of rice in the buffalo horn and blows

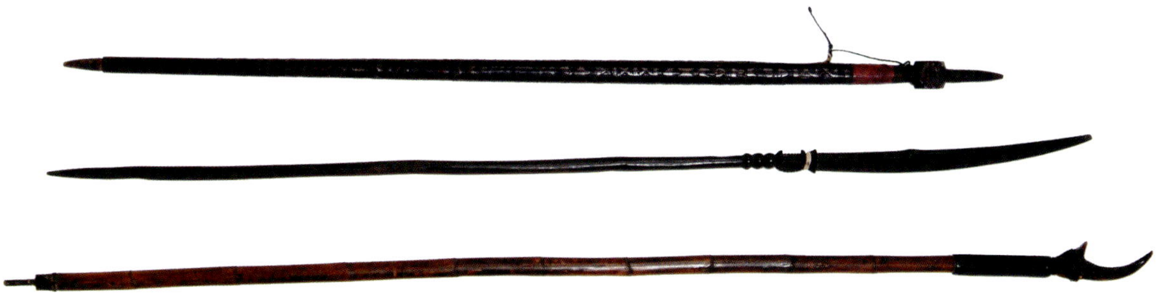

Fig. 80

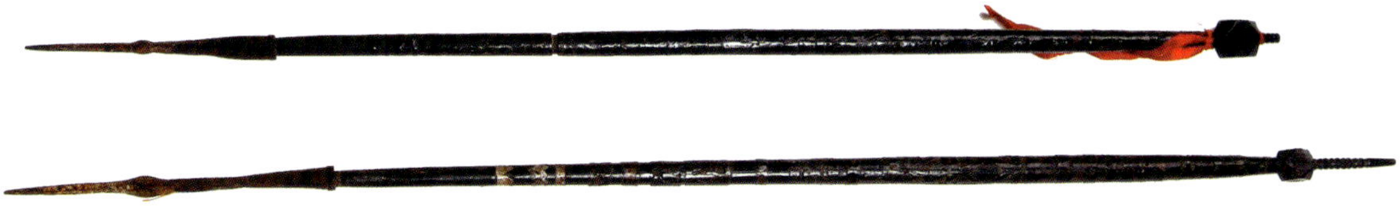

Fig. 81

them into the postulant's mouth. The latter then chews and swallows them as if they are magic pills. All these symbolic rites and gestures accentuate the transmission of the spiritual energy and magical power from the master to the disciple. After that, two assistant priests use special Daoist staffs called *sanyuan* (Figs. 80, 81) to lift the postulant up from his seated position.[49] Symbolically, the new postulant can now stand firmly on his own feet, as he is fully mature and has become a full member of Yao society, a true descendant of Pan Wang. Hereafter, the new postulant must obey his father and must venerate the chief shaman priest who illuminated his life with wisdom and magic power.

After this ceremony, the postulant is presented with an ordination certificate called 牒 (*die*) or 戒 牒 (*jiedie*). It is a large piece of paper, written in classical Chinese and Nôm, with his birth and religious names, his birthday, his parents' names, and his reasons for being initiated into the Daoist spiritual path. It also includes the teachings (prayers, vows, oaths, and prohibitions), the names of the three shaman priests and their ranks (stamped with their own

Fig. 77
Yin-yang divination blocks (2 sets), c. early 20th century
Hmong, China or Vietnam

Fig. 78
Yin-yang divination blocks, c. early 20th century
Nùng, Vietnam

Fig. 79
Yin-yang divination blocks, c. early 20th century
Coin (Tiền) Yao, Vietnam

Fig. 80
Ceremonial staffs, c. early 20th century
Yao, Vietnam

Fig. 81
Ceremonial staffs, c. early 20th century
Coin (Tiền) Yao, Vietnam

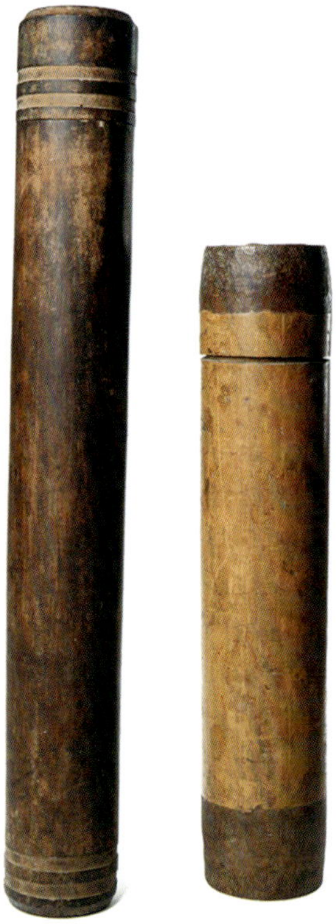

Fig. 82

seals), and the date and place of the ceremony.[50] Two copies are made: one for life and the other for death. The first copy is burned after the initial ceremony as a way to inform the Three Pure Ones and other members of the Celestial Administration that he is now an official member of the Yao Daoist order, and his soul can go to the Daoist heavens after passing away. The second copy, kept in a bamboo tube (Fig. 82) placed next to the family altar, is burned after death.[51] In practical terms, this certificate is considered a license for him to practice basic shamanic rituals such as healing the sick, performing other simple ceremonies, and achieving social status within the Yao community.[52]

Fig. 82
Scroll tubes, c. mid-20th century
Coin (Tiền) Yao, Vietnam

Fig. 83
High priest's hat, c. early 20th century
Yao, China or Vietnam

5. Group Dancing

Near the end of the two-day ritual, after enduring many hardships (including fasting, strictly observing ethical rules and regulations, kneeling for a long period of time, and sleep deprivation), it is time to celebrate the great achievement. The chief priest teaches the postulants seven traditional dances, including the dance movements used to reenact the story of the Yao's first ancestor, Pan Wang, a dance honoring the local God of the Earth, a dance asking the forest deity for protection, etc. Some of the dance movements are strong and dramatic, reflecting the rituals of using ceremonial weapons to chase demons away. During the long period of dancing, various musical instruments are taken out and played. The shaman priests and the postulants wear masks and impersonate deities and legendary figures. This exciting and lively performance can last for many hours, and the public is invited to participate.[53]

6. Concluding Ceremony and Honoring Pan Wang

Pan Wang is considered the progenitor of the Yao. For this reason, there is a concluding ritual to honor and celebrate him at the end of the initiation ceremony, aimed at all Yao ancestors, for the purpose of protecting the clan and family. Votive offerings are displayed on the ancestral altar. With all the participants wearing ceremonial dresses, crowns, and streamers, all the ritual and ceremonial tools and weapons, such as festival banners and flags, iron swords, magical daggers, wooden knives, and scimitars, are employed in different dances. Two fat pigs and many chickens are killed as sacrifices offered to Pan Wang and the ancestors, and for the banquet at the end of the ritual. The three main shamans presiding over the ceremony blow buffalo horns to invite the Jade Emperor, other heavenly deities, Pan Wang, and the clan's ancestor to join the ceremony. With this, the shaman priests reenact the life of the first ancestor's activities in different dances. Two pairs of virgin boys and girls stand in two rows behind the shamans to welcome gods, deities, and the spirits of the clan ancestors. An important part of this ritual is the priest's recitations from a book narrating Pan Wang's epic story and the Yao's migration across the South China Sea. At various intervals during the recitations, the boys and girls sing songs. At the end, a tray of food is offered outside the main door. The shaman priests pray to the deities to bless all clan members with good health, abundant crops, multiple cattle, and prosperous lives. Finally, the host gives thanks to the participants, and pays an honorarium to the priests and their assistants. One Vietnamese scholar has remarked that the telling of the story of Pan Wang emphasizes the unity of all Yao people at the end of the rituals. It can be seen as a method of reinforcing Yao solidarity and religious belief. Thus Daoism is a means of connecting the Yao, whether they are nearby or scattered across southern China or Southeast Asia.[54]

The Seven-Star Hanging Light Ceremony (掛 七 星 燈)

The Seven-Star Hanging Light Ceremony is perhaps the most important ritual for a Yao man, after he has received the initial Three-Lamp Hanging Ritual and wants to become a high Daoist shaman priest. After this ceremony he is fully ordained, can possess the full set of seventeen or eighteen scrolls, and can add even more ritual paintings for religious services, including a long horizontal scroll called *The Dragon Bridge of the Great Dao* or *Praying for Salvation for the Dead*, the Four Heavenly Messengers, the Forebears, the Enforcers of Fasting and Chasity, Pan Hu's Five Banners of Knights, and several sets of paper masks. He is also entitled to wear a high priest's hat made of human hair (Fig. 83) and a dragon robe, symbols of great status. With this ritual he becomes a specialist and spends his life as a high shaman priest.

Unlike the initial ceremony, which is intended for unmarried young men, the Seven-Star Hanging Light Ceremony is meant for a married Yao adult. This ritual ceremony requires the participation of seven high shaman priests, seven priest assistants, and many other helpers. It is lengthy, lasting five to seven days and nights, and beyond the initial ceremony it includes five additional rites: 1) Introduction to the Jade Emperor, 2) The Second Wedding, 3) Honoring the Rice Spirits, 4) Visiting the Heavenly Palace (Rebirth), and 5) Mounting the Sacred Platform to Honor Heaven. Each is outlined below, followed by a description of its procedures and the symbolic significance of lighting the seven candles. As with the first ordination, the Seven-Star Hanging Light Ceremony concludes with celebratory dancing and a ceremony honoring Pan Wang.

During this ceremony, seven priests hold candles corresponding to parts of the postulant's body. The chief priest sets the first candle on the candidate's head, while others position candles on the right shoulder, hands, and knees, with the last placed on the ground beneath the candidate's chair. The first two candles, on the head and right shoulder, represent the sun and moon, while the five other candles symbolize the five planets and five elements of the Chinese Daoist cosmos: Venus (金 星) for metal; Jupiter (木 星) for wood; Mercury (水 星) for water; Mars (火 星) for fire; and Saturn (土 星) for earth. The candle signifying Saturn—the earth element—is the one placed on the ground.[55] These seven stars correspond to the seventh of the ten vows the postulant took when he received the Three-Lamp Hanging Ritual: "I vow the Seven Stars protect (me)." The five stars representing the five planets and elements correspond to the fifth of the ten prayers:

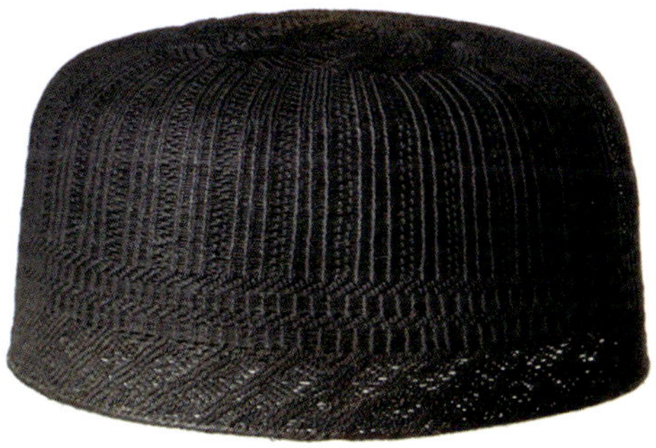

Fig. 83

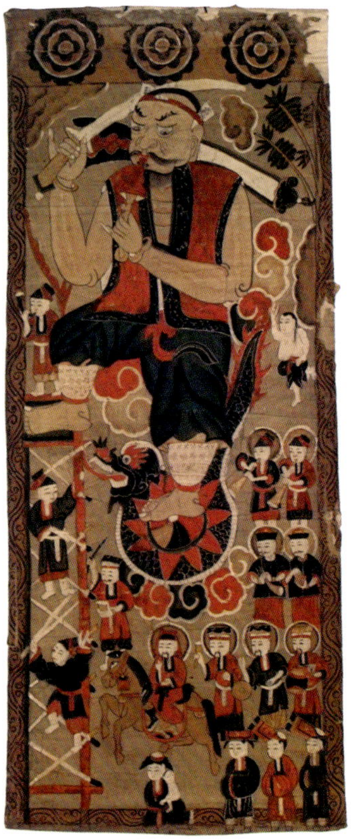

Fig. 84

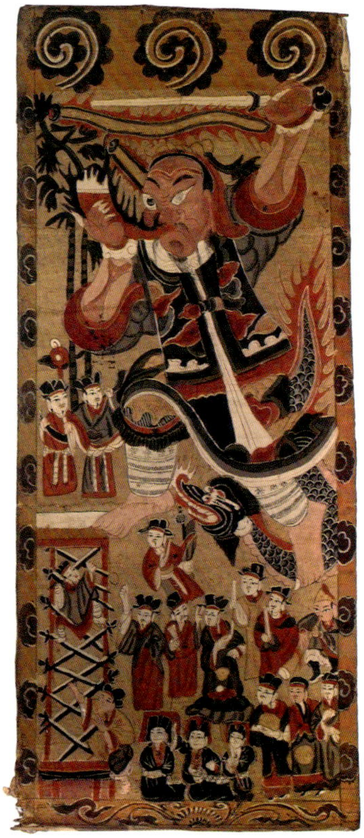

Fig. 85

"May the five stars illuminate." The symbols of the seven stars are always depicted on the back of the dragon robe: the sun and moon above, the others surrounding the Great Net Heaven, indicated by Chinese characters, radiating light flames at the center (Figs. 63, 75, 159).

The seven lights probably refer to the seven vortexes of vital energy in Daoism. A true Daoist would practice meditation techniques to channel the energy in his body, believing that, with the right practice, he could achieve extra longevity or even become an immortal. In his study of Yao shamanic practice, Đặng Nghiêm Vạn observed that though the Yao priests in Vietnam followed Daoism as a religious practice, they did not cultivate the traditional Dao methods of meditation, breathing, and dieting required to become an immortal. He remarked, however, that many of their religious rituals parallel the early practices of the Daoist high priests.[56]

1. Introduction to the Jade Emperor

After the candle-lighting ritual, the postulant climbs a ladder to a high platform made of bamboo or wood, located in front of the house, which represents the Daoist heavens and demonstrates that, as a high priest, the shaman is capable of communicating with the Jade Emperor and other celestial deities.[57] The rite starts with the second priest blowing a buffalo horn, inviting the Jade Emperor to descend to the sacred platform as a witness. Then the chief priest helps the postulant climb the ladder. In ancient times the steps of this ladder were made of swords, and the postulant was supposed to step on them without being hurt. This was to demonstrate his magical skills and a high level of concentration, a concept that is visible in Major Hoi Fan scrolls (Figs. 84, 85). After climbing the ladder, the candidate lies face down on the platform floor, flanked by two assistant priests. The chief priest recites the candidate's biography and asks the Jade Emperor to bestow magic seals upon the newly ordained priest. One must be engraved with the phrase "By expedited order of the Grand Supreme Elder Lord" (太

Fig. 86

Fig. 87

Fig. 88

上 老 君 急 勅) or "The amalgamated energy of the Grand Supreme Elder Lord" (太 上 老 君 氣 合) (Figs. 86–88). During the candidate's subsequent career as a high shaman priest, these seals will be the authorized emblems for him to use in subduing demons or warding off evil forces.

2. The Second Wedding

This rite, involving the future wife of the postulant, is one of two that incorporate Yao women. Immediately after introducing the newly ordained priest to the Jade Emperor, the chief shaman performs a spiritual wedding for the couple. While they stand next to one another, the priest continues to offer prayers and chants. After tying the couple's hands together with a piece of new red cloth, the priest pronounces that they are married not only in this life but also in many lives to come. The couple is now officially recognized as truly husband and wife under the eyes of the deities. After death they are to return to their ancestral land and live out their eternal lives.[58] The priest bestows seventy-two spirit soldiers upon the husband and thirty-six upon the wife. (After ordination, whenever her husband—the high priest—travels away from home to perform ritual services, the wife must offer incense and take care of the spirit soldiers at home.) The chief priest gives them two copies of a religious certificate. One is burned immediately after the ritual, which sends the document to the Daoist heavens for official registration, and the other is kept by the couple. The spouse who dies last will have a relative burn the second certificate, which will find the spouse who passed away first so that the couple can be united in the Daoist heavens.

3. Honoring the Rice Spirits

Rice is the main food of the Yao, and they believe that each bunch of rice has its own spirit and needs to be properly cared for. The rice spirits live happily together when they are in rice paddies, but when the rice is harvested, brought home, and stored in the house, some of the spirits are left behind in the

Fig. 84
Major Hoi Fan, 1819
Red Yao, China

Fig. 85
Major Hoi Fan, 1829–30
Red Yao, China

Fig. 86
Seal, c. late 19th–early 20th century
Yao, China or Vietnam

Fig. 87
Turtle seal and box, c. late 19th–early 20th century
Yao, China or Vietnam

Fig. 88
Seal, c. late 19th–early 20th century
Sán Dìu, Vietnam

fields. Consequently, after each harvest the Yao hold a rite calling all the rice spirits, so that they may be united with their relatives in the house. If the rite of honoring rice is conducted properly, according to Yao belief, the grower will continually have abundant harvests.[59]

4. Visiting the Heavenly Palace (Rebirth)

For this rite the shaman lies down on a mat placed on the floor in front of the main altar, while the chief shaman and assistant priests chant rituals accompanied by musical instruments. The intonation of the chanting, the steady rhythm of the drumbeats, and other mesmerizing sounds from handbells, cymbals, and oboes put the postulant into a cataleptic trance, during which the chief shaman, transmitting his magic power into the postulant's soul, leads him on a visit to the Jade Emperor's heavenly palace. Part of the rite includes the chief shaman placing two power sticks (Figs. 89, 90) on the postulant's stomach and chest to empower him on his journey. Afterward, the shaman covers the postulant's face with a memorial written in Chinese, which acts as an authorized document to help him pass through all the gateways on the journey toward the heavens. After a couple of hours, the chief shaman wakes the postulant up and questions him about life in the heavens.[60] Once this ritual is complete, the postulant is believed to be totally transformed and to have become a true Daoist shaman priest, his old body purified and his old soul dead. With rebirth of a new soul, he is on the new spiritual path of Daoism. He is now ready to serve the Dao.[61]

5. Mounting the Sacred Platform

Though this rite is called "Mounting the Sacred Platform to Honor Heaven," parts of it take place in front of the major altar inside the house, and on the floor of the sacred platform outside the house. It is a serious ritual performance, almost at the end of the ceremony. The chief shaman priest and his two assistants wear ceremonial dragon robes, don head-ties (Figs. 168, 169), and place a piece of white cloth around their belts. The chief priest also wears ceremonial shoes (Fig. 91), if he can afford a pair. He holds a ritual sword or a knife (Figs. 92, 184), and two commanding banners inscribed with many talismans and sacred spells on red paper are placed on the belt behind his back. The sacrificial offerings include seven candles, seven cups of wine (made of rice), seven bowls of rice, and eight big live roosters.

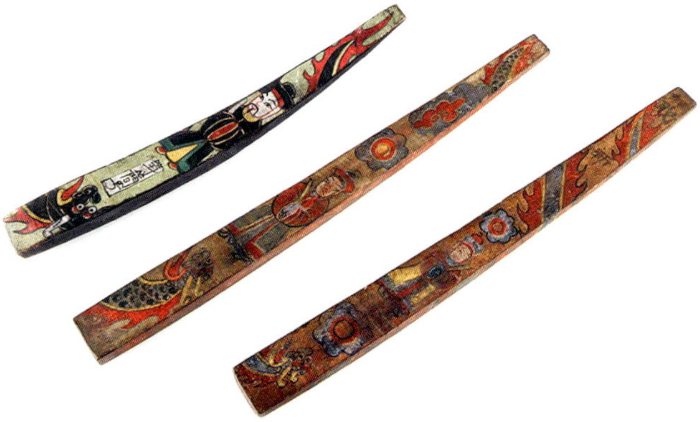

Fig. 89

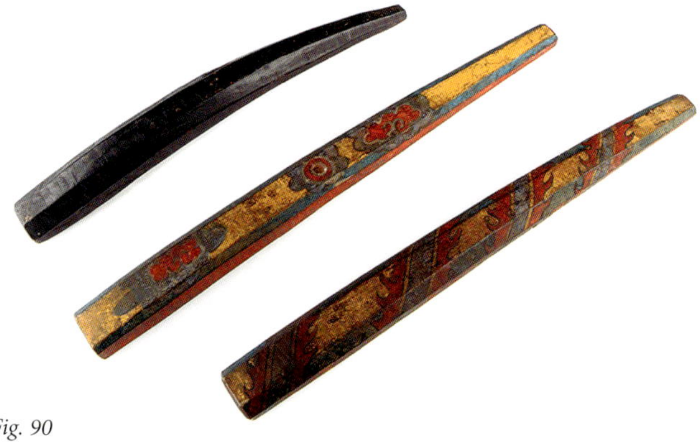

Fig. 90

Figs. 89, 90
A set of three power sticks (front and rear views), c. mid-20th century
Red Yao, China or Vietnam

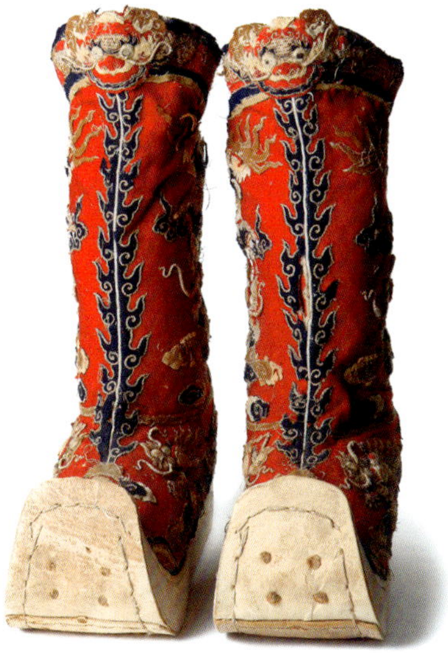

Fig. 91

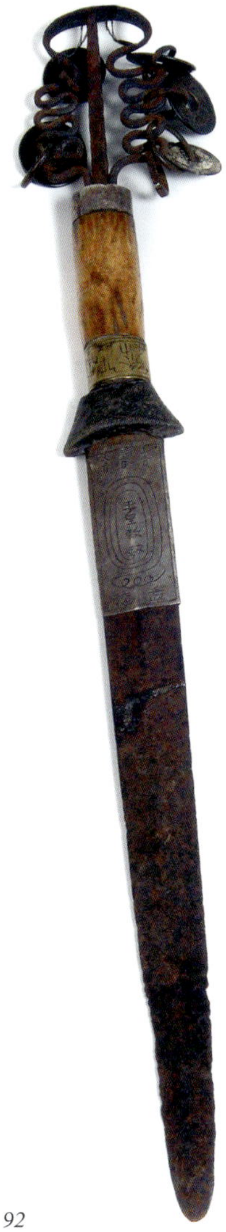

Fig. 92

First, they perform the ritual in the front of the main altar inside the house, with chanting and dancing to honor the Three Pure Ones and other Daoist deities. The three shaman priests (the chief and his two assistants), each holding the legs of a live rooster, dance around three times, and, using a sharp knife, cut the three roosters' throats to drip some of their blood into three baskets of spirit paper money, into baskets full of talismans, onto the petitions written on ceremonial papers, and into a basket of rice used in the previous ritual. After dripping the rooster blood, the shamans burn the spirit money and talismans in the front courtyard. They then pray that the sacrifices will reach the deities, who then would bless them and the newly ordained priest.

After performing the ritual in the house, they move to the makeshift platform, where the bowls of rice, wine, and candles are properly arranged. Each postulant ritually climbs the platform amid the sound of ceremonial music. Standing on the sacred platform, the three priests chant rituals, blow the buffalo horns, and pray to the Jade Emperor, thanking him. Then the chief priest cuts the throat of another rooster and offers it to the supreme deity. Next, the two assistant shamans cut the throats of the four remaining sacrificial roosters and offer them to the Lords of the Four Cardinal Directions. They perform the final chanting and dancing, and bow down three times to conclude the formal ritual.[62]

The Seven-Star Hanging Light Ceremony is concluded with grandeur and a joyful celebration honoring Pan Wang in a partylike festival.

The Twelve-Star Hanging Light Ceremony (掛 十 二 星 燈, Gua shi er xing teng)

This is the highest grade of the Yao Daoist rituals. The ceremony is very long, taking as many as nine to twelve days. The candidate must invite twelve high shaman priests who have already undergone the ceremony. In addition, he must invite many assistant priests who have received the Seven-Star Hanging Light ordination. All the ritual programs are exactly the same as in the second-degree ordination.

This ceremony also involves many sets of paintings, numerous ritual manuals, at least two fat pigs for sacrificing, and many chickens to be eaten during the ceremonial process.[63] The major difference is that the priest and his wife are granted the largest number of spirit soldiers of all the ceremonies, two hundred ten for the husband and seventy-two for his wife. In Vietnam, it has been very rare in the past few decades for a shaman to receive the Twelve-Star Hanging Light Ceremony.[64]

Conclusion

Shamans play an important role in the life of the ethnic groups in northern Vietnam. Functioning as the cornerstone of culture and society, they fulfill the practical and spiritual needs in the lives of everyone, rich and poor, offering aid during sorrowful events and helping to celebrate festive occasions. Through their presence in this range of familial and cultural occurrences, they create and nourish bonds among their people.

As these societies are gradually changing, due to the influence of Vietnamese government policy and the infiltration of Western lifestyles, the roles of shaman priests and priestesses are also changing. In addition, Vietnam is in a time of peace, allowing the country to be more open. As a result, these groups of people, their societies, religious events, and cultural activities are more accessible to field researchers and scholars. Consequently, more study has been conducted and more research published in recent decades.

Fig. 91
Ceremonial shoes, c. late 19th–early 20th century
Yao, China or Vietnam

Fig. 92
Ritual sword with rattle, c. late 19th–early 20th century
Cao Làn–Sán Chi (Sán Chay), Vietnam

NOTES

1. Hoàng Bé, Hoàng Hữu Bình, et al., *Các Dân Tộc Tày Nùng ở Việt Nam*, p. 242.

2. For further study of this subject, see Vi Văn An, "Tục lệ tang ma của người Dao thanh pháp ở Quảng Ninh [The funeral rites of the Indigo-clad Yao subgroup in Quảng Ninh]," pp. 93–101; and Lý Hành Sơn, "Nghi lễ ma chay của người Dao tiền ở Cao Bằng [Funeral rituals of the Coin Yao subgroup in Cao Bằng]," pp. 102–111, in *The Culture and Social Development of the Yao*.

3. Trần Hữu Sơn in his 2006–2009 survey (funded by the Ford Foundation) of all the Yao communities in Cao Bang province (which has the largest Yao population), counted approximately ten thousand books written in Chinese and Yao-Nom script. He classifies them into six major categories: 1) religious and ritual texts; 2) Chinese Daoist astrology, and feng shui books and manuals; 3) instruction manuals containing rites to honor ancestors; 4) medical texts, including talismans and charms for healing the sick; 5) texts and manuals for funeral rites; and 6) books of myths, stories, and poetry. Of these six subjects, books and manuals on the Daoist religion and rituals constitute roughly 90%. See *Sách Cổ Của Người Dao* [The Traditional Books of the Yao], pp. 29–46.

4. See Bế Viết Đẳng, Nguyễn Khắc Tùng, et al., pp. 279ff; Jess Pourret, pp. 52–54; see also Nguyễn Thị Yên, p. 71.

5. See Hoàng Bé, Hoàng Hữu Bình, et al., pp. 238–239. On the other hand, Trần Hữu Sơn, Director of Culture, Sport and Tourism Department of Lao Cai Province, also a Yao specialist, classifies two kinds of Yao ceremonial masters (*thầy cúng*). The first is the 道 公 (*daogong*), a ritual master who worships the Three Pure Ones, and specializes praying for the souls of the dead and well-being for the living. The second, called 師 公 (*shigong*), honors the Three Origins (Sanyuan). He is an exorcist, specializing in the rituals of warding off malicious forces, catching evil spirits, praying for rain and children for childless couples, etc. *The Traditional Books of the Yao*, vol. 1, pp. 31–32.

6. *Thầy tào*, in Chinese 道 師 (*daoshi*, or *tao-shih*), is a high priest, a Daoist master who specializes in religious rituals. Kristofer Schipper renders this term as Dignitaries of the Dao, which is a complex title, as "dignitary" consists of different meanings in the original Chinese Daoist contexts, and is unlike the common term used among the Yao and other ethnic groups in northern Vietnam. See his *The Taoist Body*, (Berkeley: University of California Press, 1993), pp. 55–60.

7. See Triệu Thị Mai.

8. Phan Ngọc Khuê, *Taoist Painting*, p. 65.

9. In Vietnam, and elsewhere in Asian countries, people believe that old trees have their own spirits and are also the dwelling place of invisible spirits. Thus, when cutting down a tree, they pray for the spirits to depart, so they do not harm the people who are destroying their habitat.

10. For samples of the exorcist master *thầy mo's* outfit, see Jess Pourret, plates 69, 70, 71, 72, and 73, pp. 46–48.

11. Phan Ngọc Khuê, *Taoist Painting*, p. 71.

12. Op. cit.

13. According to Nguyễn Thị Yên, the term *then* has its origin in the Chinese character 天 (*thiên*), meaning the heavenly deity who manifested in the earthly realm to help release human beings from suffering.

14. See Vũ Khánh, pp. 137–138, 146–147, and 160–165.

15. The Yao, Nùng, and Tày consider the ritual of opening a new house to be extremely important. Traditionally a house was built with a large quantity of good timber and took several years to complete. During the grand opening, members of the family clans and the village were invited to be thanked for their help and to celebrate the new house. The opening had to be presided over by a shaman priest or priestess. See also Hoàng Quyết, *Từ Điển Văn Hóa Cổ Truyền Dân Tộc Tày* [Dictionary of Tày Tradition and Culture] (Ho Chi Minh City, Nxb Thanh Niên, 2012), pp. 42–43.

16. See Chu Thái Sơn and Hoàng Hoa Toàn, p. 87–90; see also Hoàng Quyết, p. 24.

17. For example, see Vũ Khánh, p. 148.

18. Ibid., pp. 133, 152, 161, and 162.

NOTES CONTINUED

19. Phan Ngọc Khuê, *Taoist Painting*, p. 65.

20. Nguyễn Thị Yên, pp. 16–17.

21. Triệu Thị Mai, pp. 16–17.

22. For images of Tày shaman priests' and priestesses' ritual garments and musical instruments, see the special section of documentary pictures in Nguyễn Thị Yên's *Then Tày*. (This section is unpaginated).

23. Lã Văn Lô and Hà Văn Thư, pp. 29–30. See also Tuyen Thi Doan, *The Reemergence of Spirit Mediums: Then Practice among the Tay in Contemporary Vietnam*. Ph.D. diss., University of Washington, 2011. p. 69.

24. See Hoàng Quyết for a short description of the *pụt* promotion ritual, p. 61. Tuyen Thi Doan, in her unpublished dissertation, gives a detailed account and description of the *then* promotion ritual, which is very similar to that of *pụt*. See *The Reemergence of Spirit Mediums*, pp. 68–100.

25. Lã Văn Lô and Hà Văn Thư, pp. 28–29.

26. Nguyễn Thị Yên, p. 61.

27. In her work Nguyễn Thị Yên provides original ritual texts chanted by the *then* shaman priests/priestess of the Tày, pp. 309–473, and gives a translation of the text into modern Vietnamese, pp. 477–646. Tuyen Thi Doan also has a chapter entitled, "A Doctor for Disease, a Shaman for the Soul," explaining the important role and relating several stories of *then* practitioners as healers; see pp. 102–121.

28. Phan Ngọc Khuê, *Taoist Painting*, p. 65.

29. Ibid. p. 17.

30. Nguyễn Thị Yên, p. 49.

31. Kristofer Schipper, p. 59.

32. For example, there is a compelling account by Hoàng Hựu, a grandson of a high shaman priest, about his learning and experience within the family tradition. Hoàng Hựu, "Đôi nét liên quan đến tôn giáo của dân tộc Tày-Nùng, vai trò của thầy trò *Tào* trong ma chay, cúng bái [Some major religious features of the Tày-Nùng: Roles of the Daoist Shaman priest and his acolytes in funeral rites]," Journal of Han-Nom Study 5 (96), pp. 54–57.

33. Triệu Thị Mai, p. 15.

34. See Tuyen Thi Doan's "Chapter 3: Journey to a Given Destination: An Insider's View on Becoming a Then," which relates many true stories of several *then* shaman priestesses, as well as her analysis within the cultural, social, and religious contexts of the Tày people, pp. 44–67.

35. Nguyễn Thị Yên, p. 93

36. Bế Viết Đẳng, Nguyễn Khắc Tùng, et al., *Người Dao ở Việt Nam* [The Yao in Vietnam] (Hanoi: Social Sciences Publishing House, 1971), p. 279.

37. For visual images, see Jacques Lemoine, pp. 25–26; see also Jess Pourret, p. 51.

38. Thái Sơn and Võ Mai Phương, pp. 77–78.

39. Lý Hành Sơn, *Các nghi lễ chủ yếu trong chu kỳ đời người của nhóm Dao Tiền ở Ba Bể, Bắc Kạn* [The Main Ceremonies and Rituals in the Life of the Yao People in Ba Bể, Bắc Kạn] (Hanoi: Social Sciences Publishing House, 2003), pp. 94–95 (hereafter, *The Main Ceremonies and Rituals in the Life of the Yao People*).

40. Ibid., see also Phan Ngọc Khuê, *Lễ cấp sắc của người Dao Lô Giang ở Lạng Sơn* [The Ceremony of the Hanging Lamps of the Yao in Lô Giang, Lạng Sơn] (Hanoi: Culture and Information Publishing House, 2003), pp. 178–179 (hereafter, *Ceremony of the Hanging Lamps*).

41. Jacques Lemoine, *Yao Ceremonial Paintings*, p. 27.

42. Phan Ngọc Khuê, *Ceremony of the Hanging Lamps*, pp. 150–152. Lý Hành Sơn, in his study *The Main Ceremonies and Rituals in the Life of the Yao People*, describes in great detail how the Yao in Bắc Kạn province carefully prepare for the initiation ritual. This includes choosing auspicious days, raising pigs for sacrifice, choosing the right women for making clothes, preparing all kinds of food, making spirit money, selecting virgin boys and girls for singing and reciting poetry, and arrangements for the invited shaman priests. He also devotes a section to how the chief priest makes all preparations before the actual ritual takes place. See pp. 106–119.

43. For a lengthy discussion on preparations for the ritual event, see Phan Ngọc Khuê, *Ceremony of the Hanging Lamps*, pp. 98–100.

44. Chu Thái Sơn and Võ Mai Phương, pp. 92–95.

45. See Phan Ngọc Khuê, *Ceremony of the Hanging Lamps*, pp. 128–130. See also Lê Sĩ Giáo, "Tục cấp sắc của người Dao và tính giáo dục của nó [The Yao initial ceremony and its educational values]," in *The Culture and Social Development of the Yao*, pp. 161–162.

46. The language of the ten prayers is very obscure and hard to understand. Originally it was written in classical Chinese, and it has been transmitted over many generations. However, many Vietnamese authors and field researchers have transliterated the Vietnamese pronunciation from the Chinese without providing the written characters. Thus it is difficult to completely discover the true meanings. I translated the ten vows from the Vietnamese words *thập độ*. If this is written as 十 度, it literally means the "ten laws." But if it is written as 十 渡, it means the "ten deliverances," or "ten salvations."

47. In the Buddhist tradition, true Buddhists must take Three Refuges (in the Buddha, the Dharma, and the Sangha) and adopt the Five Precepts. They then receive a dharma name, known as 法 洺 (*faming*) in China. This raises the question of whether the Yao Daoist belief system was influenced by these Buddhist practices—taking the Three Refuges, observing the Five Precepts, and receiving the religious name.

48. Jacques Lemoine, *Yao Ceremonial Paintings*, p. 24.

49. Jess G. Pourret, plate 78, p. 59.

50. Lê Sĩ Giáo, "The Yao initial ceremony and its educational values," pp. 159–163.

51. Jacques Lemoine, p. 28.

52. Lý Hành Sơn, pp. 93–94.

53. Op. cit., pp. 125–127.

54. Đặng Nghiêm Vạn, "Vai trò tôn giáo tộc người trong việc thống nhất ý thức cộng đồng người Dao" [The religious functions in unifying all the Yao communities], in *The Culture and Social Development of the Yao*, pp. 126–134.

55. Phan Ngọc Khuê, *Ceremony of the Hanging Lamps*, pp. 142–143.

56. Đặng Nghiêm Vạn, p. 134.

57. See Phan Ngọc Khuê, plates 18 and 19, page 119, in *Taoist Painting*, for examples of the high platform built for the Seven-Star Hanging Light Ceremony.

58. For further discussion on the rite of the Second Wedding, see Phan Ngọc Khuê, *Ceremony of the Hanging Lamps*, pp. 148–149.

59. See Bế Viết Đẳng and Nguyễn Khắc Tụng, p. 261–2; see also Phan Ngọc Khuê, *Ceremony of the Hanging Lamps*, pp. 150–152.

60. Phan Ngọc Khuê, *Ceremony of the Hanging Lamps*, pp. 150–152.

NOTES CONTINUED

61. For a full description of the rite of visiting the heavenly palace, see Bế Viết Đẳng and Nguyễn Khắc Tụng, pp. 286–288. Phan Ngọc Khuê has a detailed description of this ritual in *Ceremony of the Hanging Lamps*, pp. 153–156.

62. For further discussion on this rite, see Phan Ngọc Khuê, *Ceremony of the Hanging Lamps*, pp. 156–160.

63. Đặng Nghiêm Vạn, pp. 126–134.

64. For example, in 2001 Lý Hành Sơn interviewed many Yao who were over eighty years old, and all stated that in this life they had only heard of shamans receiving the Twelve-Star Hanging Light Ceremony, but had never witnessed one. Lý Hành Sơn, pp. 122–123 and 132. In another study among various Yao communities in Vietnam, two authors (one a Yao native) concluded that each community used to have four or five people who received the Seven-Star Hanging Light Ceremony, but now this was extremely rare. In the distant past, in a region with many large Yao communities there might have only been one person who achieved this status. The high shaman priests of the Yao community in Lô Giang, of Lạng Sơn province, also agree that there are no Twelve-Star rituals nowadays, because it is rare that any priest has been ordained at the highest level. It is evident that this ritual has since then been abandoned. See Bế Viết Đẳng and Nguyễn Khắc Tụng, p. 272.

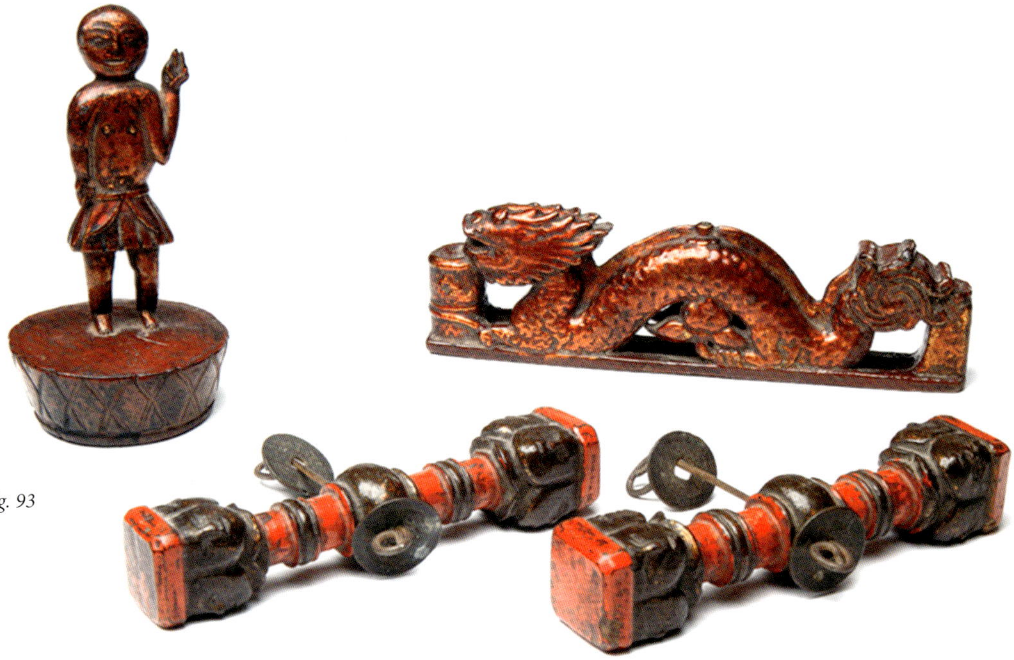

Fig. 93

Fig. 93
Ritual instruments, c. late 19th–early 20th century
Sán Dìu, Vietnam

Fig. 94
Ritual headdress, c. late 19th–early 20th century
Tày, Vietnam

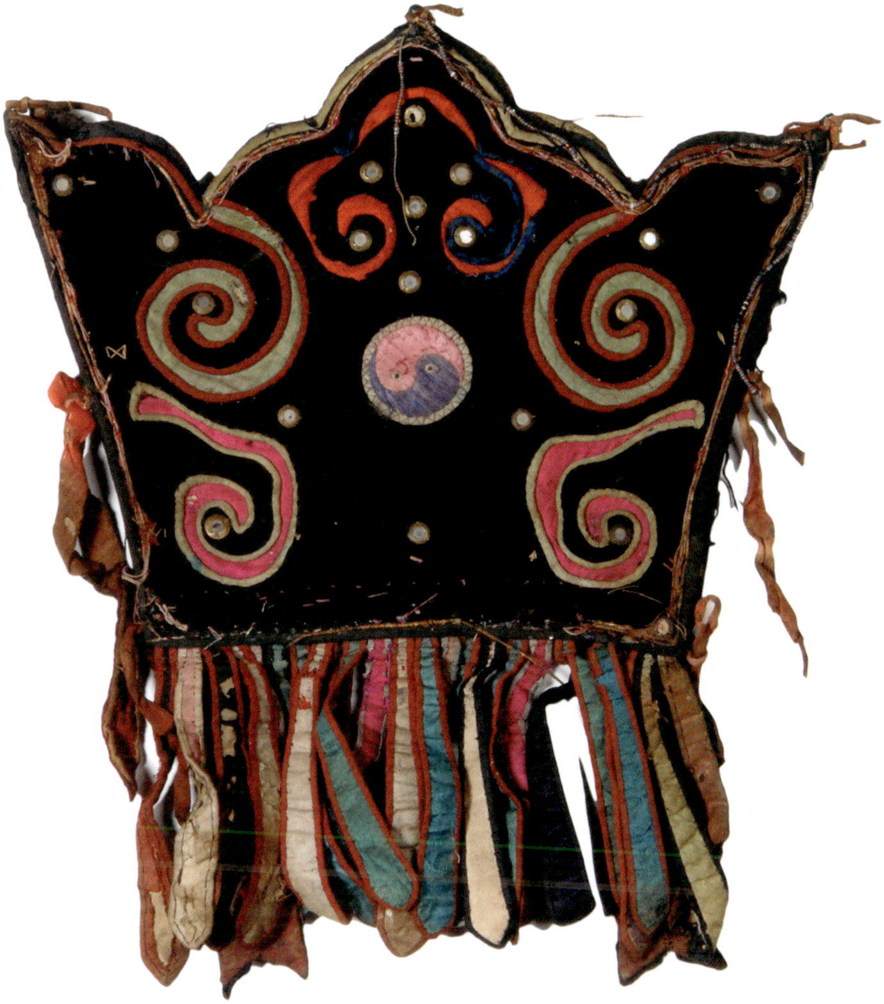

Fig. 94

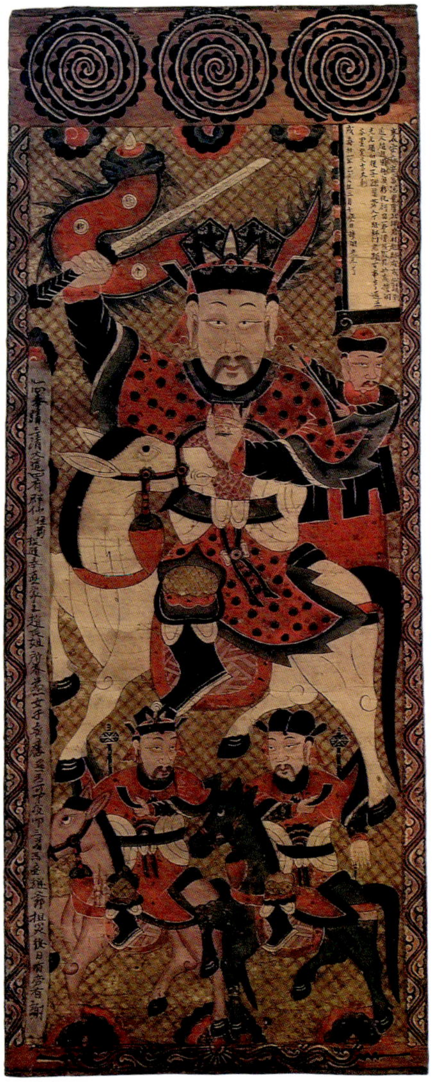

Fig. 95

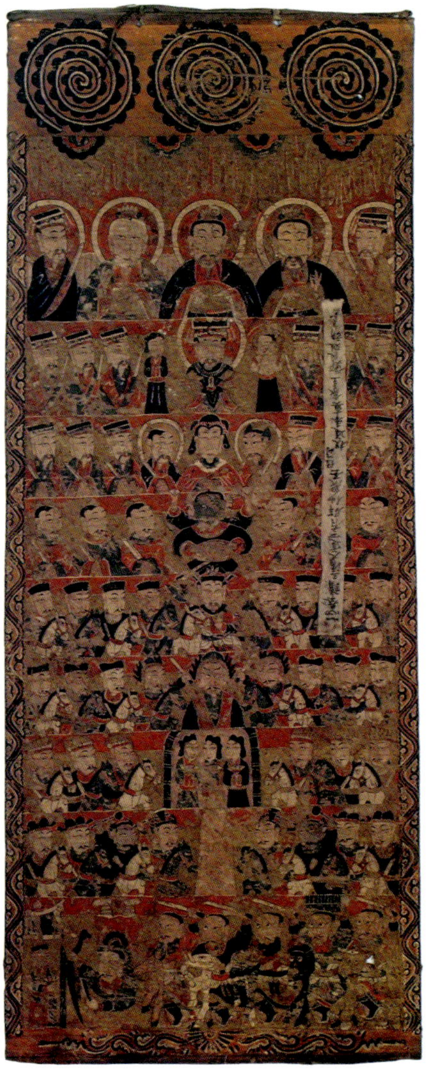

Fig. 96

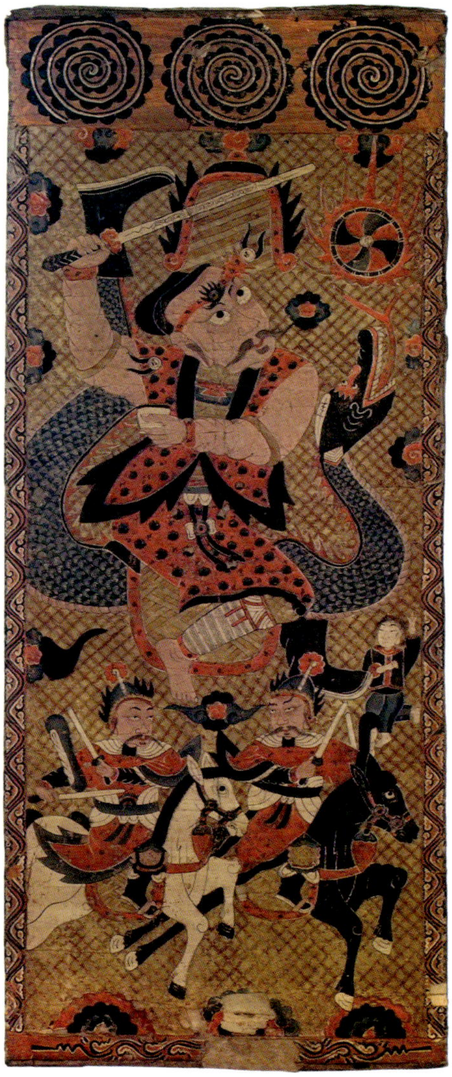

Fig. 97

INITIATION INTO THE SPIRITUAL PATH OF THE DAO:
The Three Basic Painting Scrolls of the Yao

The possession of this set of three paintings (Figs. 95–97) is a minimum requirement for a newly ordained Yao shaman. This acquisition is followed by being initiated into the Three-Lamp Hanging Ritual, a ceremony in which the new postulant is flanked by a three-stemmed candelabrum. After being initiated, the postulant must study, understand, and practice certain Daoist rituals, religious hymns, magic spells, and the names and functions of deities in order to perform basic spiritual services.[1]

Not all Yao males possess or want to possess a basic set of paintings when they receive the initial ordination. In a Yao family, only the eldest son can inherit a set from his father. His siblings must commission a new set if they wish to practice shamanistic rituals and move upward into the higher priesthood.[2]

Without exception, the beginner set must include: 1) the God of the Sea, commonly known as the Minor Hoi Fan (小 海 旛, Xiao Hai Pan, Tiểu Hội Phan); 2) the Ancestors (祖 宗, Zuzong, Tổ Tông), also known as the Administration, or Heavenly Host (行 祠, Heng Fei, Hành Từ); and 3) the High Constable, or Tai Wai (太 尉, Taiwei, Thái Úy). When a new postulant performs the basic ritual ceremonies, the Ancestors painting is placed between Minor Hoi Fan and the High Constable on the wall behind the main altar. The structure of the set, the deities painted on the scrolls, and the fixed arrangement are related to concepts of birth, life, and death.

The High Constable, Tai Wai (太 尉, Taiwei, Thái Úy)

The left-hand scroll painting, the High Constable (Fig. 95), is painted in color and has an unusual gold backing, indicating it once belonged to an important and affluent young Yao postulant. The High Constable scroll symbolically represents the Palace of Life. In the traditional Daoist system, as well as in ancient Chinese astrology, the Southern Dipper, otherwise identified as the Stellar Lord of the South Pole, keeps a record book of human life as he administers the Palace of Life (生 宫, Shenggung, Sinh Cung). It is believed that whenever new human beings come into worldly existence, their souls are registered and kept in the Palace of Life. The palace is preserved and protected by the Supreme Pure One.

The scroll depicts the High Constable as a formidable commanding officer riding a white horse, holding a magical sword in his right hand and a seal of command in his left. Behind his head is a dragon-shaped military banner inscribed with the words "Imperial Order" (勅 令), which indicates that as commander general he can order his army to protect the ritual precinct and to ward off evil forces. On his left is an attendant dressed in Manchurian

Figs. 95, 96, 97
The three basic scrolls of a Yao priest
From left: The High Constable, the Ancestors/Heavenly Host, and Minor Hoi Fan, dated 1899.
Red Yao, Vietnam

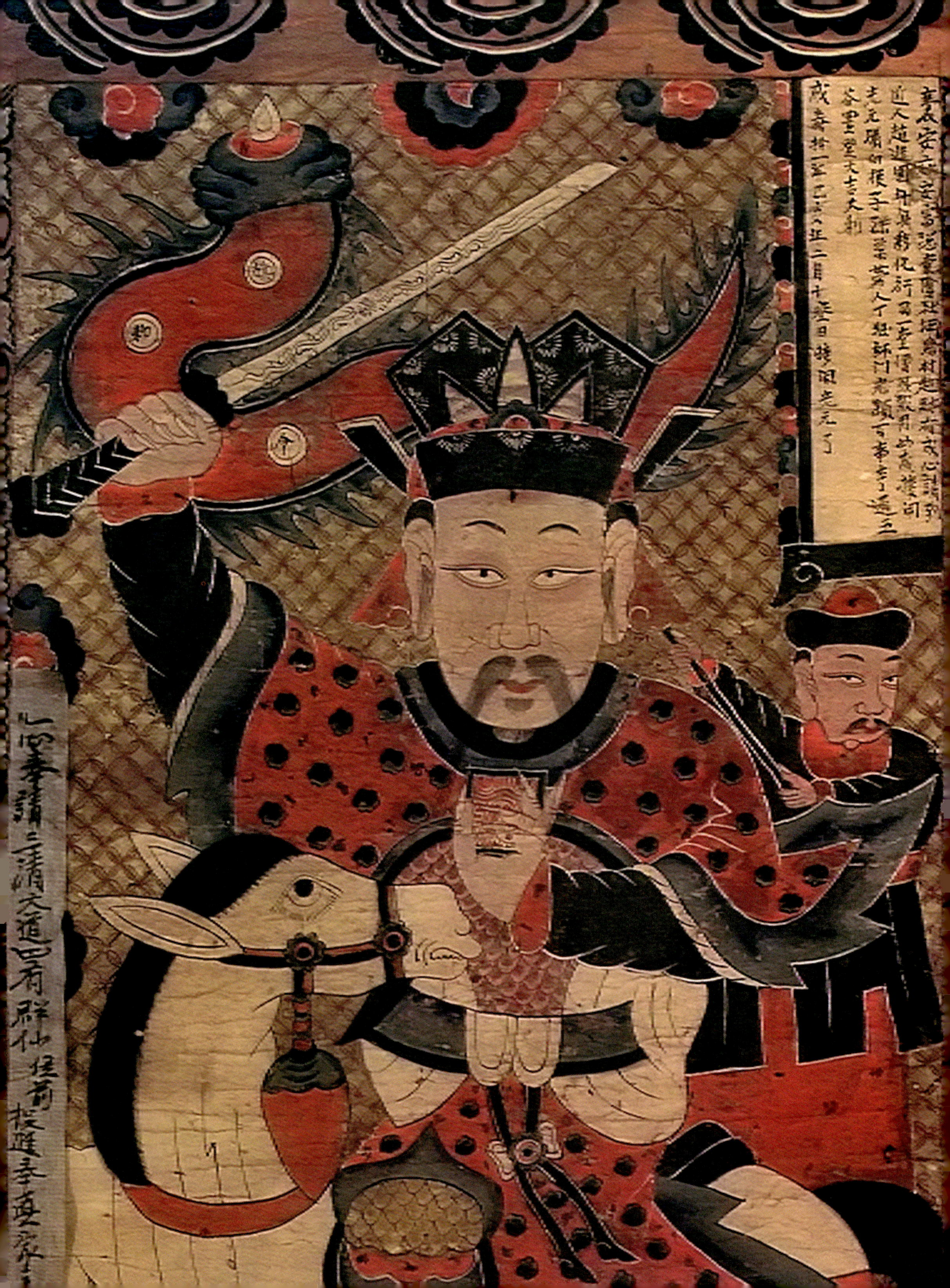

clothes and holding a small canopy. Below him are two generals, Shanyuan (上 元, Thượng Nguyên) and Xianfeng (前 鋒, Tiền Phong), riding pink and blue horses, each with a ritual buffalo horn in his hand and a sacred staff behind his back. Originally, the two generals were henchmen, but with the help of Tai Wai, they were canonized into the Daoist pantheon, where they assist the High Constable in protecting the holy precinct.[3]

Minor Hoi Fan, God of the Sea (小 海 旛, Xiao Hai Pan, Tiểu Hội Phan)

The painting of the Minor Hoi Fan (Fig. 97) symbolically signifies the Palace of Death (死 宮, Sigung, Tử Cung), governed by the Northern Dipper, also known as the Stellar Lord of the North Pole. In this palace everything concerned with death, such as illness, the issuing of death warrants, lifespan and time of death, and the records of a person's fate are administered. The Palace of Death is preserved and protected by the Grand Pure One, as his role within the traditional Daoist belief system.[4]

Minor Hoi Fan, or the God of the Sea, on the right, symbolically represents a spiritual master. The deity is a mysterious figure connected to the legend of the Yao, who crossed the South China Sea, migrating first to southern China and later to Vietnam.[5] Hoi Fan often appears twice, as Minor Hoi Fan in the basic set of three paintings and as Major Hoi Fan in large scroll sets of seventeen or more paintings. Here, as Minor Hoi Fan, he protects the body of the postulant, bestows magic powers upon him, and guides him during his learning period. In this painting he holds a magic sword in his right hand, a cup of water for purification in his left hand, and wears a headband with a large buckle on his forehead. The sword and cup of water are the required tools for a shaman to perform ritual services. A sun disk (日) and a moon disk (月) are tied to the ends of his headband, representing the dualities of day and night, yin and yang, and the concepts of time and the year. These attributes are the signature emblems of Taisui, the Deity of the Year. Legend has it that when Hoi Fan crossed the sea, he lost his right shoe, which was retrieved by a large serpent. True to form, the scroll shows his right foot as bare, and the lost shoe hangs from a serpent's tail on the left next to his sword-holding hand. A flying wheel of fire whirls above the serpent's tongue, and the deity's prominent eyes stare directly at the fireball. For unknown reasons, in the basic set of three paintings Tai Wai and Hoi Fan appear twice, once in large scale, and another time in smaller scale. Here, underneath the image of the God of the Sea, Tai Wai is riding a white horse and Hoi Fan is riding a black horse, both of whom gallop toward the right. Both of these small figures play the role of army generals with hands brandishing swords, as these two important deities protect the sacred platform during the ordination ritual.

There are two different Hoi Fan scrolls, which serve different purposes. The first one is called the Minor Tribute (小 堂), which is the Minor Hoi Fan in the basic set of three paintings. The second scroll is called the Major Tribute (大 堂), referred to as the Major Hoi Fan, which is commissioned for the complete set of paintings, as discussed in the next chapter.

The Ancestors (祖 宗, Zuzong)/ Administration/Heavenly Host (行 祠, Heng Fei)

The center painting (Fig. 96) depicts the Palace of Human Destiny, known as the Ancestors, the Administration, and the Heavenly Host, and also as the Central Government, or the Whole Tribute. This scroll includes the cohort of gods ranging from major deities—the Three Pure Ones, the Jade Emperor, the Master of the Saints, the Two Celestial Masters, and Guanyin—to lesser ones, such as the local God of the Earth, the Five Orderlies, and the guardian deities in charge in this central office. The deities of the Administration keep the universe harmoniously balanced. Related to human destiny and the life force, they are believed to be in charge of diseases and their cures, longevity, fortune, prosperity, abundant harvests, and marriages. When a shaman priest

Detail of *Fig. 95*

writes a memorial prayer to the Daoist gods and a postulant commissions a set of paintings, human destiny can be altered if the proper rites and sacrifices are correctly performed.[6]

The Administration scroll is divided into three strata according to the functions and responsibilities of the Daoist gods, rather than their divine status. Following ancient Daoist beliefs, the scroll organizes this system in descending order: the Heaven, the Earth, and the Underworld, or the Upper, Middle, and Lower Tributes. Each tribute has three levels, making nine in total (九 重 台, *cửu trùng đài*), which are arranged in hierarchical order. Each tribute is presided over by a group of superior deities or one single, divine being. The Upper Tribute is the realm of the supreme deities, or the primordial upper administrators, consisting of the Three Pure Ones, the Jade Emperor, the Master of the Saints, the Two Celestial Masters, the Four Celestial Marshals, the Lords of the Northern and Southern Dippers, the Governors of the Four Realms, and others. The Middle Tribute is the realm of the subordinate gods, headed by the God of the Year, Taisui, the High Constable, and the Three Dragon Phoenix Ladies. The Lower Tribute comprises the heavenly messengers, the local God of the Earth, the Five Orderlies, and many more.[7]

These deities were chiefly based on the administrative system of the Chinese imperial dynasty. Each tribute has its supreme deity positioned at the center and flanked with attendants on both sides and at lower levels. Often they have a courtlike appearance, with a sense of authority and seriousness appropriate for ceremonial rituals. With the exception of the Three Pure Ones, placed at the center of the top row, and the local God of the Earth and Five Orderlies, placed in the lowest row, the positions and arrangements of the figures are not fixed. Consequently, no two scrolls are alike.

The Yao believe that the supreme deities of Daoism created and continue to manage the universe. They also consider the deities' ancestors from a religious perspective rather than from a clan's or a family's ancestral lineage. The following list will assist with identifying deities and understanding the iconography of this complex painting.

Identification of the Deities

(Top to Bottom)

1st row: The Three Pure Ones, with the Lord of the Living and the Lord of the Dead

2nd row: The Jade Emperor flanked by boy and girl attendants, and the Lords of the Six Directions

3rd row: The Mysterious Lady of the Ninth Heaven and the Celestial Masters Zhang and Li, attended by the Lords of the Six Directions

4th row: Taisui, attended by eight mounted officials

5th row: The High Constable, attended by eight mounted officials

6th row: The Deity of the Big Dipper, attended by eight mounted officials

7th row: The Three Dragon Phoenix Ladies, attended by six mounted officials

8th row: The Eight Messengers

9th row: The local God of the Earth, an accountant, and the Five Orderlies

Description and Explanation

The top row depicts the Three Pure Ones, the supreme deities in the Daoist pantheon. Yen Si is in the center with his hands held together. On his right is To Ta, and on his left is Leng Pu, with one hand raised and the other placed at chest level, as if he is holding something. All three figures wear crowns and have sacred halos framing their heads. Symbolically, they represent the universal forces, yin and yang, which create balance within the universe. The figure dressed in a black robe on the left is the Lord of the Underworld (陰 天 王, Yin Tian Wang, Âm Thiên Vương), who administers the souls of the dead. The figure wearing the yellow robe on the right is the Lord of the Living (啓 天 王, Kai Tian Wang, Khải Thiên Vương). These two lords help the Three Pure Ones govern the world.[8]

The Jade Emperor is in the second row. Wearing a cardboard hat with a halo around his head, he is in charge of the heavenly realm, as well as all saints, deities, sages, the worthy (the famous Chinese rulers and heroes who were honored and deified), and living beings. With heavenly power and the supreme command indicated by his jade scepter, the Jade Emperor punishes the bad and rewards the good. A Golden Page attends him on his left, a Jade Maiden on his right, and three of the Lords of the Six Directions (north, east, west, south, zenith, and nadir) are on each side. They are identifiable as lords by their imperial robes, regal cardboard hats, and scepters.

The third row depicts the Mysterious Lady of the Ninth Heaven (九 天 玄 女, Jiu Tian Xuan Nu, Cửu Thiên Huyền Nữ). In Chinese mythology she is the deity who constructed the world and stopped a flood by patching the heavens. Considered as the only disciple of the Queen Mother of the Western Heaven, she is the prime symbol of femininity among the female deities present in the nine levels of the sky. She is portrayed with black hair. Unlike the gods above her, she does not have a halo. To her sides are the two Celestial Masters, Zhang and Li, the last two figures with sacred halos. The former was the reformer of Daoism and is in charge of everyday life in heaven, and the latter is responsible for life on earth and the heavenly military. Around them are the Lords of the Six Directions, all holding ceremonial tablets. (Sometimes the same deities appear twice within a Yao scroll).

Presiding over the fourth row is Taisui (太 歲, Thái Tuế), the God of the Year, President of the Celestial Ministry of Time and the traditional Chinese cycle of sixty years.[9] He assists the Jade Emperor by taking charge of the well-being of the living world. Featuring six arms and three heads, his frontal face is always painted blue. The concepts of time, day and

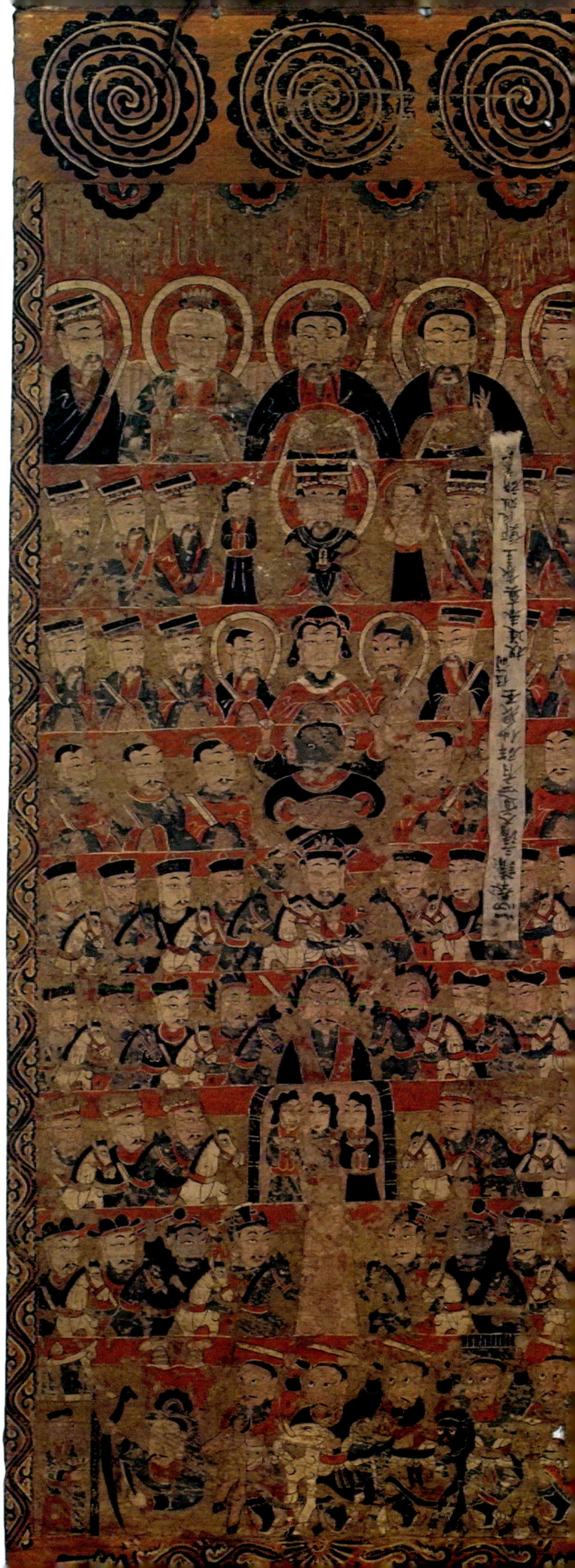

Detail of *Fig. 96*

night, and yang and yin are symbolically represented by the sun he holds in his upper right hand and the moon in his upper left hand. Daoist priests pray to him for peace and good fortune throughout the year. He is attended by six officials.

The High Constable is the central figure of the fifth row. Riding a white horse, he is flanked by eight mounted officials wearing Manchurian hats, whose horses face toward him. From this level down, all the depicted deities deal with the human world and are joined by mounted officials.

The central figure presiding over the sixth row is the Deity of the Northern Dipper (北 斗 七 星, Beidou Qixong, Bắc Đẩu Tinh Quân), the chief and brightest star in the constellation also known as Ursa Major, the Great Bear, and the Big Dipper. Daoists believe that this constellation is the seat of the celestial bureaucracy of the gods. Priests often pray to this deity to extend a person's lifespan, particularly on their birthday. In some Daoist ritual manuals circulated among the Yao, the Big Dipper is prayed to for the removal of obstacles and for the prolonging of life and happiness. Like the High Constable, he is attended by eight mounted officials.

The Three Dragon Phoenix Ladies (龍 鳳 三 娘, Long Feng Xan Nieng, Long Phượng Tam Nương) appear in the "moon window" in the center of the seventh row, attended by mounted officials and cavalry. These deities are protectors of all living things and play a major role in bestowing happiness and beauty to women.

At the center of the eighth row is a ritual furnace (obscured by wear in this example). The furnace is used by the Chinese to burn paper money, whose smoke is mixed with incense smoke, which then travels to the celestial treasuries and the Three Dragon Phoenix Ladies. Facing the furnace are the Eight Messengers, four on each side mounted on horseback, who collect peoples' wishes and offerings and report to the deities of heaven. They are also in charge of carrying messages back from the gods to humans.

The ninth and final row exhibits the deities concerned with things related to this world. First, the local God of the Earth, a white-bearded old man, stands in a small shrine and is attended by an accountant. His duty is to gather information about events taking place in his regional jurisdiction. Brandishing swords and riding on various animals are the Five Orderlies, who inflict injuries and misfortunes on those who violate moral codes. Also known as the Lords of the Five Directions—east, west, north, south, and zenith (possibly related to the Lords of the Six Directions)—their mounts are a pink buffalo, a white elephant, a blue lion, a black unicorn, and a yellow tiger. Often associated with the five poisons—from snakes, scorpions, centipedes, toads, and spiders—these figures march toward the local God of the Earth, ready to receive information about the people in his jurisdiction.

Provenance, Artist, Ownership, and Dating of This Scroll Set

There is an important inscription written on the cartouche of the High Constable painting (Fig. 95) providing useful information on this scroll set. Written in the upper right corner of the scroll, it identifies the name and address of the shaman-owner, the name of the artist, the purpose and cost of the commission, and the date that the set was consecrated:

> 襄安附安富總堂陰社坪為村趙財有成心請到匠人趙進國舟身彩
> 化行司一堂價银弍月女成接開光元滿向後子孫萬帶人丁旺師门
> 光顯百事亨通五谷豐登大吉大利
>
> 成泰拾一年己亥年二月十參日接開光元了
>
> *Mr. Triệu Tài [10] of Bình Vi village, Đường Âm commune,[11] An Phú canton, Nhượng An district,[12] invited artist Triệu Tiến Quốc to paint an administrative set (hành tứ, xingci). It took a couple of months until the pieces were done. The set was fully consecrated. May the future generations, children, grandchildren, all the male decendants be prosperous; may teachers and students be glorified, all things be favorable and beneficial. The five cereals always be more abundant. May happiness and prosperity return!*
>
> *The consecration was completed on the thirteenth day of the second month, Kỷ Hợi year, the eleventh year of Thành Thái's era (24-3-1899).*

In addition, there are two long bands of rice paper loosely attached to the left side of the High Constable scroll and the right side of the Ancestors scroll. The first offers prayers for a man who requested the shaman's services, invoking the supreme Daoist deities to ensure his well-being, abundant harvests, and the safety and prosperity of his family, descendants, and domestic animals. It reads:

> 一心奉請三清大道四有群仙位前投進奉真家主趙氏姐所养苐心女
> 子病患無方可叩投叩三清爲疕繼𠂉担災後日有劳有謝.
>
> *We sincerely invite the Three Pure Ones of the Great Dao, all the immortals in the four realms come to bless the true images of the hostess Triệu Thị Thư* (趙 氏 姐, Zhao Shi Jie), *whose daughter is very sick. We sincerely prostrate and pray to the Three Pure Ones to cure her sickness and eradicate the disaster. In the future for your miraculous work we will be thankful.*

The inscription written on the Ancestors scroll:

> 一心奉請大四有群仙衆圣位前投進奉真家主鄭氏姐群所养
>
> *We sincerely invite the Three Pure Ones of the Great Dao, all the immortals in the four realms come to enter the image of the hostess Trịnh* (鄭 Zheng).

From these inscriptions we learn that the set later changed hands. It no longer belonged to Triệu family (趙, Zhao), as originally written in the cartouche, but is now owned by the Trịnh family (鄭, Zheng). In Yao traditions, if the owner of a painting set passed away without a son to follow his father in becoming initiated, the set was customarily deconsecrated and either destroyed or passed to a new owner. If the latter course of action took place, a high shaman had to perform a ceremony inviting the deities to reenter and take residence in thc paintings.

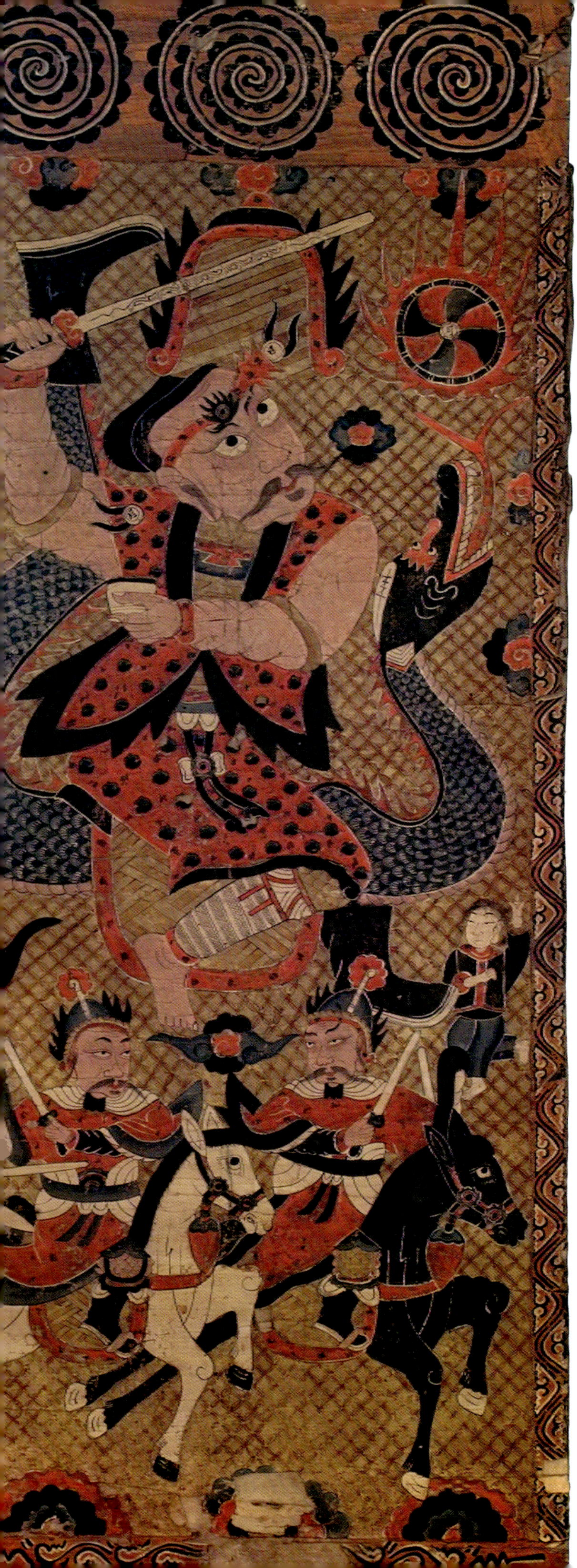

Conclusion

In traditional Yao Daoist communities, men are initiated into the spiritual path through the Three-Lamp Hanging Ritual. After being ordained, introduced into the Daoist pantheon, granted a religious name, and accepted as a full member of Yao society, the postulant has achieved the first degree in the clerical hierarchy. To perform basic rituals, he must possess the basic set of three paintings. This example displays a high level of craftsmanship by a known artist, using traditional pigments and highly refined brushwork on high-quality handmade paper.

Detail of *Fig. 97*

NOTES

1. Jacques Lemoine, *Yao Ceremonial Paintings*, p. 42.

2. Ibid., p. 34.

3. For more detailed discussion of Tai Wai and Sanyuan, see Jacques Lemoine, pp. 79–82 and 123–124; see also Jean Cormerais, pp. 156–159 and 177–181; and Phan Ngọc Khuê, *Taoist Painting*, p. 104.

4. Phan Ngọc Khuê, *Taoist Painting*, p. 31.

5. According to the myth known as the Sea Journey, frequently mentioned in Yao documents and poetic epics, various Yao groups migrated by boat across the Dongting Lake, in the northeast of Hunan province, to arrive in Guang Dong. Other Yao groups from Fujian province migrated across the South China Sea, arriving Hainan and northern Vietnam. For further discussion on this topic, see Jacques Lemoine, *Yao Ceremonial Paintings*, pp. 15–18; see also Jess Pourret, pp. 20–22.

6. Phan Ngọc Khuê, *Taoist Painting*, p. 29–30.

7. For more discussion of Daoist deities and their functions, see Jacques Lemoine's chapter 15, "The Ancestors," in *Yao Ceremonial Paintings*, pp. 125–120. See also Jean Cormerais's chapter "Heng Fei: Le pantheon divin," in *Les Chemises des Dieux: l'Univers Magique de la Peinture Yao* (Paris: Tribal Héritage, 2011), pp. 182–190. However, Cormerais pays more attention to the legend of the goddess Guanyin, rather than discussing the significance of other Daoist deities.

8. Here I use an unpublished manuscript by Phan Ngọc Khuê to identify these two deities and their main functions.

9. For a quick reference on Chinese astrology and the sixty-year calendar cycle, see en.wikipedia.org/wiki/Chinese_astrology. See also Derek Walters, *The Chinese Astrology Bible* (New York: Sterling, 2008), pp. 36–37.

10. The last name of the owner and artist is Triệu (趙, Zhao), one of the twelve common last names among the Yao people. Although there is no additional information about artist Triệu Tiến Quốc, he was probably active in that part of Vietnam in the late nineteenth and early twentieth centuries.

11. The name of the Đường Âm commune has not changed since then, but it now belongs to Bắc Mê, of Hà Giang province, northern Vietnam. This area is dominated by different ethnic groups, mainly the Red Yao.

12. It is located in Hà Giang province, northern Vietnam, not far from Guangxi province in China.

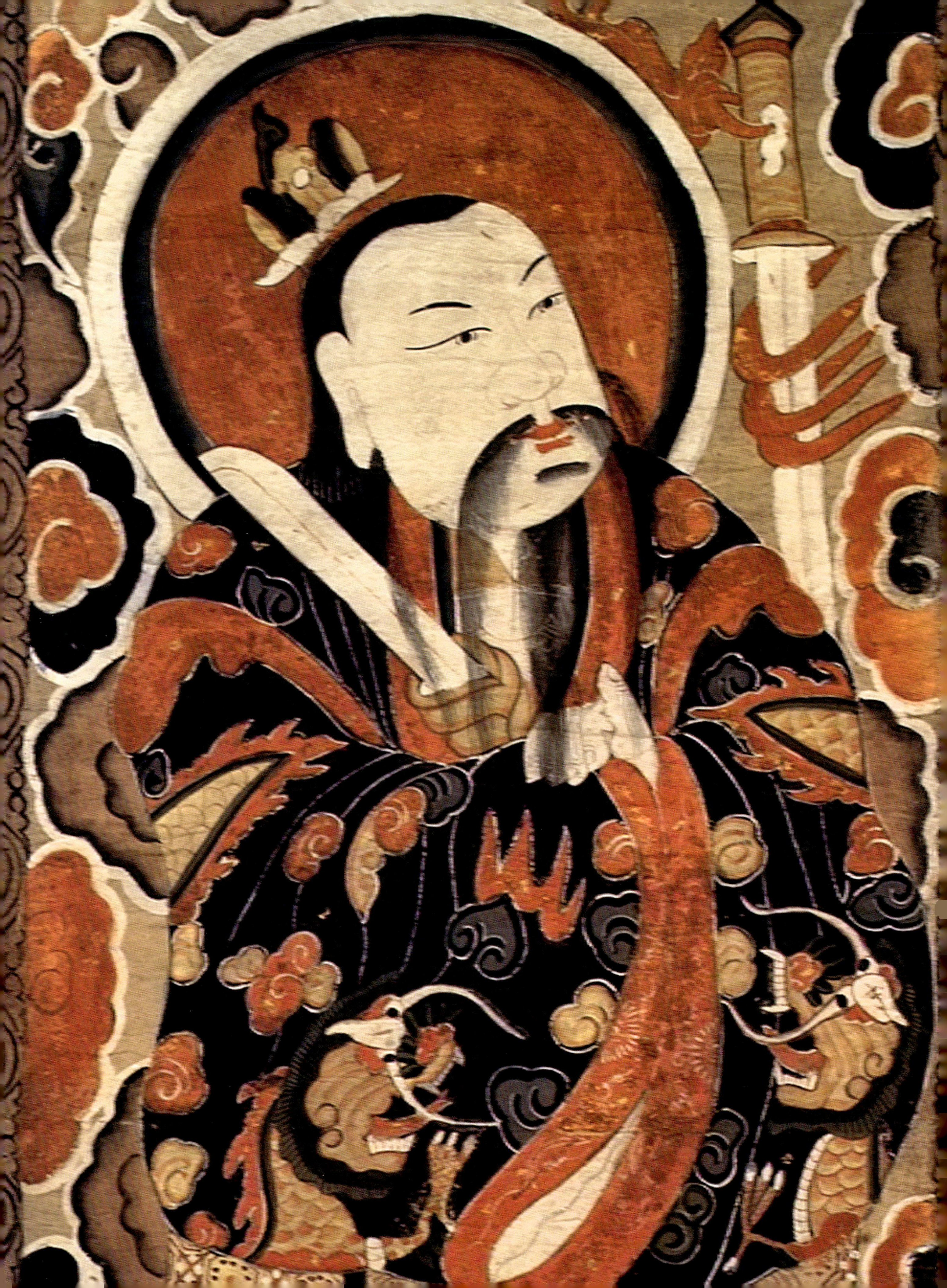

A FULL SET OF EIGHTEEN PAINTINGS:
The Pantheon of a Fully Ordained Shaman Priest in the Yao Tradition

This set of eighteen Daoist paintings (Figs. 98-115) once belonged to a high shaman that had been ordained with the Seven-Star Hanging Light Ceremony. After receiving ordination and obtaining a full set of paintings, he could offer services to the Yao community, such as leading the ritual of praying for the souls of the dead, performing exorcist rituals that expel demons from the sick, and participating in ceremonies of ordaining other Yao men. Since the paintings were portable, the full set could be used to set up a temporary altar or a makeshift shrine wherever needed for ritual and ceremonial services. The full set of paintings not only represents major and minor members of the Yao Daoist pantheon, but also reveals the rituals and other elements of cultural significance to the Yao people.

The full set usually consists of fourteen painting scrolls added to the basic set of three. According to Jacques Lemoine, the list includes:

A. The basic set of three:

The High Constable, Tai Wai (太 尉, Thái Úy)

The Ancestors/Administration/Heavenly Host (祖 宗, Tổ Tông)

The Minor Hoi Fan, God of the Sea (小 海 旛, Tiểu Hải Phan)

B. Fourteen paintings added to complete the set:

The Grand Pure One (太 清, Thái Thanh), To Ta (道 德)/The Virtue of Dao

The Jade Pure One (玉 清, Ngọc Thanh), Yen Si (元 始)/The Original Beginning

The Supreme Pure One (上 清, Thượng Thanh), Leng Pu (靈 寶)/Sacred Jewel

The Jade Emperor (玉 皇, Ngọc Hoàng)

Master of the Saints (星 主, Tinh Chủ)

Celestial Master Zhang (張 天 師, Trương Thiên Sư)

Celestial Master Li (李 天 師, Lý Thiên Sư)

Detail of *Fig. 103*

Celestial Marshal Deng (鄧 元 帥, Đặng Nguyên Soái)

Celestial Marshal Zhao (趙 元 帥, Triệu Nguyên Soái)

The Major Hoi Fan/God of the Sea (大 海 旛, Đại Hải Phan)

The Ten Kings of the Underworld (拾 殿 冥 王, Thập Điện Minh Vương)

The Officials of Heaven and the Underworld (天 府 地 府, Thiên Phủ Địa Phủ), or the Palace of the Left's Treasure (左 殿 庫 官, Tả Điện Khố Quan)

The Officials of Earth and Water (陽 間 水 府, Dương Gian Thủy Phủ), or the Palace of the Right's Treasure (右 殿 庫 官, Hữu Điện Khố Quan)

The Family Forebears (家 先, Gia Tiên)

C. An additional painting:

The Three Generals (元 帥, Nguyên Soái)

This particular set consists of eighteen paintings. However, the original set was made up of seventeen (as stated in the inscription on the back of the Yen Si scroll).[1] It is rare to have the Three Generals included.[2]

The Arrangement

The specific arrangement of a full set of painting scrolls during Yao Daoist ceremonies and rituals is hierarchical: the scrolls containing the most important deities, such as the Three Pure Ones, the Jade Emperor, and the Master of the Saints, occupy central positions, and other scrolls, representing lesser deities and other personages, are fanned out on both sides. The Governors of the Four Realms (heaven, underworld, earth, water) and the Celestial Marshals are positioned on the ends.[3] Since many of the deities are depicted in pairs—the Jade Emperor with the Master of the Saints, and Celestial Master Li with Celestial Master Zhang, for example—they are arranged symmetrically, with each member of a pair the same distance from the center, to the left and to the right.

Based on firsthand research by scholars and artists, various ideal arrangements have been proposed, taking into account traditional practices among Yao communities. Age-old customs were usually passed down orally from teachers to students, from older to younger generations, without written records, so alterations due to mistakes or forgetfulness would be passed along as well. In this way it has become the case that different Yao communities arrange the scrolls somewhat differently.

Taking into account the deities' religious roles, hierarchical order, and artistic depictions, I propose the following arrangement (see Appendix on p. 208):

Q	O	M	K	I	G	E	C	A	B	D	F	H	J	L	N	P	R

A. The Jade Pure One (Fig. 100)

B. The Supreme Pure One (Fig. 101)

C. The Grand Pure One (Fig. 99)

D. The Jade Emperor (Fig. 98)

E. Master of the Saints (Fig. 102)

F. Celestial Master Zhang (Fig. 104)

G. Celestial Master Li (Fig. 103)

H. The Ten Kings of the Underworld (Fig. 105)

I. The Ancestors/ Administration/ Heavenly Host (Fig. 106)

J. Major Hoi Fan, God of the Sea (Fig. 108)

K. Minor Hoi Fan, God of the Sea (Fig. 107)

L. The High Constable/ Tai Wai (Fig. 109)

M. The Three Generals (Fig. 110)

N. The Officials of Heaven and the Underworld, or the Palace of the Left's Treasure (Fig. 112)

O. The Officials of Earth and Water, or the Palace of the Right's Treasure (Fig. 111)

P. Celestial Marshal Zhao (Fig. 114)

Q. Celestial Marshal Deng (Fig. 113)

R. The Officials (Fig. 115)

To begin with, the Three Pure Ones must be placed in the middle, with the Jade Pure One (Yen Si) at the very center (A). On his left (viewer's right) would be the Supreme Pure One (Leng Pu) (B), and on his right (viewer's left) the Grand Pure One (To Ta) (C). The Three Pure Ones are the highest gods in the Daoist pantheon, considered the creators of the universe and the origin of all beings. The next two deities are the Jade Emperor (D), to the right of Leng Pu, and the Master of the Saints (E), to the left of To Ta. These are the supreme rulers of heaven and earth, and the givers of life and death. Next are the two Celestial Masters, almost identical in their depictions, who are the upholders of Daoism, the masters of Daoist teaching and of all ritual rules and principles. Celestial Master Zhang (F) is to the viewer's right of the Jade Emperor, and Celestial Master Li (G) to the viewer's left of the Master of the Saints; both face toward the center. The next two scrolls depict the most complex subjects in the set. The Ten Kings of the Underworld represent punishment, reincarnation, and salvation, suggesting the path one should follow and warning of things that should be avoided. The Ancestors/Heavenly Hosts introduce possible salvation through a wide range of Daoist deities who address different needs of the masses. The Ten Kings of the Underworld are placed next on the right (H) and the Ancestors next on the left (I).

When a Yao man receives the Seven-Star Hanging Light ordination to advance to a higher level of the priesthood, he is allowed to obtain the Major Hoi Fan as part of the large set of Daoist ritual paintings, which indicates that he has advanced from the lower level of the Three-Lamp Hanging Ritual, when he could receive only the basic set of three paintings. The Hoi Fan pair should be arranged on opposite sides, the Major on the right (J) and the Minor on the left (K). The High Constable (L) and the Three Generals (M) are high-ranking military officers whose duty is to provide security, keeping evil demons and spirits from entering the sacred tribune area. They are security officials of the inner circle, while the six marshals (presented by two scrolls) offer security to the outer circles (P and Q). The Officials of the Four Realms are stationed between them and fulfill their obligations to govern the world, both above and below (N and O). To assist them are local officials who are positioned at the outer edge (R). According to the inscription, there were originally only seventeen paintings, so this painting was added later to the full set.

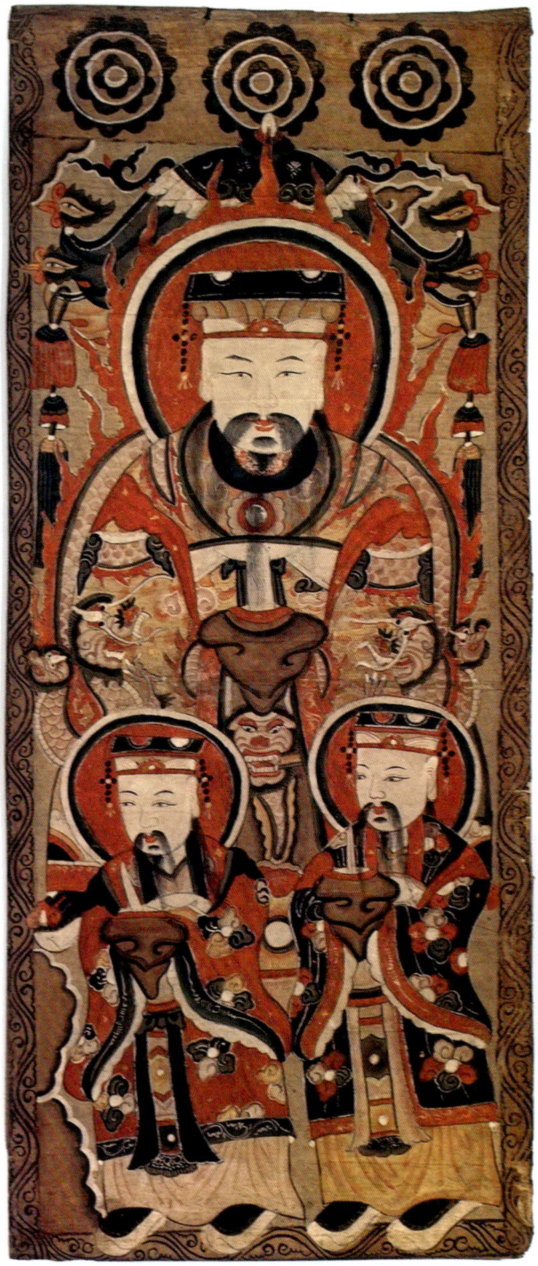

Fig. 98
The Jade Emperor, 1819
Red Yao, China

The traditional Chinese organizational system always respects the primary principles of symmetry as a way of creating harmonious balance. This is also true with traditional pictorial interpretations of Yao ritual paintings. Thus the set of eighteen paintings follows this long-established principle in anchoring the triad of the Three Pure Ones at the center with seven pairs of paintings fanning out, each pair almost identical. (For some unknown reason, the painting of the Three Generals was added later and was placed on the left side). It is important to note that any such proposed arrangement is idealized, and only works in a setting large enough to display the full set. In reality, many times when an ordination ritual takes place in a home, there is not enough room, and the paintings are layered.[4] For example, during large group ordinations such as the Great Net Hanging Light Ritual, as discussed in "The Shaman Priest and Priestess," the high Daoist shaman priests bring all the scrolls with them, displaying one layer on top of another on the walls around the main sacred platform.[5] In this case, it is more important to have all the images of the deities witnessing, protecting, and blessing the postulants than to have the symmetrical arrangement described above.

The Three Pure Ones (三 清; Sanqing)

The Three Pure Ones are the highest gods in the Daoist pantheon. They represent the manifestation of the Dao, the creation of the universe, and the origin of all beings. They are: the Jade Pure One (Fig. 100), also identified as the Universally Honored One of Origin (元 始 天 尊, commonly referred to as Yen Si); the Supreme Pure One (Fig. 101), known as the Universally Honored One of Divinities and Treasures (靈 寶 天 尊, also known as Leng Pu); and the Grand Pure One (Fig. 99), often recognized as the Universally Honored One of Dao and Virtues (道 德 天 尊, To Ta), or sometimes called the Grand Supreme Elder Lord (太 上 老 君, Thái Thượng Lão Quân). This trinity represents different incarnations of the Dao presiding over the Three Realms (三 清; Tam Thanh). It was from the primordial breath that the creator Pangu[6] emerged to create the world in which the Three Pure Ones rule. The Jade Pure One is paramount among the supreme echelon of the Daoist pantheon. The second, the Supreme Pure One, is omnipotent, capable of infinite transformation, and can bestow salvation when opportunity arises or when adversity strikes. He is commander of the second great epoch, when chaos dissipated and yin and yang became discernible. The third, the Grand Pure One, manifests himself as Laozi, the founder of Daoism, the ancient and most eminent ruler.[7]

Scrolls depicting the Three Pure Ones are usually centrally displayed and anchor the full painting set. They are often portrayed as elderly deities; each holds a sacred object in one hand and makes a sacred gesture with the other. In this set they are seated on thrones surmounted by wreathed canopies. Divine flames radiate from their heads. Each deity wears a typical golden crown of the type that Yao postulants receive from the high shaman. Each is dressed in loose robes embroidered with a dragon and a phoenix, symbolizing imperial rank. Their bodies are bound by dragons, and each deity is accompanied by two attendants. Yen Si—the Jade Pure One (Fig. 100)—is attended by two female jade servants holding a vase with flowers supported by a long tablet that rests on a lotus flower. Inscribed is a short phase in Chinese characters, blurred from use and age but nevertheless legible: 當 今 皇 帝 壽 萬 歲 萬 萬 歲, meaning, "Long live the current emperor!" On his right (viewer's left) is To Ta, the Grand Pure One (Fig. 99), joined by a general holding a long spear and female attendant holding a scepter. Leng Pu—the Supreme Pure One (Fig. 101)—is on Yen Si's left side (viewer's right), accompanied by a civil and a military attendant. The attendants on either side face Yen Si at the center. The Jade Pure One scroll is identified by two Chinese characters: 玉 清 (Yuqing, or Yen Si), written on the back, along with two long lines of vital information. The line on the right side reads:

> 沐 浴 丹 青 号 西 思 恩 武 緣 累 � 人 潘 進 敏 彩 画 神 像 大 堂 小 堂 共 有 壹 拾 柒 張 價 四 両 久 錢 正.
>
> *The Daoist Master named Si Xiang Wu Yen invited the painter Pan Jin Min (潘 進 敏) who created the spirit scrolls consisting of a large tribune set (大 堂) and a small tribune set (小 堂), altogether seventeen pieces. They cost 2.9 taels of silver money.*

The line on the left side reads:

> 嘉 慶 二 十 叁 年 孟 冬 十 一 月 初 八 日 馮 成 有 眷 近 遠 父 子 論 議 成 心 有 意 新 習 神 像 大 小 一 堂 保 家 人 丁 旺 兴 五 谷 豐 登 六 畜 滿 物 年 年 發 利 李 李 平 安 後 代 子 孫.
>
> *On the day in the middle of the winter, the eighth of the eleventh month, the twenty-third year of Jiaqing's (1796–1820) era, 1819, Mr. Feng (馮), father, and his son together discussed the subject matter carefully. Henceforth, they sincerely invited the painter to make the whole set including the small and large tribune of the sacred paintings.*
>
> *May all the male descendants be prosperous and the five grains always be more abundant! May the six domestic animals become flocks! May happiness and prosperity return every year! May the four seasons be peaceful! May future generations be glorified and prosperous!*

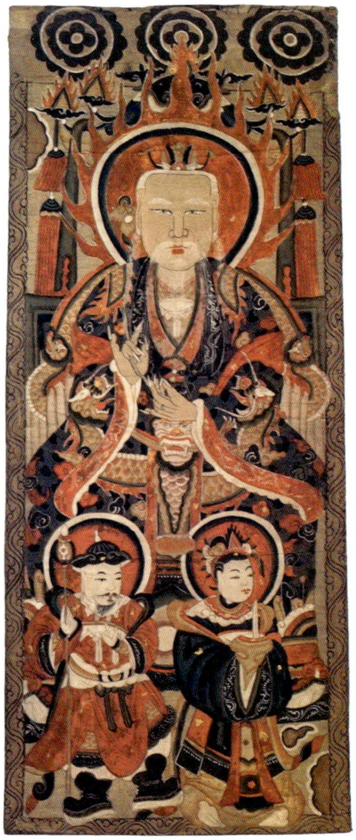

Fig. 99

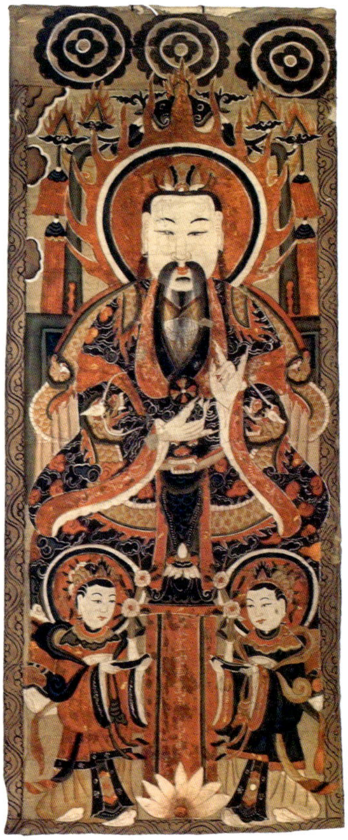

Fig. 100

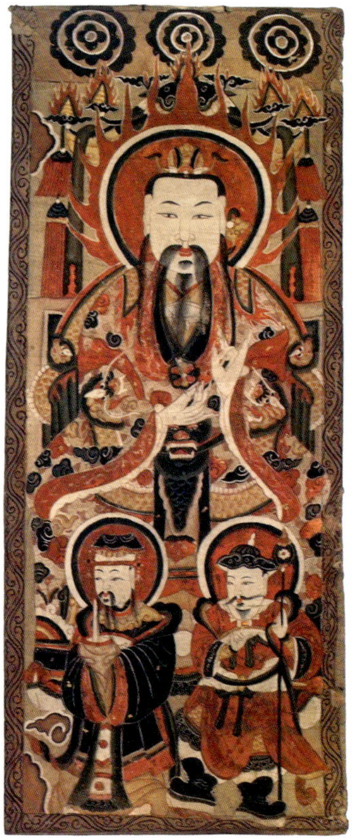

Fig. 101

The Jade Emperor (玉 皇) and the Master of the Saints (星 主)

The Jade Emperor (Fig. 98) and the Master of the Saints (Fig. 102) are shown as a nearly identical pair in this set. Their general features, costumes, and their two attendants are almost indistinguishable, with the small exception of the color of their robes. In each scroll the deity is seen sitting on a canopied throne, wearing an imperial dragon robe and a regal headdress surmounted by a mortarboard with strings of pearls hanging from the sides. Each is holding a *kuei* (圭), a ceremonial scepter, and is flanked by dragons that resemble chair arms. Each deity is accompanied by two male attendants dressed in imperial court robes and bearing ceremonial tablets. A small animal, probably a lion-dog, holds a folded scroll in its mouth, acting as a spirit messenger between the attendants and the supreme deity. Since the painting of the Jade Emperor is positioned on the right, his two attendant officials are looking toward the left; whereas the painting of the Masters of the Saints is positioned on the left, so his are facing toward the right, another example of the principle of symmetrical order.

In Daoism, the Jade Emperor is the supreme ruler of the universe, with the power to appoint, dismiss, reward, and punish other divinities as well as human beings. He resolves problems for humans in their conflicts with the realms of water, the heavens, the underworld, and the earth. In Yao Daoist rituals, when a shaman invokes the heavens he must first pray to the Jade Emperor, who then communicates with other deities.

Since the two figures are virtually indistinguishable, the Master of the Saints is identified by an inscription written on the back of the scroll. As a reflection of the Jade Emperor, he was appointed as the Heav-

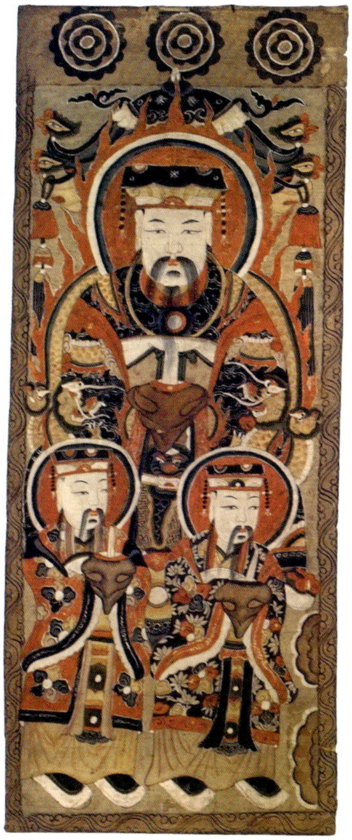

Fig. 102

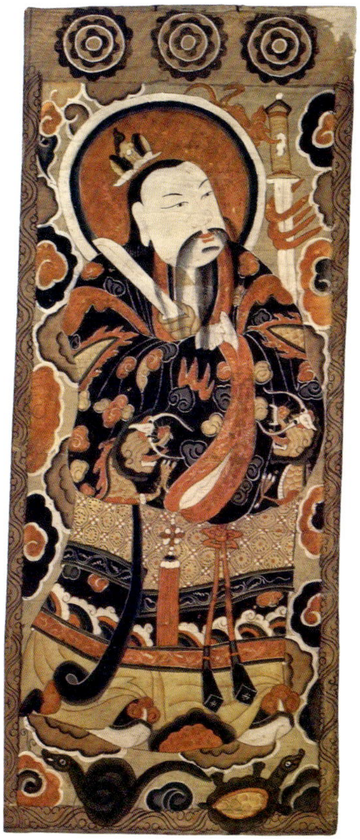

Fig. 103

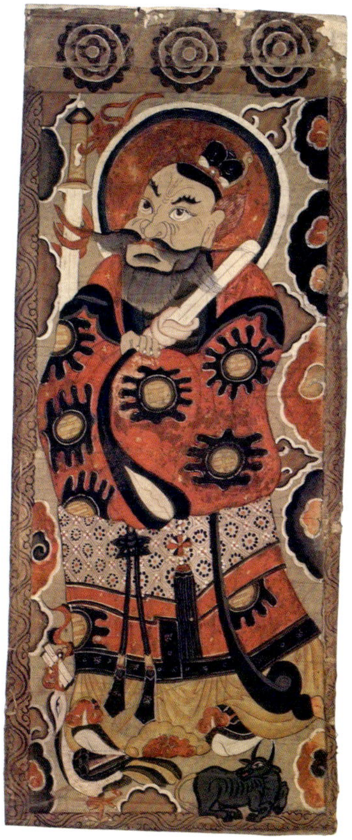

Fig. 104

enly Worthy and Perfect Lord to govern three periods of the year, to take charge of the twenty constellations, and to have the power to terminate evil and bring happiness. It was believed that the Master of the Saints had the ability to determine each person's fate: being rich or poor, having good fortune or bad, and living a short or a long life.[8] In Yao ritual texts this deity is always invoked after the Jade Emperor, because of his position as a medium between the Jade Emperor and human beings.[9]

Celestial Master Zhang (張 天 師) and Celestial Master Li (李 天 師)

The two Celestial Masters are either historical or legendary figures that have been immortalized and subsequently canonized into the Daoist pantheon. They are required paintings in the set of seventeen or eighteen scrolls, because the two Masters play important roles in Yao rituals and ceremonies. Celestial Master Zhang (Fig. 104) is a historical figure. His real name was Zhang Ling (張 陵), popularly

Fig. 99
The Grand Pure One, 1819
Red Yao, China

Fig. 100
The Jade Pure One, 1819
Red Yao, China

Fig. 101
The Supreme Pure One, 1819
Red Yao, China

Fig. 102
Master of the Saints, 1819
Red Yao, China

Fig. 103
Celestial Master Li, 1819
Red Yao, China

Fig. 104
Celestial Master Zhang, 1819
Red Yao, China

known as Zhang Daoling (張 道 陵; 34–156) of the Late Han dynasty (25–220). At first he studied the Five Classics canon, but was unsatisfied. Later he studied the Yellow Emperor's *Nine Cauldron Alchemy Scripture*.[10] He is credited as the founder of the principal school of Daoism and the Way of the Celestial Masters of Daoism, commonly referred to as the Way of the Five Pecks of Rice (五 斗米 道). Master Zhang taught that a universal energy, *qi*, pervaded everything and that a person who practices the Dao can nourish it by preserving, correcting, and harmonizing the balance of *qi* within the body, which can eventually lead to achieving immortality. Master Zhang imparted that a true Daoist should practice meditation, avoid sex, and observe a strict diet to cultivate internal energy.

Knowledge of Zhang Ling's life and work comes mostly from later scripture and hagiography. It is said that he was a descendant of Zhang Liang, the strategist who helped Liu Pang establish the Han dynasty. According to legend, in 142 Zhang announced that Laozi had appeared to him and presented him with liturgical books, a sword, and a seal—all common tools used in rituals by Yao shamans—and taught him magic mudras, or ritual gestures. He mastered all the Daoist scriptures and became an immortal, the First Celestial Master.[11] Regarded as the leader of spiritual forces and the patron saint of literature, Master Zhang serves as the key attendant to the Three Pure Ones and the Jade Emperor.[12]

In shamanic ceremonies the scroll of Celestial Master Zhang is positioned on the right, so he is facing toward the center. Dressed in a red sacerdotal robe embroidered with eight trigram motifs in circles that resemble the sun, Master Zhang clutches a ceremonial tablet in a regal manner. His magical sword, entwined with flames, hangs next to his right shoulder. According to legend, this sword can destroy evil spirits and demons. Though his vehicle mount is a tiger, a water buffalo is present in the bottom right corner of this painting. The back of the scroll is inscribed with seven Chinese characters (張 天 師 馮 成 有 号) identifying Celestial Master Zhang and providing the name of the owner, Mr. Peng.

The scroll of Celestial Master Li (Fig. 103) is on the left and facing toward the center, in a position corresponding to that of Master Zhang on the right. The iconographic details are almost identical with those of Master Zhang, with the exceptions that he wears a black ceremonial robe decorated with two flying dragons, and his hair hangs down onto his shoulders.

There are three different accounts of the origins of Master Li, from different periods. In the first, he was a historical figure named Li Jing (李 靖, 571–640), a great general and once a chancellor of the Tang dynasty (618–907). Born to a middle-level officer in an administrative family, he was trained in literary and military matters. A very talented and ambitious man, he first served under the Sui dynasty (581–618), but later served Li Yuan—the founder of the Tang dynasty—as a general in charge of many military campaigns to pacify and unify the country. Under the Emperor Taizong (626–649) he was promoted to be minister of justice, then minister of war, and, finally, chancellor. Li Jing is credited with helping to establish and stabilize the Tang dynasty, and was bestowed with the honorific title of Assistant God in Founding the State (開 國 功 神). In later periods he was canonized and became a high deity in the Daoist pantheon.[13]

A second account, from Chinese mythology, regards Master Li as one of the Four Heavenly Kings. His attribute is a magical pagoda that can capture evil spirits and help the Jade Emperor in guarding the Heavenly Gate. Li Jing was a high-ranking commanding officer of the Shang dynasty (c. 1600–c. 1050 BCE), who studied magic at Mount Kunlun and achieved great powers. He aided the Jade Emperor in subduing evil forces, demons, and sinners. Li Jing had three sons. The youngest, Nata, had supernatural powers that surpassed his father, but he was disobedient and rebellious, using his powers to disturb the superior gods and even his own father. Infuriated with his son, Li Jing had many terrific battles with him, and ultimately killed him. However, Li Jing was granted a golden pagoda with the capacity to preserve life, and he was able to save his son. The Jade Emperor bestowed him with the title Heavenly Prince and named him Guardian of the Heavenly Gate.[14]

In the third account, Master Li was a Dark Warrior who came into being in 1118. It was under the influence of Daoist Master Lin Lingsu that Emperor Huizong created Master Li as a counterpart to Master Zhang. One story states that the Dark Warrior appeared to the emperor amid thunder and lightning accompanied by an enormous snake and a huge tortoise. The deity was dressed in a black robe with pendant sleeves and carried a sword. As a skilled painter, the emperor rendered his portrait, which afterward became the model for his depiction.[15] In Daoism, the Dark Warrior (玄 武, Xuan Wu) is a powerful god who controls the elements, is capable of great magic, and helps believers to cultivate the Dao. In the classical novel *Journey to the West*, the Dark Warrior was the Heavenly King of the North, named Li Jing, who had two great generals serving under him: the Tortoise General and the Snake General (similar to the aforementioned story).

As with many gods, the stories of the Celestial Masters mix history, legend, and semilegend, and are a combination of popular religion and Daoism. In this depiction of the Celestial Master Li, the tortoise and the snake are illustrated at the bottom of the painting. These iconographic features closely resemble the third account.

These brief accounts reveal striking differences between Master Li and Master Zhang in terms of a binary and symmetrical opposition: civil versus military, right versus left, patronage of the magic arts versus patronage of the military. One is counterposed to the other in order to bring harmonious balance.

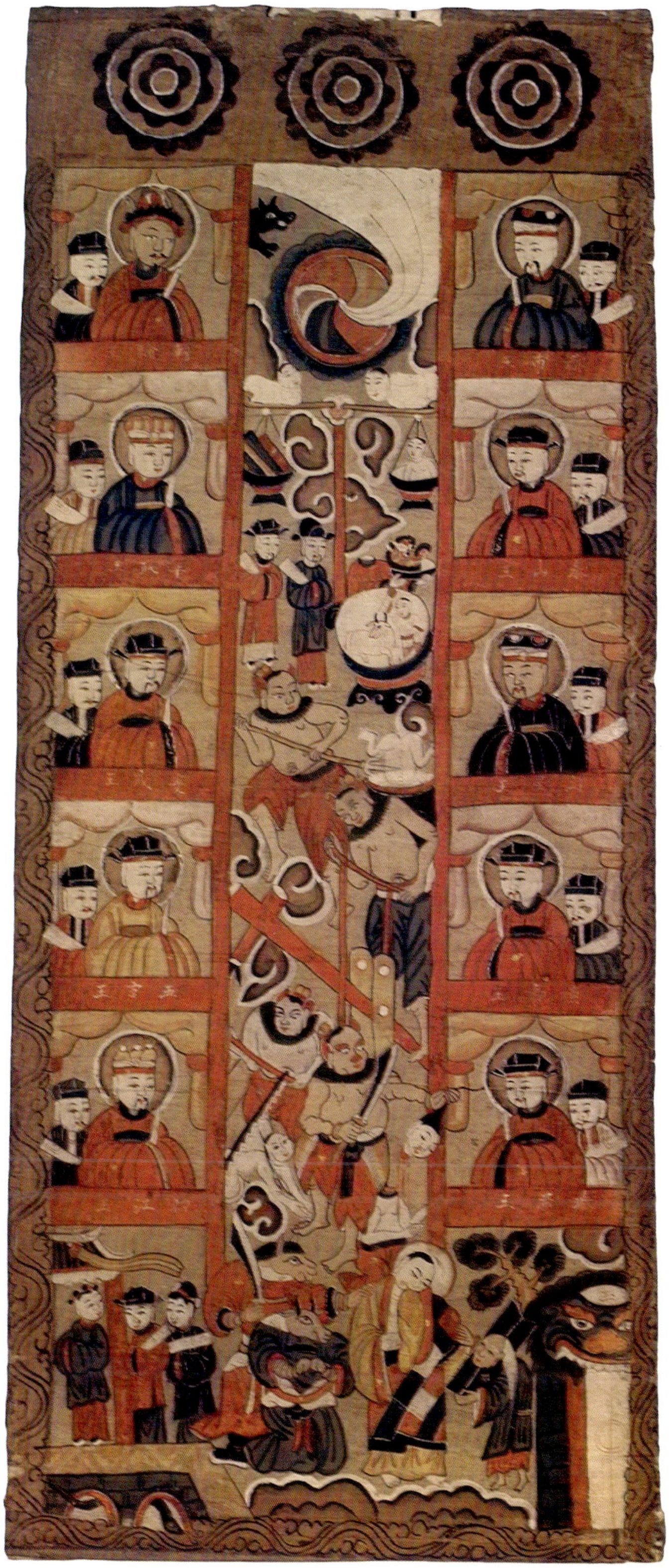

Fig. 105
The Ten Kings of the Underworld, 1819
Red Yao, China

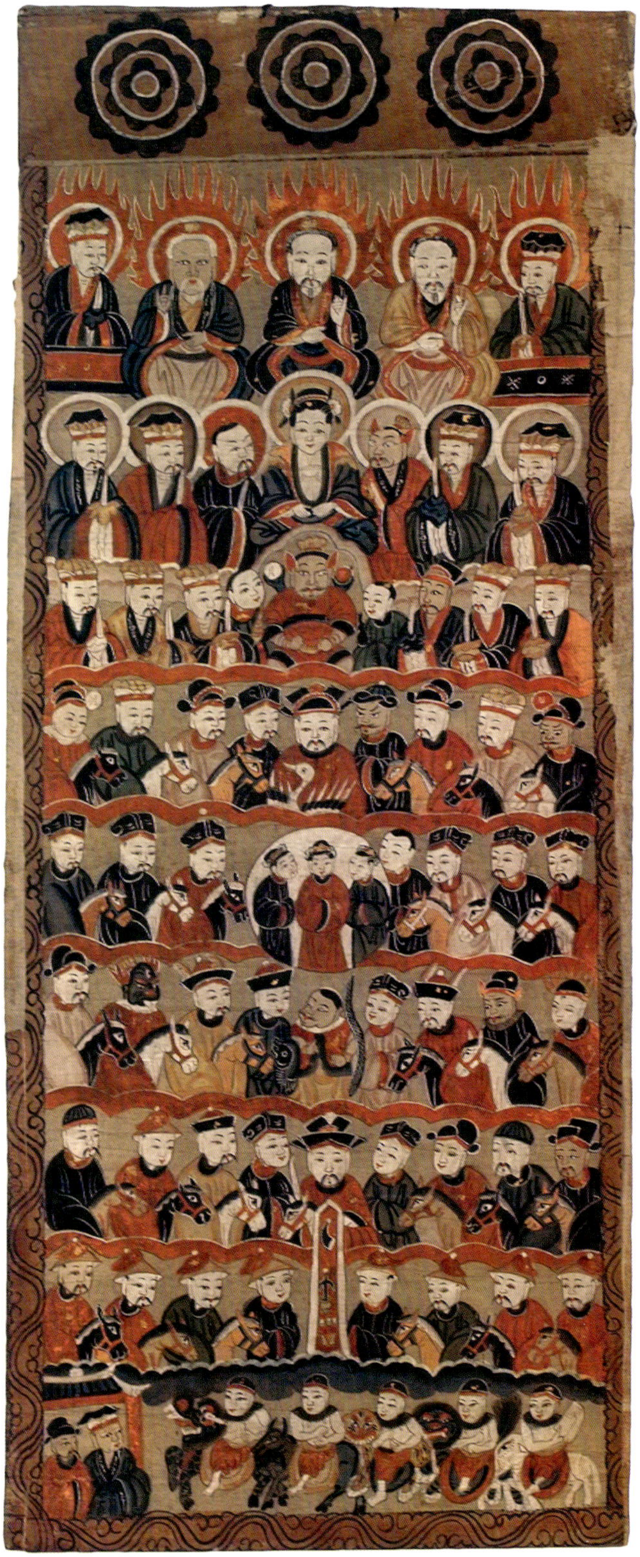

Fig. 106
The Ancestors/Heavenly Host, 1819
Red Yao, China

Ten Kings of the Underworld (拾 殿 冥 王, Thập Điện Minh Vương)

The painting of the Ten Kings of the Underworld (Fig. 105) is an important part of the whole series. Commonly placed on the right side of the set, it is divided equally into three vertical parts, with a small introductory section at the bottom. The middle section depicts the journey of the soul of the dead, starting from the bottom with the two constables Oxhead and Horseface, named after their physical appearances. In this painting, the two animal-headed constables (whose heads here more resemble donkeys), come to fetch the soul of a dead person and bring him to the underworld. The deceased is forced to swim the River Nai, under the Bridge of No Resource. If the soul, who is symbolically depicted as an old white-haired figure whose head is locked in a long black cangue (a portable pillory), is escorted by Bodhisattva Kṣitigarbha (wearing a monk's robe with a halo and standing in front), it is exempted from crossing the bridge. Contrarily, if the soul has no support from the savior deity, it could fall into the river, be attacked by fierce animals, and drown. From there, the sinner is depicted in various scenes of horrible torture in hell: beheaded by a sharp knife, cut into pieces by a large saw, pounded with a heavy pestle, and boiled in hot oil. Illustrated near the top is the popular story of a shaman who was ordained but did not observe the prohibition of not killing domestic animals. In his former life on earth, he slaughtered a cow with a knife, an act that is reflected in the magic mirror. Two officials stand by the beheaded figure holding his records. Finally, the soul of the dead is weighed in the scale of merit, as portrayed near the top of the scroll. If the soul creates merit in life, or if his close relatives organize a ritual ceremony and transfer merits to him, he can then be reincarnated into the next life. At the top of the center column two small naked figures, resembling two human embryos, are about to be reborn under the turning Wheel of Reincarnation. (In the Kitnick Collection there is another full set of seventeen scrolls; in the Ten Kings scroll there is a Daoist deity positioned at the top of the middle section, called the Lord of Merits, who controls the Wheel of Reincarnation. He is the deity who makes the final decisions regarding rebirth, instead of King Yama, as in the Buddhist tradition.)

Flanking the journey of the dead's soul through the tortures of hell is the court of the Ten Kings of the Underworld, stacked five on a side and rendered in a stylized manner. Each king holds a ritual scepter in both hands, wears a formal robe, has a halo, and is attended by a court clerk. The kings are arranged in a zigzag order, starting from the bottom right corner and proceeding from right to left, row by row, to the top of the scroll. This arrangement is in accord with the sequential route of the soul from the bottom to the top. The Tenth King of the Underworld is the deity who assigns the reincarnation of the soul's next life, symbolically represented by a black pig jumping into the turning wheel, so his court is arranged in the upper top left corner. The religious functions and meanings of the Ten Kings of the Underworld are fully discussed in their own chapter.

The Ancestors/Heavenly Host/Administrator (祖 宗, Tổ Tông)

A painting of the Ancestors/Heavenly Host has been explored in detail in the previous chapter. However, this painting (Fig. 106) highlights some different deities, which are identified in the list below, from top to bottom.

1st row: The Three Pure Ones, flanked by the Jade Emperor and Master of the Saints, or possibly the Lord of the Living and the Lord of the Dead

2nd row: Bodhisattva Guanyin, flanked by Celestial Masters Zhang and Li and the Governors of the Four Realms

3rd row: Taisui, attended by a Golden Boy and Jade Girl, and by the Lords of the Six Directions

4th row: Unknown deity riding a goose, attended by eight mounted officials

5th row: Three Dragon Phoenix Ladies, attended by a lady (probably the Third Lady, Empress Zhao) and six mounted officials

6th row: The Deity of the Big Dipper, attended by eight mounted officials

7th row: The High Constable, attended by eight mounted officials

8th row: The Eight Messengers

9th row: The local God of the Earth and the Five Orderlies

Among the deities appearing in the cohort, Bodhisattva Guanyin (觀 世 音 菩 薩) is a figure needing brief discussion here. Initially, Guanyin was a popular Buddhist bodhisattva, known as Avalokiteśvara, originating in India. Over time, the deity was incorporated into Daoism and widely worshipped. In the early Indian Buddhist tradition, Avalokiteśvara, whose name means "the lord who looks down," perceives the sounds of suffering and the lamentations of all sentient beings in this world. His religious vows and supernatural powers that can save sentient beings are described in chapter 25 of the *Lotus Sutra*. In India Avalokiteśvara is manifested as a male deity. After Buddhism was introduced to China, this bodhisattva increasingly became a prominent figure, whose popularity has pervaded many legends, tales, and manifestations of Chinese Buddhism as well as those of various folk religions. After the eleventh century, this compassionate deity gradually transformed into a female deity, and is now often referred to as the Goddess of Mercy.[16] A legend that appeared during the eleventh century tells the story of Guanyin as the Third Princess, named Miaoshan, the beautiful daughter of a cruel king. The king wanted her to marry, but she refused her father's order. Instead, she wanted to enter a Buddhist temple and become a nun. Out of anger her father asked the abbot to give her heavy chores beyond her abilities, so she would tire of working day and night without rest and would want to return to the palace. However, animals helped her accomplish all of her tasks. The king burned down the temple, but a tiger came to rescue Miaoshan and took her to a cave in the Fragrant Mountain. There she practiced the Buddhist religion for many years and finally achieved enlightenment. Years later her father fell terribly ill, and nothing could cure him except the eyes of a person who had never become angry. No such person existed in this world except for the Third Princess, Miaoshan. Out of compassion she offered her eyes, mixed with medicine, to save her father. Miraculously, his sickness was cured. The king then went to the Fragrant Mountain to give thanks to the person who sacrificed their eyes for him. He encountered a lady in the cave, who told the king that it was his own daughter. The legend concludes with Princess Miaoshan transforming into the Thousand-Armed Guanyin, who fights to save the people of the world from enduring massive suffering.[17]

In later periods Guanyin was integrated into Daoism as an immortal deity. In popular Buddhism, and generally in Daoism and folk beliefs, Guanyin is worshipped as the Goddess of Mercy and Compassion and as a source of unconditional love. She hears suffering voices, answers cries, and pleases all sentient beings by liberating them from their own karmic woes. Furthermore, she also appears to childless women as the giver of children.

In the Heavenly Host scroll, Guanyin occupies a very high position. She presides over the second row of the Upper Tribune, the highest position after the Daoist supreme deities, the Three Pure Ones.

The God of the Sea (海 旛, Hoi Fan), Minor and Major

The deity Hoi Fan, God of the Sea, is one of the three deities in the basic set. He appears twice in the set of seventeen scrolls, as Minor and Major Hoi Fan. His role as the Major Hoi Fan is important to Yao men who have already completed the Three-Lamp Hanging Ritual. Now, after years of training, practicing Daoist rituals and ceremonies, getting married, and establishing a family, they are ready to advance on the path of becoming a Daoist shaman. After receiving the Seven-Star Hanging Light ordination, the fully ordained shaman priest can acquire additional paintings and ritual items. In the Minor Hoi Fan scroll (Fig. 107), the deity dominates the painting. While it includes two small figures, generals on horseback, there are no scenes of ceremonial activities. In the Major Hoi Fan scroll (Fig. 108), half of the painting portrays the ceremonial activities of the Seven-Star Hanging Light ordination. On the left edge, postulants ascend the sword ladder, guided by many high Daoist shamans. The chief shaman stands on the side of the sword ladder with one hand holding a magic dagger and other holding a bowl of charmed water to purify the area and ward off evil influences. At the top of the ladder is another high shaman blowing a water-buffalo horn and leading the postulants up the sword ladder to salvation. To the right, seven priests form a musical orchestra of oboes, cymbals, drums, gongs, and a chime to assist with the ritual. One of the important parts of the Seven-Star Hanging Light ordination is the ritual of the Second Wedding, which officially recognizes the wives of the Yao men, so that after passing away they may join their husbands in heaven (see "The Shaman Priest and Priestess"). This is often depicted as a husband and wife being carried in a palanquin on the path toward heaven. Here, in the painting of the Major Hoi Fan, a postulant's wife, dressed in formal

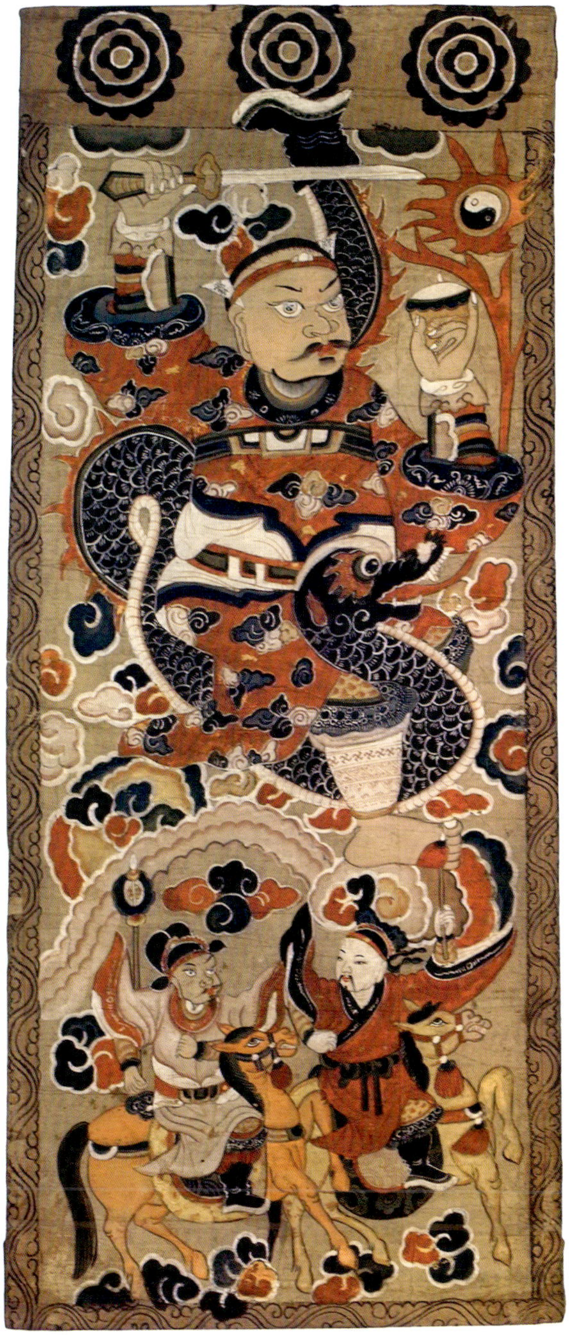

Fig. 107

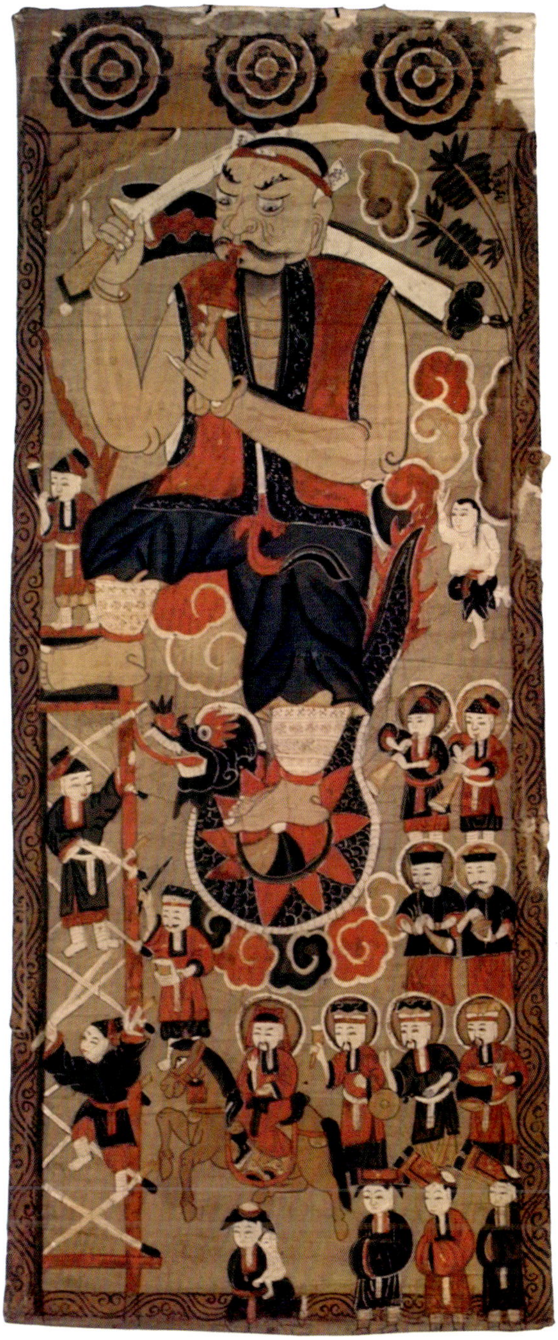

Fig. 108

Fig. 107
Minor Hoi Fan, 1819
Red Yao, China

Fig. 108
Major Hoi Fan, 1819
Red Yao, China

clothes, is depicted at the bottom of the scroll holding a baby. Standing to the right are three female assistants, who help her during the ceremony.

The High Constable (太 尉 Tai Wai) and the Three Generals (三 大 將 軍, Tam Đại Tướng Quân)

The religious function and ritual significance of the High Constable (Fig. 109) was discussed in detail in the previous chapter. The iconographic features and pictorial layout of this scroll are very similar to the painting shown in Fig. 95 from the three-scroll set. Briefly, Tai Wai is depicted as a formidable commanding general riding a white horse, holding a magical sword in his right hand, and attended by a civil official, who holds a banner above him. He is accompanied by two generals riding horses below. Tai Wai grips a long buffalo horn in his left hand, as do the two generals in Fig. 95.

The Three Generals (Fig. 110) are almost as important as the High Constable. They are on horseback, wearing heavy armor, brandishing swords, and are accompanied by guards running behind them. Since the Three Generals are almost identical, with the exception of the color of their clothing and horses, each is identified by the characters written on a banner that flies behind him. The first is Tang Hong (唐 宏, Đường Hoành), illustrated at the top; the second is Ge Yong (葛 雍, Cát Ung); and the third is Zhou Wu (周 武, Châu Vũ). The flying banners are used as dividers between figures, organizing the painting

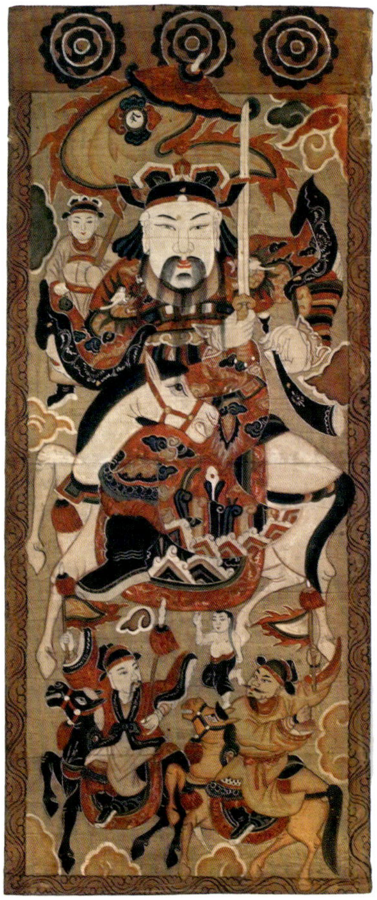

Fig. 109

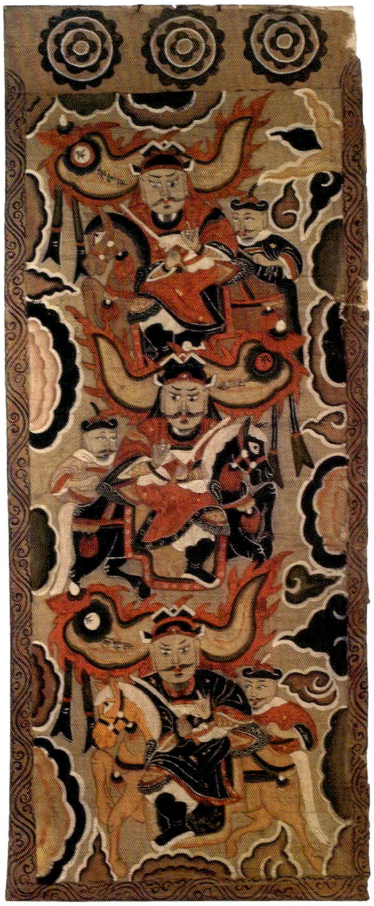

Fig. 110

into three equal sections. These generals were originally historical figures who served King Li of the Zhou dynasty in the tenth century BCE, and later took refuge in the Wu state when they were at odds with the king. They fought heroically for their new ruler and were heavily rewarded, but they refused the royal gifts and honorific titles. Finally, when their former ruler, King Li, passed away, they returned to their own state and were restored to their former ranks. Thereafter, they aided the new king in maintaining security for their country and helped people with just causes.[18]

Because of their heroic deeds and legendary fame, Emperor Zhenzong (r. 997–1022) of the Song dynasty bestowed them with the power to rule heaven, earth, and water; they are also known as the Three Origins (三元, Sanyuan, Tam Nguyên), or the Three Officials. The emperor built a temple on Mt. Tai to memorialize their heroic and benevolent deeds.[19]

The Four Officials of Heaven, Earth, Water, and the Underworld (天府 陽府 水府 地府)

The Yao divide their world into four realms, each ruled by an official. A unique aspect of the two paintings depicting these four officials is that they are not portrayed individually. The Official of Earth and the Official of Water are shown together in one scroll (Fig. 111), while the Official of Heaven and the Official of the Underworld are paired in the other (Fig. 112). The paintings have a similar struc-

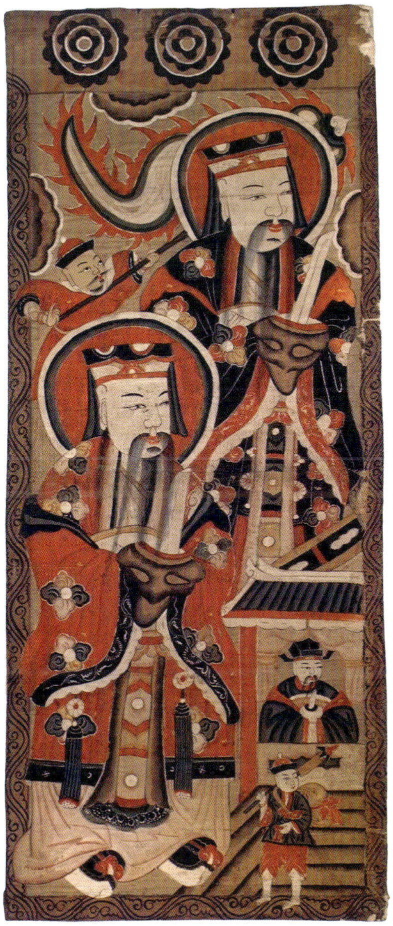

Fig. 111

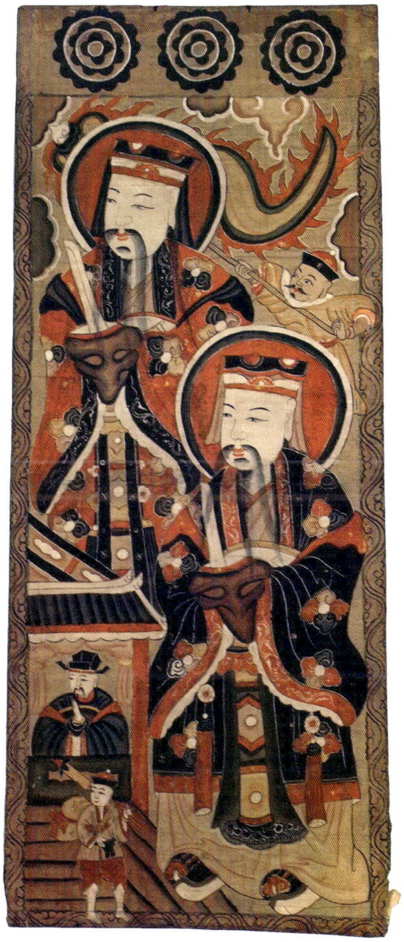

Fig. 112

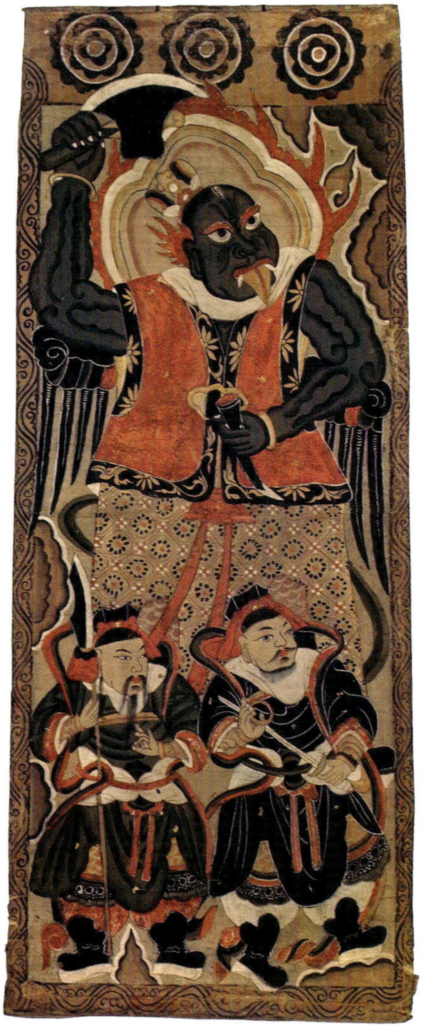

Fig. 113

Fig. 109
The High Constable, 1819
Red Yao, China

Fig. 110
The Three Generals, 1819
Red Yao, China

Fig. 111
The Officials of Earth and Water, 1819
Red Yao, China

Fig. 112
The Officials of Heaven and the Underworld, 1819
Red Yao, China

Fig. 113
Celestial Marshal Deng, 1819
Red Yao, China

Fig. 114
Celestial Marshal Zhao, 1819
Red Yao, China

ture. At the top are three wheels or spirals, which are recurring symbols in many Daoist paintings of the Yao. Usually all four officials have similar clothing, demeanors, and gestures. They occupy a large portion of each painting and are dressed in beautifully elaborate robes. Because of their divine status, a halo surrounds their heads and they calmly gaze into the distance. Each of them clasps his hands around a ceremonial *kuei* scepter. In the background on the upper half of each painting, a guard waves a flying banner. The whole image is usually framed by organic patterns or flowers. At the bottom and toward the side is a building housing a minor official, and an optional subsidiary figure. The building is positioned in the corner that the main officials face. Although their attire may vary, their robes are consistently colored in red, gold, green, or black.

The Official of Earth stands in the upper section, wearing a red robe and a mandarin bonnet with pearl pendants. Standing solemnly just below him is the Official of Water, dressed in the same fashion. To the right of the lower half of his body is a small building known as the Treasury of the Right. Inside is a treasury official in formal attire. A young man holding a folded parasol and carrying a traveling bag is on his way to collect money.

The painting of the Official of Heaven and the Official of the Underworld (Fig. 112) faces in the opposite direction but is almost identical with the previous one. The Official of Heaven stands in an elevated position and wears a red robe, while the Official of the Underworld is dressed in darker attire. Both wear imperial bonnets. The Official of the Underworld is in charge of executioners that attend the dead souls. He works closely with the Ten Kings of the Underworld. The building on the side is the Treasury of the Left, which is analogous to the Treasury of the Right.

The Official of Heaven understudies the role of the Jade Emperor, including overseeing the Golden Palace in the Thirty-Third Heaven, the Sun and the Moon, the Three Rulers, the Pantheon of the Three

Pure Ones, the two Saints Huang and Chao, the Sovereign of the Heavenly Mansions (or the Great Net Heaven), the two judicial officers of the Two Treasuries of Wealth and Salaries, the Enforcer of Fasting, and other deities of this level.

The Celestial Marshals (元 帥, Nguyên Soái)

The Daoist pantheon is replete with celestial marshals charged with protecting the Dao. In the context of Yao religious ceremonies, their presence protects the holy precinct and wards off evil forces. There are six marshals, who are often exhibited in two separate scrolls, each headed by a major marshal who is accompanied by two others.[20] In this set Marshal Deng (鄧, Đặng) is accompanied by Marshal Kang (康, Khang) and Marshal Xin (辛, Tân), while Marshal Zhao (趙,Triệu) is attended by Marshal Ma (馬, Mã) and Marshal Zhang (張, Trương). They are the most popular military figures represented in the set. In an eighteen-painting series, Marshal Deng and Marshal Zhao often appear as a pair that mirror one another, the first positioned on the extreme left and the second to the extreme right.

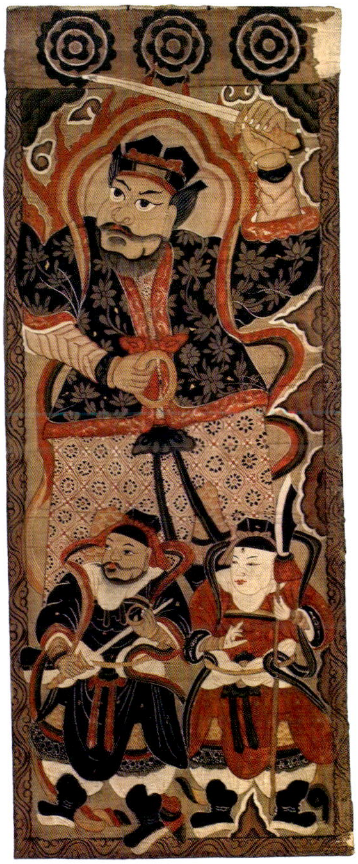

Fig. 114

Marshal Deng (Fig. 113), the fearful Thunder God, controls all natural phenomena. Portrayed with dark blue skin, tongue sticking out, two tusks, and bulging eyes, and holding a hatchet above his head, he symbolizes the power to punish corrupt officials and the unfaithful. His left hand holds a stiletto, which is his weapon to attack devils and evildoers. He wears a sleeveless jacket and a long sash with a ribbon tied near the waist. It is believed that the Jade Emperor orders the Thunder God to punish evil spirits and earthly mortals guilty of secret crimes. Flickering flames surround his head like a sacred halo, but they also represent the flashing light created when he sends lightening bolts across the sky. In Yao rituals, Marshal Deng is believed to protect the ceremonial altar and the Four Supreme Divinities of Daoism: the Three Pure Ones and the Jade Emperor.[21]

At the feet of Marshal Deng stand two other generals: Marshal Xing and Marshal Kang, who are dressed alike. Holding a long-handled scimitar, Marshal Kang is positioned on the left. On the right, Marshal Xing brandishes a sword with both hands and his feet trample on flying clouds. In Yao ritual, Marshal Kang was appointed by the Jade Emperor to protect the country, save worthy folks, and ward off evil influences. Meanwhile, Marshal Xing investigates the good and bad deeds of mankind.[22]

Marshal Zhao (Fig. 114), whose real name is Zhao Gongming (趙 公 明, Triệu Công Minh), is a semi-legendary figure of the Shang dynasty (c. 1600–c. 1050 BCE). Legend has it that King Wu asked a famous political thinker and military strategist named Jiang Ziya (姜 子 牙, Trương Tử Nha) for help. The latter recommended the magician Zhao Gongming, who would go on to use his magical weapons and supernatural power to assist King Wu in winning battles. When the King of Qin founded the Qin dynasty (221–206 BCE), he withdrew to the mountains and cultivated the Dao to become an immortal. Soon after, the Jade Emperor bestowed him with the title of Vice Marshal of the Divine Clouds (神 霄 副 元 帥, Shenxiao Fu Yuanshuai).[23]

In Chinese Daoism and folk religions, Celestial Marshal Zhao has been venerated as the God of Wealth (財 神). The deity is widely believed to bestow riches on his devotees when they pray to him. During the Chinese New Year celebration, people often joyously exchange the traditional greeting "May you become rich" (*Gongxi facai*). Such a tradition is closely associated with this deity, who is also in charge of the Ministry of Wealth in the Daoist pantheon.[24]

The scroll depicts him brandishing a magic sword in his left hand and a *chakram*—a circular shaped weapon for throwing—in his right. Wearing an iron hat and standing in a threatening posture, his military manner is enhanced by his bulging eyes, luxuriant moustache, and beard. His most crucial function is to dispel pestilence and ward off natural disasters. He also works as a judge who rectifies unjust verdicts, and is appealed to as the God of Money. In Yao rituals his purpose is to guard the ceremonial platform and to lead other marshals in their protection duties.

Beneath Marshal Zhao are Marshal Ma and Marshal Zhang. Celestial Marshal Ma belongs to the Thunder Ministry and is closely related to fire. In this scroll he appears relatively young, without a beard or mustache, but with a third eye featured at the center of his forehead. The general is armed with a long-handled Chinese scimitar entwined with a long black piece of cloth like a snake moving on the edge of his robe. According to a Yao folktale, after becoming a deity Marshal Ma acquired the power to see through to the underworld, and to emit fire from his third eye; he can burn the devil and other harmful spirits, bringing safety to people. He symbolizes the element of fire and is the central figure in the Yao fire ceremony.[25]

Standing to the left is Marshal Zhang. He is dressed in a black robe and is wielding a sword in his right hand and small ring in his left. His face has a darker complexion, closely resembling that of Marshal Zhao. In any case, he is the object of little ritual attention.

The Officials (各官, Các Quan)

This painting (Fig. 115) is identified as the Officials by two Chinese characters, 各 官 (*Geguan*), written on the back. Note that it is not one of the seventeen items mentioned in Lemoine's list above, but was added, instead of the Family Forebears, to become part of a set of eighteen scrolls. If the evidence of the inscription is correct, the two figures are the local magistrates who rule, judge, and solve problems for the people under their jurisdictions. Not only are they responsible for delivering peace, security, and justice in their realms, but they also preside over the proceedings of criminal cases, both minor and major. According to Yao Daoist belief, the local officials are the second tier of the divine pantheon, who govern different terraces, caverns, mountains, rivers, and other locations.[26] They work closely with the local God of the Earth, recognized as the white bearded personage often depicted in the long horizontal scroll *The Dragon Bridge of the Great Dao* (Fig. 143).

However, according to Jacques Lemoine's list of the large painting set, this scroll would represent the Palace of the Right's treasurer.[27] It depicts palacelike architecture, a treasurer who assists two clerks, and two people presenting money. On the top left, the treasurer is seated behind a bureau, wearing a mandarin's hat and making some judgment with a brush in one hand and paper in other. Seated in an armchair is another official, who appears very relaxed, sitting with his legs crossed. Between the officials are clerks holding abacuses and calculating amounts of money, an idea reinforced by two small figures, one carrying two large, heavy strings of silver coins on a

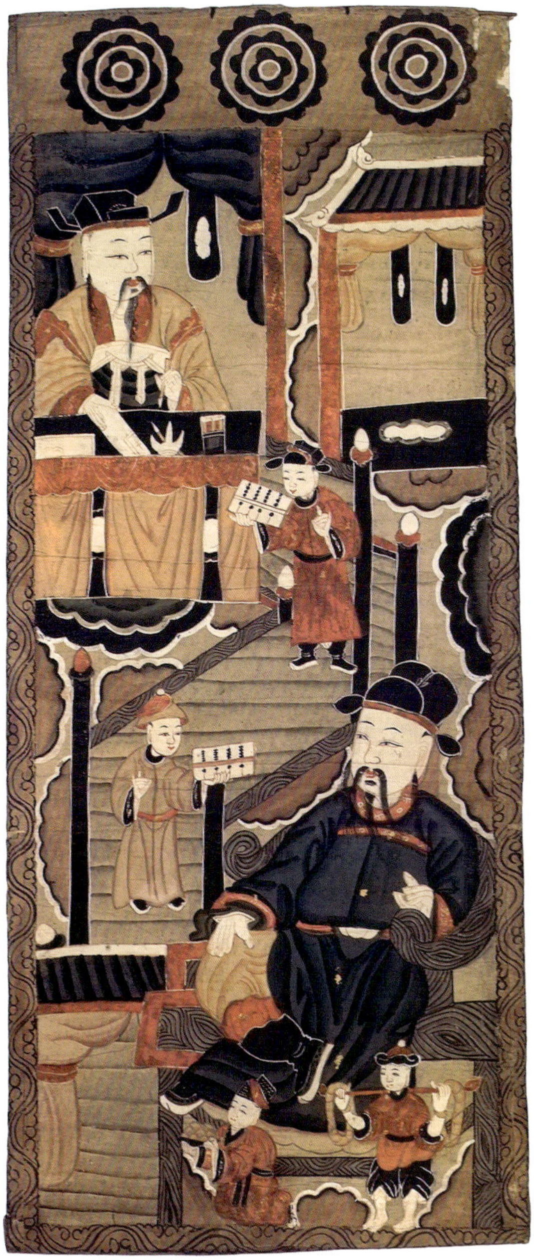

Fig. 115

pole, and the other a minor official kneeling to present a tray full of gold.

It is interesting to note that money plays an important role in Yao ritual. Spirit paper money must always be made before any ceremony (this is discussed in "Finding the Way to Heaven"). In the long vertical scroll *Guiding the Soul* (Fig. 142), the soul of the recently deceased must pay a fee to the treasury at the beginning of his journey on the road to heaven (lower section).

Conclusion

These scroll paintings are an example of a significant complete scroll set, and are important Daoist ritual items. Originally the Feng family, father and his son, commissioned it in 1819, during the twenty-third reigning year of Emperor Jiaqing (1796–1820) of the Chinese Qing dynasty (1644–1912). Though the inscription does not state its original provenance, the whole set must have come from some area in Southern China with a large Yao community.

The inscription also indicates that this is the oldest set in the collection and, more importantly, provides additional valuable information: the names of the owner and artist, the cost of commissioning the set, and general prayers and wishes. A full set of paintings always consists of two groups: the small basic set called the Small Tribune (小 堂), which has three paintings, and the large set of fourteen or fifteen called the Large Tribune (大 堂). This full set could have been commissioned all at once, if we surmise that the Small Tribune was for the son and the Large Tribune for the father. Such a cost-saving practice served two purposes: avoiding the problem of finding a good artist to paint additional scrolls at a later time, and having the complete set of seventeen or eighteen to use for large ceremonial rituals. For these rituals, the paintings would be organized into two levels: the initial level for the Three-Lamp Hanging Ritual for the son, and the advanced Seven-Star Hanging Light Ceremony for the father. The inscription states that prior to and during the painting of the set, the painter must purify himself physically and mentally, so that after the high shaman priest consecrates the set, it would become a sacred dwelling place for the deities.

Artistically, since the whole set was painted by the same person, it has a unified artistic style, using the same kind and quality of paper, and all the paired paintings strictly obey the principles of a symmetrical and balanced order.

Fig. 115
The Officials, 1819
Red Yao, China

NOTES

1. For a brief discussion of the full arrangement of Daoist deities within a whole set of the Yao ceremonial paintings, see Jacques Lemoine's chapter 4, "The Celestial Chessboard," pp. 46–47. Here he arranged all seventeen painting scrolls from left to right, starting with Marshal Deng (or Teng in Yao Mien pronunciation), and ending with Marshal Zhao (Chao). All the images of the seventeen hanging scrolls, plus the Four Heavenly Deities, the Forebears, the Enforcer of Fasting, and a long scroll of the *Dragon Bridge of the Great Dao* are illustrated between p. 48 and p. 49. See also Jean Cormerais, pp. 86–87.

2. According to Jacques Lemoine, it is rather rare to have the painting scroll of the Three Generals included in a full set, something he had seen only twice during his ten years of research during the 1980s, p. 47.

3. For a brief discussion of the arrangement, see Jacques Lemoine, "Yao Taoist Paintings," in *Arts of Asia* (Jan–Feb, 1981): 67–69.

4. For example, see Jess G. Pourret, images on pp. 51 and 214; see also the frontispiece of Phan Ngọc Khuê, *Taoist Painting*.

5. For example, see the pictures illustrated in Jacques Lemoine's *Yao Ceremonial Paintings*, pp. 27, 30, and 31.

6. In Chinese mythology, Pangu (盤 古, Bàn Cổ) was the first living being and the creator of the earth, sky, sun, moon, and the entire universe.

7. For full discussion of the Three Pure Ones, see Jacques Lemoine, *Yao Ceremonial Paintings,* pp. 53–63. For paintings of the Three Pure Ones in the Chinese Daoist tradition, see catalogue nos. 65, 66, and 67 in Stephen Little, *Taoism and the Arts of China* (Berkeley: University of California Press, 2000), pp. 228–231.

8. Phan Ngọc Khuê's unpublished manuscript.

9. For the further functions and legends of the Master of the Saints, see Jacques Lemoine, pp. 67–68.

10. For a brief hagiography of Master Zhang, see Thomas Cleary, trans. & ed., *Alchemists, Mediums and Magicians: Stories of Taoist Mystics* (Boston: Shambhala, 2009), pp. 39–40.

11. For the story of Master Zhang's encounter with Laozi, his receiving the Daoist teachings and practices, and his religious establishment, see Stephen Bokenkamp, *Early Daoist Scriptures* (Berkeley: University of California Press, 1997), pp. 115–218.

12. Jacques Lemoine, pp. 74–78.

13. See Phan Ngọc Khuê, *Taoist Painting*, pp. 38–39.

14. Ibid., and Jacques Lemoine, pp. 74–75.

15. Jacques Lemoine, pp. 72–73.

16. For a good discussion of this subject, see Chun-fang Yu, "Guanyin: The Chinese Transformation of Avalokitesvara," in *Latter Days of the Law: Images of Chinese Buddhism 850–1850*, ed. Marsha Weidner (Honolulu: University of Hawaii Press, 1994), pp. 151–181.

17. For full translation of the original Chinese text into English and a discussion of the historical development, see Glen Dudbridge, *The Legend of Miao-shan* (London: Oxford University, 1978).

18. For further discussion and images of the Three Generals, see Lemoine, pp. 123–124. Phan Ngọc Khuê's *Taoist Painting* has a good discussion of the Sanyuan festivals and their meaning, pp. 144–146. See also Cormerais, 177–181.

19. The concepts of primordial origins and time were first propagated by Master Zhang Daolin of the Han dynasty, but then bestowed to the Three Generals when Emperor Zhenzong canonized them. The emperor also built a temple on Mt. Tai to remember their heroic and benevolent deeds. Accordingly, they were worshipped during the three full-moon days according to the Chinese lunar calendar. These three full-moon days have become important annual festivals in China. The Shangyuan (上 元, Thượng Nguyên), or the Upper Prime, is when people pray for happiness, good fortune, and prosperity, which is on the fifteenth day of the first month. This is also the Lantern Festival, fifteen days after the Chinese New Year. The Zhongyuan (中 元, Trung Nguyên), or the Middle Prime, is dedicated to praying for all sins to be pardoned and exonerated, which is on the fifteenth day of the seventh month. It also coincides with the Buddhist festival, All Souls Day, an important day in East Asian Buddhism. Traditionally, it is the day that Buddhist monks complete three months of summer retreat, and also the day that

families pray for their ancestors to be reborn into heaven or the Buddhist Pure Land. Finally, the Xiayuan (下元, Hạ Nguyên), or the Lower Prime, is on the fifteenth day of the tenth month, when people pray for eliminating seen and unforeseen misfortunes and for longevity. Perhaps the best discussion related to the historical development of Shanyuan, and the three major annual festivals and their significance, is by Shih-Shan Susan Huang, *Picturing the True Form: Daoist Visual Culture in Traditional China* (Cambridge: Harvard University Press, 2012), pp. 296–299.

20. For an extensive discussion of the history, iconographic features, and functions of the Celestial Marshals in Yao Daoist ritual paintings, see Jacques Lemoine, pp. 115–122.

21. Ibid., pp. 121–122.

22. Ibid., pp. 118–119; see also Phan Ngọc Khuê, *Taoist Painting,* p. 39

23. Jacques Lemoine, pp. 122; see also Jean Cormerais, pp. 175–176.

24. Jacques Lemoine, pp. 115; see also Phan Ngọc Khuê, *Taoist Painting,* pp. 39–40.

25. Jacques Lemoine, pp. 115–118; Cormerais, pp. 175–176; see also Phan Ngọc Khuê, *Taoist Painting,* p. 40.

26. Phan Ngọc Khuê's unpublished manuscript, and also his book, *Taoist Painting,* plate 98, and a short explanation, p. 186.

27. Jacques Lemoine, p. 46.

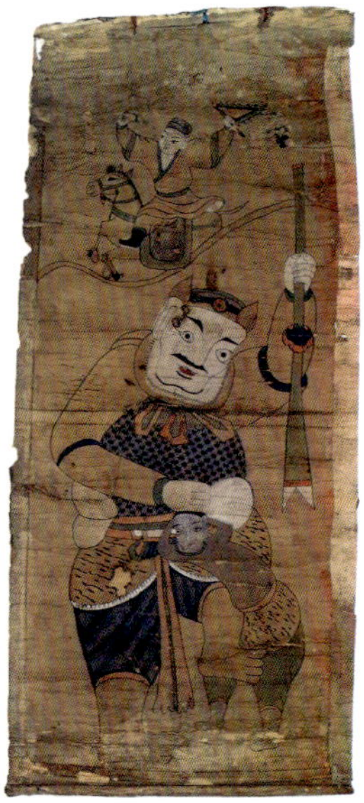
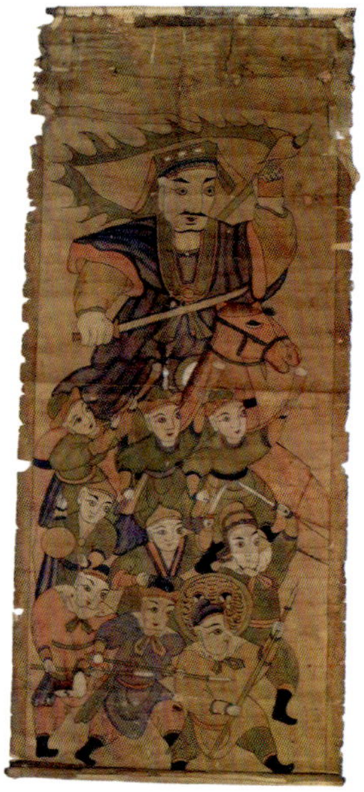
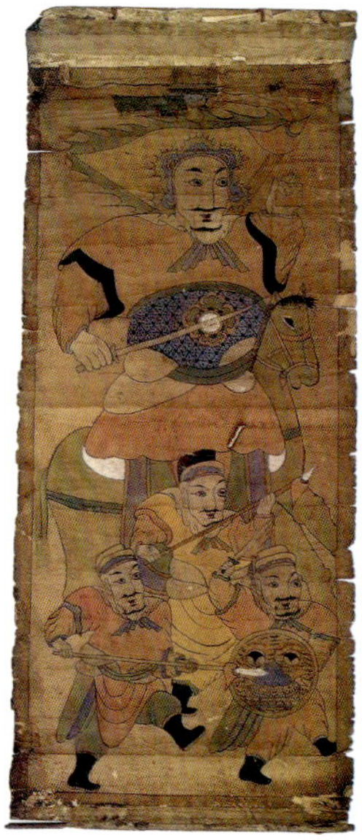
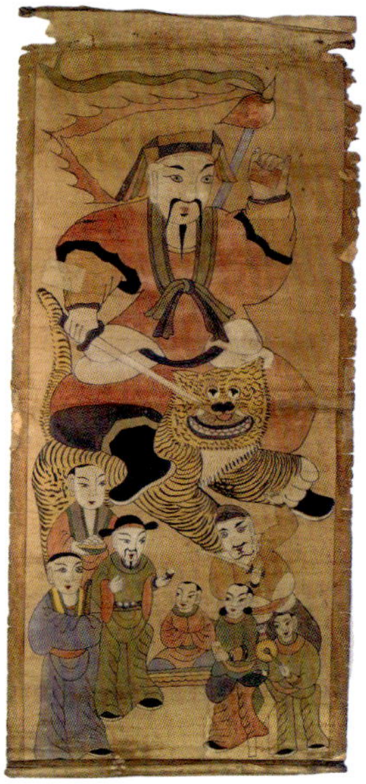
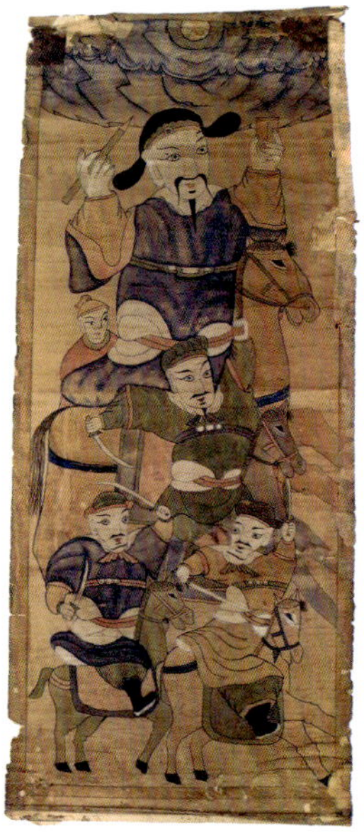
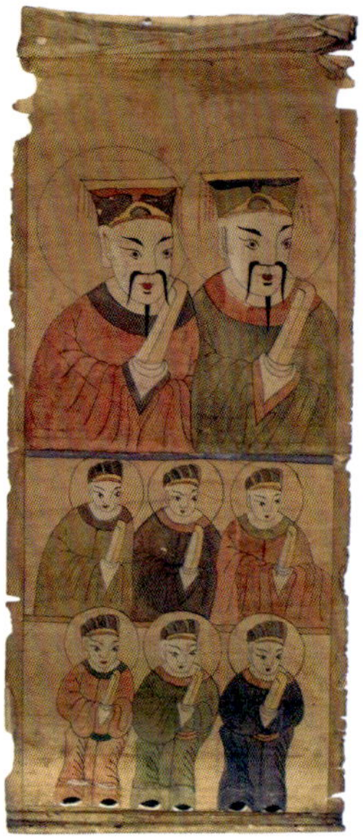
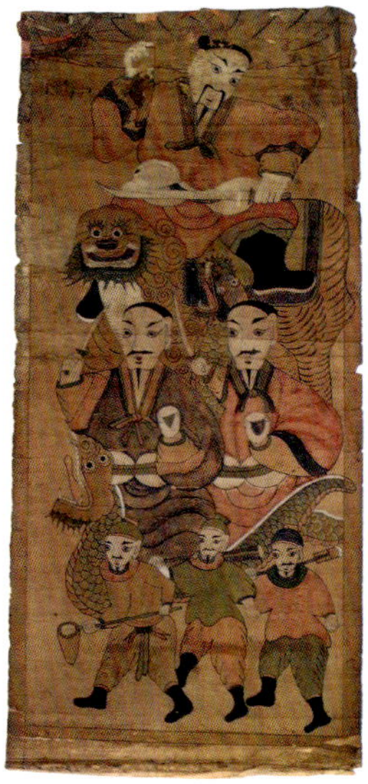
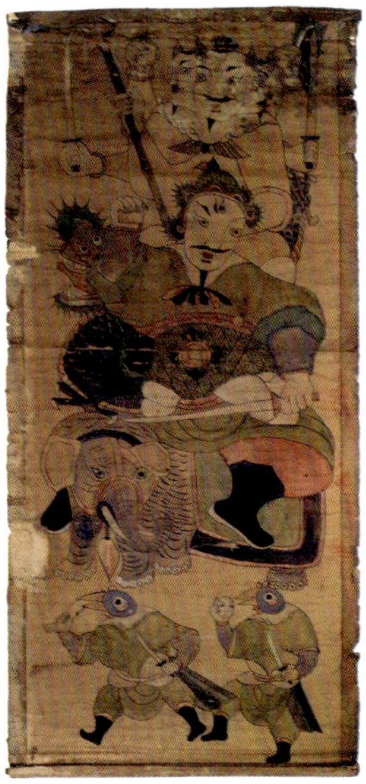
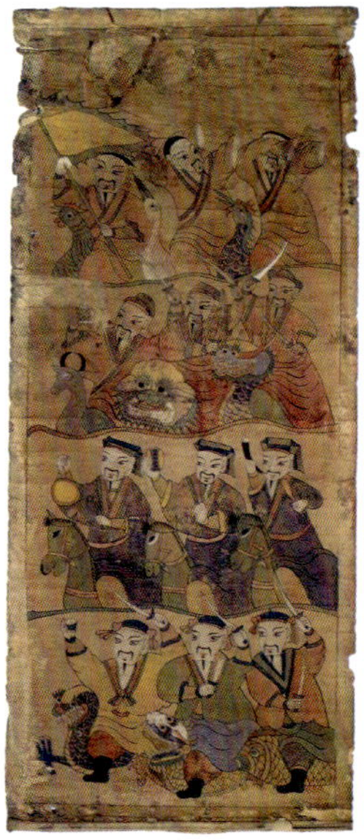
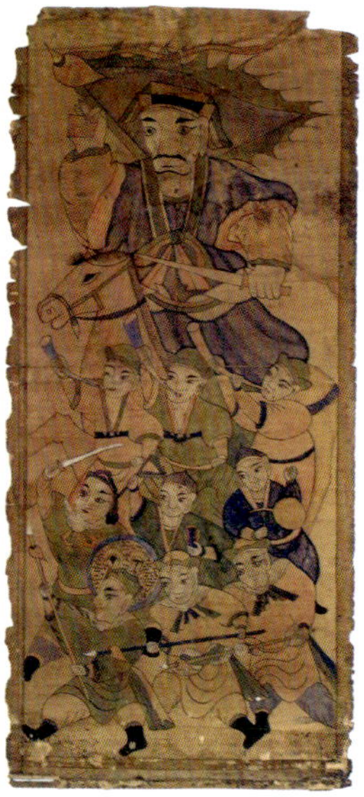
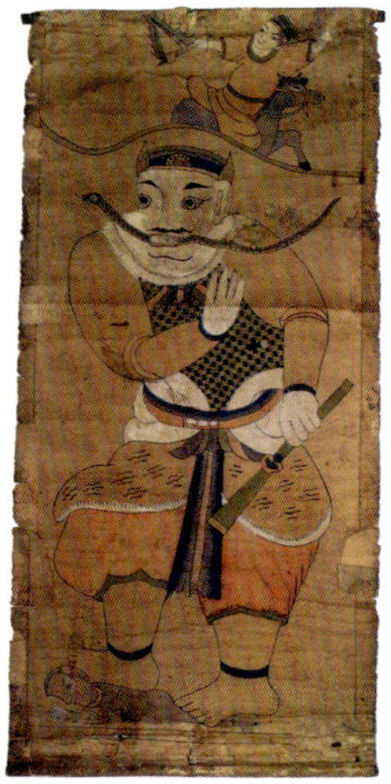

THE TWELVE GUARDIAN DEITIES:

Healing the Sick, Warding off Evil Forces, and Providing Protection for the Household and Community

As introduced earlier, the Sán Dìu people are a distant subgroup of the mountainous Yao who believe in an amalgam of religions, mainly Daoism, but mixed with major elements of Buddhism, Hinduism, animism, and ancestral worship.[1] These combinative elements are clearly illustrated in this set (thought to be originally composed of twelve painted scrolls; regarding missing scrolls, see below). Often, as is the case with this set, each deity is symmetrically paired with another having corresponding clothes, weapons, attributes, and the same or a similar number of attendants, though there are a few exceptions. The following identifications and arrangement are based on their religious functions, their artistic depictions, their iconographic features, and Chinese characters written on the backs of the paintings.

| A | B | C | D | E | F | G | H | I | J | K | L |

A. The Guardian Deity of the Left (Tả Đẩu Đà) (Fig. 125)

B. Governor of the Earth Soldiers (Địa Tiên Binh) (Fig. 121)

C. Lord of the Three Caves (Tam Động Vương) (Fig. 117)

D. The Medicine God (Trị Bịnh Công Tào) (Fig. 123)

E. Deity of Early Chinese Writing (Tả Đẩu Tự Thần) (Fig. 119)

F. The Official of Heaven and the Official of Earth (Thiên Đế, Địa Đế) (Fig. 116)

G. The Official of the Underworld and the Official of Water (Địa Phủ Đế, Thuỷ Đế) (missing)

H. Celestial Master Li (Lý Thiên Sư) (Fig. 120)

I. Brahma and Indra (Phạm Vương and Đế Thích Thiên) (Fig. 124)

J. The Twelve Divinities (Thập Nhị Sứ) (Fig. 118)

K. Buddha's Soldiers (Phật Tiên Binh) (Fig. 122)

L. The Guardian Deity of the Right (Hữu Đẩu Đà) (Fig. 126)

The organization presented here is different from that of Phan Ngọc Khuê, a Vietnamese expert in the religious paintings of ethnic communities in the mountainous regions of Northern Vietnam. In one of his handwritten notes, he proposes "the order of the ritual ceremonies performed by the Sán Dìu shaman priests,"[2] and his arrangement is as follows, reading from left to right: (A) Official of Heaven and Official of Earth, (B) Official of the Underworld and Official of Water, (C) the Guardian Deity of the Right, (D) Lord of the Three Caves, (E) Governor of the Earth Soldiers, (F) Deity of Early Chinese Writing, (G) Medicine God, (H) Brahma and Indra, (I) Celestial Master Li, (J) Buddha's Soldiers, (K) the Twelve Divinities, and (L) the Guardian Deity of the Left.

Note that his arrangement seems to reflect a modern system. In the traditional Chinese manner, important deities were always positioned at the center and the lesser deities generally placed on the outer right and left. If arranged in the traditional way, the Guardian Deity of the Left and the Guardian Deity of the Right would have been positioned at A and L, not C and L. Furthermore, carefully reading the short notes written in Chinese characters on the backs of three painted scrolls, it is clear that there are several paintings missing, not a single scroll (as stated by a previous dealer). The inscriptions state that the Brahma and Indra scroll (H) is number 4 from the right (右 第 四); the Medicine God (D) is number 7 on the left (左 治 病 功 曹 第 七); and the Official of Heaven and Official of Earth (F) was arranged as number 8 from the left (左 二 帝 第 八). If this is the case, the present set of eleven paintings in fact originally had at least sixteen (eight on the left and eight on the right) or perhaps more paintings, as can be seen in another collection.[3] Therefore, the paintings of the Three Pure Ones, Celestial Master Zhang, the Sanyuan, and the Official of the Underworld and the Official of Water are missing.

The group of twelve deities can be placed into six pairs, as follows:

> The Official of Heaven and the Official of Earth pairs with the Official of the Underworld and the Official of Water.
>
> The Lord of the Three Caves pairs with the Twelve Divinities.
>
> The Deity of Early Chinese Writing pairs with Brahma and Indra.
>
> Buddha's Soldiers pairs with the Governor of the Earth Soldiers.
>
> The Medicine God pairs with Celestial Master Li.
>
> The Guardian Deity of the Left pairs with the Guardian Deity of the Right.

All of them are equipped with weapons, including swords, spears, shields, pestles, and thunderbolts, for defensive purposes and protection.

The Official of Heaven and the Official of Earth

This painting depicts the two Officials of Heaven and Earth (Fig. 116) with their six attendants (minor deities) below them. The two officials are represented similarly; each wears a conventional cardboard hat with tassels, surrounded by a halo, and each holds a ceremonial tablet. Sán Dìu Daoist shamans usually use this painting, along with one depicting the Official of the Underworld and the Official of Water (missing from this set), to invoke the respective spirits. Originally it was believed that these four deities existed before the establishment of Daoism. Subsequently the Three Pure Ones and the Jade Emperor became the supreme deities in the Daoist belief system.[4] Individual paintings of the Three Pure Ones are missing from this set as well.

The Lord of the Three Caves and the Twelve Divinities

The painting of the Lord of the Three Caves (Fig. 117) symbolically represents the heavenly realm (Thiên Động), the earthly realm (Địa Động), and the human realm (Nhân Động). These are the three basic philosophical factors interwoven into and influencing not only human life, but also a myriad of natural and universal forces. In this painting, the Lord of the Three Caves is riding a horse and holding a sword in his right hand, a seal in his left, and carrying a banner on his back. Marching alongside the horse and representing each realm are three armed attendants.

In addition to these three realms, another Daoist belief divides the world into four realms: sky, earth, forests/mountains, and water. A lord, assisted by three divine attendants, governs each of these realms, as seen in the painting of the Twelve Divinities (Fig. 118). Here, the groups of divinities are arranged in hierarchical order, with the three for the Lord of the Sky at the top riding a rooster, a crane, and a peacock. The next row depicts the three divinities of the Lord of the Earth riding a cow, a lion, and a dragon. In the third row are the divinities of the Lord of Forests/Mountains, riding on horseback and holding a gong, a drum, and a water-buffalo horn. The divinities on the bottom row, riding two dragons and a carp, assist the Lord of Water. Thus, the birds represent the sky; the cow, lion, and dragon the earth; the horses the forests and mountains; and the dragons and carp the water. According to Phan Ngọc Khuê, these twelve divine beings, divided into four groups, also represent the four cardinal directions, four seasons, and the twelve months of the year.[5]

The Deity of Early Chinese Writing (倉 頡 Cangjie) and Celestial Master Li

In the minds of the Sán Dìu people, the Deity of Early Chinese Writing (寫 斗 字 神) (Fig. 119) is the figure who created the oracle-bone script employed during the Shang dynasty (c. 1600–1050 BCE) as a means of divination and a way to communicate with the ancestors. He was also thought

Fig. 116

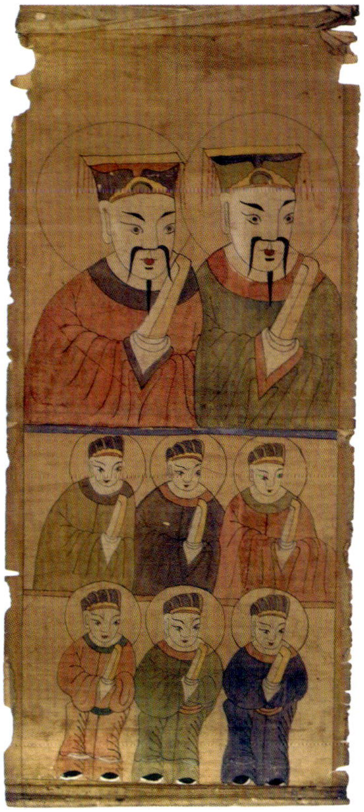

Fig. 117

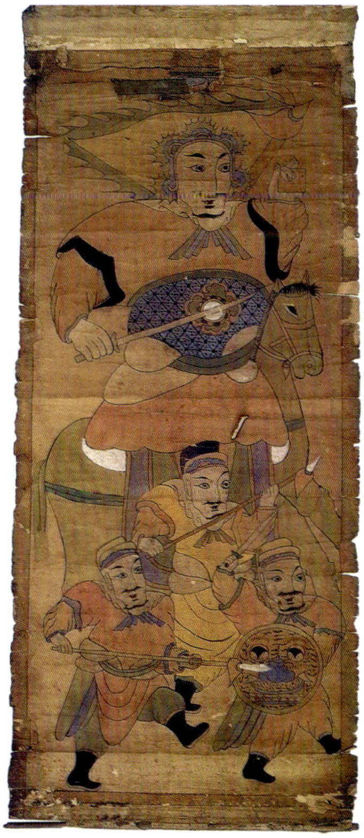

Fig. 118

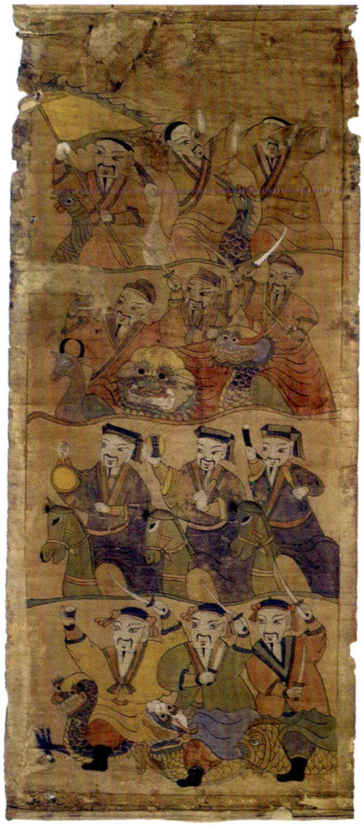

Fig. 116
The Official of Heaven and the Official of Earth,
c. early 20th century
Sán Dìu, Vietnam

Fig. 117
Lord of the Three Caves,
c. early 20th century
Sán Dìu, Vietnam

Fig. 118
The Twelve Divinities,
c. early 20th century
Sán Dìu, Vietnam

Fig. 119
The Deity of Early Chinese Writing,
c. early 20th century
Sán Dìu, Vietnam

Fig. 120
Celestial Master Li,
c. early 20th century
Sán Dìu, Vietnam

Fig. 121
Governor of the Earth Soldiers,
c. early 20th century
Sán Dìu, Vietnam

Fig. 122
Buddha's Soldiers,
c. early 20th century
Sán Dìu, Vietnam

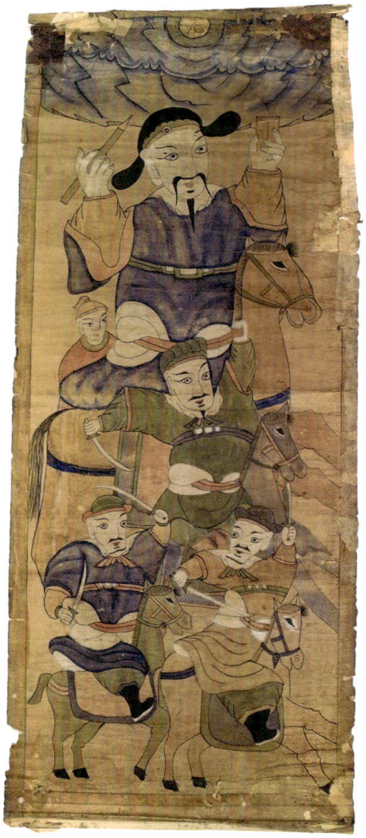

Fig. 119

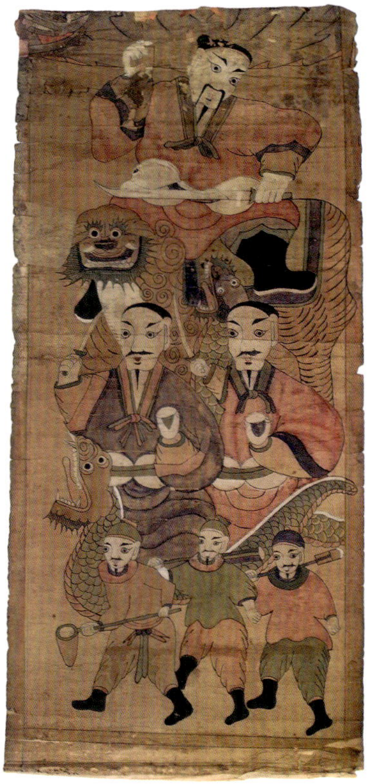

Fig. 120

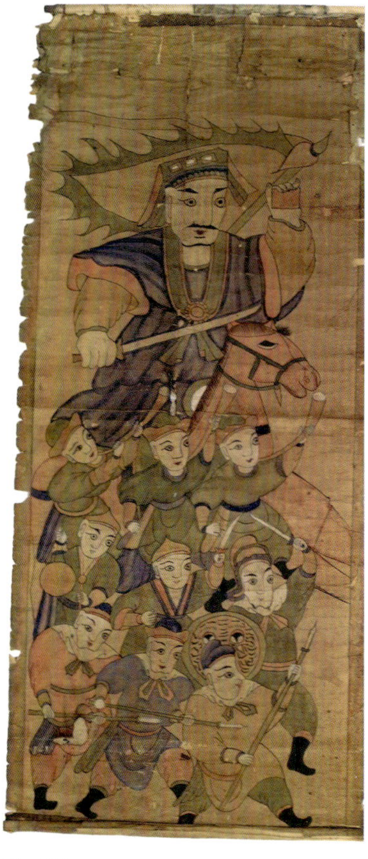

Fig. 121

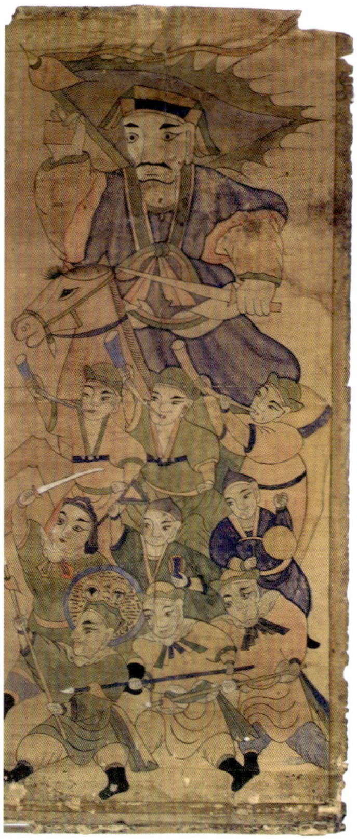

Fig. 122

to have later been promoted to become the god of writing.[6] According to Chinese mythical history, he is Cangjie (倉 頡), the cultural hero who invented Chinese characters and an official historiographer of the Yellow Emperor. Legend has it that Cangjie had four eyes with remarkable vision and ability. By examining constellations, the footprints of birds and animals, and other aspects of nature he developed pictographic signs and created Chinese characters.[7]

In this scroll the deity wears a loose blue mandarin's robe, a black mandarin's hat, and a belt, and rides a galloping horse. His signature characteristic is the large Chinese writing brush he holds in his right hand. His left hand holds a sacred seal, a feature often seen with the other deities of this set. He is accompanied by three military generals on horseback holding swords, and an attendant follows closely behind.

The only clue given to assume that the painting of Celestial Master Li (Fig. 120) is paired with the Chinese writing deity is the curtainlike canopy on the top of both scrolls, which resembles thick auspicious clouds protecting the divine beings. Only these two scrolls have such a feature. Holding a magical sword in his left hand, Master Li is riding on a striped yellow tiger with a lion-featured face. He is accompanied by two large figures riding on the backs of dragons, each holding a sword and a small cup. Below them are three small figures, each carrying a farming tool.

The Governor of the Earth Soldiers and Buddha's Soldiers

If these paintings weren't known to be from the Sán Dìu people in Vĩnh Phúc province from the labeling on their backs, it would be difficult to know which represents the Governor of the Earth Soldiers and which Buddha's Soldiers, because they are nearly identical in every detail. In this pair of scrolls the figures in the left-hand painting, the Governor of the Earth Soldiers (Fig. 121), face toward the right, whereas the figures in the right-hand painting, Buddha's Soldiers (Fig. 122), face toward the left. In the left-hand scroll the lord himself, dominating half of the painting, rides a horse and holds a sword in his right hand, a heavenly seal in his left, and has a triangle-shaped war banner on his back. Beneath the lord are nine soldiers arranged in three rows—three holding long horns in the upper row, one holding a gong and two holding swords in the middle row, and three holding long spears in the bottom row. All are fearlessly charging forward. The nine soldiers symbolically represent the eight cardinal directions plus the center. In this case, it is hard to know which one is the leader, but it is possibly the one holding the gong.

The Medicine God, and Brahma and Indra

The Medicine God (Fig. 123) is portrayed riding on the back of a yellow-striped tiger, holding a sword in one hand and a piece of paper in the other. In Chinese mythology, there is no particular healing god. Healing was associated with Shennong, the mythical emperor who spread the knowledge of herbal medicine and taught his people how to cure diseases.[8] Later, sometimes divine healing figures were associated with the Daoist chemists, the Elder Zhang Guo and Iron Crutch Li, two of the Eight Immortals. In this painting, the figure that seems to represent the patient is seated in the center on a dais, surrounded by six figures. Each is holding something except for the female figure on the patient's left side. There is an inscription written on the back of the painting saying that the medicine god scroll is placed seventh from the left for ritual ceremonies.

Paired with the Medicine God is the scroll depicting two supreme Indian gods, Brahmā and Indra (Fig. 124). Brahmā is the Hindu god of creation and is part, along with Vishnu and Shiva, of the Hindu trinity. He is regarded as the progenitor of all living beings. Traditionally, Brahmā is portrayed with four heads, four faces, and four arms. Often, as in this painting, only three faces are visible, because the fourth, on the back of his head, cannot be seen. In this scroll, Brahmā has four arms. Each arm wears a bracelet; two hands hold swords, the others bear a trident and something which looks like a small dagger. In Indian and Southeast Asian traditions, his *vāhana*, or animal vehicle, is a *hamsa*, usually depicted as a swan or a goose. However, in this painting, he is riding a dragonlike animal with four-clawed feet and blue scales. Beneath Brahmā is Indra Śakra (帝 释 天), leader of the gods and Lord of Heaven in Hinduism, riding his elephant *vāhana*. He is one of the earliest Indian Vedic deities, known as the god of rain and thunderstorms. Instead of holding his standard attribute, a lightning thunderbolt, he holds a sword and a seal in this painting. Further, this painter mistakenly drew a third eye in the center of Indra's forehead, an iconographical attribute of Shiva. At the bottom are two bird deities that represent the sun and the moon, or day and night. In Chinese mythology, a crown represents the sun, while a lady's face represents the moon.[9] In Buddhism, these two supreme deities accompanied the Buddha from his birth, appearing many times during his dharma lectures. On the back of the scroll four Chinese characters state that the painting is arranged fourth from the right. Unlike the other pairs of paintings, these two do not have any parallel or common symmetrical features. Rather, each functions as an independent scroll with its own merits.

The Guardian Deity of the Left and the Guardian Deity of the Right

Phan Ngọc Khuê identifies these guardians as Đầu Đà deities,[10] and says that they are Chinese Buddhist monks who were highly trained in martial arts in order to protect the Buddha dharma and Buddhist temples. They are often associated with Bodhidharma, the founder of Chan (Zen) Buddhism, who sat for nine years in meditation facing a wall in the Sha-

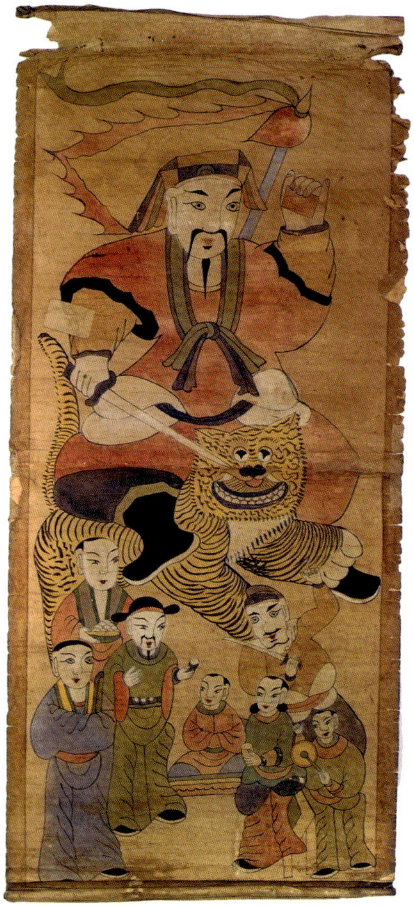

Fig. 123

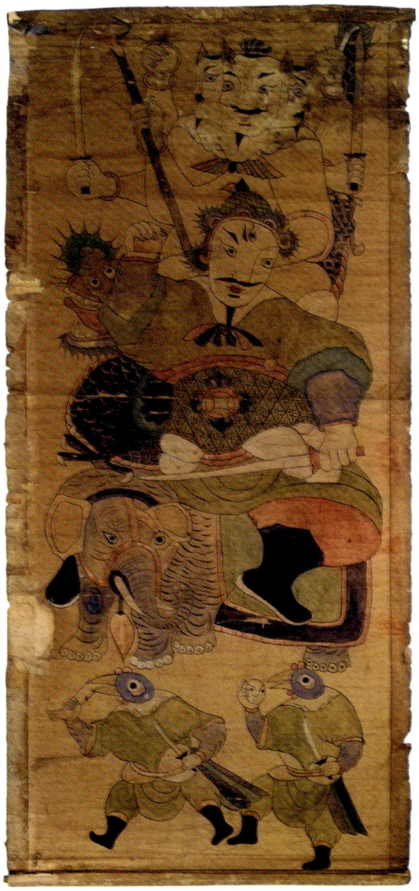

Fig. 124

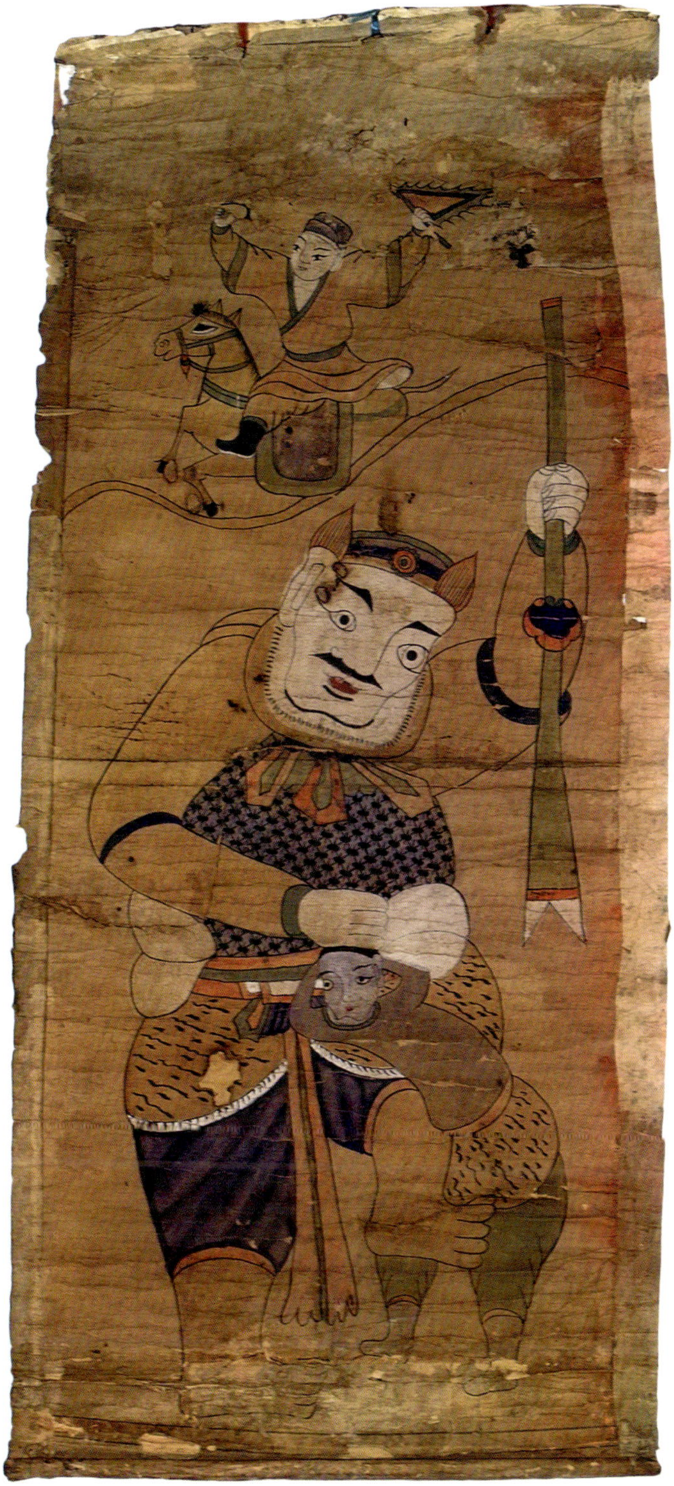

Fig. 125

oling Temple in Henan Province, China.[11] Đầu Đà is a transliteration of the Sanskrit word Dhūta (頭 陀), which literally means "shaken off" and refers to the monk's ascetic practice when he is shaking off his desire for good food, clothing, and shelter.[12]

In fact, the pair are probably representations of Vajrapani, originally a Hindu god, who was incorporated into Buddhism as a protector against evil spirits. In East Asian Buddhist countries, including Vietnam, this pair of protectors commonly stands guard outside temple gates, one on either side. The protector deity depicted with an open mouth, as if shouting, is always to the right side of the entrance, and the one with a closed mouth stands to the left. Their fierce appearance is meant to ward off evil spirits and keep the temple grounds free of demons and thieves.

In this pair of paintings, the Guardian Deity of the Right (Fig. 126) grips a live snake between his teeth and stamps on a demon with his bare feet. The Guardian Deity of the Left (Fig. 125) holds a pestlelike object in his left hand while his right hand is about to smash a demon that he is kicking with his left leg. At the top of both paintings, a figure on horseback holds a banner in one hand and seal in the other. Both deities wear costumes that are not related to Buddhist monks or esoteric deities, but are stock examples of ethnic clothing.

These deities are also similar to Vajradhara, the "thunderbolt bearer," known in Chinese esoteric Buddhism as the "diamond pestle holder" (金 剛 杵, Kim Cương Chùy), a reference to the weapon in his hands.[13]

Fig. 123
The God of Medicine, c. early 20th century
Sán Dìu, Vietnam

Fig. 124
Brahma and Indra, c. early 20th century
Sán Dìu, Vietnam

Fig. 125
The Guardian Deity of the Left, c. early 20th century
Sán Dìu, Vietnam

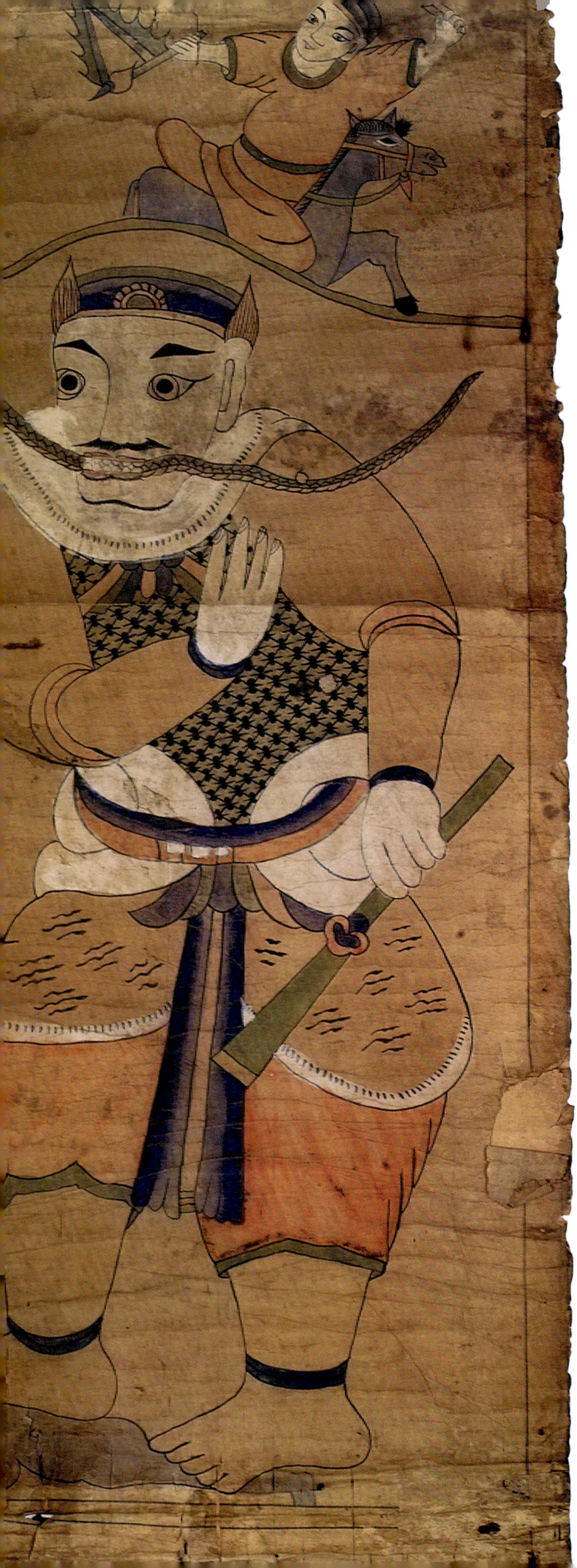

Conclusion

As noted in the introductory essay, it is a common practice among Sán Dìu families to have at least one son become a shaman priest, whose main duties are to protect the family, ward off evil forces, and heal the sick in his community. In undertaking such a noble role, he would draw power from all religious sources—Hinduism, Buddhism, Daoism, and Chinese mythical and legendary figures—into his own spiritual system.

As traditions are passed down from one generation to the next, backed by devotional belief but lacking factual references, later generations may mistakenly identify the deities and thus wrongly inform field researchers, and subsequently collectors. Or perhaps the artist himself portrayed the divine beings based on whatever was in his own collection, without knowing their original identities. Even so, a strong belief in the power of guardian deities is more important than their accurate iconographical depiction, in the minds of the Sán Dìu shaman priests.

Fig. 126
The Guardian Deity of the Right, c. early 20th century
Sán Dìu, Vietnam

NOTES

1. For a brief discussion of the Sán Dìu religious belief system, see Phan Ngọc Khuê, *Taoist Painting*, pp. 70–71.

2. Phan Ngọc Khuê's unpublished manuscript.

3. There is a similar set of twelve paintings of the Sán Dìu from Tuyên Quang province, Vietnam, published in Phan Ngọc Khuê, *Taoist Painting*, pp. 176–178. Thus, Khuê based his argument on this set. However, in Phạm Đức Sĩ's collection, there is a set of twenty-eight guardian deities, also of the Sán Dìu ethnic people, though six of them are missing. On each part there is a Chinese inscription providing the identification of each deity and the prescribed position, either on the left or on the right. *Vietnamese Ceremonial Paintings: Pham Duc Si's Collection, 2001–2009* (Hanoi: Icon Communications, 2009), pp. 92–109.

4. Phan Ngọc Khuê's unpublished manuscript.

5. Ibid.

6. Ibid.; also, *Taoist Painting*, p. 178.

7. For the full description of the myths and legends of Cangjie, see Lihui Yang and Deming An, *Handbook of Chinese Mythology* (Santa Barbara: ABC-CLIO, 2005), pp. 84–86.

8. According to Chinese myth, Shennong was the person who developed Chinese medicine by tasting hundreds, or even thousands, of herbs in order to discover their characteristics and functions. He also invented the system of yin and yang as an integral part of the body, which is closely connected to nature. He was depicted as the first person to carefully study the pulse of the body, and started the therapies of herbal medicine, moxibustion, and acupuncture. Ibid., pp. 72–73.

9. For example, as early as the Former Han dynasty (206 BCE–9 CE), the sun was depicted with a bird in the circle on the right side, and the crescent moon with a jumping frog on the left side of a painted silk banner discovered in the Mangwang Tomb I in Hunan. For the image and full description, see Robert L. Thorp and Richard Ellis Vinograd, *Chinese Art and Culture* (New York: Abrams, 2001), pp. 145–147.

10. In Phan Ngọc Khuê's unpublished manuscript, he writes that these two deities are Chinese Buddhist monks, known as Đầu Đà, because they were associated with ancient Indian Buddhist monks of the Theravada tradition, who observed the twelve rules (as explained in note 12, below), and also later associated with Chinese martial art monks from Shaolin Monastery in Henan, China. However, in *Vietnamese Ceremonial Paintings: Pham Duc Si's Collection,* the Chinese inscriptions identify these two as the Snake Head, 頭 它, not 頭 陀, meaning Dhūta. In fact, the Vietnamese pronunciation of these two words are Đầu Xà, and Đầu Đà. If not carefully reading the Chinese characters, it is easy to make errors. For reference, see Phạm Đức Sĩ, the two images on pages 93 and 107.

11. Phan Ngọc Khuê's unpublished manuscript. See also *Taoist Painting*, pp. 178–179.

12. The twelve rules are: (1) begging for food; (2) begging for food from one door to the next without discrimination; (3) eating only one meal a day, at noon; (4) eating in moderation; (5) no solid food after lunch; (6) wearing clothes made of castaway rags; (7) keeping only three garments; (8) living in a quiet, remote area; (9) living among graves; (10) living under a tree; (11) sitting on open ground under the open sky; and (12) sitting all the time without reclining. See William Edward Soothhill and Lewis Hodous, *A Dictionary of Chinese Buddhist Terms* (Delhi: Motilal Banarsidass, 1977), pp. 453–454.

13. For example, see Penelope Manson, *History of Japanese Art*, 2nd ed. (Upper Saddle River, NJ: Person-Prentice Hall, 2005), fig. X16, p. 187.

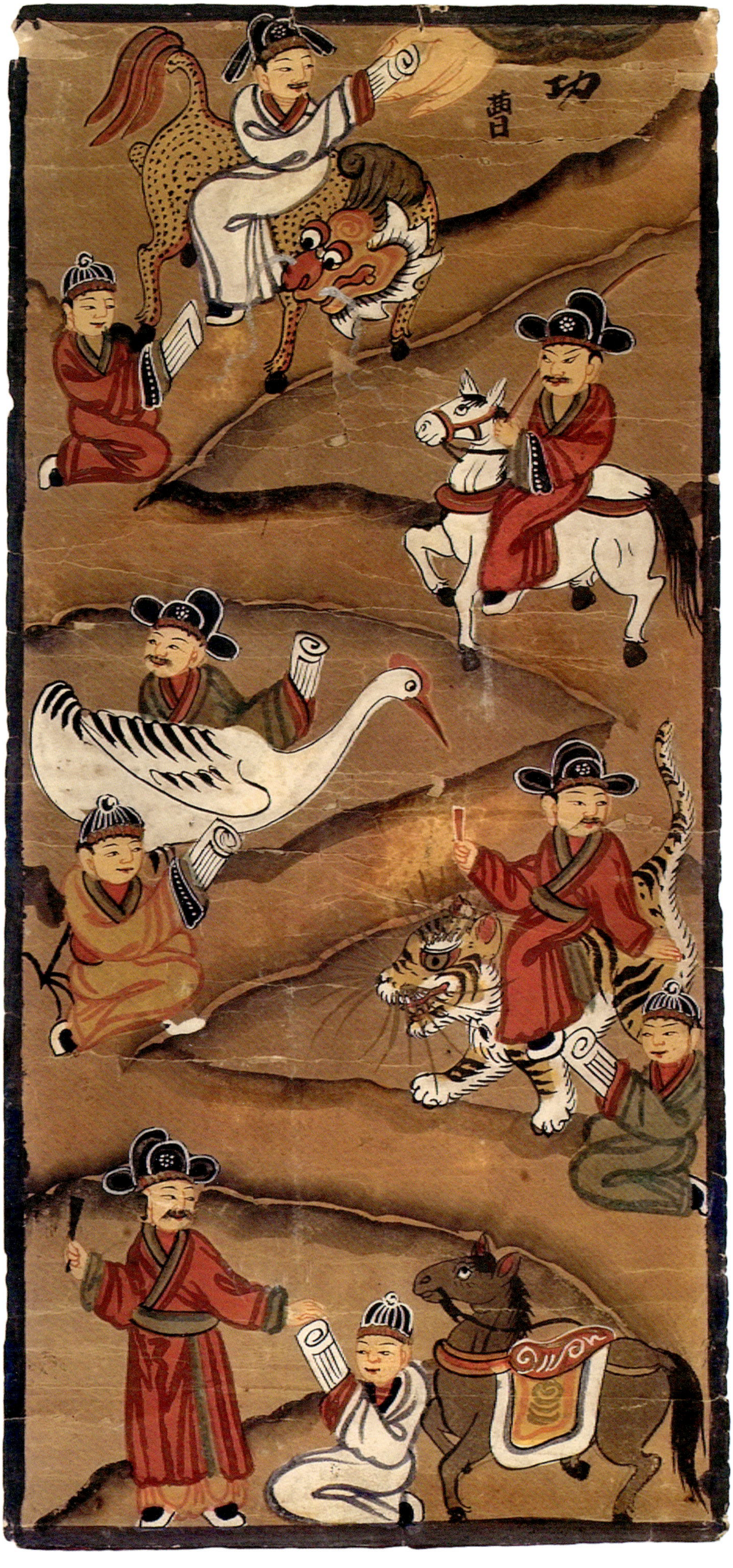

Fig. 127

THE FOUR HEAVENLY MESSENGERS:
The Liaison Officials of Time and Space

The Four Heavenly Messengers (四 直 公 曹, *Tứ trực công tào*) are minor Daoist deities in charge of the year (値 年, *trực niên*), month (値 月, *trực nguyệt*), day (値日 *trực nhật*), and hour (値 時, *trực thời*).[1] In the Han dynasty (206 BCE–220 CE), a messenger was a minor district official whose main tasks were to keep a magistrate's records of good and bad deeds as well as credits for rewards, punishment, promotion, and demotion of both citizens and staff. During the Ming dynasty (1368–1644), Daoist exponents incorporated the position into their religious system by installing four messengers into the service of the Jade Emperor's court in heaven.[2] Paintings of the Four Heavenly Messengers by the Yao and other ethnic groups were probably influenced by these Ming dynasty beliefs. The Four Heavenly Messengers work for the Governors of the Four Realms. Namely, they are the messengers from the sky, the underworld, the earthly realm, and the realm of water.[3]

According to ancient Chinese astronomy, the sky around the ecliptic (the plane of the earth's rotation) and the celestial equator (the plane of the earth's orbit) are divided into twenty-eight regions, or twenty-eight lunar lodges, known in Chinese as 二 十 八 宿 (*Er shi ba xiu, Nhị thập bát tú*). Each region is one *xiu* 宿, or constellation. These constellations are organized into four groups of seven, corresponding to the four cardinal directions. Within each major division, a central constellation is selected to represent both its cardinal direction and a time unit.[4]

In the traditional Chinese system one twenty-four-hour day is divided into twelve units, each represented by an animal in the Chinese zodiac. As a result of all this, it is believed that the Four Heavenly Messengers carefully monitor and record everything in each hour around the clock, during the four seasons, during every month of the year, and everywhere in the four cardinal directions within the four realms. Their task is to make final reports on all actions, including good and bad deeds, to the high supreme deities in the court of the Jade Emperor, so that the good can be rewarded and the bad punished.

Although they are considered minor deities, their presence is necessary during any major ceremony of the ethnic groups in northern Vietnam and southern China. In such ceremonies, the Daoist priests write and recite petitions on behalf of a family, a clan, or the whole community. This written document is then burned on a tray that is either held on the head by the family host or placed on the ground. The local God of the Earth transmits all the documents to the messengers, who then ride animals and fly through the clouds to deliver the messages to the heavenly court.

Pictorially speaking, the Four Heavenly Messengers correspond to four animals representing the four cardinal directions. However, in paintings of the Yao and other minority groups there are some variations from traditional Chinese animals. The black tortoise (*xuanwu*) is a vehicle for the First Heavenly Messen-

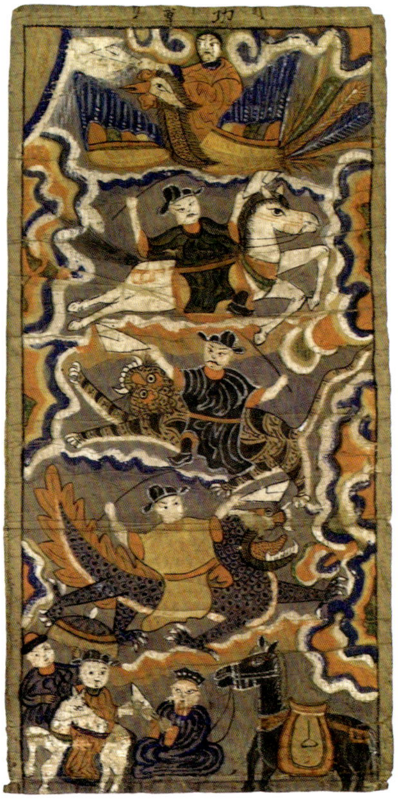

Fig. 128

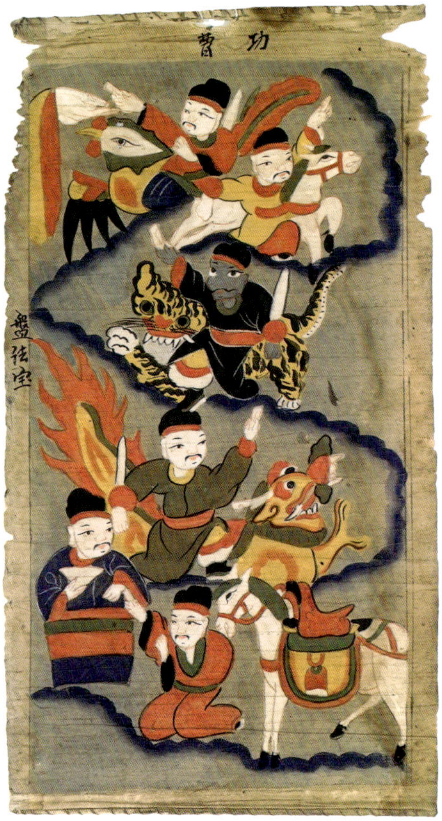

Fig. 129

ger, the year deity, and that of the heavenly realm. In the last few centuries of Chinese tradition the black tortoise has been a symbol of bad fortune, so to accord with folk belief the tortoise has been replaced with a phoenix, a goose, a rooster, or even a unicorn (麒 麟, *kỳ lân*)—a mythical, auspicious animal. A red bird (*zhuque*) is the vehicle for the Second Heavenly Messenger, the month deity, and that of the underworld. However, it has been replaced by a white horse, regarded as more auspicious. The green dragon (*zhinglong*) is the mythical animal for the Third Heavenly Messenger, the day deity, and that of the water realm, but in a Tày painting of the Four Messengers (Fig. 127), the dragon has been replaced by a large goose, a propitious animal of their particular mythology.[5] Finally, the white tiger (*baihu*) is the vehicle for the Fourth Heavenly Messenger, the hour deity, and that of the earthy realm. The white tiger, however, is very rare in Vietnam, and is considered the most sacred and fearful animal of the jungle; therefore a yellow-black striped tiger, which is more abundant, is often depicted instead. The positions of the tiger and dragon are not fixed, thus in a majority of the paintings (Figs. 128-131, 133-135), the deity riding the dragon is at the bottom. Alternatively, in the Tày scroll the animals, arranged from the top down, are: Chinese unicorn, white horse, large goose, and yellow-striped tiger.

The Kitnick Collection has ten representations of the Four Heavenly Messengers with various dates, in conditions ranging from excellent to relatively good. The Yao most often depict them in a single scroll. Compositionally, each painting is organized into five triangular sections in a zigzag line running from the bottom to the top. The bottom section depicts the local God of Earth, with the figure kneeling between the deity and a horse being regarded as a shaman or court messenger; thus these two figures are not Heavenly Messengers. The artistic style and execu-

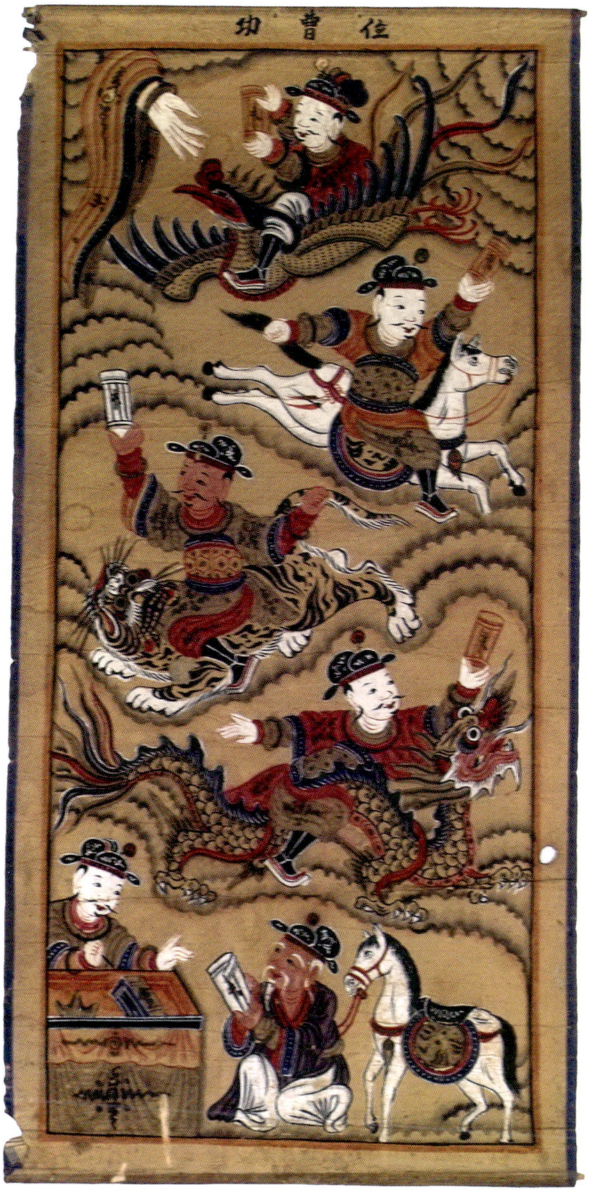

Fig. 130

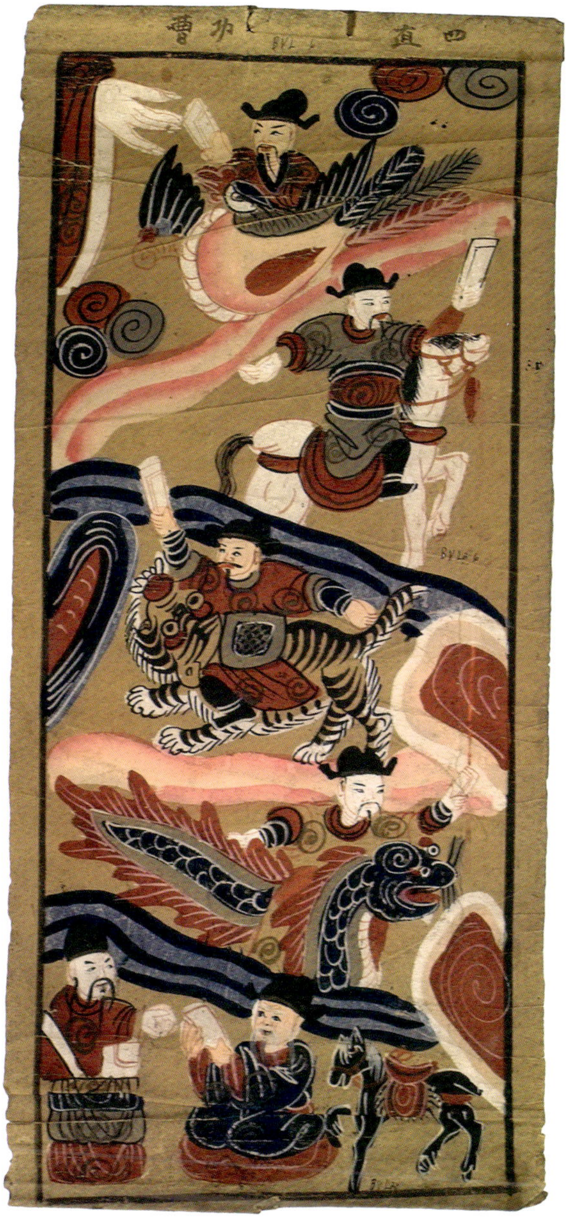

Fig. 131

Fig. 127
Four Heavenly Messengers, c. early to mid-20th century
Tày, Vietnam

Fig. 128
Four Heavenly Messengers, c. early to mid-20th century
Sán Dìu, Vietnam

Fig. 129
Four Heavenly Messengers, c. early to mid-20th century
Sán Dìu, Vietnam

Fig. 130
Four Heavenly Messengers, c. early to mid-20th century
Cao Làn–Sán Chi (Sán Chay), Vietnam

Fig. 131
Four Heavenly Messengers, c. early to mid-20th century
White Trouser (Quần Trắng) Yao, Vietnam

tion of each painting vary greatly: some were painted by highly skilled artists, while others possess a folk quality. For example, in Fig. 135 the third messenger differs from the others, as he has a blue face with a strong facial expression. In this painting the messengers wear similar clothing and are mainly distinguishable by their color, whereas in other scrolls (Figs. 128–130, 133) their clothing is quite differentiated. In some paintings the messengers have a pleasant demeanor, while in others they are stern looking, or simply calm.

In general, all Heavenly Messenger paintings, from whatever ethnic group, feature the local God of the Earth (土 地 神, Thổ Địa Thần). In Fig. 132 he is depicted in the standard manner as an old man with a mustache, wearing a special uniform and riding, or standing next to, a horse. However, in other paintings (Figs. 127, 135), the artists characterized him as a younger man without a white beard. In the Tày painting (Fig. 127), for example, the local God of the Earth is handing, or has handed, a scroll to each messenger, with the exception of the second one from the top. Each deity, carrying a message scroll, rides on his animal vehicle and flies toward heaven. After rushing through the sky, the top messenger, the year deity, delivers the message to heaven. His

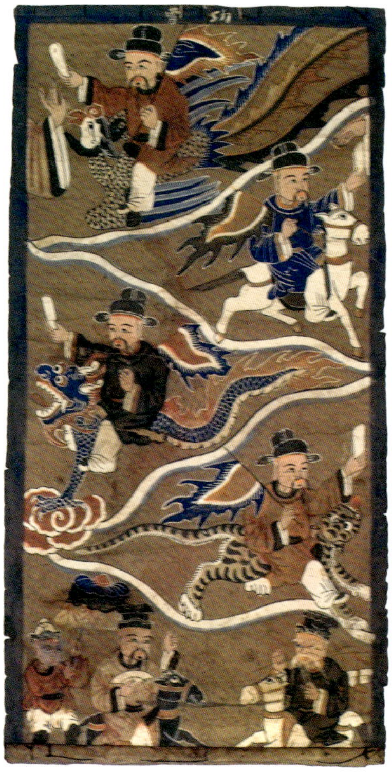

Fig. 132

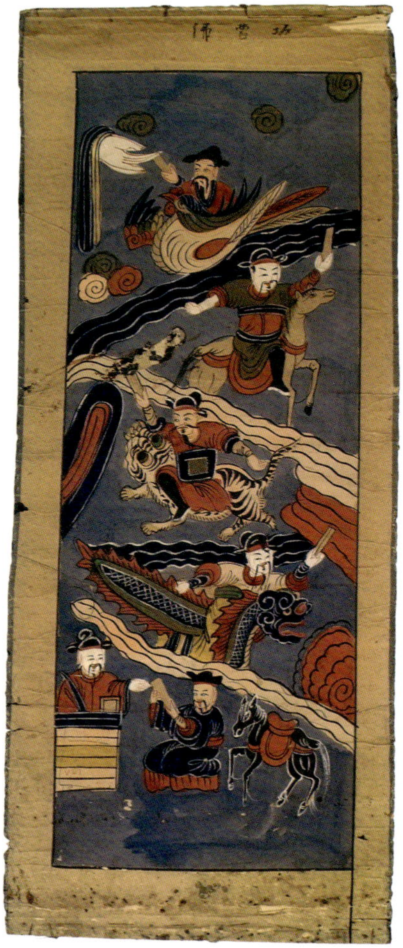

Fig. 133

message is received by a large hand, visible at the top of the painting. The arrangement of the four deities may also be read from top to bottom, because they receive messages sent down from the Jade Emperor regarding rewards and punishments.

The scrolls of the Four Heavenly Messengers imply the continuous movement of time. They represent time units, from the smallest to the largest, which are in perpetual transformation, since everything on earth is altering in every single moment.[6] This idea is symbolically painted at the bottom of each scroll: the local God of the Earth watches everything happening in his territory. He then reports to the hour deity, who reports to the day deity, and he to the month deity, and he to the year deity. In a continuation of traditional Chinese customs, the Yao and other ethnic peoples hold annual celebrations as a result of these reports. These four deities are considered important in rituals of receiving initiation, the New Year festival, the new harvest, and many other annual celebrations.

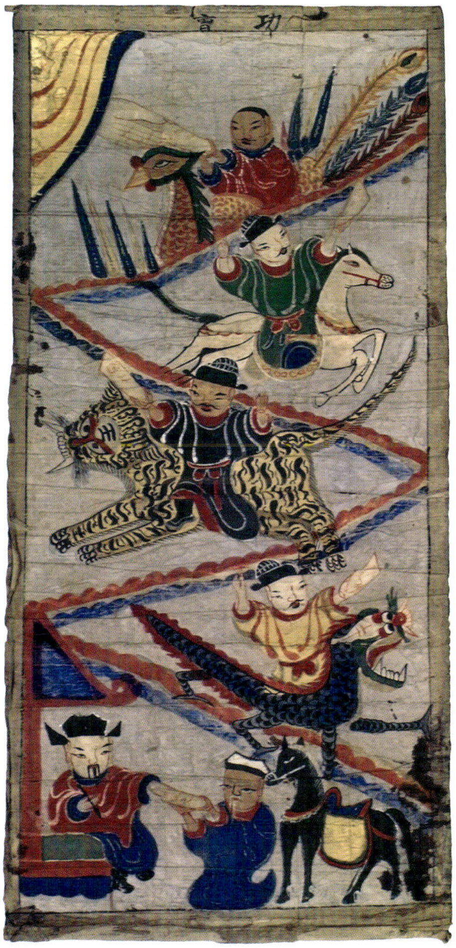

Fig. 134

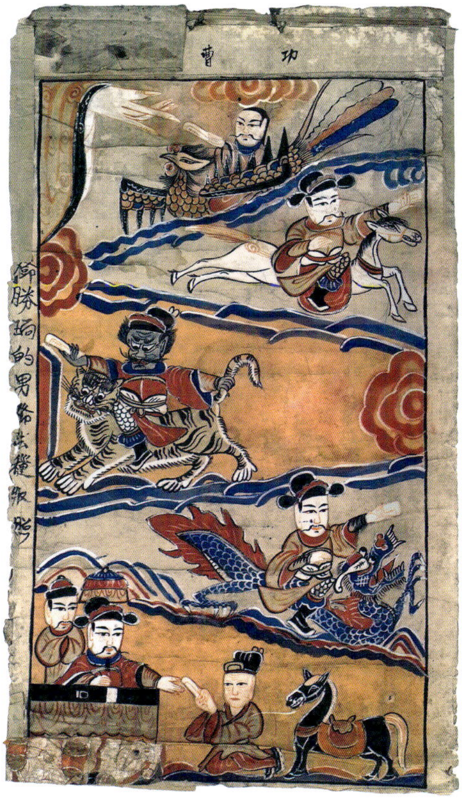

Fig. 135

NOTES

1. Because of their functions, the Chinese named them Li Bing (李 丙, Lý Bính), the year deity; Chen Yi (承 乙, Thừa Ất), the month deity; Zhou Teng (周 登, Châu Đăng), the day deity; and Liu Hong (劉 洪, Lưu Hồng), the hour deity. See 四 值 功 曹 [Si zhi gong cao], http://baike.baidu.com/view/302166.htm (accessed 7/15/2013).

2. For a more elaborate discussion related to the historical development of the Four Heavenly Messengers in the Daoist tradition as well in Chinese folk belief, see the web page cited in note 1. For a brief discussion about the Four Messengers and their functions within the Yao tradition, see Phan Ngọc Khuê, *Ceremony of the Hanging Lamps*, pp. 56–58.

3. Ibid., p. 56.

4. For further discussion on this topic, see Thomas F. Aylward, *The Imperial Guide to Feng Shui and Chinese Astrology* (London: Watkins, 2007), pp. 95–102.

5. Author interview with Phan Ngọc Khuê in Hanoi, June 2013.

6. *Tìm Hiểu Về Tứ Trực Công Tào* [Helping Understand the Four Heavenly Messengers] http://huyenthuat.com/index.php/vi/dien-dan/48-d-o-giao/242-tim-hi-u-v-t-tr-c-cong-tao (accessed 7/15/2013).

Fig. 132
Four Heavenly Messengers, c. early to mid-20th century
Indigo Clad (Thanh-y) Yao, Vietnam

Fig. 133
Four Heavenly Messengers, c. early to mid-20th century
White Trouser (Quần Trắng) Yao, Vietnam

Fig. 134
Four Heavenly Messengers, c. early to mid-20th century
Indigo Clad (Thanh-y) Yao, Vietnam

Fig. 135
Four Heavenly Messengers, c. early to mid-20th century
Indigo Clad (Thanh-y) Yao, Vietnam

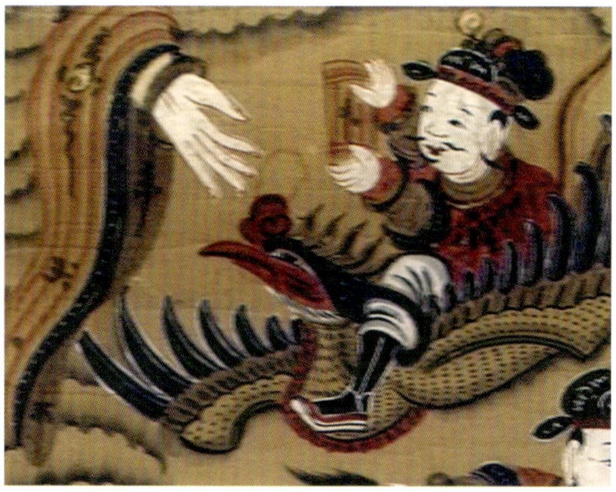

Detail of *Fig. 130*

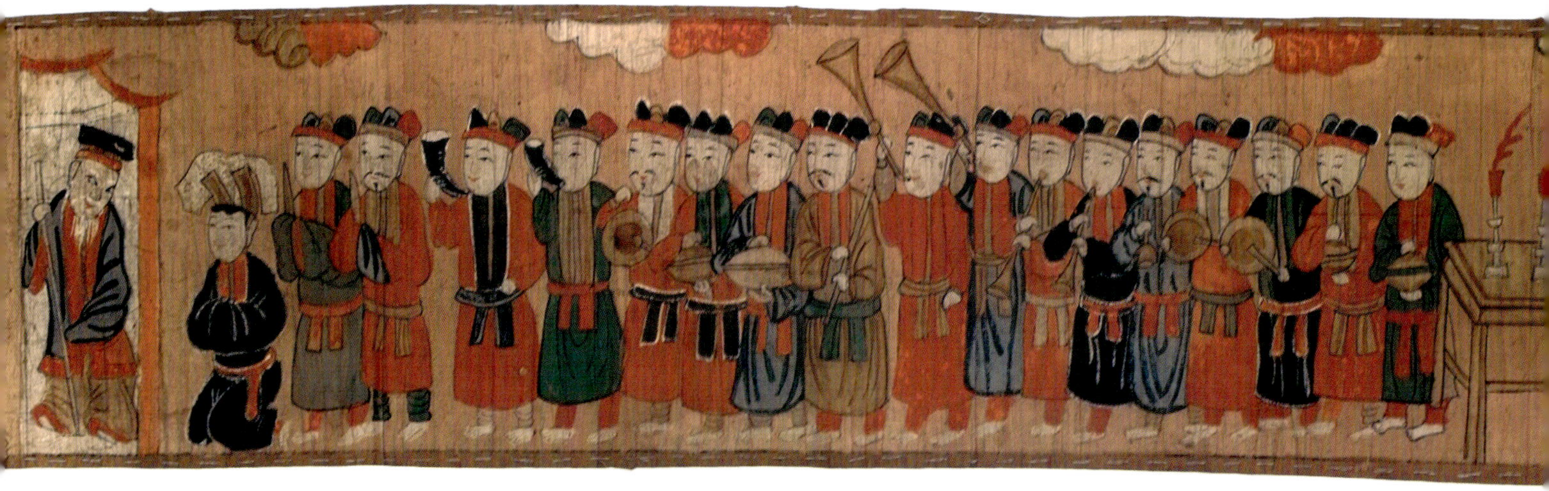

Fig. 136

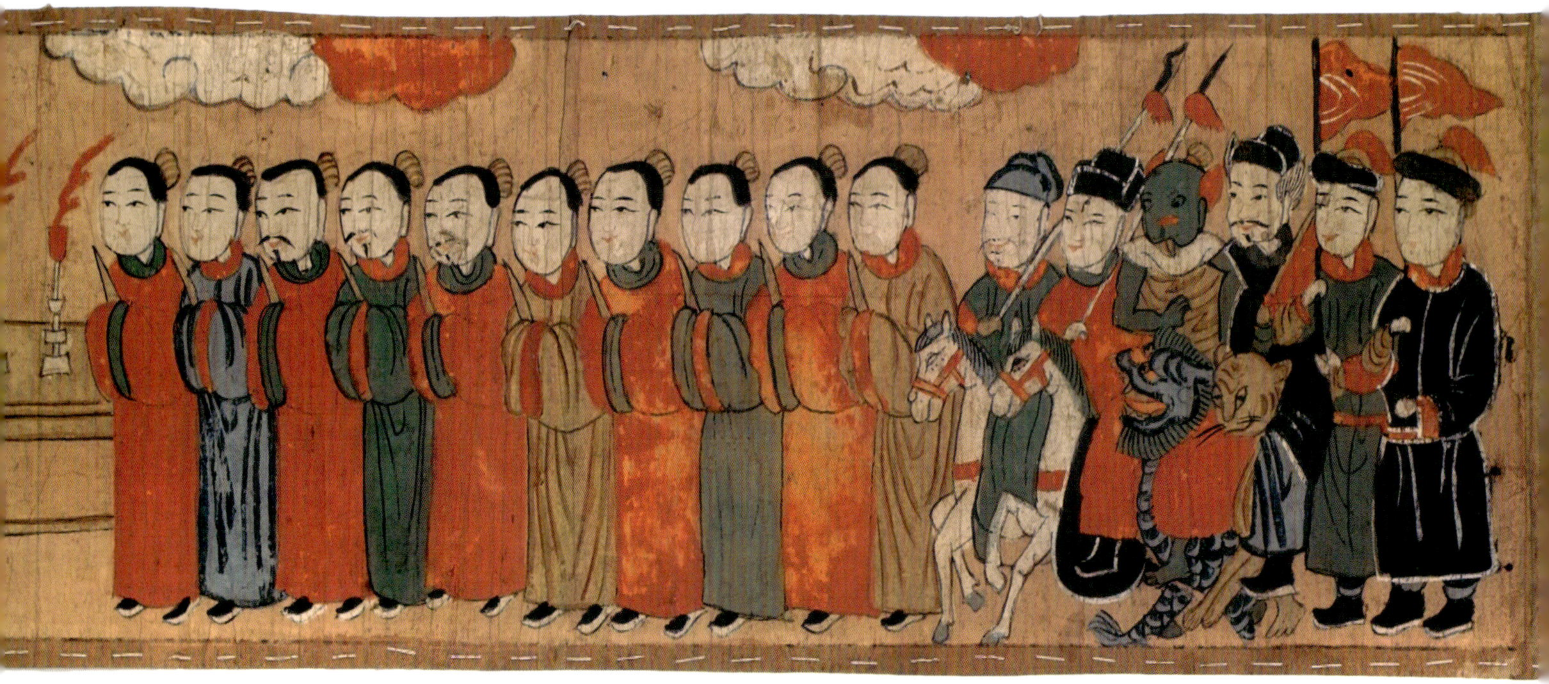

Fig. 137

FINDING THE WAY TO HEAVEN:
The Long Painting Scrolls

This chapter examines four major types of long scrolls in the Kitnick Collection. The first type is *The Dragon Bridge of the Great Dao* (大 唐 僑, 大 道 龍 僑, *Đại đường kiều* or *Đại đạo long kiêu*), of which the collection has three handscrolls (Figs. 136–140, 143). The second type is *Guiding the Soul* (引 香 路, *Dẫn hương lộ*) (Fig. 142). The third is *Praying for Salvation for the Dead* (度 靈, *Độ linh*), the longest scroll in the collection (Fig. 141a-q). The last type has two subcategories: *Respectfully Welcoming the Saints* (恭 迎 聖 駕, *Cung nghinh thánh giá*) (Fig. 144) and *Respectfully Welcoming the Buddhas* (恭 迎 佛 駕, *Cung nghinh phật giá*) (Fig. 145). Of all the paintings, these seven long scrolls reflect the greatest diversity in terms of the range of deities represented. Vietnamese artist Đỗ Đức remarks that while each long scroll differs artistically, all were used for the same purpose: to pray for the dead and guide their spirits into heaven.[1]

In general, these four types of scrolls reflect the cultural and religious differences among the ethnic groups. The oldest tradition is that of the Yao, represented in three scrolls titled *The Dragon Bridge of the Great Dao*. These are relatively pure works reflecting the Daoist pantheon, without Buddhist influence, since the Yao people had adopted Chinese Daoist rituals and, being the last of the ethnic groups to migrate, resisted integration with the new local culture. This type of scroll accurately depicts Yao costumes and musical instruments. The Tày painting *Guiding the Soul* (Fig. 142), on the other hand, combines elements of the Daoist pantheon with Chinese folk belief and includes many Chinese inscriptions identifying deities and places. *Praying for Salvation for the Dead*, also a Tày scroll, shows a great mixture of the Daoist pantheon with Buddhist figures and concepts of the afterlife. Finally, the two Sán Dìu scrolls represent two distinct aspects of their religion. *Respectfully Welcoming the Saints* depicts only Daoist deities and the clan ancestors, whom the shaman priests and the host family invoke to witness the family ceremonies. *Respectfully Welcoming the Buddhas*, on the other hand, depicts the historical Buddha, the Buddhas of the Three Periods, and the Three Pure Ones, along with ancestors to bless the religious service.

There are three major long-handscroll formats represented in the Kitnick Collection. The first is horizontal and arranged from left to right, as seen in the three *Dragon Bridge of the Great Dao* scrolls. In this arrangement the painting usually depicts the local God of the Earth in a shrine at the left (Fig. 136) and finishes with the Three Pure Ones on the right (Fig. 140), or symbolically represented by the wheels (Fig. 139). The second format, as seen in *Guiding the Soul* and *Respectfully Welcoming the Buddhas*, is a vertical layout, in which the deities are organized in hierarchical order, the supreme beings at the top and lesser ones beneath. The third is a combination of these two formats within a single scroll. For example,

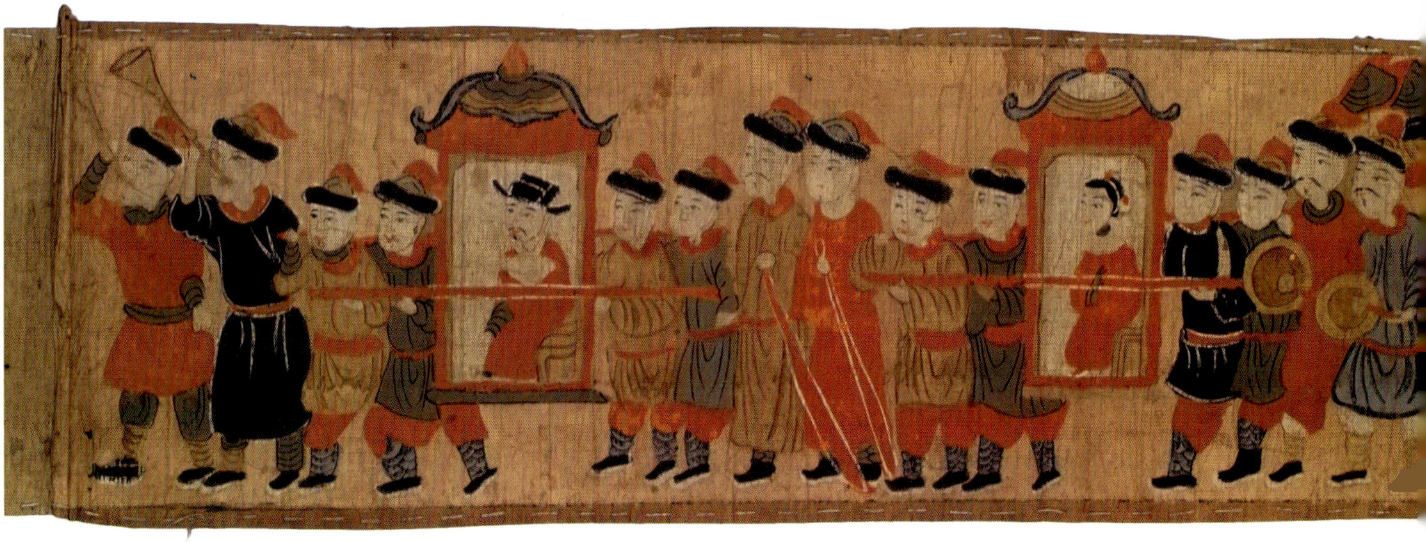

Fig. 138

in *Respectfully Welcoming the Saints*, there are seven human figures painted horizontally at the left of the scroll, with their heads pointing to the right, while the rest of the figures are arranged vertically. The longest scroll, *Praying for Salvation for the Dead*, also has a mixed composition, with the figures of the grand procession arranged vertically in the left portion as well as in horizontal groups, heads pointed to the left, in the right portion.

The traditional Chinese practice is to view a scroll from left to right, interpreting the imagery as a series of continuous scenes. This follows the principles of Chinese writing, brought from China by the Yao and other groups, which is read from left to right and top to bottom. This pictorial system is used, for example, at the left of *Praying for Salvation for the Dead*. While most of the long scrolls adopt the Chinese system, undoubtedly following the model of early but now lost scrolls, the Yao, Tày, and Sán Chay artists have also had the freedom to develop their own pictorial layouts, as they rearranged the order from right to left, or combined both horizontal and vertical formats within a single handscroll as in the scrolls just mentioned. There needs to be further research to fully explain these changes. It is possible that exposure to Western paintings has influenced these later artists and their styles.

In general, the long scrolls are used for funerals, memorial services, and praying for the dead's salvation. However, these services are not necessarily performed immediately after the death of a family member, but can take place whenever the family has the means to invite the high priests, prepare sufficient offerings (pigs, chickens, sweet rice, delicacies made from sticky-rice flour, etc.), and supply enough food for everyone who attends. For Yao Daoist priests with advanced training and experience, long horizontal scrolls, such as *The Dragon Bridge of the Great Dao*, can be added to their sets of seventeen, eighteen, or twenty-three. In the latter case the priest must add five or six scrolls to his set of seventeen or eighteen, including scrolls of the Four Heavenly Messengers, one long scroll of *The Dragon Bridge of the Great Dao*, scrolls of the Enforcers of Fasting and Chastity, and a scroll of Pan Hu's Five Banners of Knights. But these are not part of the basic set of paintings for low-ranking shamans.

In these ceremonies the long horizontal scroll is hung above the entire large set of scrolls, connected to the walls with a long piece of white cloth and framed with bamboo. The long vertical scroll usually extends from the main entrance of the shrine to the principal altar in the house, also connected by a piece of white cloth.

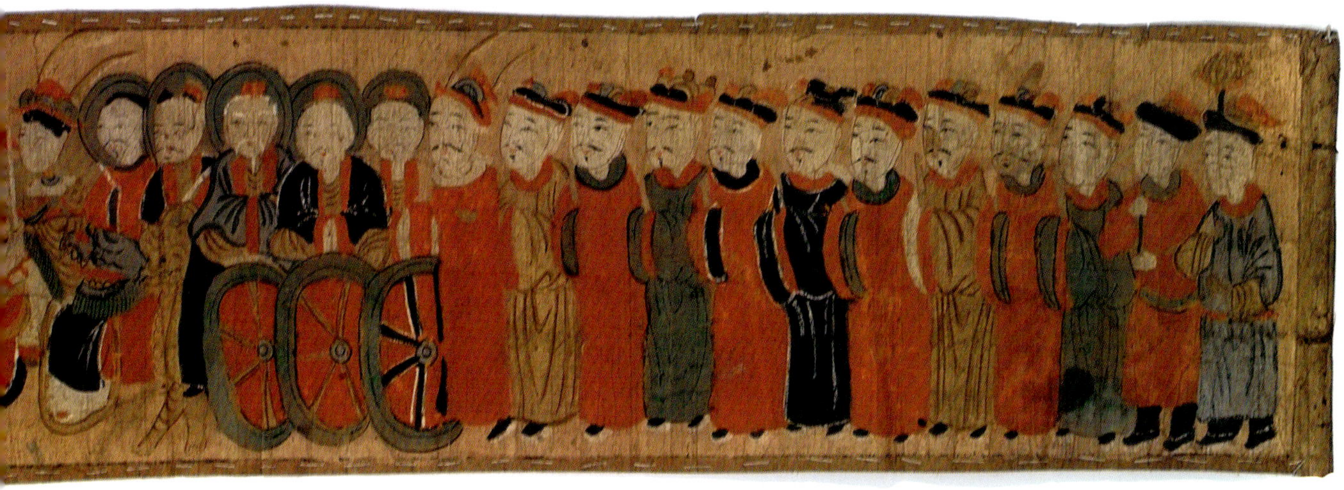

Fig. 139

1. The Dragon Bridge of the Great Dao (大 道 龍 僑, Đại Đạo Long Kiều)

The Dragon Bridge of the Great Dao may represent the most important theme of the Yao long scrolls.[2] The long scroll is a mandatory component for forming a complete large scroll set, added later to the set of seventeen or eighteen paintings. The scroll is a symbolic bridge connecting this world with eternal life in heaven, restoring health and virtue, and prolonging life. It is used a few months after the death of a member of the community, or whenever the family of the dead has the means to invite the Daoist shamans to pray for the spirit of the dead ascending to heaven.[3] For the Yao, sometimes heaven means their ancestral land in Yangzhou, where the soul is united with deceased relatives.

The collection has three versions of *The Dragon Bridge of the Great Dao*. Of the scroll types discussed in this chapter, these have the highest artistic quality and are clearly painted by professional artists. They are also thought to be the oldest ones, depicting multiple human figures and animals with a great deal of detail and a very refined use of color. In general, these paintings depict the procession of the soul of the recently deceased as it travels from the earthly world to heaven, led and accompanied by important members of the Daoist pantheon, includ-

Fig. 136
The Dragon Bridge of the Great Dao (part 1),
c. late 19th–early 20th century
Red Yao, China

Fig. 137
The Dragon Bridge of the Great Dao (part 2),
c. late 19th–early 20th century
Red Yao, China

Fig. 138
The Dragon Bridge of the Great Dao (part 3),
c. late 19th–early 20th century
Red Yao, China

Fig. 139
The Dragon Bridge of the Great Dao (part 4),
c. late 19th–early 20th century
Red Yao, China

ing: the local God of the Earth, a band of musicians, family members and villagers, the Four Heavenly Messengers, the Twelve Maidens, the Three Generals, the Four Celestial Marshals, and the Three Pure Ones. The arrangement and the order of the figures is not fixed. However, this type of scroll always has three main features. First, on the extreme left are the high shaman priest, a welcoming committee, and the local God of the Earth. Second, in the middle of the scroll is the body of the recently dead, carried on a sedan chair by four people. Third, in the center right or to the extreme right are the Three Pure Ones.

The first scroll (Fig. 136–139) is from the Red Yao subgroup, painted in color on handmade paper, and is part of a set of twenty-seven paintings. The grand procession can be divided into two parts. The first begins with a local God of the Earth, characterized in the standard fashion as an old man with a white beard wearing a black square cap and holding a long staff, carefully listening to a shaman priest who is kneeling and praying. The priest is assisted by two attendants, each holding a ritual scepter or court tablet, and is accompanied by a fifteen-member band, playing instruments commonly seen among the Yao: water-buffalo horns, gongs, Chinese cymbals and trumpets, oboes, a monochord, and a two-stringed instrument (Fig. 136). Following the band is a group consisting of ten people (three men with mustaches and seven women), all of whom hold court scepters. They are members of the reception committee welcoming the arrival of the long procession of gods. An offering table with a pair of candelabras separates these two groups. A group with six figures is next. The first two ride white horses and hold spears, and are followed by a green-faced deity riding a dragon, a pointy-eared deity riding a yellow tiger, and two standing figures with black and yellow robes holding banners. The figures to the left and right of the deities riding the dragon and tiger are probably attendants, for the two central figures are important divinities. The green-skinned figure sticking out his tongue is probably the Burning Mouth Deity, and the other is a brahmin (Fig. 137). These two deities are honored during the Water-Land-Air ceremony of praying for the dead, originally a Buddhist ritual but later incorporated into Daoist funeral services.[4]

The next section contains two of the three major features of a grand procession scroll. First, it illustrates a husband and wife, each in a sedan chair carried by four young men (Fig. 138). They are preceded by two musicians playing long oboes, two officers holding long staffs are between them, and two men with cymbals are behind the woman's chair. Next in line are four liaison officers riding animals. To their right are the most important deities in the scroll: the Three Pure Ones, riding chariots, which are depicted as three wheels (Fig. 139). Finally, at the far right

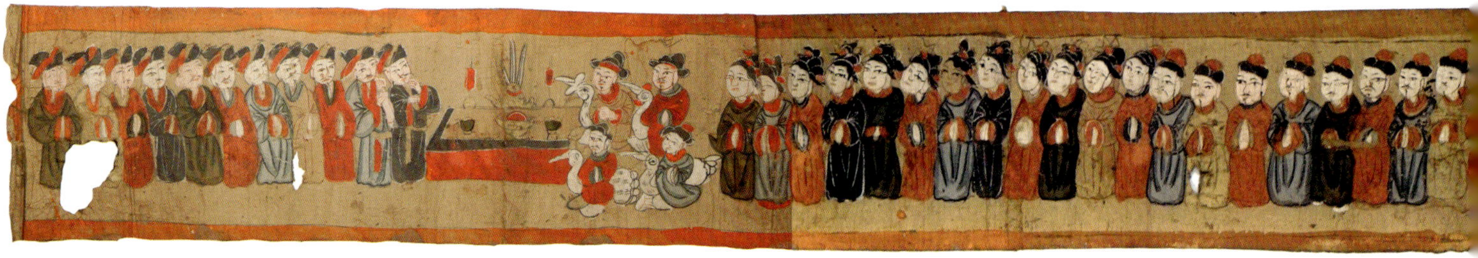

Fig. 140

there is a row of twelve figures with identical faces, who are probably either the twelve shaman priests who performed the Twelve-Star Hanging Light Ritual, the highest ordination for the Yao priesthood or the deities of the twelve months of the year.

The layout of the second long scroll (Fig. 140) resembles the first, with some minor variations. It begins on the left with the local God of the Earth and the high shaman priest facing the offering table. Leading the grand procession to the right of the table are the Four Heavenly Messengers riding large geese, followed by a reception committee of the Twelve Heavenly Maidens and ten figures before a musical band. They are most likely the Ten Kings of the Underworld. Next is the band, playing cymbals and long oboes, followed by a sedan chair, carried by four men, holding the soul of the recently deceased. This is followed by a large group of figures riding horses and other animals, probably the Celestial Masters Li and Zhang, the Governors of the Four Realms, and the Jade Emperor. Finally, near the end of the scroll, are the Three Pure Ones riding in chariots, attended by two people.

The last *Dragon Bridge of the Great Dao* scroll (Fig. 143) is complex and quite long (132½ x 9 in.; 336.5 x 22.7 cm). Only the first-described section is illustrated here. It begins with six musicians playing cymbals, a gong, a drum, a flute, and short and long oboes. The members of this group are dressed in Yao costumes with embroidered turbans, long black robes outside of long skirts, and leggings, and have bare feet. Judging from their outfits, these figures are high shaman priests praying for the dead. Kneeling before the offering table are four members of the reception committee holding court tablets. The figure closest to the table, wearing a black robe and folded black cap, is the chief shaman priest, who represents the group welcoming the arrival of the grand procession of deities. The procession is led by the local God of the Earth, depicted as a gentleman with white hair and beard, followed by the Four Heavenly Messengers riding on a crane, a striped tiger, a white horse, and a dragon; each carries a banner and a document. Three pairs of military figures precede the two sedan

Fig. 140
The Dragon Bridge of the Great Dao,
c. early 20th century
Red Yao, Vietnam

Fig. 141a-q
Praying for Salvation for the Dead (long scroll),
c. mid-20th century
Tày, Vietnam

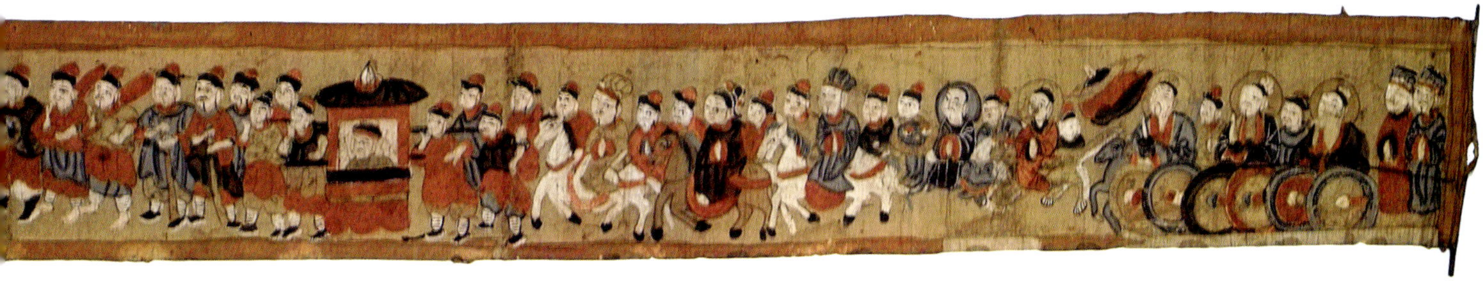

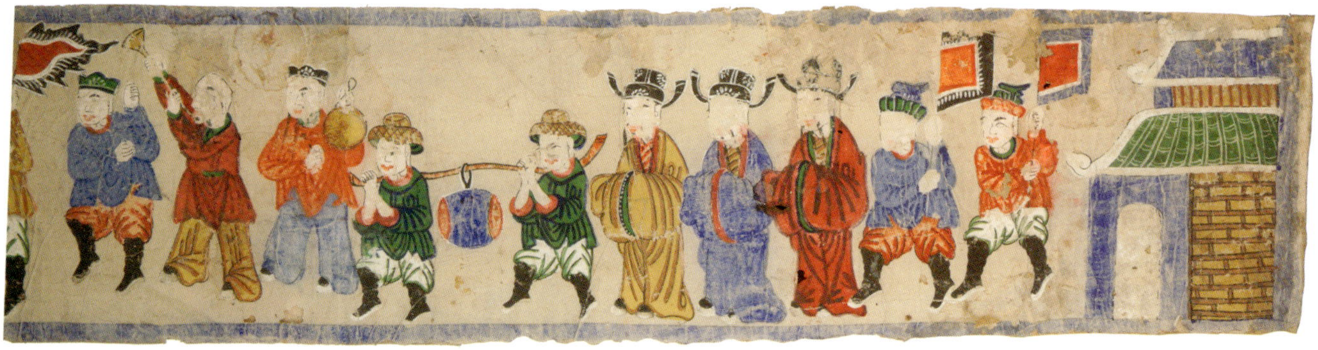

a

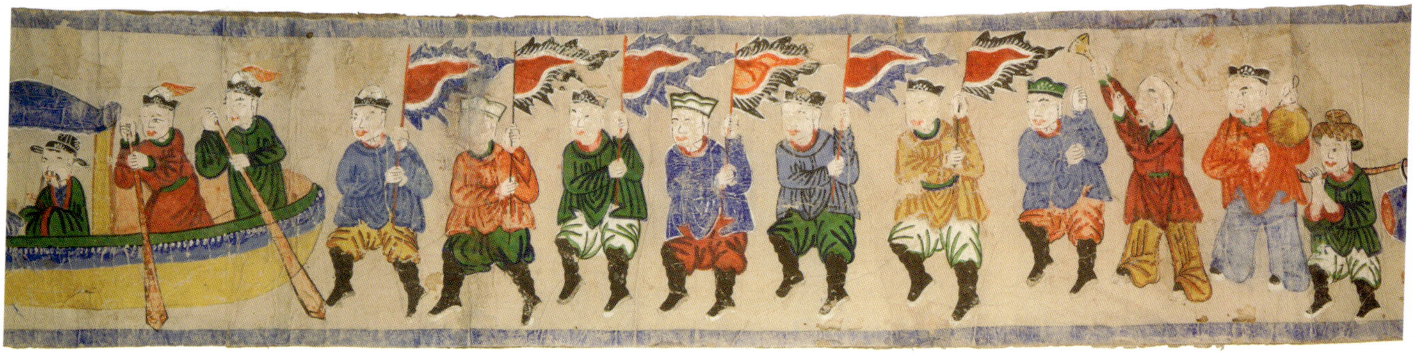

b

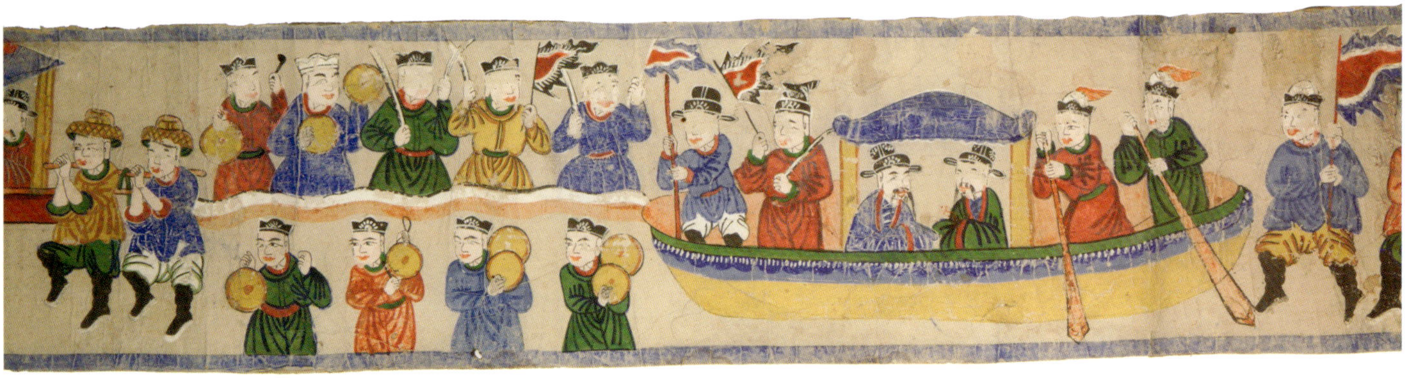

c

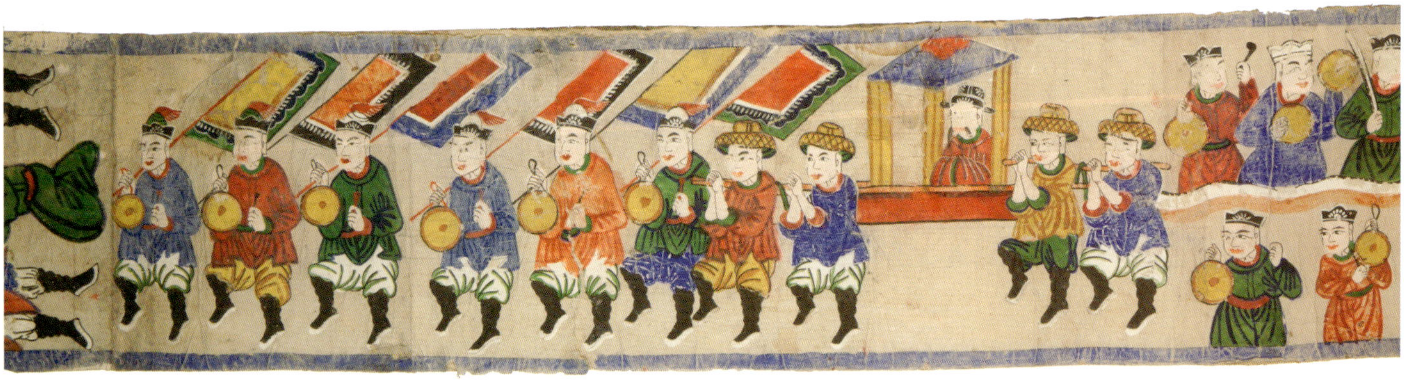

d

Fig. 141a-h

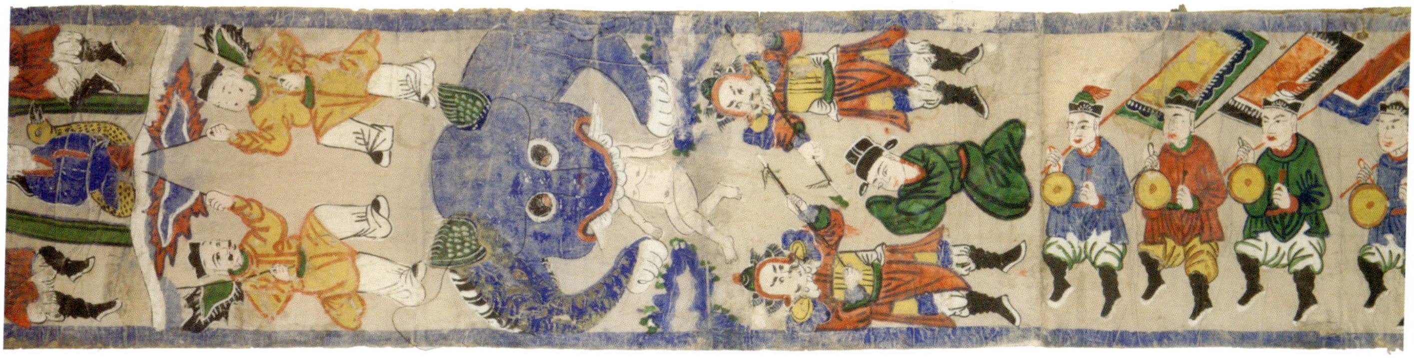

e

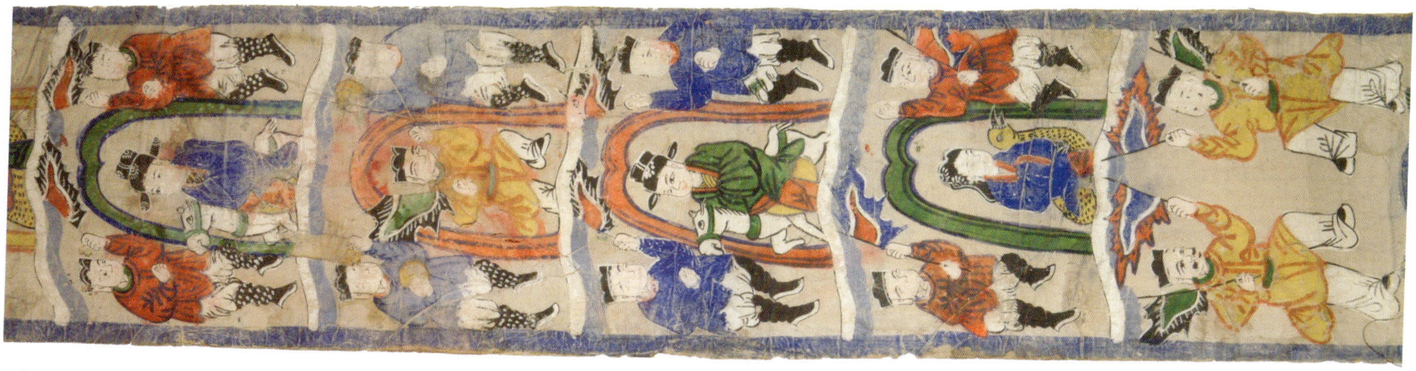

f

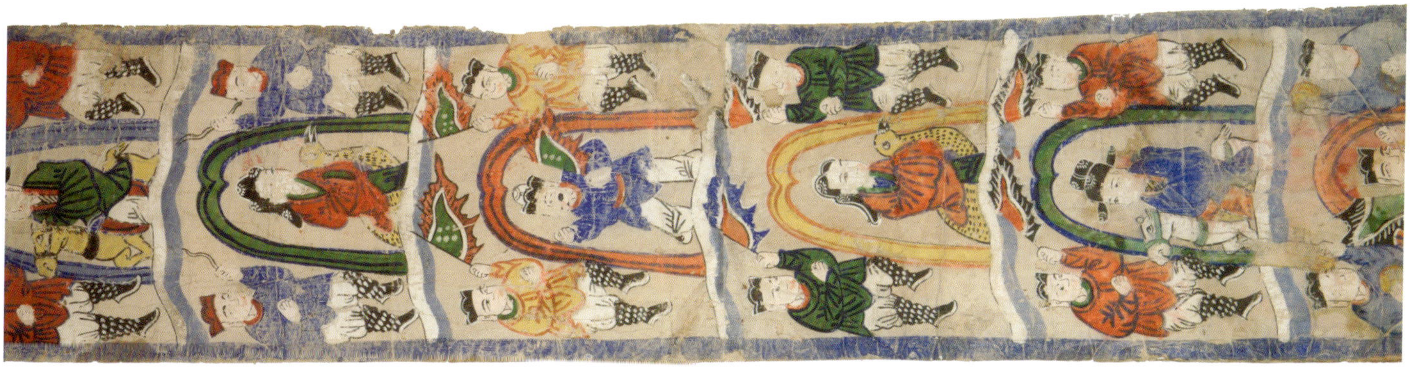

g

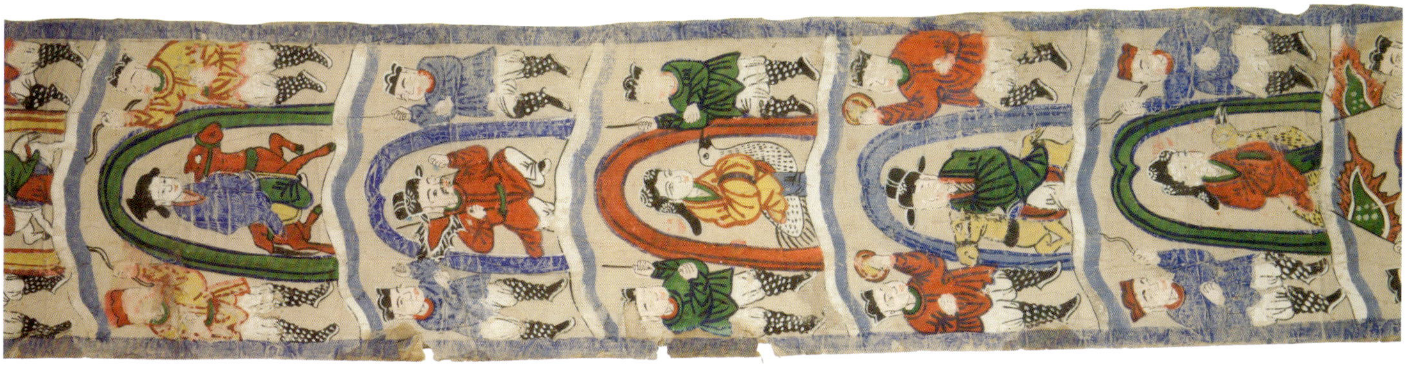

h

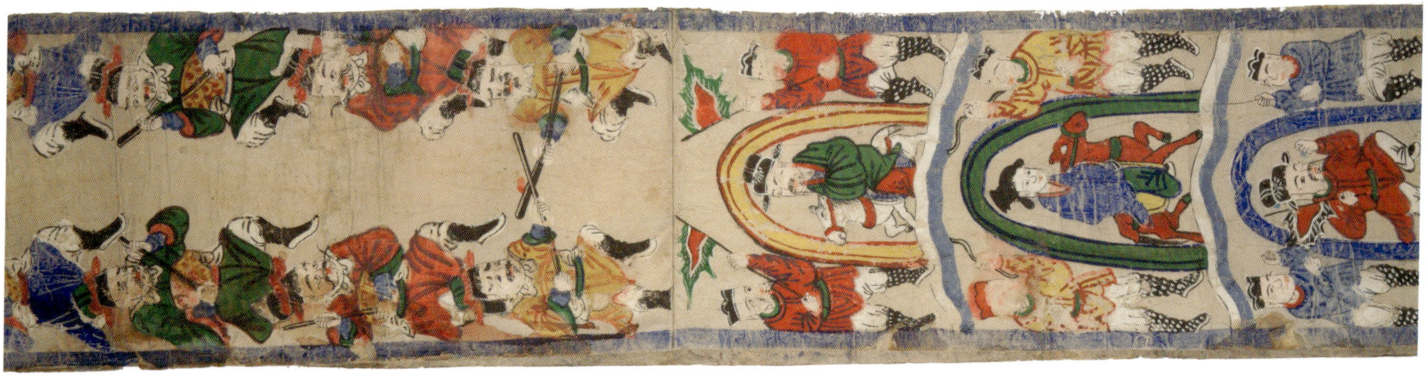

i

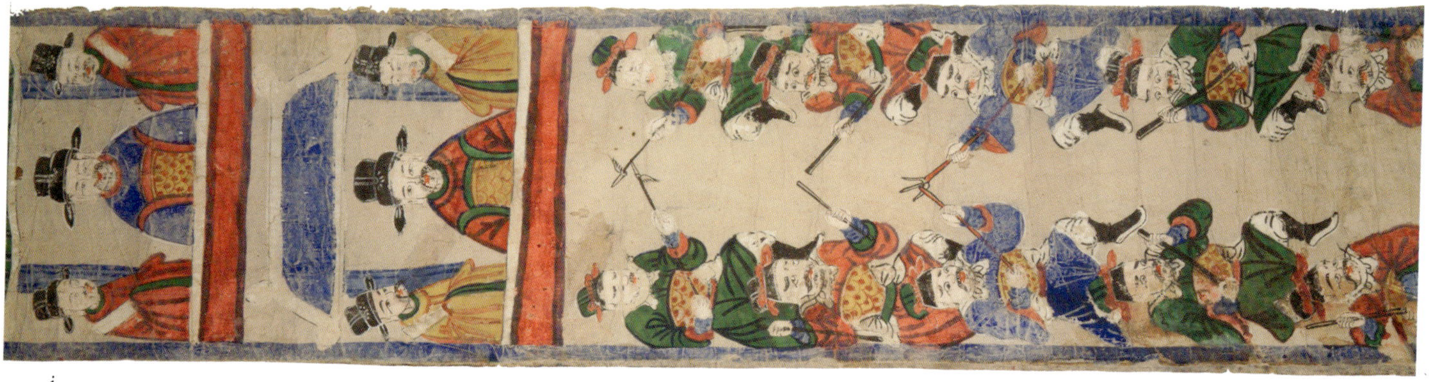

j

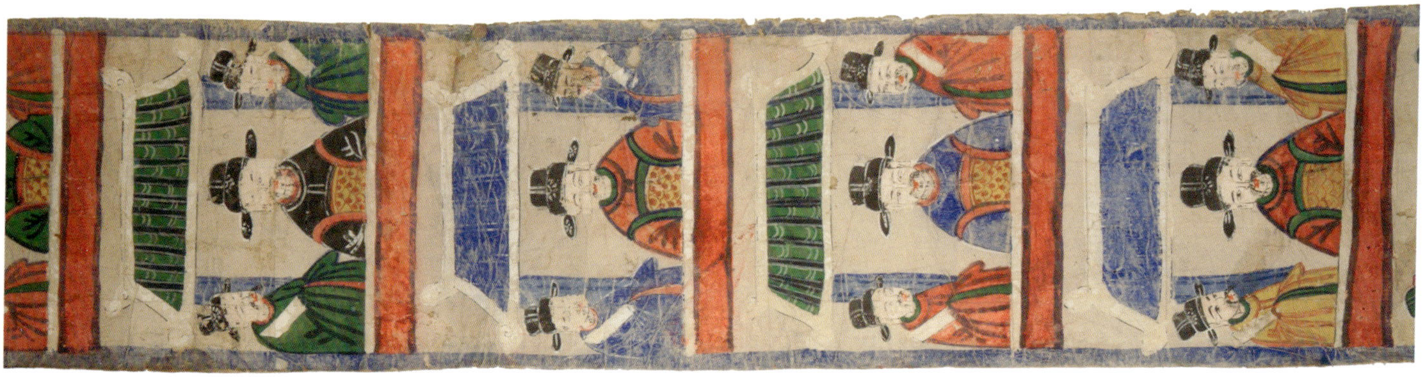

k

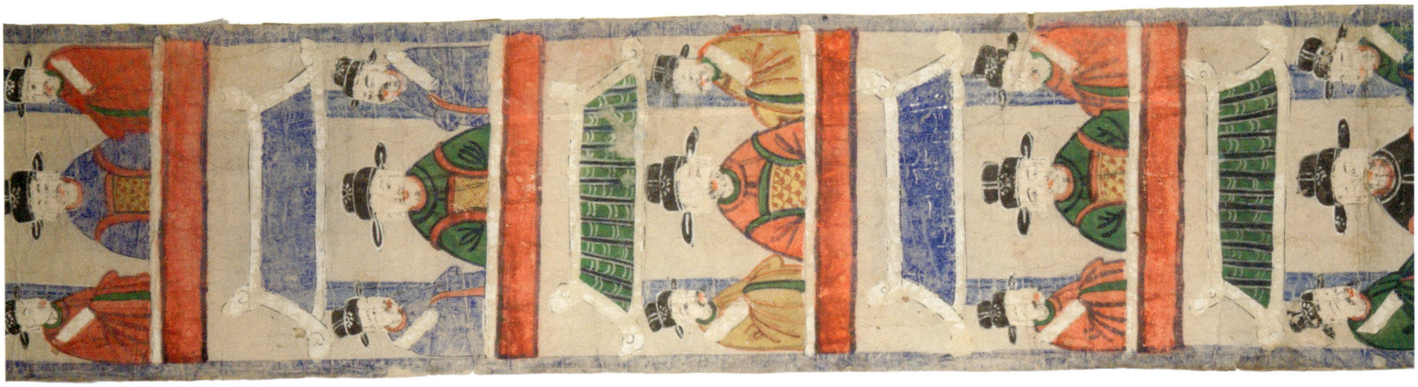

l

Fig. 141i-p

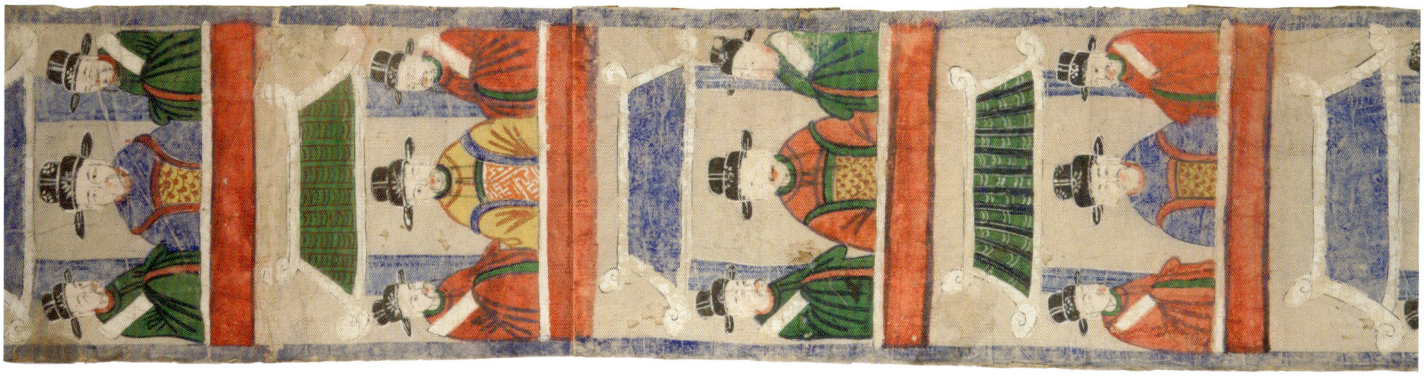

m

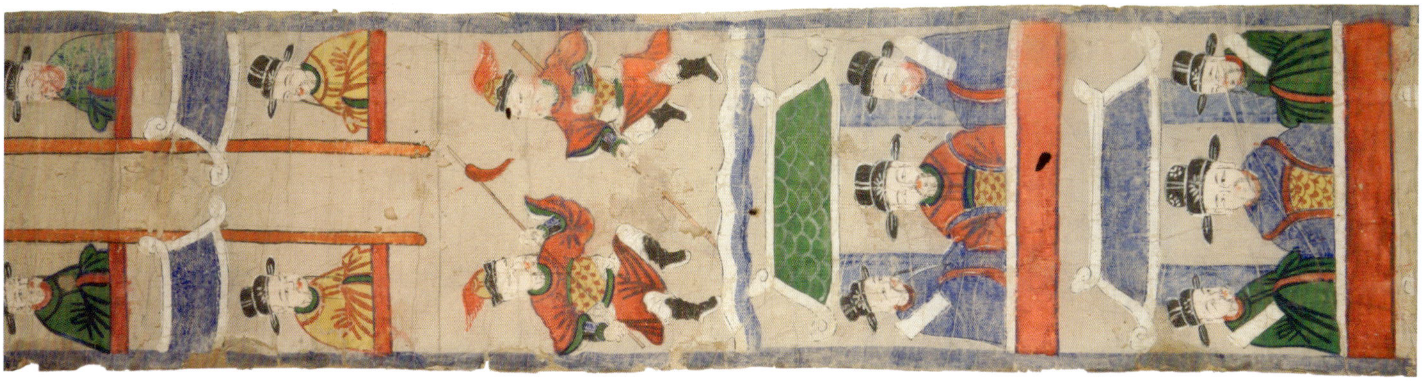

n

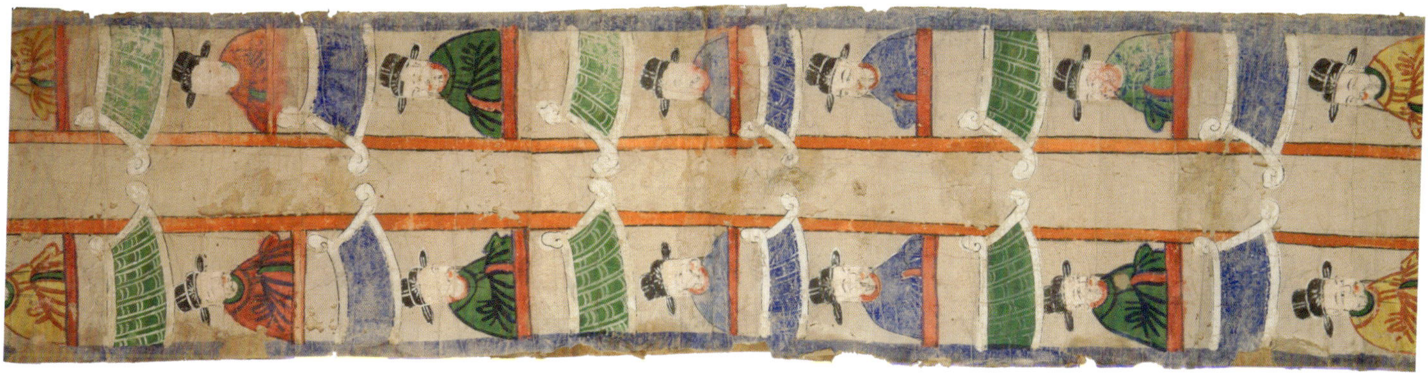

o

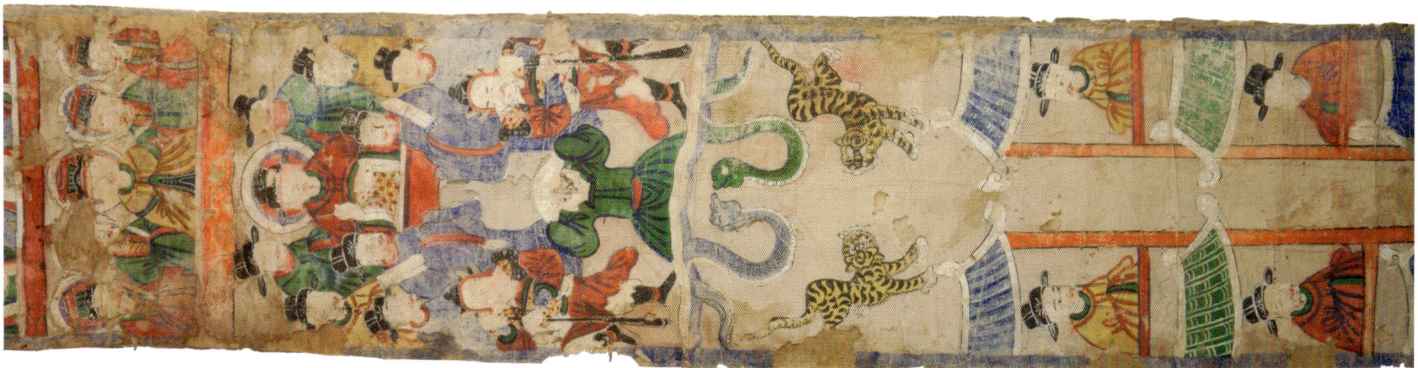

p

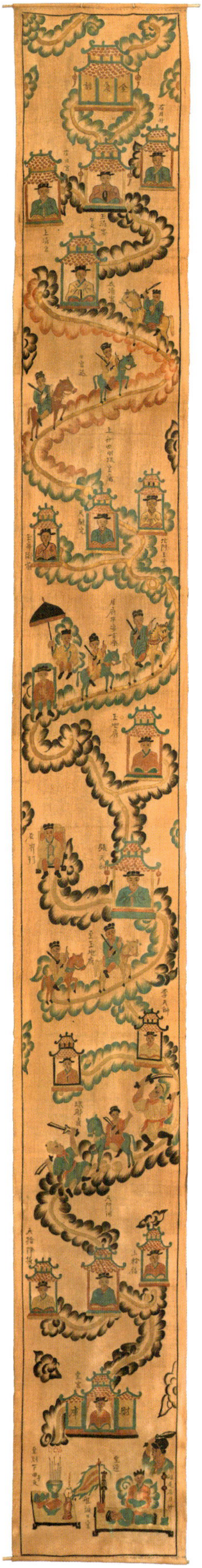

Fig. 142

chairs. Wearing Manchurian hats and very serious facial expressions, the first pair hold long fighting staffs, the middle have "cowboy" whips, and the remaining pair brandish long iron chains. One of the major features of this scroll is the depiction of the spirits of the deceased couple. Husband and wife are seated in a chair and a palanquin, each carried by figures dressed in the same fashion, with leggings, long black robe, and two-colored headdresses. A figure holding a folded black umbrella (an attribute of Yao women—Yao men do not use umbrellas—often seen in public)[5] follows the four bearers, wearing the same clothing. The four characters in the next group are difficult to identify. The first three figures, wearing helmets and riding differently colored horses, could be the three generals, Tang Hong (唐 宏, Đường Hoành), Ge Yong (葛 雍, Cát Ung), and Zhou Wu (周 武, Châu Vũ). The first two wield swords in their right hands and long spears in their left. The third holds a bow angled as if he is preparing to shoot an arrow toward the sky. The last character, a bird with green skin and a long snout, holds a small drum in his left hand and could be Celestial Marshal Deng. If this is the case, the three previous figures could be Marshals Ma, Chang, and Zhao. Following the four military characters are a group of fourteen figures, thirteen of whom resemble one another with the exception of their headgear. The first figure, with dark blue skin, could be Yama, the Fifth King of the Underworld. The next two are probably the stellar gods of the Northern and Southern Dippers. The next seven figures could be attendants of the Four Governors of the four realms (sky, earth, underworld, and water). Each wears an imperial bonnet and holds a royal scepter in his hand. The next five figures are riding animals and are accompanied by attendants carrying ceremonial parasols. They are the Jade Emperor riding a brown horse; the Master of the Saints riding a white horse; the Jade Pure One holding a fan and riding a unicorn; the Grand Pure One making a sacred gesture with his left hand and riding a white elephant; and the Supreme Pure One holding a *lingzhi* magic mushroom–shaped scepter and riding a lion.

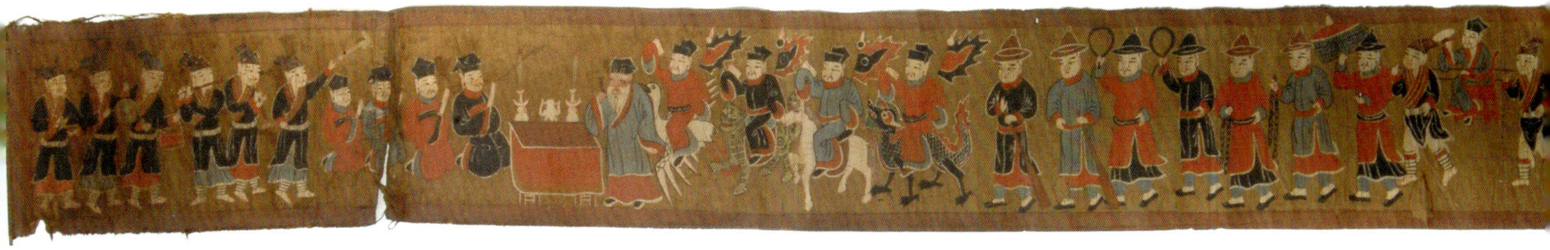

Fig. 143

2. Guiding the Soul (引 香 路, Dẫn Hương Lộ)

"Guiding the Soul" refers to the fact that the smoke arising from burning incense during the shaman's prayers shows the soul of the recently dead, departing this earthly world, how to reach heaven. The incense smoke acts as a rainbow bridge, and through the power of the sincere prayers of the high shaman priests and members of the host family, the soul of the dead would pass the difficult gates, high mountains, perilous places, and the underworld, eventually arriving in heaven. This type of long scroll belongs to the Sán Chay, Tày, and Nùng ethnic groups, but is not found among the Yao.

The *Guiding the Soul* scroll is always vertical and usually long (Fig. 142). Its sections are arranged in a hierarchical order, beginning with praying for the newly dead at the bottom and ending with the Daoist heaven at the top. The spirit must pass through many holy realms, sacred places, heavenly palaces, and obstacles, and encounter numerous saints, sages, and deities. Often all of these places are labeled with captions written in Chinese.

Compared with other *Guiding the Soul* scrolls, the one in the Kitnick Collection is short and simple, dotted with sketched pavilions and a few deity figures. The long scroll housed at the Vietnam Five Arts Museum in Hanoi, on the other hand, is a very complicated rendering, with Daoist gods, a long line of family ancestors, and full captions written in classical Chinese arranged throughout the painting.[6] Two other long scrolls, in the Phạm Đức Sĩ collection, which belong to the Tày and Nùng, are no less complicated.[7] However, all of them similarly depict the journey of the soul going to heaven.

Painted with colors on brownish paper, this scroll depicts human figures holding swords, riding on horseback up a zigzagging road that takes them through framed pavilions and gates. Also on the way are two figures bearing swords, seemingly chasing each other. All are connected with the trail of incense smoke.

At the bottom right, a high shaman is seated in a cross-legged position with hands folded in prayer. In front of him is a recently dead person lying on a low bed. In the left corner, an altar near the inscribed names of the dead holds offerings: a lit oil lamp, two bowls of food, and an incense burner. Seven incense sticks are burning to create the smoke seen rising up. The painter also labels where the head and feet should be located. In Yao tradition, when the shaman chants the sacred rituals, the local God of the Earth comes to bear witness and carry the message to the higher deities. Thus in this painting we see the deity standing to the right, above the priest. Following the incense smoke, the spirit of the recently dead travels past the Palace Treasury (財 庫), where a male figure is seated in a pavilion. The spirit then passes the heavenly fortune realm and heavenly gate, as identified by the Chinese characters, and presented by three figures seated in pavilions. His soul, depicted as riding on a blue horse and chased by two figures swinging their swords, reaches the first fork as a test: whether he will go straight or be

Fig. 142
Guiding the Soul, c. early–mid-20th century
Tày, Vietnam

Fig. 143
Dragon Bridge of the Great Dao (detail), c. late 19th century
Yao, China

Fig. 141q

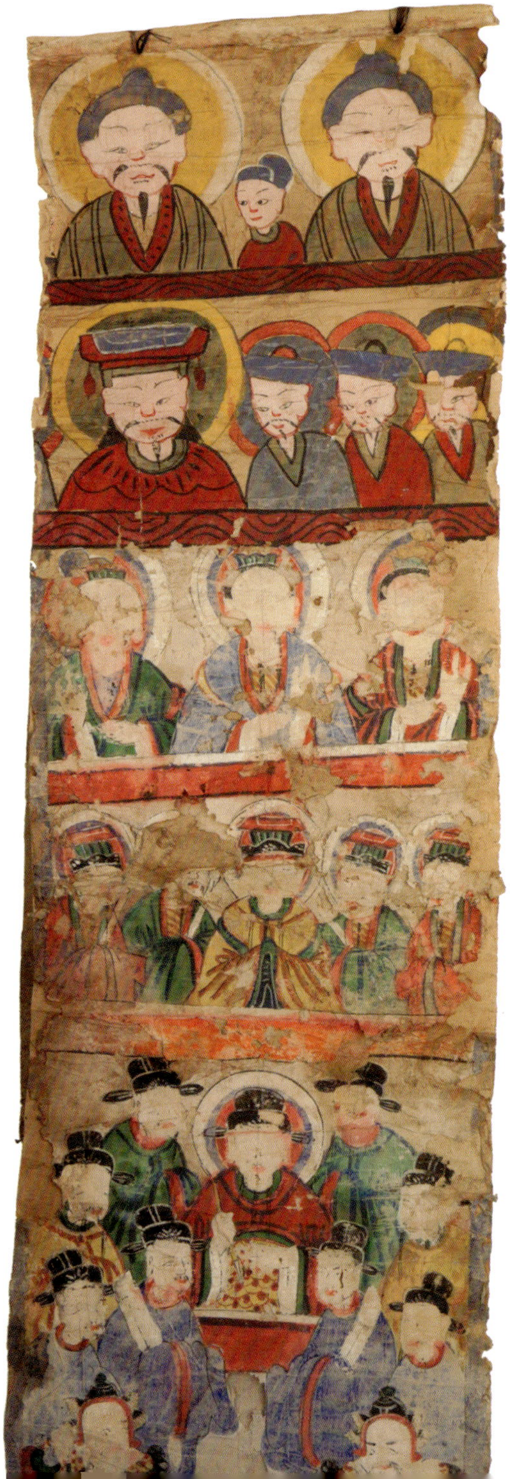

lured to other attractions. One road leads to the Lord of the Jade Underworld (至 玉 地 府); the other leads to heaven. With the help of the Celestial Master Li (labeled by his name written in Chinese: 李 天 師), wearing a light yellow robe, black hat, and seated in the pavilion, the soul of the recently dead is advised to go straight. On the way he encounters Celestial Master Zhang (identified by a label written in Chinese: 張 天 師), and before long he is again confronted with a choice: up to heaven or down to the underworld. With the aide of Celestial Master Zhang, he reaches the Jade Earth Palace (玉 地 府) and the Palace of the Peaceful and Auspicious Moon. Once again, the soul is challenged with diverging ways. On one path, he happens upon the Jade Emperor (玉 帝 御 前); on the other the gatekeeper of the Heavenly Palace. He passes the gate and heads toward the brilliant treasury and the Sun Palace. From now on, the soul encounters no more obstacles. He reaches the Palaces of the Grand Pure One, the Supreme Pure One, the Jade Pure One, and the Sun and Moon Palaces. By completing this journey, he is able to unite with his ancestors and becomes an eternal resident of heaven.

3. Praying for Salvation for the Dead (度 靈, Duling, Độ Linh)

The painting of *Praying for Salvation for the Dead* is similar to *Guiding the Soul*. Functionally, the main purpose is to pray for the spirits of the dead to enter heaven. Pictorially speaking, they are quite different. In *Guiding the Soul*, the pathway of incense smoke that leads souls to heaven is also used as a vertical pictorial device. *Praying for Salvation for the Dead*, on the other hand, visually alludes to carrying the spirits of the dead on a boat across the ocean of suffering, or on a sedan chair traveling over land, in order to achieve salvation (度 靈). Other features, like musical bands accompanying the spirits and the inclusion of various Daoist and Buddhist deities, vary from one scroll to another, depending on the artist's imagination, cultural and religious orientation, and access to previous scrolls for study and a repertoire of images.[8]

In shamanic practice, candlelight and boats made of paper or leaves are alternatively used to guide the souls of the dead. Prior to the memorial ceremony, family members, guests, and the shaman priests' assistants fold paper or banana leaves into small boats, placing candles or little lamps inside. They are lit and put along a route from the graves of the recently dead to the family altar. These lighted paper or leaf boats show the spirit the way back to his family, so he can enjoy the offerings and hear the prayers from the priests.[9]

This *Praying for Salvation for the Dead* scroll (Fig. 141a-q), from the Tày people of northern Vietnam, is painted on handmade paper and is more than forty-two feet long. It can be divided into two major parts. The first part is a grand procession of the departed souls, accompanied by bands of musicians playing a large drum, gongs, oboes, clarinets and Chinese cymbals. Two main features of this section are: a long boat carrying two men seated in the center in a square-shaped frame, rowed by two women in the rear, navigated by a man holding a long pole in front, and a guardian holding a banner and sword (Fig. 141a-c); and an old man—the spirit of the recently dead—seated in a sedan chair and carried by four young able-bodied men (Fig. 141d). All three figures—probably the souls of a clan whose family members finally had the means to organize a lavish ceremony for them—are escorted by different groups of people holding colorful banners, long swords, native gongs, and Chinese cymbals. They joyfully march toward the gate of heaven. The procession in the first segment depicts a group departing from their brick house on earth at the extreme right edge of the scroll and travelling to the heavenly gate in the middle (Fig. 141a-d).

The second part begins with the heavenly gate and finishes with the reunion of the departed souls and their ancestors in heaven (Fig. 141e-q). Unlike the first part, all sections of the second part are painted with figures depicted horizontally. Although the second part continues the procession begun in the first part, the viewer must turn ninety degrees in order to continue viewing the painting, as if the two parts were separate works joined together as one. The disjuncture emphasizes that the end of the grand procession is only half of the journey, with the commencing of judgment and reunion with ancestors making up the second half.

The first section of the second part (e) depicts the local God of the Earth in a customary black cap, wearing a green robe, kneeling and making a report to two military guards. Presented as a naked body, the departed soul is devoured by the dark blue Kāla, a monster of time and death who consumes everyone, underlining the fact that nobody on earth can escape this horrible reality. After passing through Kāla, the deceased soul is welcomed by two men holding banners and dancing joyfully (Fig. 141e). The next section depicts twelve figures presumably on a long journey to heaven, both men and women, riding big birds and galloping horses under arched gates. These figures, which may be departed souls, are identical except for the colors of their garments and the animals they ride. They are each accompanied by two attendants holding different attributes—colored banners, swords, disks, staffs, robes, and snakes (Fig. 141f-i). In the third section, the departed souls must pass through six pairs of marshals holding long canes, tridents, and spears, solemnly positioned in front of the judges (Fig. 141j). The souls are judged by twelve magistrates, in the fourth section, seated in a pavilion and staffed by two court clerks (Fig. 141k-n). In the fifth, seven pairs of officials stand, hands folded, inside a roofed pavilion. These officials are identically painted in a generic manner and lack labels, so their identities are uncertain (Fig. 141o-p). However, they could be the fourteen masters in charge of leading the spirits of the dead to the infinite and limitless realm of the Daoist Pure Emptiness.

The final section is the most complex and represents the climax of the long journey toward heaven (Fig. 141p). Here the gate to heaven is heavily guarded by two yellow striped tigers and two snakelike dragons. The departed souls, one by one (although only one is represented in the painting), kneel before the final tribunal, which is presided over by a judge holding a brush. The judge is assisted by two military marshals, four court clerks, and two deputies. The figure above the judge is probably the Jade Emperor, watching over the final judgment and welcoming the departed souls to unite with the Three Pure Ones, who are illustrated in the next scene, and the ancestors, found in the two final scenes (Fig. 141q).

In brief, the scroll *Praying for Salvation for the Dead* has two major parts. The first focuses more on the religious beliefs practiced among the Yao and other minority groups in Vietnam. Their garb and accessories—long robes tied with waist sashes, various black caps, black boots with leggings, musical instruments, and flying banners—are prominent. The second part reveals the traditional Daoist belief that departed souls must undergo a long journey and be judged before being united with their ancestors in heaven. From an artistic viewpoint, the human figures are stylized. They do not express any individual characteristics or interact with each other, but are rather rigidly placed within framed boxes, as if the artist used templates to create the different types of people and deities, with the exception of the color of their garments. This work was perhaps created by a modern-day amateur Tày or Vietnamese artist, who did not have a good knowledge of the Chinese writing system. A well-trained traditional artist would have labeled the names of the deities with Chinese characters in a scroll like this one. Such an artist would have been exposed to a repertoire of earlier scrolls, which would have served as models.

4. Respectfully Welcoming the Saints (恭迎聖駕, Cung Nghinh Thánh Giá) and Respectfully Welcoming the Buddhas (恭迎佛駕, Cung Nghinh Phật Giá)

Both of these long painting scrolls are from the Sán Dìu ethnic group. Unlike the Yao, the Sán Dìu always include Buddhist figures—Buddhas, bodhisattvas, and other guardian deities—in their paintings.[10] In the way that it is hung and read, the first scroll is primarily horizontal, whereas the second is vertical, but they similarly present the imagery. At the beginning, or left, of *Respectfully Welcoming the Saints* (Fig. 144), a shaman priest is kneeling, facing inward, and praying to the saints and other divine beings above him. (These first figures at the left of the scroll are painted with their heads pointed to the right.)

With his two assistants—one blowing a buffalo horn and another clapping cymbals—and the four-person welcoming committee, he awaits the arrival of the saints, sages, heavenly ladies, and maidens. The welcoming procession begins with two guardian deities known as Đầu Đà, or the Guardian Deity of the Right and the Guardian Deity of the Left, as discussed in "The Twelve Guardian Deities." Their signature attributes are a wooden pestle in the hand, a black snake in the mouth, and the six eyes that appear on their arms and legs.[11] A long line of saints riding on horseback is led by a chief sage holding a sacred seal in one hand and a prayer document in the other. Following him are twenty-four figures, male and female, holding sacred seals, swords, bowls, water-buffalo horns, rosary beads, and fly-

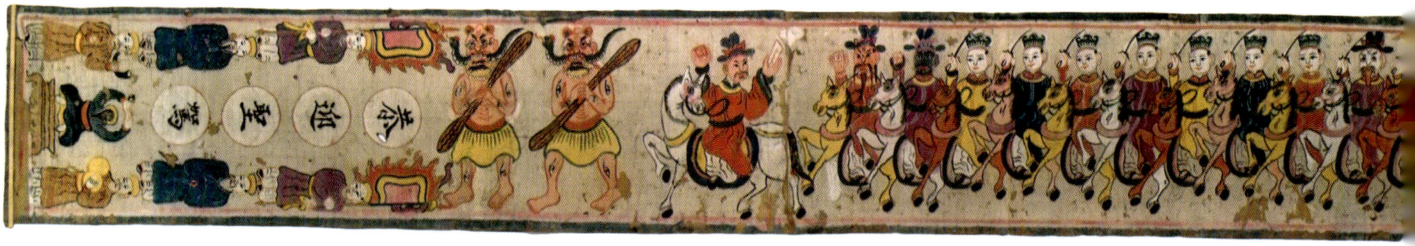

Fig. 144

whisks. Next are the ten sages, wearing caps with boards and tassels, who are capable of perceiving the invariable ways of the *Dao* manifested in nature. The last and most important figure rides on the back of a white elephant. This figure is Laozi, the founder of Daoism, according to Phan Ngọc Khuê, who further asserts that all the ethnic groups, with the exception of the Yao, represent Laozi on a white elephant, instead of the cow or buffalo always seen in traditional Chinese imagery.[12]

In *Respectfully Welcoming the Buddhas* (Fig. 145) the shaman priest is positioned at the beginning, or bottom, praying to the Buddhas, the Three Pure Ones, and other deities above. Flanked by two acolytes playing musical instruments and chanting hymns, the shaman recites a petition to welcome the whole pantheon. The title of the scroll, written with four Chinese characters (恭 迎 佛 駕) centrally located above the priest, is surrounded by four officials in formal attire, respectfully giving welcoming gestures (Fig. 145b). The procession of the worthies, sages, heavenly maiden, saints, and Buddhas begins with an animal—a white horse in the Saint scroll, a white elephant in the Buddha scroll—led by two marshals. At the other end of the scroll, the most important figures—Laozi and the Buddha—come to witness and bless the service.

Respectfully Welcoming the Buddhas depicts the infant Buddha in Lumbini Garden at the top (Fig. 145a), his left hand pointing toward the sky and his right toward the earth. The figures below are the Buddhas of the Three Periods, seated on lotus flowers, with snaillike curly hair and saintly halos. Below the Buddhas are the Daoist Trinity, the Jade Pure One, the Supreme Pure One, and the Grand Pure One, seated on flat thrones with halos. The eight figures appearing in pairs beneath them could be identified as the eight Daoist immortals, or lords of the eight directions. However, their representation is so generic that it is difficult to determine. The fifteen ladies grouped in four rows, eight figures on the left and seven on the right, are likely the heavenly maidens, or the ladies-in-waiting of Queen Maya, Buddha's mother, who dreamed that a white elephant entered her body when she conceived the future Buddha. King Suddhodana (the Buddha's father) called the sages and soothsayers to interpret the dream, a scene that is represented by fifteen ladies (Fig. 145b).

This type of painting is usually used first to petition the saints, sages, and Buddhas to come witness and help the spirits entering heaven. Unlike the Yao, as we have said, the Sán Dìu and other ethnic groups include members of the Buddhist pantheon and Buddhist legends in their religious paintings and services. They mix Buddhist and Daoist deities and utilize the auspicious animals—dragon, phoenix, tiger, white horse, cow, goose—as a backdrop to the primary figures in the scroll painting.

Fig. 144
Respectfully Welcoming the Saints, c. mid-20th century
Sán Dìu, Vietnam

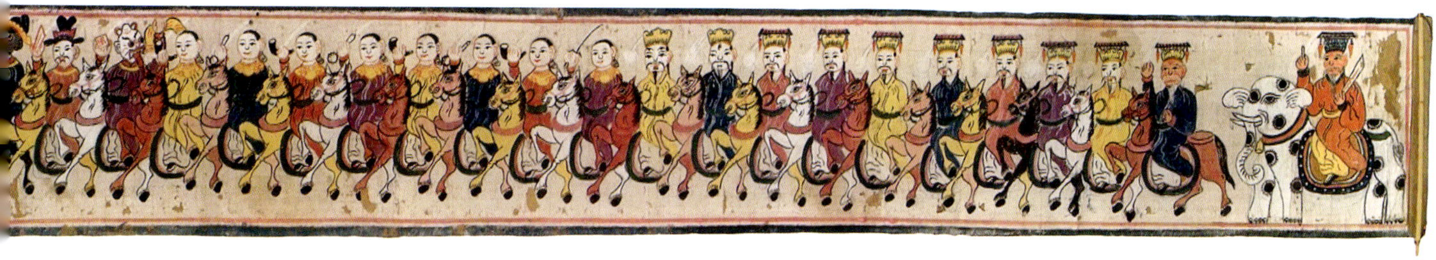

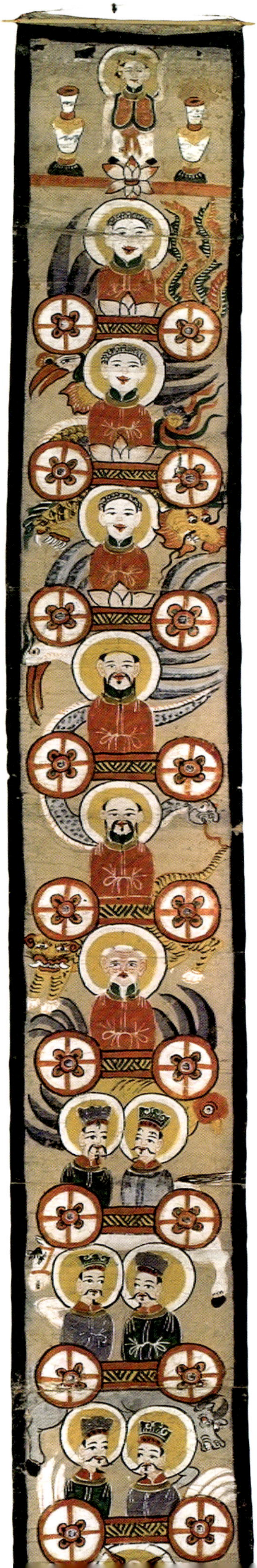

a

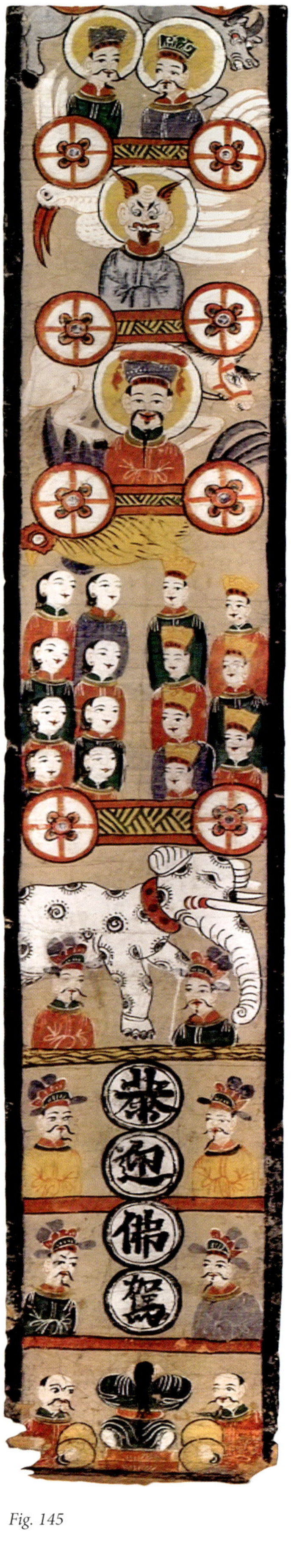

b

Fig. 145

Conclusion

When viewing the four types of long painting scrolls together, one can see many interesting features that vary from analogous to quite distinct. The local God of the Earth is always present in the first three types of long scrolls, as his role of conveying prayers from the chief shaman priest to the heavenly administrative deities is crucial. The Three Pure Ones are the most sacred figures, so they are always depicted, though in symbolically and artistically varying ways. Many of the deities that may appear in a scroll are not fixed. Instead they are often presented in groups bearing the same features, rendering them difficult to differentiate. In the grand procession there are always male musicians. In fact, the shaman priests and their acolytes play various instruments, because music enhances spiritual powers as well as encouraging the expression of the participants.

In this group of long scroll paintings, one can discern various cultural manifestations and artistic qualities. Funeral rites play an important role, since it is believed that if the dead do not go to heaven, they do not become ancestors and therefore remain on earth to haunt the family, clan, and the community at large. For those who die prematurely from accidents or other causes, the family members must organize elaborate funeral rites by inviting many high shaman priests to pray for their wretched souls to become liberated, reborn into a better realm or in heaven. For those who die a natural death, funeral prayers for their souls are always a crucial part of the social and cultural life of the living.

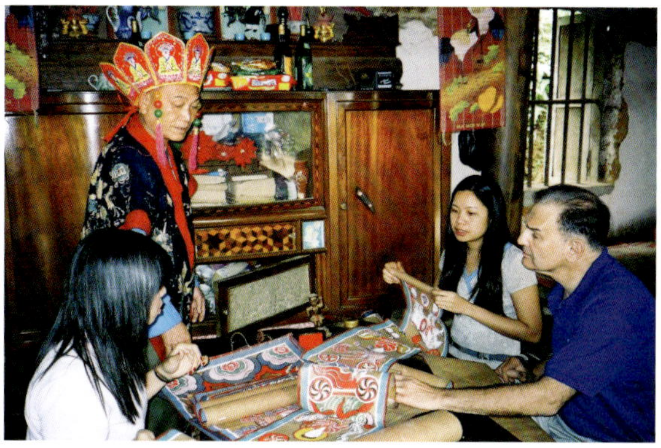

Shaman, Cao Làn–Sán Chi (Sán Chay), Thái Nguyên province, Vietnam, 2006.

Aesthetically, some of the scrolls are of superb quality and were undoubtedly painted by trained artists (Figs. 136–139, 143). Others were more likely painted using a template, evident in the indistinct human figures that lack facial expression (Figs. 144, 145). The quality of Yao, Tày, and Sán Dìu shamanic art in general has declined over time to the point where paintings are now seldom created in a sacred environment by trained professional artists, but instead are mostly made by local Vietnamese amateurs.

Fig. 145
Respectfully Welcoming the Buddhas, c. mid-20th century
Sán Dìu, Vietnam

NOTES

1. Đỗ Đức,"Worship Pictures Depict the Spiritual World," in Phạm Đức Sĩ, *Vietnamese Ceremonial Paintings: Pham Đức Sĩ's Collection 2001–2009* (Hanoi: Icon Communications, 2009), pp. 98–99.

2. The *Dragon Bridge of the Great Dao* is the most popular theme of the long painted scrolls among the Yao, seen in many other collections. This type of scroll is often the most beautiful and is always exquisitely executed on high-quality paper, reflecting high artistic and cultural values. For a range of this type of long scroll, see Phan Ngọc Khuê, *Taoist Painting*, plates 29, 30, pp. 130–133; Phạm Đức Sĩ, pp. 68–69; see also Jean Cormerais, pp. 198–200; and Pourret, plate 592, pp. 228–229.

3. See Jacques Lemoine, *Yao Ceremonial Paintings*, pp. 135–141.

4. For a brief discussion of the ritual service, see Trian Nguyen,"Images of Anatapindika and Ananda in Vietnamese Buddhist Tradition," in *Arts of Asia* 36, no. 6 (Nov.–Dec. 2006): 114–125.

5. For example, see Vũ Quốc Khanh, *The Yao People*, pp. 42, 122, and 160–161.

6. See Phan Ngọc Khuê, *Taoist Painting*, plate 1, pp. 76–83.

7. Phạm Đức Sĩ, pp. 156–157.

8. For example, in Phan Ngọc Khuê's *Taoist Painting*, he provides two long paintings of *Praying for Salvation for the Dead*, each consisting of forty-two groups of deities; see plates 2 and 3, pp. 84–89. An extremely long scroll of the same subject in another book has more than thirty-four groups of deities; see Phan Cẩm Thượng, et al., *Graphic Art of Vietnam* (Hanoi: Fine Arts Publishing House, 1999), pp. 80–86. Since these scrolls are very long and full of deities and places, they all have captions to identify the deities, their functions, and locations.

9. Phan Ngọc Khuê, *Taoist Painting*, pp. 129–130.

10. In Phạm Đức Sĩ's collection there are two beautiful examples of *Respectfully Welcoming the Buddha*, which are very similar to the piece in the Kitnick Collection.

11. See Phan Ngọc Khuê, *Taoist Painting*. This figure is clearly depicted in the painting numbered 86, page 178, of the same Sán Dìu ethnic group.

12. Ibid., pp. 128–129.

Detail of *Fig. 141e*

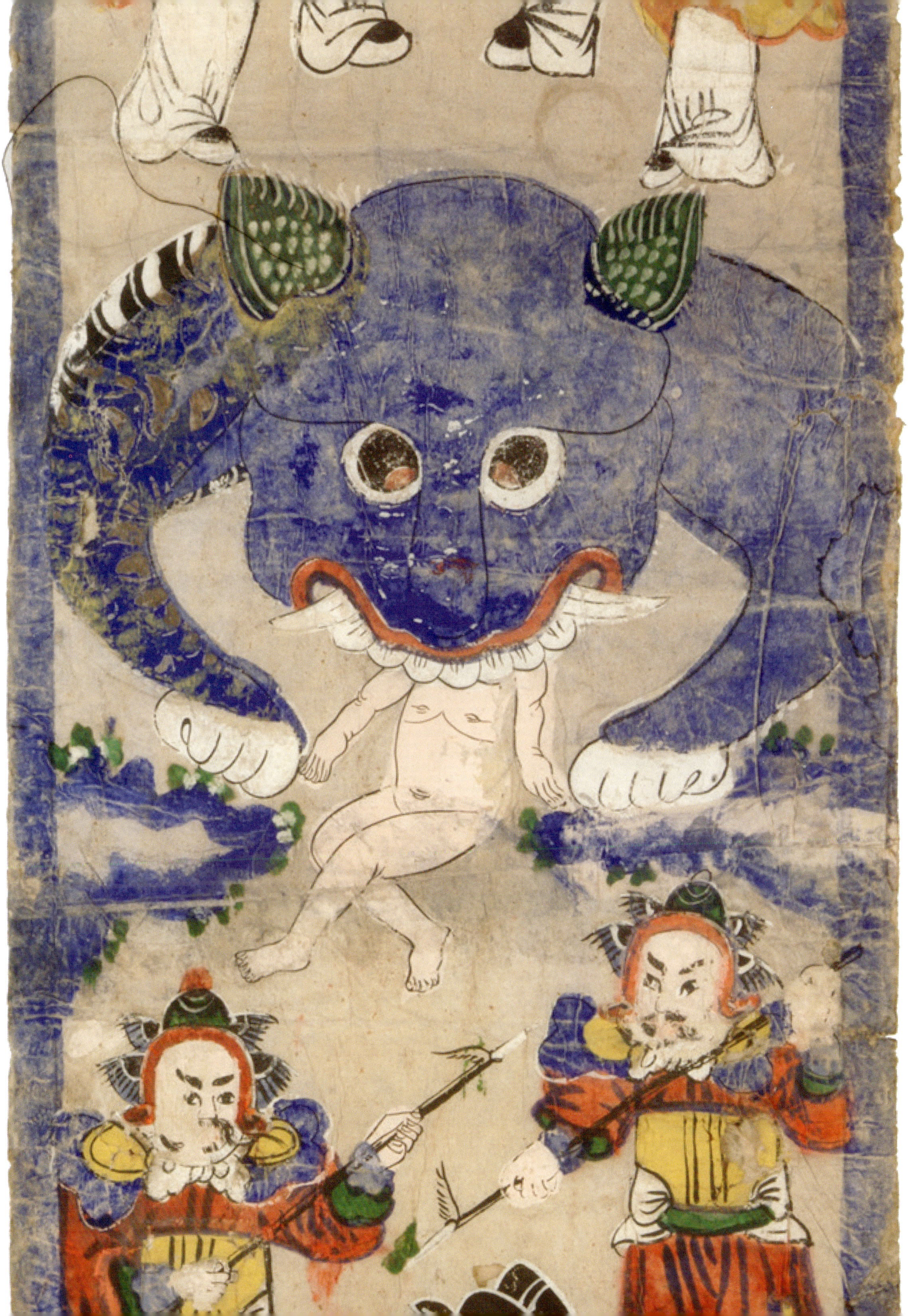

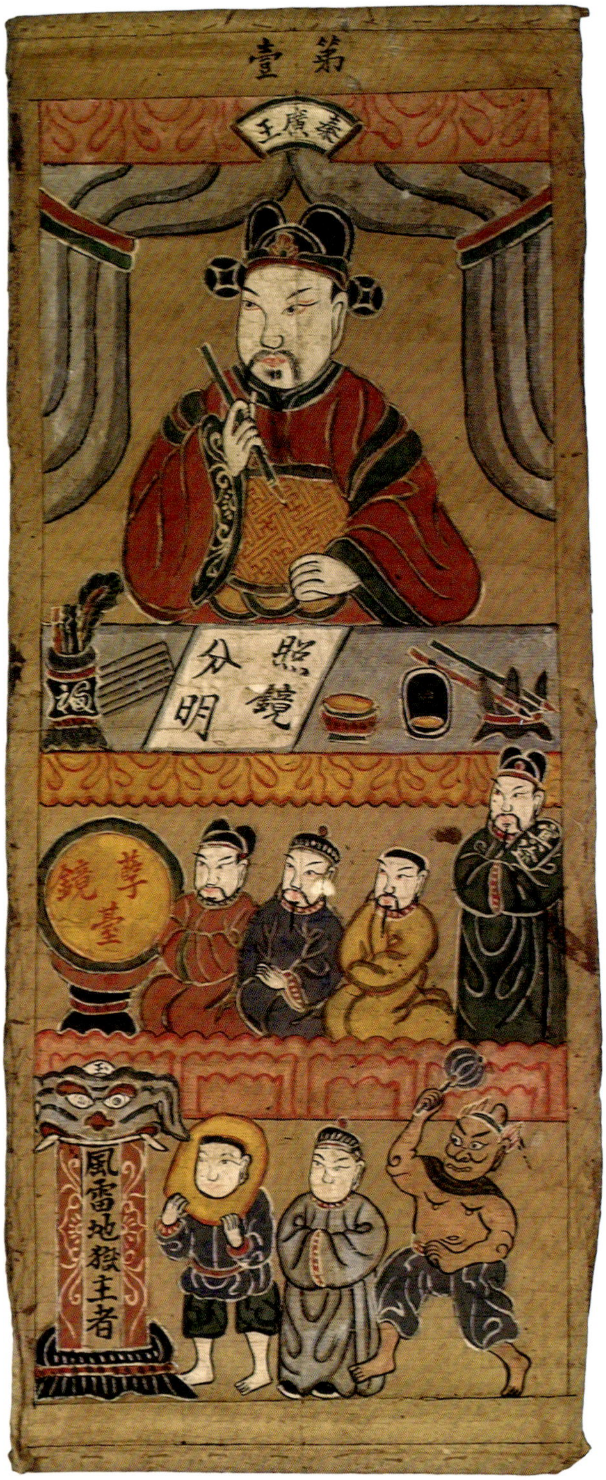

Fig. 146

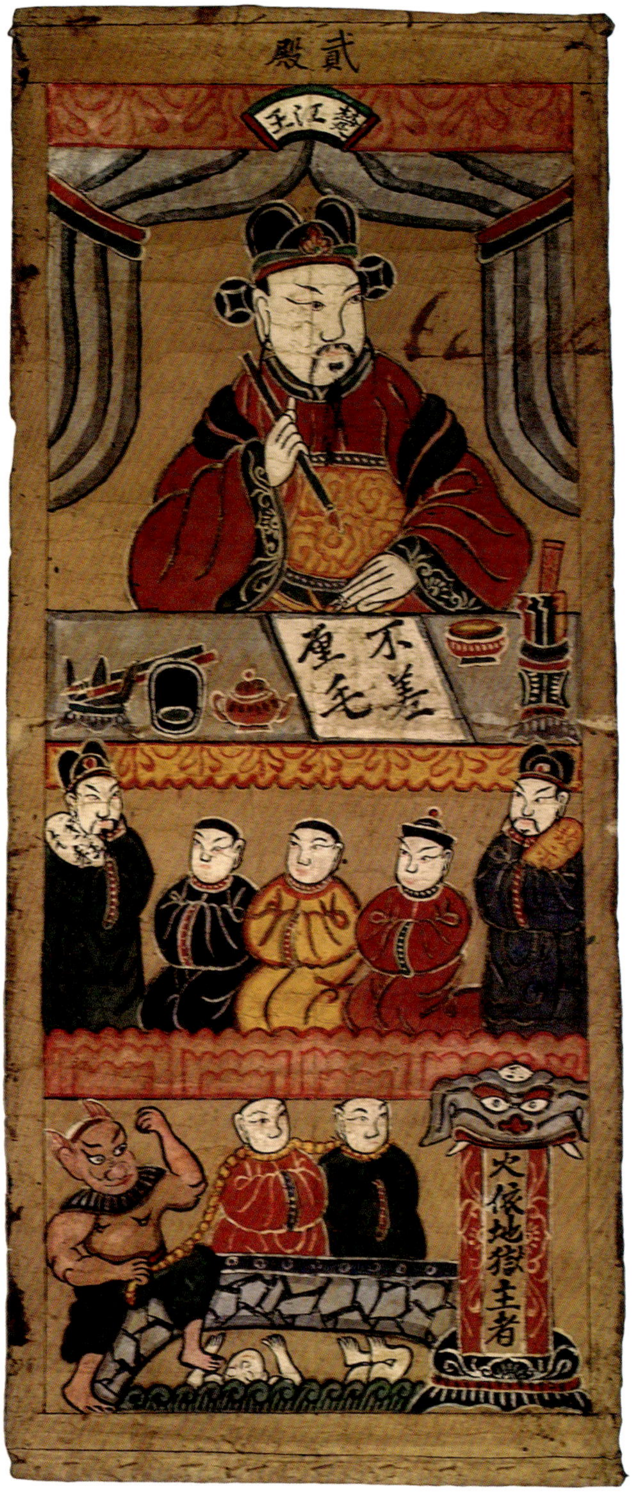

Fig. 147

GOING THROUGH THE DARK COURTS:

The Ten Kings of the Underworld

The ethnic groups in northern Vietnam worship a wide spectrum of gods, ranging from those responsible for the creation of the universe to those with a more direct influence on everyday life. Although many paintings depict heavenly deities, others represent the gods of the underworld. The Ten Kings of the Underworld play a significant role in the afterlife, as they, according to Quitman E. Phillips, "symbolize the promise of salvation as well as the threat of damnation."[1] The Ten Kings of the Underworld are visualized differently across East Asian cultures, in popular Buddhist belief, in Chinese Daoism, and also in folk traditions. The concept of the Ten Kings has been rooted in China since the first half of the tenth century and has spread since then with many cultural modifications.[2]

The Yao and the Tày have interpretations of the Ten Kings that slightly differ from the Chinese version.[3] Before dead souls can come before the kings, they have to pass the Thirty-Six Caverns of Mt. Mei (Meishan) in Hunan Province.[4] On this long journey, with many difficult hurdles, the dead souls are guided by spirit escorts to the dark world.[5] Once arriving before the tribunal of the Ten Kings, the path into the afterlife proceeds in a fashion similar to that of Chinese tradition.

Although it was originally believed that the Ten Kings stood for both salvation as well as damnation, the latter gradually dominated over time. They are often portrayed alongside scenes of torture and punishment, a trend that is prevalent in painting scrolls of the Yao, especially in sets in the Kitnick Collection. Each painting of the Ten Kings in this Tày set (Figs. 146–155) is divided into three levels.[6] The top third presents the king seated in a three-quarter view behind a bureau, looking slightly to left or right of center, and surrounded by brushes, brush holder, inkstone, water vase, and a piece of paper inscribed with four characters, a warning or an ethical motto for the living. In front of them are scenes of the inquisitorial process. The facial expression of each king is similar, very calm and composed.

Generally, the middle level depicts scenes of the recently dead, who are accompanied by two court clerks holding scrolls on their shoulders, as if to present evidentiary records; other functionaries, who announce sentences; and the dead themselves, who present the petitions and are being judged. In this case the scroll of the first king (Fig. 146) has only a single clerk holding a sign reading "The dark path" (冥 途), whereas the two clerks depicted in the scroll of the tenth king (Fig. 155) are saying farewell to those in the process of being born into the six realms. The middle levels of the scroll

Figs. 146, 147
The First King and the Second King of the Underworld,
c. late 19th–early 20th century
Tày, Vietnam

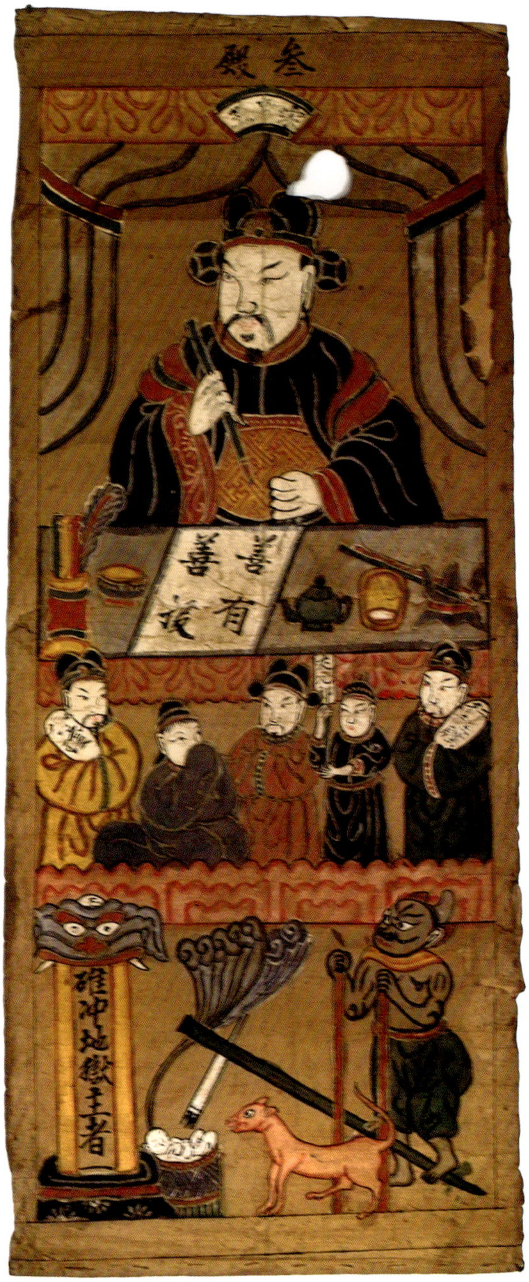

Fig. 148

paintings of the sixth and seventh kings (Figs. 151, 152) depict two well-known episodes from Chinese popular literature, which would be easily understood by a general audience. These stories concern the journey to hell and emphasize concepts of judgment and filial piety.

The bottom level contains a cartouche inscribed with seven Chinese characters, labeled as hell, or purgatory. This section exhibits vivid scenes of demonic prison guards punishing sinners. In some the dead are placed in yokes and dragged about to face judgment, then torture, and even bodily destruction.

In Buddhism, hells are plural, not the single hell of Christianity. They are equivalent to purgatory, an "intermediate realm of the immediate judgment and expiatory punishments,"[7] and are usually referred as "the dark region" (冥 府, 冥 界, *minh phủ*, *minh giới*) or "the underworld" (陰 界, âm giới), as is written in the scroll of the tenth king. Buddhist hells would be understood by ordinary people as "a simple binary opposition: damnation in underground hells versus salvation in a celestial paradise."[8]

It is interesting to note that these hanging scrolls often depict roosters, horses, and buffalos as the accusers. The scrolls also include a few important rules that postulants receive when they are ordained into the Daoist path. Throughout the scroll set, the scenes depicted in the middle registers are dynamic and diverse, while the top and the bottom sections follow a fixed format in a relatively consistent manner. The inscribed cartouches in all ten paintings provide helpful identification of the kings, a short religious or ethical statement, and the names of the various hells.

Though the set of kings is numbered from one to ten, it does not follow a linear progression of development. The first king, King Guang of Qin, (秦 廣 王, Qinguangwang, Tần Quảng Vương) (Fig. 146), receives the dead souls as they initially pass into the afterlife, and directs them onto their next path after examining their balance of good and evil deeds. He

Fig. 148
The Third King of the Underworld, c. late 19th–early 20th century
Tày, Vietnam

also checks the record book of birth and death for the deceased's foreordained lifespan. If it has not been reached, they may be sent back to earth to complete their lives. The first king wears a red robe and holds a brush in his right hand to make notes in a book reflecting the deeds of each soul. The four characters in front of him (照 鏡 分 明, *Chiếu cảnh phân minh*) refer to a magical mirror that clearly reflects all past deeds—good, bad, neutral—from the sinner's life. In the middle, three recently deceased people are kneeling in front of this "mirror of deeds" (孽 鏡 臺), viewing their own past transgressions and successes, as the court clerk, clad in a formal robe, stands behind them. The sinner's punishment is illustrated in the lower register: a large cangue[9] (similar to a pillory or yoke) is placed around his neck, while the thunder god is holding a large metal ball in his hand. The small inscription, written vertically on the left as if vomited by the animal head above it, states, "The thunder god is in charge of this hell" (玉 風 雷 地 獄 主 者). The soul is then sent to the second king for further judgment. In the case of an innocent soul, the path leads to the tenth king, where it is prepared for reincarnation.

The second king, Chujiangwang (楚 江 王, Sở Giang Vương) (Fig. 147), the King of the First River, primarily handles the dead sent from the first king. As implied by his title, the dead must cross the River Nai (奈 河, Nại Hà), also known as the River of No Recourse. They are hurled into the serpent-infested water by two demons. The best cross the bridge, the average ford at the shallow place, and the worst must swim, as depicted at the bottom of the hell (see Fig. 7). The second king also wears a long crimson court robe, a mandarin hat, and holds a Chinese brush in his right hand. All of his office utensils are neatly arranged on the table: a brush holder, inkstone, water pot, and small bowl of water. The four-character motto, presumably written by the king, states that not even a tiny hair is incorrect (不 差 重 毛). In other words, all of his judgments are extremely fair, truthful, and without bias. Instead of facing a magic mirror, the spirits of the dead are

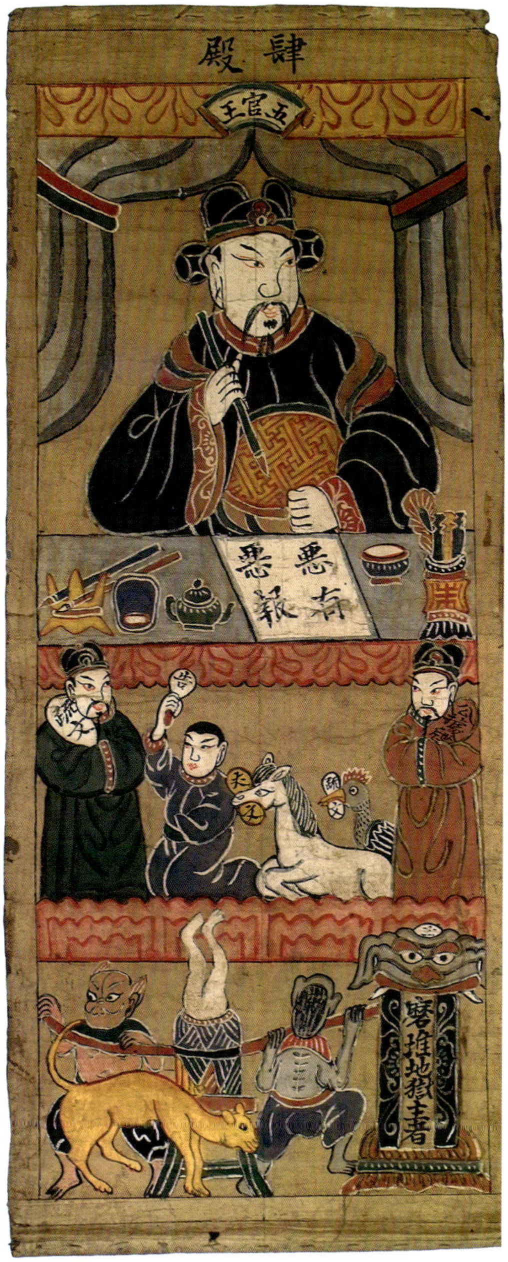

Fig. 149

Fig. 149
The Fourth King of the Underworld,
c. late 19th–early 20th century
Tày, Vietnam

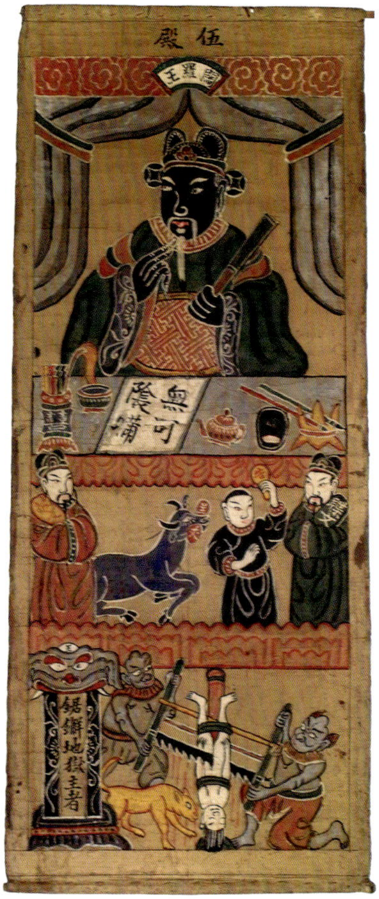

Fig. 150

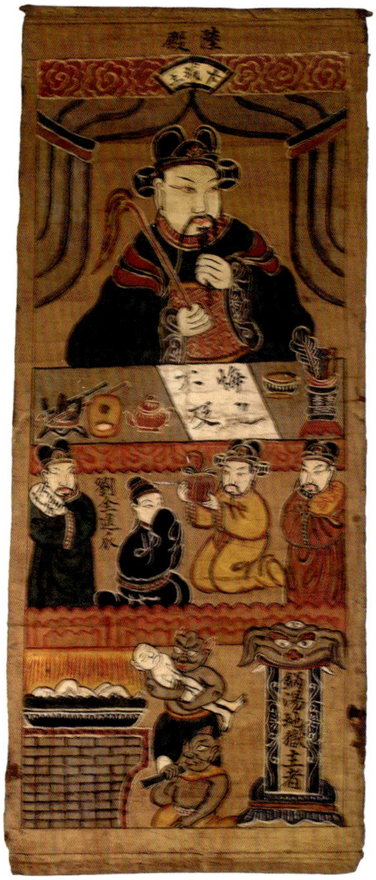

Fig. 151

kneeling at the center, escorted by the two court clerks and awaiting further judgment. If they have committed any bad acts, they will be burned alive by means of extremely hot charcoal. In this scroll the demonic prison guard, who sports two pointed horns, grasps a long iron chain tied around the necks of the two criminals sent from the first king, who are about to drop into the hot pit hell labeled by the six characters 火 催 地 獄 主 者. Beneath the pit is a sinner being tortured.

The third king (宋 帝 王, Songdiwang, Tống Đế Vương) (Fig. 148), the King of Song, judges individuals with lesser crimes, such as corrupt officials, ungrateful commoners, and troublesome wives. These individuals have usually failed to respect their ancestors. In this painting, the king is wearing a black robe. The writing in front of him says, "Those who sowed the good seeds will harvest the good results" (善 有 善 報). Influenced by Buddhism, this reflects the concept of karma, the law of cause and effect, applied to one's actions in successive incarnations, never ending until a person achieves enlightenment. In the center, the two court clerks (recognizable by the scrolls they carry on their shoulders) are preparing to send the sinner, the woman in a kneeling position, to hell, while the lifespan of the standing person, probably her husband, is being checked. The two clerks are functionaries, one keeping the record of good deeds, the other of bad deeds,[10] who help the king make his judgment. The bottom section illustrates a scene in which a demon is pounding the sinner, depicted as a baby, in a stone mortar guarded by a hell dog. This is the hell of pounding (碓 冲 地 獄 主 者).

The fourth king (五 官 王 Wuguanwang, Ngũ Quan Vương) (Fig. 149) is known as the King of the Five Offices. He is a standard member of the infernal bureaucracy, who collates the reports on evil actions sent by lower-level functionaries. Like the third king, he wears a black robe, but faces in the opposite direction. The words of warning written on his table are the opposite of those in front of the third king. The characters state, "If one caused evil in the past, he will harvest a horrible outcome in the future" (惡 有 惡 報). This is also a karmic concept: that nobody can escape the consequences of their evil actions. The center register depicts two court officials listening to complaints made by a horse and a chicken as they each hold documents in their mouths. The clerk's assistant kneels in front of the green-robed clerk (疏 文) and publicly announces (告) the presence of the two animals, while the official clerk to the right holds the documents over his shoulder, indicated by the characters 公 據 牒. The bottom section depicts two demonic guards grinding the sinner in a stone mill by pulling the rope back and forth, as described in the inscription on the stone tablet (磨 摧 地 獄 主 者).

The fifth king (閻 羅 王, Yanluowang, Diêm La Vương) (Fig. 150), King Yama, is easily identified by his black skin. In this scroll he is painted with a white beard, wearing traditional robes, and sporting a judge's cap. Unlike kings one through four, rather than holding a brush in his right hand, he instead gestures, as if making a judgment, pointing two fingers toward his beard, while his left hand holds an unopened fan. The character of the fifth king originated in India; Yama is the deity of death and the ruler of the departed. He was later adopted into the traditional Chinese religious system as the central figure of the court, the highest ranking of the Ten Kings. With his insight, wisdom, and power the spirits of the dead cannot be fraudulent or trick him, as stated in the Chinese inscription, 無 可 陰 瞞. In the middle segment, a bull makes his way to the court, as the clerk's assistant holds a "public announcement" sign (告) facing toward the court clerk at the right. The bottom section depicts the gruesome torture of the sinner by two demons, who cut him in half with a large saw. The sinner is tied to a wooden pole and guarded by a yellow dog. The

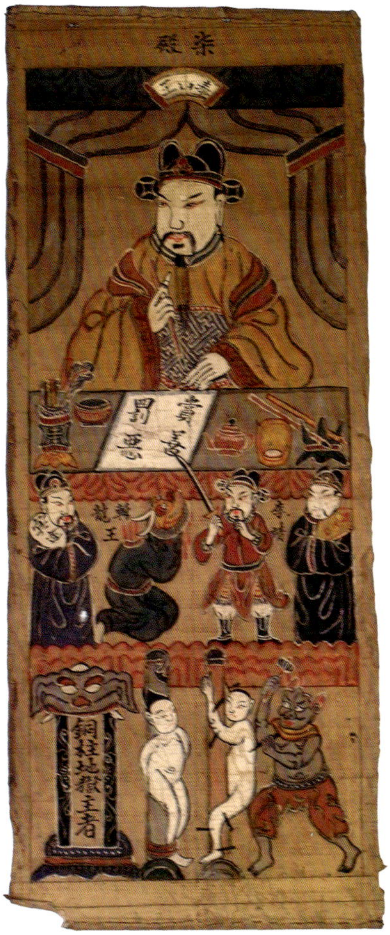

Fig. 152

Fig. 150
The Fifth King of the Underworld,
c. late 19th–early 20th century
Tày, Vietnam

Fig. 151
The Sixth King of the Underworld,
c. late 19th–early 20th century
Tày, Vietnam

Fig. 152
The Seventh King of the Underworld,
c. late 19th–early 20th century
Tày, Vietnam

individuals judged in the fifth king's realm include sinners who have committed adultery, been murderers, burned religious books, and been blasphemers of Daoism and its gods. By this stage, the dead soul has no chance for redemption or reincarnation, having been tarnished to the extent that it can no longer be sent back to the world of the living. Punishment may include being sent to a terrace where one must watch the legacy of one's wicked deeds unfold among family members.[11]

The sixth king, King of the Transformation (卞 城 王, Bianchengwang, Biến Thành Vương) (Fig. 151), is similar to the fifth king. In his right hand he holds a Daoist fly-whisk, while his left hand strokes his long beard. He wears a dark green robe and a judge's cap. The motto in front of this king states that at this point it is too late for the sinner to repent for his bad acts (悔 過 不 及). However, the moral of the story depicted in the middle level is that if a person sincerely and willingly atones for his bad deeds, it is not too late. This scene simply visualizes the tale (行程) of Liu Quan Delivering Melons (劉 全 進 瓜). Briefly, this story begins with the Tang Dynasty Emperor Taizong, who, after having been wrongly accused and sent to hell, meets the Ten Kings. Before leaving hell, he asks if they want something from the living world. The Ten Kings say that they would like to taste southern melons. Taizong promises to send them some when he returns to his nation. At his court, he seeks a volunteer to deliver the watermelons. Depressed because of having accidentally driven his wife to commit suicide, Liu Quan steps forward. He is poisoned to death, after which he descends into hell with the melons. The Kings of the Underworld reward Liu Quan by reuniting him with his wife. However, after three months of death, his wife's body has decayed, so she cannot return to it. But Yama lets her soul enter the body of the Emperor Taizong's younger sister, recently deceased. The emperor marries off the princess to Liu Quan and heavily rewards him for fulfilling his promise.[12] The bottom register is the hell where sinners are boiled in a copper cauldron (锅 湯 地 獄 主 者). One demon is throwing a sinner into a cauldron that already holds another, while a second demon blows fire through a tube to make it hotter.

The seventh king is King of Mount Tai (泰 山 王, Taishanwang, Thái Sơn Vương) (Fig. 152). In traditional Chinese belief, Mount Tai was recognized as the administrative seat of death, so he was the Lord of the Land of the Dead. But with the introduction of Buddhism into China, Yama gradually usurped his place and became the new Lord of the Underworld.[13] Confucianism regarded this mountain as the holy place for emperors to carry out important sacrifices to heaven and the royal rites of a benevolent ruler. Clad in a traditional Chinese yellow robe, the seventh king holds a brush in his right hand, while his left touches a piece of paper on the desk, which states, "Reward the good, punish the bad" (賞 善 罰 悪). The most thought-provoking aspect of this painting is the narrative illustrated in the middle level. The person holding a sword and dressed in full armor is identified as Li Ding (李 靖), an outstanding military general, theorist, and hero of the early Tang dynasty. As a commander, he participated in battles that reunified the country and resolved border disputes. The story is from chapters 10 and 11 of the important late-sixteenth-century Chinese epic *Journey to the West*. In this episode, the Dragon King of the Jing River (溼 河 龍 王), commonly regarded in Chinese mythology as the divine ruler of water, is painted with a human body and a dragon's head. The Dragon King offends the Jade Emperor by controlling the time and nature of rainfalls to be inefficient and useless, so he then seeks protection from Emperor Taizong. However, the Jade Emperor sends a heavenly messenger to instruct Li Ding to persecute the Dragon King at noon the next day. Emperor Taizong wanted to keep his promise by inviting Li Ding to play chess with him in the palace all day, hence preventing him from killing the Dragon King. Nonetheless, Li Ding takes a nap at noon during the chess game with the emperor. While asleep, his spirit goes to the river and beheads the Dragon King. Feeling betrayed by the human emperor, the spirit of the Dragon King goes to the underworld to file a court complaint with the Ten Kings. Taizong is summoned to the underworld for judgment.[14] The verdict declares him innocent, and he is given a chance to tour hell and learn about its torture and punishments. He also promises the Kings of the Underworld that he will deliver watermelons (as discussed earlier). The bottom section is the hell of the hot copper pillars (銅 柱 地 獄 主). This painting shows a demon nailing one sinner onto a hot copper pillar, while a second is tied to another pillar.

The eighth scroll depicts the King of the Capital and Market (都 市 王, Dushiwang, Đô Đế Vương) (Fig. 153) and his court. Wearing a dark blue robe and holding a brush in his right hand, he has the contemplative expression of a more critical judgment. At this stage all sentences are completed, as stated by the four characters 功 果 完 滿, meaning all innocent souls are soon to be assigned for reincarnation in the court of the tenth king. In other words, all the bad and good deeds of the past have been judged by the previous seven kings. In the central scene it appears that the two court clerks, together with the three central figures, are gathered for final discussions. The sign held by the court clerk on the left says "Punish them" (罸 度), while the clerk on the right holds a sign saying "Free them" (赦 文), both of which probably mean that the dead here are ready to send to the tenth king for processing. The five figures display the same demeanor and are dressed alike, except for the color of their robes. The lower section depicts the hell of cutting a sinner's body into pieces (刀 扎 地 獄 主 者), as two demonic prison guards operate a large iron knife to dismember the body of a dead soul.

The ninth king (平 等 王, Pingdengwan, Bình Đẳng Vương) (Fig. 154) is similar to the seventh: he wears a yellow robe and writes a four-character note

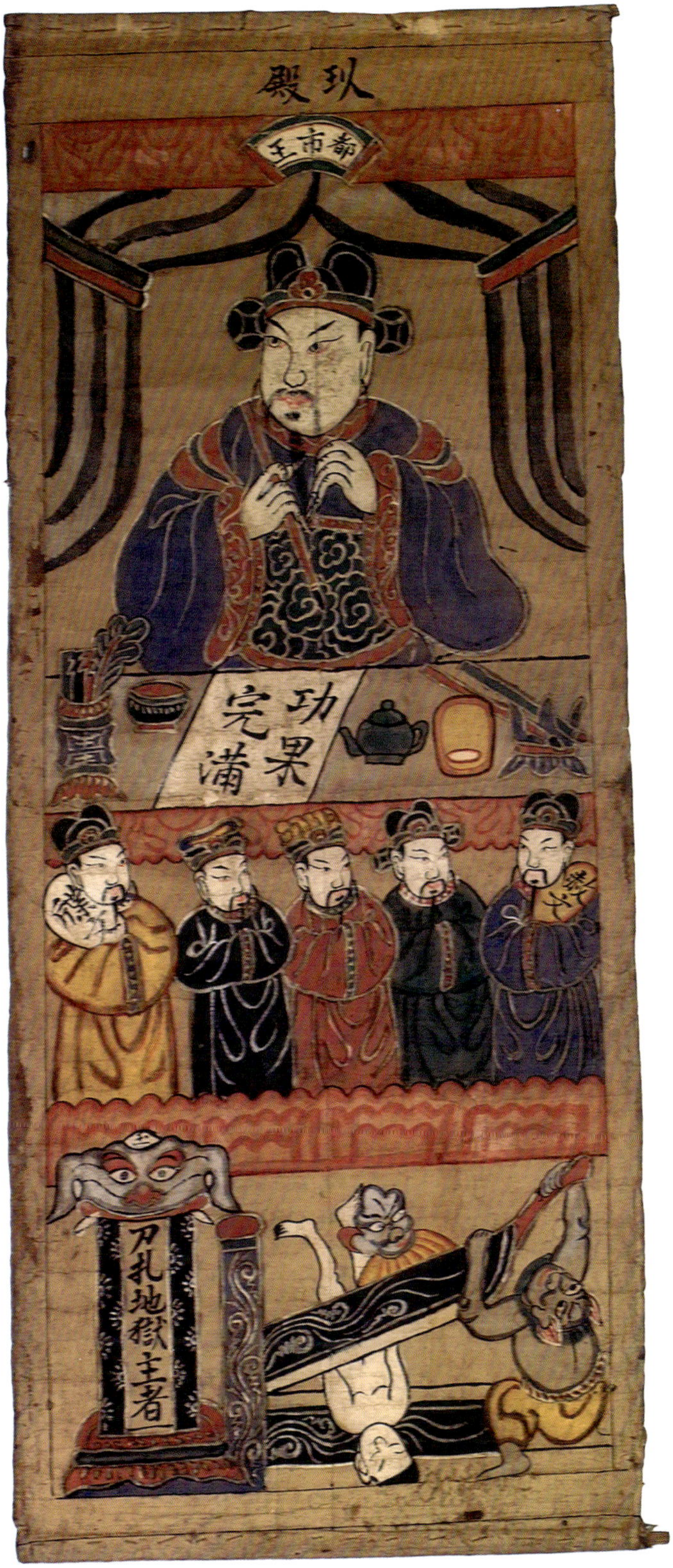

Fig. 153

Fig. 153
The Eigth King of the Underworld, c. late 19th–early 20th century
Tày, Vietnam

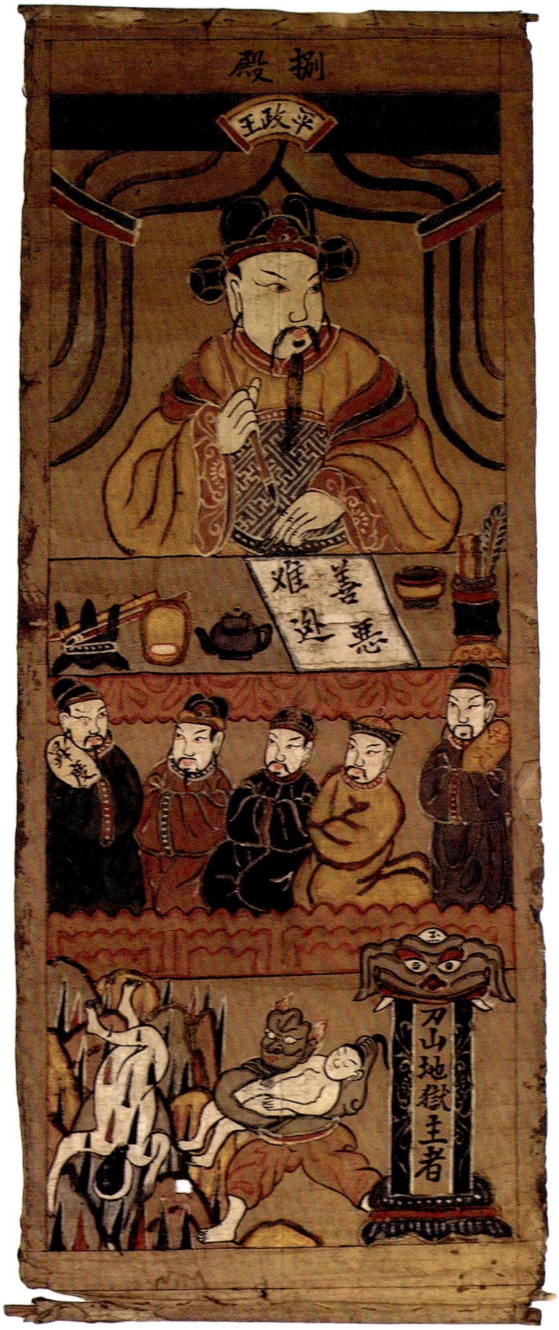

Fig. 154

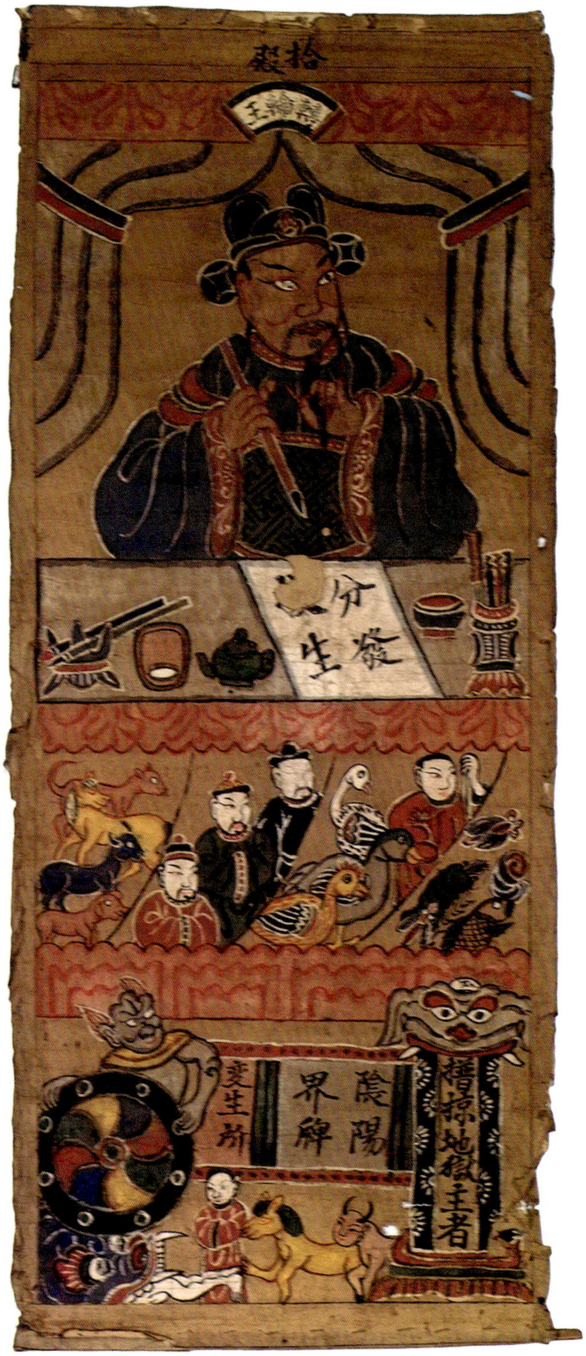

Fig. 155

with the brush in his right hand. The note says that the ruling must be equitable, taking into account both wholesome and unwholesome deeds (善 悪 難 遞). Therefore, the court councils on both sides debate the deeds of the three people kneeling at the center of the middle section. One label states that they are being released. In the bottom section, those who committed cardinal crimes are being punished by a demon who is throwing them onto mountains of sharply pointed blades and spikes (刀 山 地 獄 主 者), a disturbing and horrendous scene of torture.

The tenth scroll is of the King of the Wheel of Law (轉 輪 王, Zhuanlunwang, Chuyển Luân Vương) (Fig. 155). As the last judge of the purgatory court, his duty is to make the final judgment by sending the deceased back to the world of living. In this painting, his facial complexion is much darker than the other kings, with the exception of the fifth. The four characters on his desk state that he is the person who assigns all beings to be reborn into different realms (分 發 再 生). In the middle register, both humans and animals —dogs, cows, ducks, chickens, fish, and shrimp—are mingling, waiting to be assigned for rebirth. All face toward an invisible force to the right, which is pulling them to the next scene, at the bottom. The sign reads, "This is the borderline between the underworld and the living world" (陰 陽 界). Here a large demon is turning the wheel of life, pushing all the dead spirits to be reborn into one of the six realms, according to their accumulation of virtuous or bad deeds. Referring to Buddhist beliefs, if they were bad, they would be reborn into one of the three lower realms: in hells, as hungry ghosts, or as animals. If they were good, they would be born into one of the three upper reals as *asuras* (a powerful type of deity), as humans, or as heavenly beings. The demon is helping the tenth king with the procedures for reincarnation, as signaled by the three Chinese characters: 变 生 所. Unlike paintings one through nine, no torture is displayed in the court of the tenth king.

When these ten hanging scrolls are viewed as a complete set, one can see some overall patterns. All odd-numbered kings face to the left, while all even-numbered kings face to the right. This reflects the tradition of the symmetrical arrangements of scroll sets. Most importantly, the odd-numbered kings are always hung on the viewer's right side of a central picture, say the image of Buddha Amitābha, or the spirit tablet of the recently dead; whereas the even-numbered kings are on the viewer's left.

This set of ten hanging scrolls from the Tày ethnic group was once used for funeral rites and other ritual services to aid the dead in their quest for salvation. It also acted as a reminder to the living that no one can escape the law of karma. Criminals can hide their crimes on earth, yet when forced into the underworld, all past wrongdoings clearly appear in the magical mirror. In the court of the Ten Kings of the Underworld, punishment always awaits those who have been wicked, and rewards always come to those who have been virtuous.

The set is strongly influenced by later Buddhist religious practices that allow living relatives of the dead to make offerings to the Buddhas as well as perform charitable work that can affect the karmic balance on which the kings' judgments rested. Consequently, the dead could overcome their karmic destiny, being reborn into a better realm or even into the Buddhist Pure Land or Daoist heaven.

Artistically, this set of scrolls is very much like other Tày and Nùng scrolls in terms of scheme and design. The Yao, on the other hand, never depict the Ten Kings in a set of ten separate paintings, but rather all in a single scroll.

Fig. 154
The Ninth King of the Underworld, c. late 19th–early 20th century
Tày, Vietnam

Fig. 155
The Tenth King of the Underworld, c. late 19th–early 20th century
Tày, Vietnam

NOTES

1. See Quitman E. Phillips, "Narrating the Salvation of the Elite: The Jōfukuji Paintings of the Ten Kings," in *Ars Orientalis* 33 (2003), p. 123.

2. For full discussion of the historical development and many other important issues regarding the Ten Kings of the Underworld in Buddhism, see Stephen F. Teiser, *The Scripture on the Ten Kings and the Making of Purgatory in Medieval Chinese Buddhism* (Honolulu: University of Hawaii Press, 1994).

3. For discussion of the Ten Kings of the Underworld in the Yao tradition, see Jacques Lemoine, p. 104–114; for the Yao, Tày, and other mountainous ethnic groups in northern Vietnam, see Phan Ngọc Khuê, *Taoist Painting*, pp. 188–201.

4. Jacques Lemoine, *Yao Ceremonial Paintings*, p. 104.

5. Ibid. pp. 104–105.

6. For similar hanging scrolls from the Tày and Nùng, see Phạm Đức Sĩ, pp. 146–151. See also Phan Ngọc Khuê, *Taoist Painting*, pp. 190–200, for another Tày set. However, in the Vietnamese Buddhist tradition, the format of the hanging scroll paintings of the Ten Kings of the Underworld is more complicated, as the scheme is not always similar: see Quang Huy, ed., plates 54–57, pp. 58–59, and plates 114–125, pp. 90–97.

7. Quitman Phillips, p. 123.

8. Ibid., 129.

9. A cangue is a device put around a prisoner's neck. A typical one would consist of a large, heavy board with a hole in the middle. The board consists of two pieces that are closed around a sinner's neck, then fastened shut by locks or hinges.

10. Quitman Phillips, p. 138.

11. Jacques Lemoine, *Yao Ceremonial Paintings*, p. 107.

12. The story of Liu Quan going to hell to deliver the watermelons to the Kings of the Underworld and unite with his wife is told in Anthony C. Yu., trans and ed., *The Journey to the West*, vol. 1 (Chicago: University of Chicago Press, 2012), pp. 222–269.

13. Quitman Phillips, p. 138.

14. The stories of Li Ding persecuting the Dragon King and Taizong touring hell are told in *The Journey to the West*, pp. 218–268.

Detail of *Fig. 149*

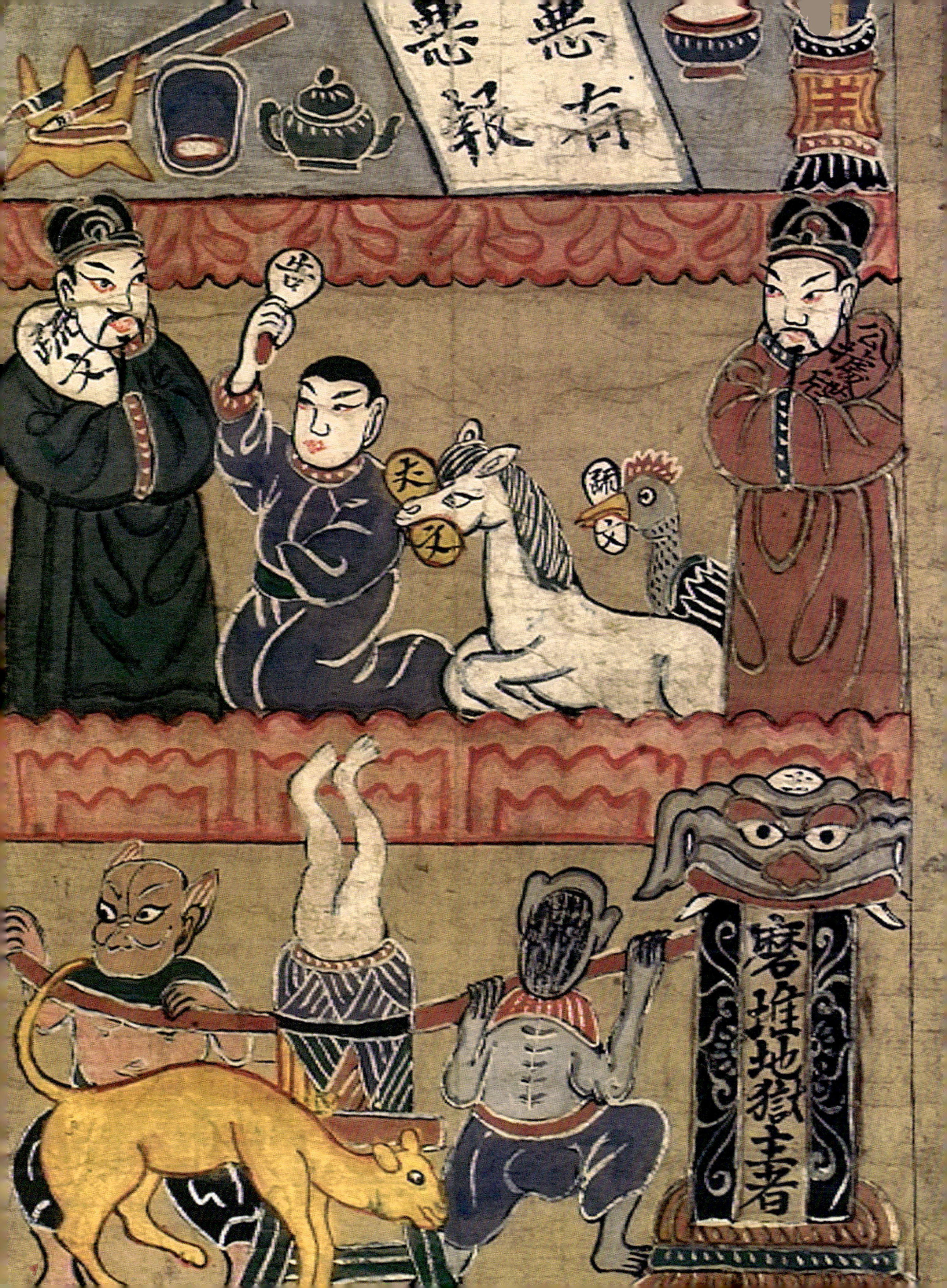
惡有惡報
疏文
告
夫文
疏文
磨推地獄書者

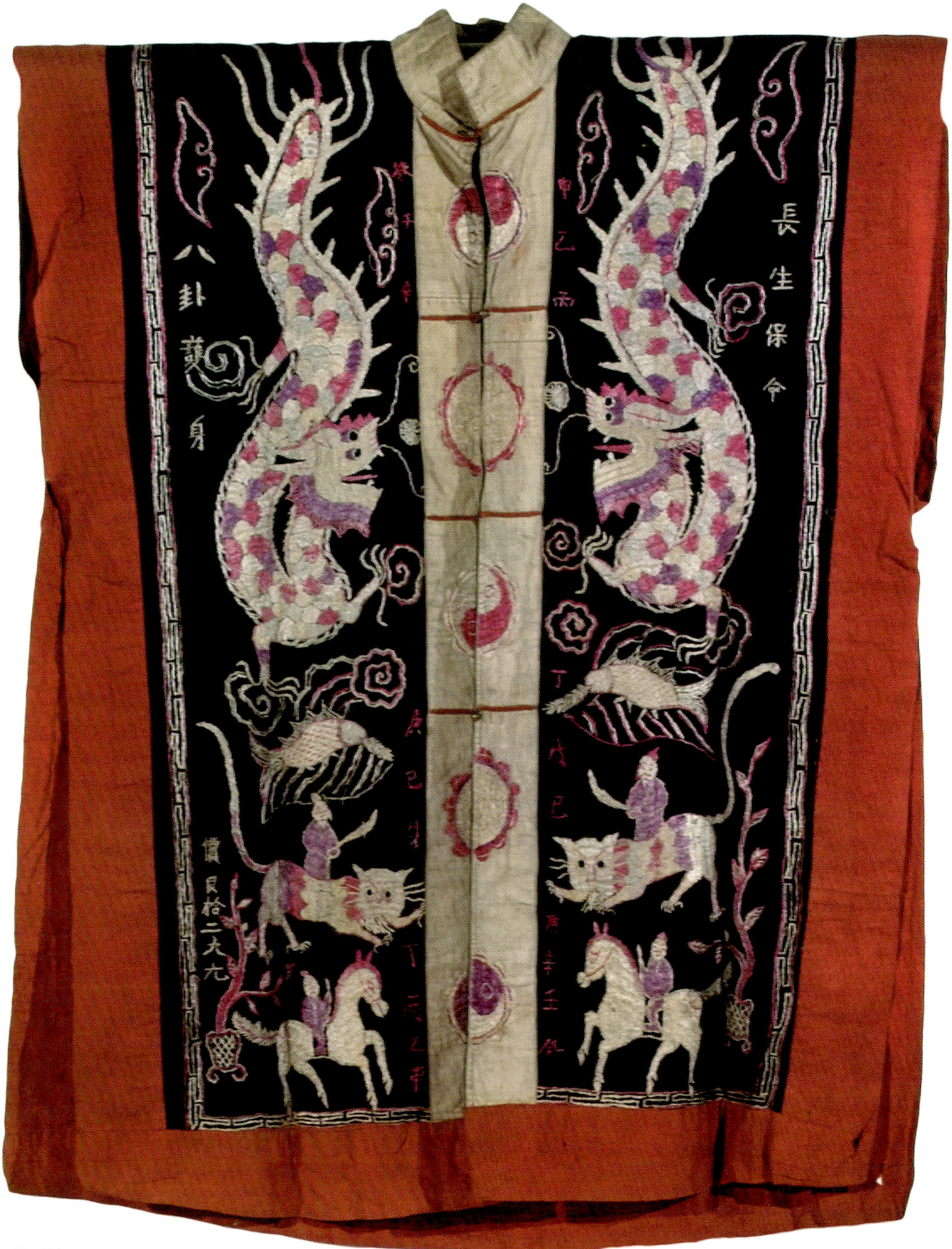

Fig. 156

WEARING THE UNIVERSE:
Shaman Robes, Garments, and Paraphernalia

A very long time ago, all Yao priests were women. Men in those days were farmers and hunters, providing food for their families; in turn, women conducted all rituals and religious services. The following legend accounts for a change in this practice: a family once invited a shaman priestess to their village to perform a prayer ritual for a sick relative. When she arrived, accompanied by her husband, she had childbirth pains and started to go into labor. The priestess then took off her robe, laid out her other ritual instruments, and asked her husband to make the offerings and pray for the sick person. Because the husband had heard his wife praying at home, and often accompanied her on religious trips, he knew the rituals, procedures, and prayers, and was well able to perform them. The sick person was cured. Since that time, people have found that as men did not have to bear and raise children, they were more powerful in praying to the deities. Gradually, the Yao men replaced the women shamans. However, the original garb of the women remained customary.[1] There are many similar legends explaining why Yao shaman priests wear female costumes.[2] Nevertheless, the transition has had a profound effect on the shamanic wardrobe, which has become the focus of artistic, spiritual, and cultural study. The ritual outfits in the Kitnick Collection are diverse, and include colorful textiles with fine embroidery and a variety of decorative motifs.

Dragon robes and crowns are elaborately embellished with images, thus special attention is given to them in the first half of this chapter. Other less-decorated parts of the full outfit will also be discussed briefly. Unlike the Yao, Tày shamans adopted many Buddhist elements and symbols into their religious services and outfits, so a final section will examine a few garments that belonged to this ethnic group.

The Shaman's Dragon Robes

Aside from painted scrolls, the traditional robes worn by Yao Daoist priests are the most visually spectacular objects in the collection. Regarding those worn by Chinese Daoist priests of the Qing dynasty, the scholar Stephen Little has remarked, "The decoration of these robes presents images of the structures of the cosmos, which are unified in the Dao and in the person of the priest himself."[3] Such an observation is paralleled in the imagery of robes worn by shaman priests among the Yao, Tày, Nùng, Sán Chay, and Sán Dìu peoples. In general, the embroidered designs on the dragon robes and some related paraphernalia reflect traditional Daoist cosmology and belief. Typical motifs include the Three Pure Ones, the Jade Emperor's heaven, the

Fig. 156
Ritual robe, c. early 20th century
Sán Chay, Vietnam

deities of the twenty-eight lunar mansions, rows of Daoist saints, sages, and immortals, the five sacred Daoist mountains in China, the yin-yang emblem (the Diagram of the Supreme Ultimate), and the twelve animal symbols of the Chinese zodiac. Animals like tigers, fishes, and horses are often employed to represent strength and good fortune, and as the mounted vehicles for the deities. The four auspicious animals—dragon, phoenix, unicorn (麒麟, *qilin*, or *kỳ lân*), and turtle—the Eight Trigrams (八 卦), and the sun and moon are also prominent motifs. Some robes have two Asian flying carp, a reference to the legend of a carp jumping over the Dragon Gate and subsequently transforming into a dragon.[4] The symbol of two fish and two dragons signifies a sudden lift in social status. In addition to Daoist designs, Buddhist symbols such as the swastika, representing the auspicious power of an enlightened being, and lotuses, suggesting mental purity and spiritual perfection, are sometimes embroidered on robes or crowns. The three popular wishes, good fortune, prosperity, and longevity, so prominently embedded in Chinese culture, are represented by the three embroidered characters 福 祿 壽 (*fu lu shou, phúc lộc thọ*). Written couplets and phrases extolling the virtues and powers of the Daoist priests are occasionally employed. When wearing their dragon robes and crowns, Daoist shaman priests embody a combination of the Dao, the structure of the cosmos, and many important Chinese concepts, thus becoming a microcosm of the universe. Jean C. Cooper, a scholar of Chinese religion, makes the following remarks about the dragon robes once worn by Chinese emperors during special occasions, which are applicable as well to the robes worn by Daoist priests:

> The magnificent dragon robes, which the emperors wore at the solstice sacrifices, symbolically clothed them in the universe and displayed all the cosmic symbols of heaven, earth and the waters, the mountains and clouds, and the waters of the ocean. The glory of these robes was not a vain adornment of the male or to add consequence and pomp to man and ceremony, but to serve as constant reminder of man's place in the universe, to recall the spiritual powers controlling heaven and earth, and to keep in mind the hierarchic order of things celestial and terrestrial, to which man must conform on its various levels and according to his varying capacities.[5]

The colors and style of each robe or ritual jacket may vary, but the primary decorations are nearly identical. It is a full-body garment that, when not being worn, resembles a large rectangular cloth folded in half. The front is split in two at the midpoint, where the robe is placed around the neck. Four long strings are used to tie it around the waist. On some robes there are additional pieces of cloth on each side, forming short sleeves. When worn, one half of the front slightly overlaps the other half. The front side is usually more simply decorated than the back, often with a pair of dragons dominating the top half and a few auspicious animals, occasionally ridden by deities, on the lower half. The back, always fashioned in one piece, is filled with the major decorative motifs previously mentioned,

The Kitnick Collection has seven dragon robes from five different ethnic groups: the Tày (Figs. 158, 162), Sán Dìu (Fig. 159), Sán Chỉ (Figs. 63, 156), Cao Làn (Fig. 157) and Nùng (Fig. 160). These robes, old and fairly worn, were made in either southern China or northern Vietnam and date to before World War II, based on several factors. Some are heavily embroidered with figures uncommon in robes made after the mid-twentieth century. One robe has an inscription (Fig. 160) saying that it was paid for in silver money, indicating that it was made in the last Chinese dynasty period, the Qing (1644–1912), since during the Republic of China (1912–1949) silver currency was no longer circulated. Furthermore, though different ethnic groups dyed their robes with distinctive colors, one or two colors were introduced by the French during the early colonial period (1887–1945).[6]

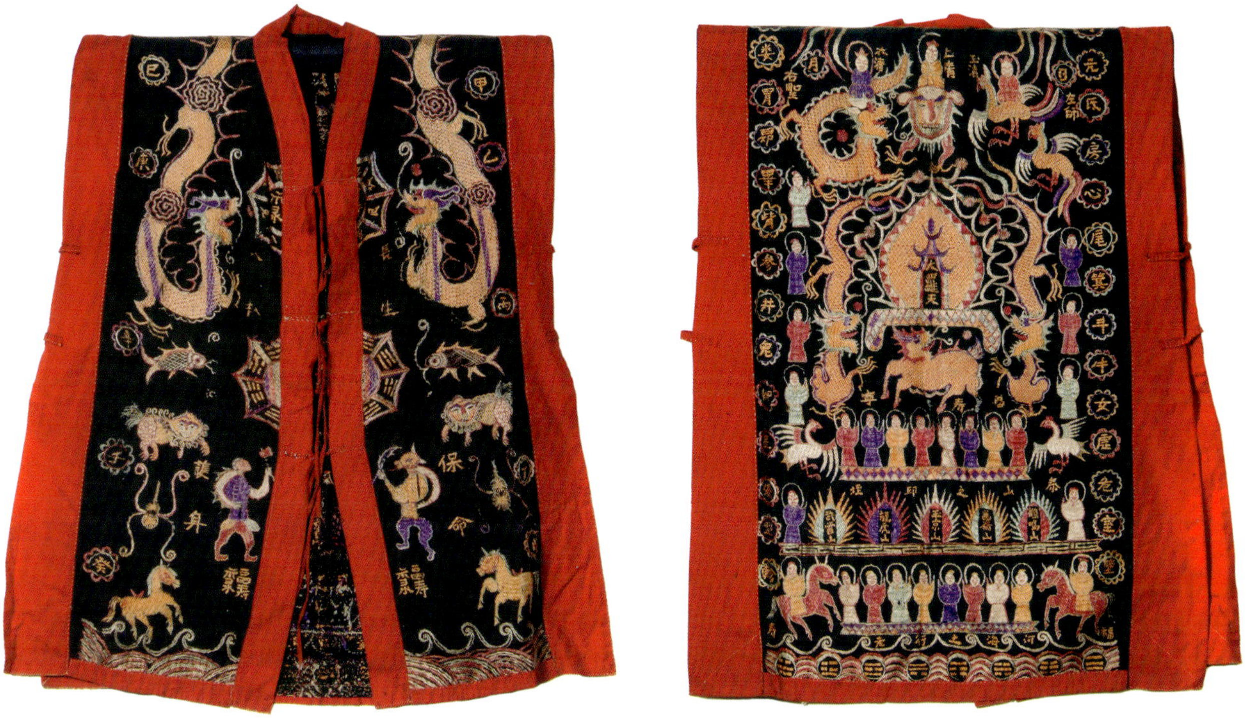

Fig. 157 (front and rear)

Dragon Robes of the Tày, Sán Chảy, and Cao Làn

These three dragon robes exhibit some common characteristics: the body is surrounded by a red or white edge and features an inner black or white border. They are worn by tying together the strings attached to the inner edge of the two frontal flaps and by fastening a cloth belt around the shaman's waist.

The frontal motifs are simple and uniform, almost always including two embroidered dragons facing the center and flying in clouds. There are minor differences in the details of the left and right sides, which otherwise appear to mirror each other. On the Tày robe (Fig. 158), below each dragon are a fish, stylized ocean waves, and a galloping horse. On the Sán Chỉ robes (Figs. 63, 156) there are four heavenly passengers riding on tigers and horses, along with a pair of fish. On the Cao Làn example (Fig. 157) are two pairs of animals without riders and the Eight Trigrams, beneath which are two heavenly deities: Celestial Marshal Ma, holding a long-handled Chinese scimitar, and Celestial Marshal Deng, holding a hatchet. Of these three dragon robes, only the Cao Làn jacket has human figures. Artistically, the needlework of the Tày and Sán Chỉ examples is more refined and elegant. The latter has an inscription on the left edge of the front flap revealing that the robe cost twelve large silver coins.

The backs of these robes are elaborately decorated with visually spectacular embroidery. In general, the designs are very alike. The surfaces are divided into two major parts. Each part is further divided into small sections or rows embellished with Daoist deities, auspicious animals, and other spiritual emblems. The topmost row often depicts the Three

Fig. 157
Ritual robe, c. early 20th century
Cao Làn-San Chi (San Chay), Vietnam

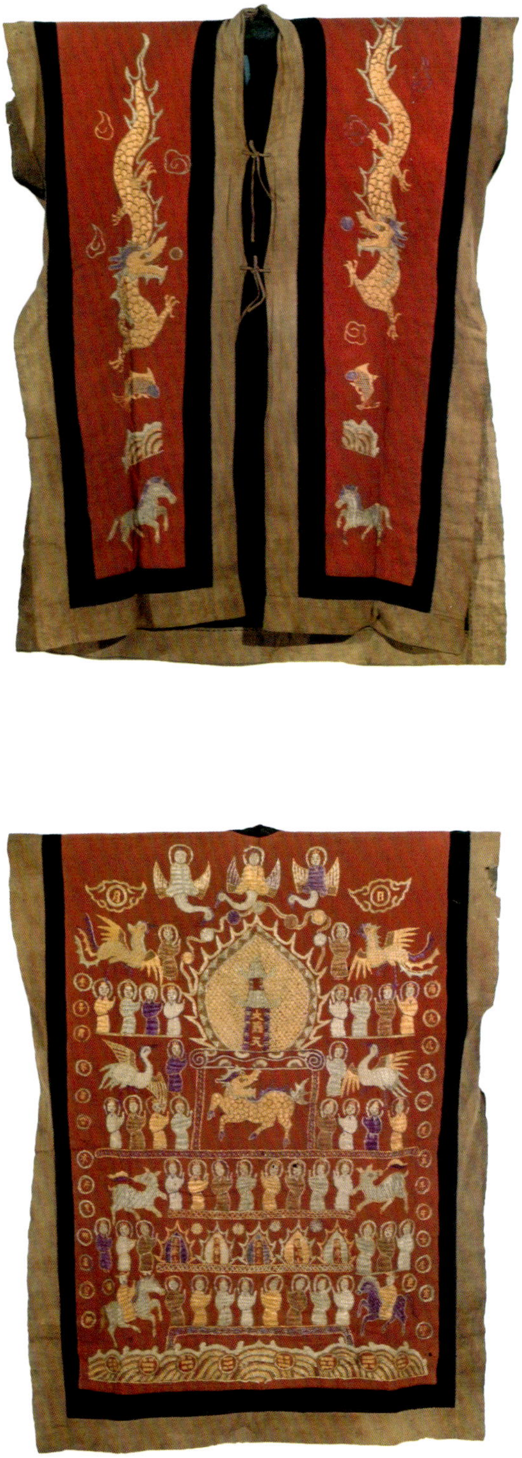

Fig. 158 (front and rear)

Pure Ones riding their auspicious animals (dragon, phoenix, and crane), flanked by the sun on the right and the moon on the left. Dominating the large section beneath the Three Pure Ones is the Great Net Heaven (大 羅 天, Đại La Thiên), the abode of the heavenly beings over which the Jade Emperor presides. A three-tiered pagoda surrounded by an oval shape framed with fire rings symbolizes this abode, while beneath it is a golden-scaled unicorn (麒 麟 *qilin*), a mythical animal denoting the appearance of a wise sage or an illustrious ruler. The whole upper part represents the heavenly realm by means of rows of deities, sages, and the immortal ones on both sides, flanked by flying phoenixes, cranes, and dragons.

The lower part contains three long registers flanked by either unicorns or cranes on the upper level. The top and bottom registers are elaborated with rows of eight, nine, or ten Daoist sages, or the immortals. The middle row is embroidered with the names of the five sacred Daoist mountains in China, framed in leaflike shapes and attended by Daoist deities on each side. The lowest section is a long, wavy ocean band dotted with the Eight Trigrams, symbolizing heaven, earth, lake, water, mountain, lightning, fire, and wind. On the edges of the lower corners are Celestial Marshals Ma and Deng on galloping horses. Finally, the names of the twenty-eight lunar deities are inscribed on both sides.[7] These are "a vital part of the Taoist pantheon,"[8] who help counteract the negative influences of other cosmic forces. They also relate to "the personalities of people born under their influences."[9]

The five sacred mountains embroidered in Chinese characters are worthy of a brief discussion. Central to Daoist cosmological belief is the concept that the sacred peaks are key locations connecting heaven and earth.[10] The five sacred mountains are located in four different regions of China, defining the four cardinal

Fig. 158
Ritual robe, c. early 20th century
Tày, Vietnam

directions and thus signifying their role as special guardians within the cosmological system.[11] Mount Wudang is in the north,[12] Mount Heming is in the south,[13] Mount Dragon Tiger[14] and Mount Yujing[15] are in the east, and the Kunlun Mountains are in the west.[16] Followers are encouraged to make pilgrimages to these places at least once during their lifetime.

Four Additional Dragon Robes

These dragon robes from different ethnic groups have the same designs with minor variations. The Sán Dìu robe (Fig. 159) is made of cotton dyed dark blue, the principal color of these people. Each of the two front flaps is adorned with a dragon, below which are the Four Heavenly Messengers in pairs, riding a dragon, a phoenix, a horse, and a tiger. The major design on the back is essentially the same as in the three previously discussed robes. On each side is a column with five roundels in the stylized shape of a pomegranate. Each roundel contains a different abstract or geometrical symbol, or the Buddhist swastika, an auspicious emblem. Two Chinese characters, 福 and 壽 (*fu shou, phúc thọ*), representing good fortune and longevity, are also a part of the design. In traditional Chinese culture, the myriad seeds of a pomegranate underscore the concepts of surplus, abundance, and fecundity.

The Nùng robe (Fig. 160) has some details that supplement this discussion. Its front flaps have four four-character phrases specifying the religious roles of a high shaman priest: to pray for protecting and prolonging life; to use the trigrams for guarding the physical body; to treasure the Daoist Three Jewels (the Dao, the Teaching, and the Master); and a fourth that is blurry and consequently illegible. On the back, names of stars and constellations are embroidered next to the figures in the two top rows. The abode portrayed in the central square, flanked by two dragons, is the Jade Emperor's palace. The rest of the design is similar to the previous robes, with the exception of the five sacred Daoist mountains, which are depicted in a lower register.

The dragon robes from other ethnic groups in the collection are not as elaborate and intricately woven. For example, the design of a robe from the Tight Trouser Yao subgroup (Fig. 161) is simpler, decorated mainly with large dragons, pairs of small horses, and unicorns. The black jacket belonging to a Tày shaman (Fig. 162) also features a less elaborate design than those in the previous section.

According to Chinese tradition, designs and decorative motifs on dragon robes are symmetrical, with all elements organized into a balanced vertical and horizontal arrangement. The two front flaps are dominated by the two dragons, while the back is always embellished with the Daoist trinity, the Jade Emperor's heaven, the twenty-eight lunar mansions, the five Daoist sacred mountains, and the Eight Trigrams. The characters for Fortune and Longevity are also noteworthy features. Their arrangement is similar to those of the Heavenly Host scroll paintings (Figs. 42, 96, 106). Everything is interconnected: the Jade Emperor administrating the world in his palace, the balancing act of the sun, moon, and constellations, the Daoist teachings, and the immortals on earth as represented by the five sacred mountains.

Paraphernalia

Besides the dragon robes, the Yao and other shaman priests need additional religious items to complete their full ritual outfits. These include cloth or paper crowns, hats, turbans, pendants, streamers, skirts, belts, and leggings. Some of these items are embroidered but are not as richly and meticulously designed as the dragon robes.

Crowns

The high priests' crowns come in different forms and feature various decorative symbols, from simple to very complex. Some crowns are made of painted paper, while others are made of cotton with carefully embroidered figures. The crowns of Yao Daoist priests are always decorated with the Three Pure Ones, which distinguishes them from the other

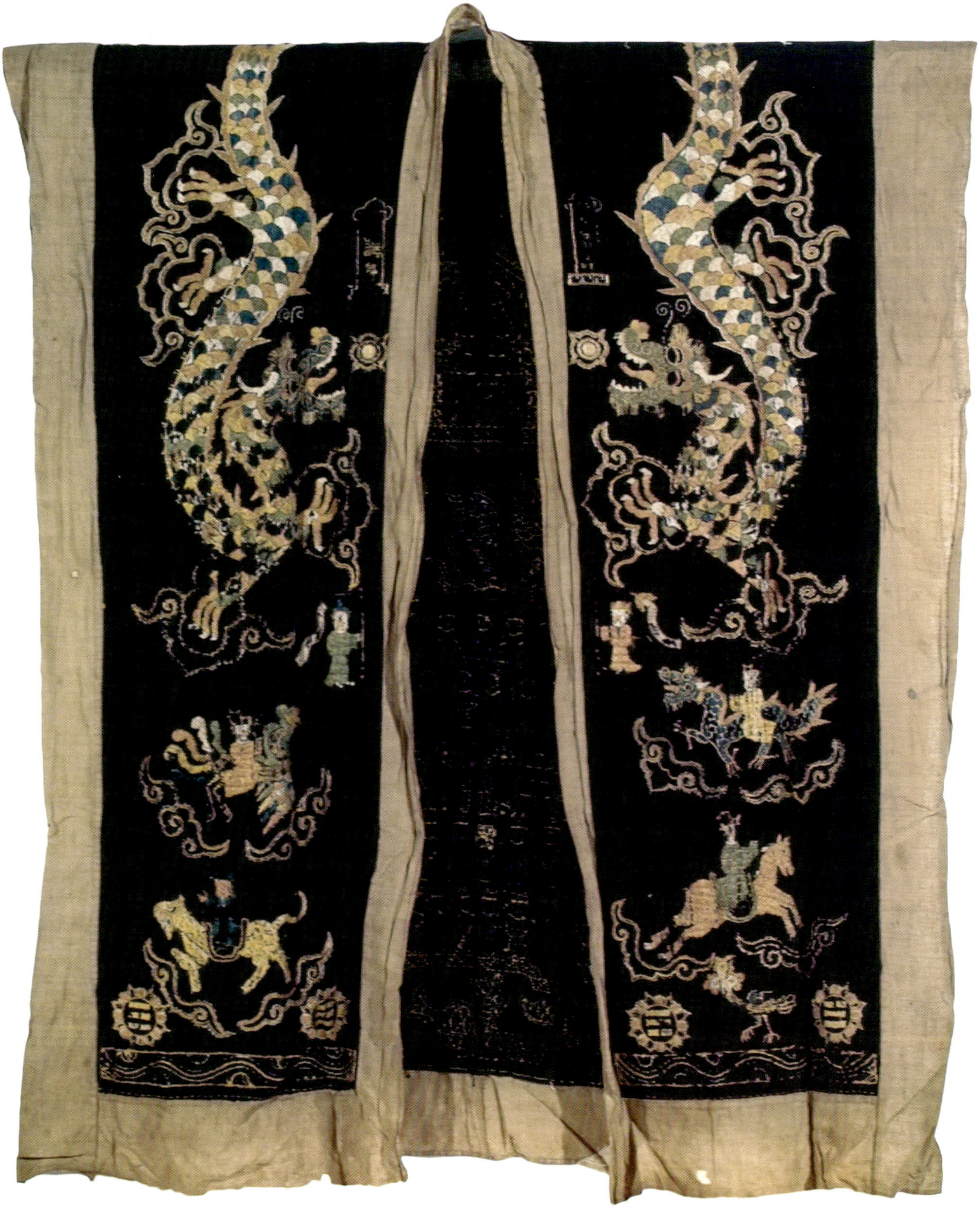

Fig. 159 (front and rear)

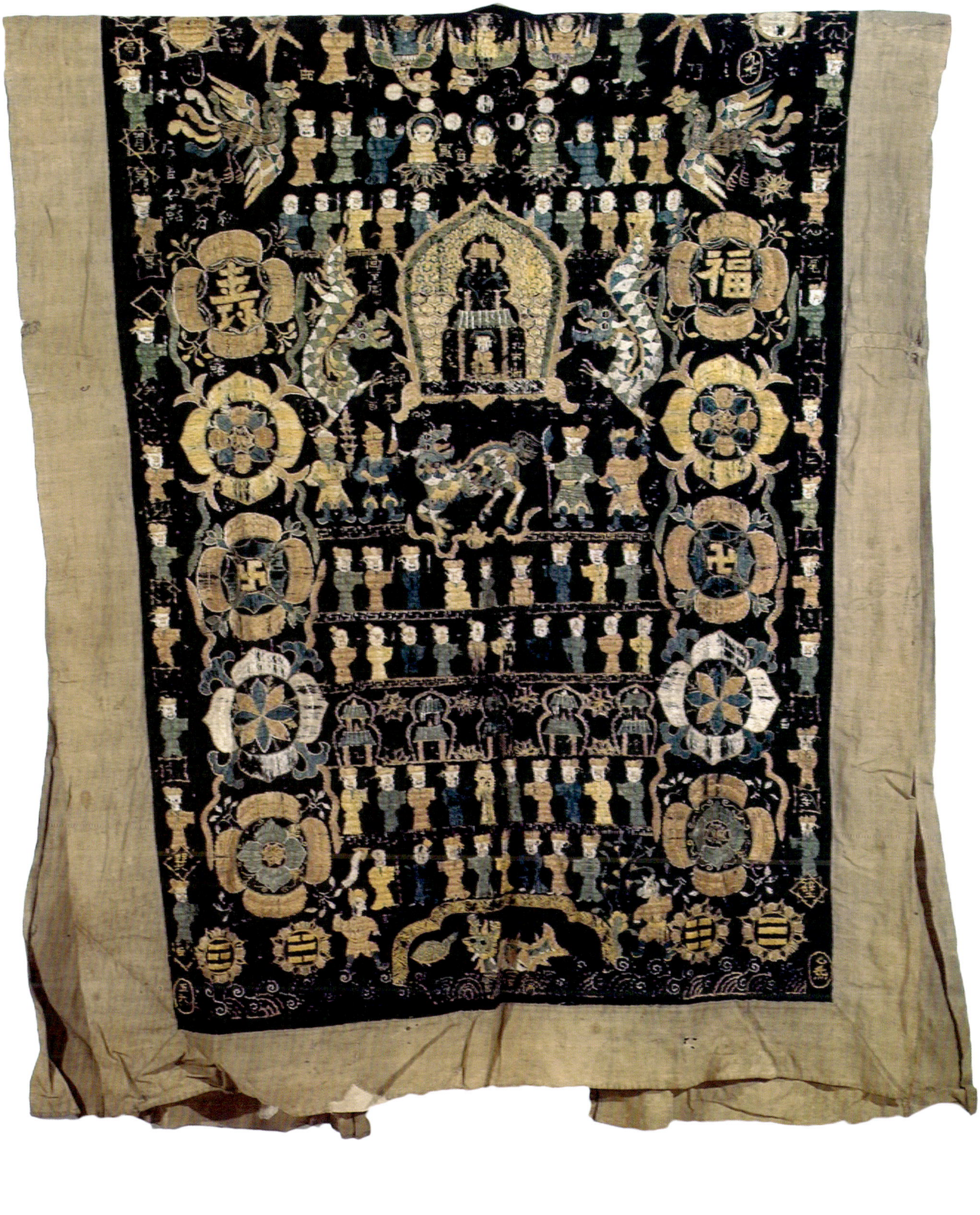

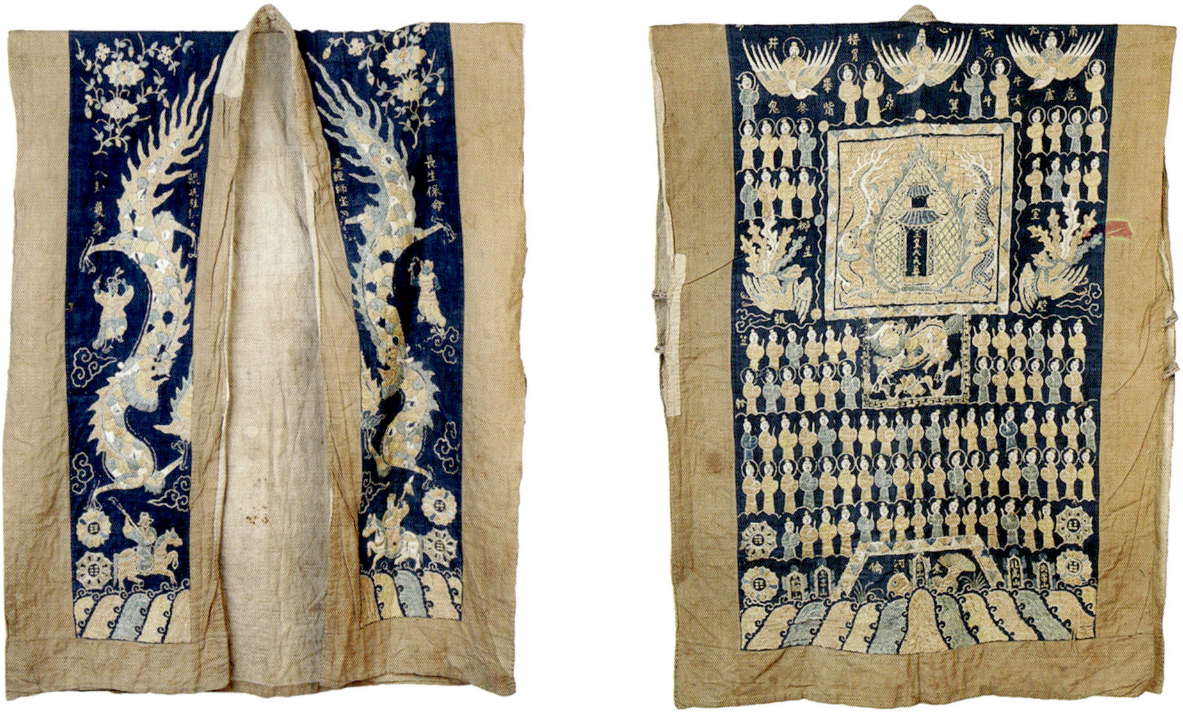

Fig. 160 (front and rear)

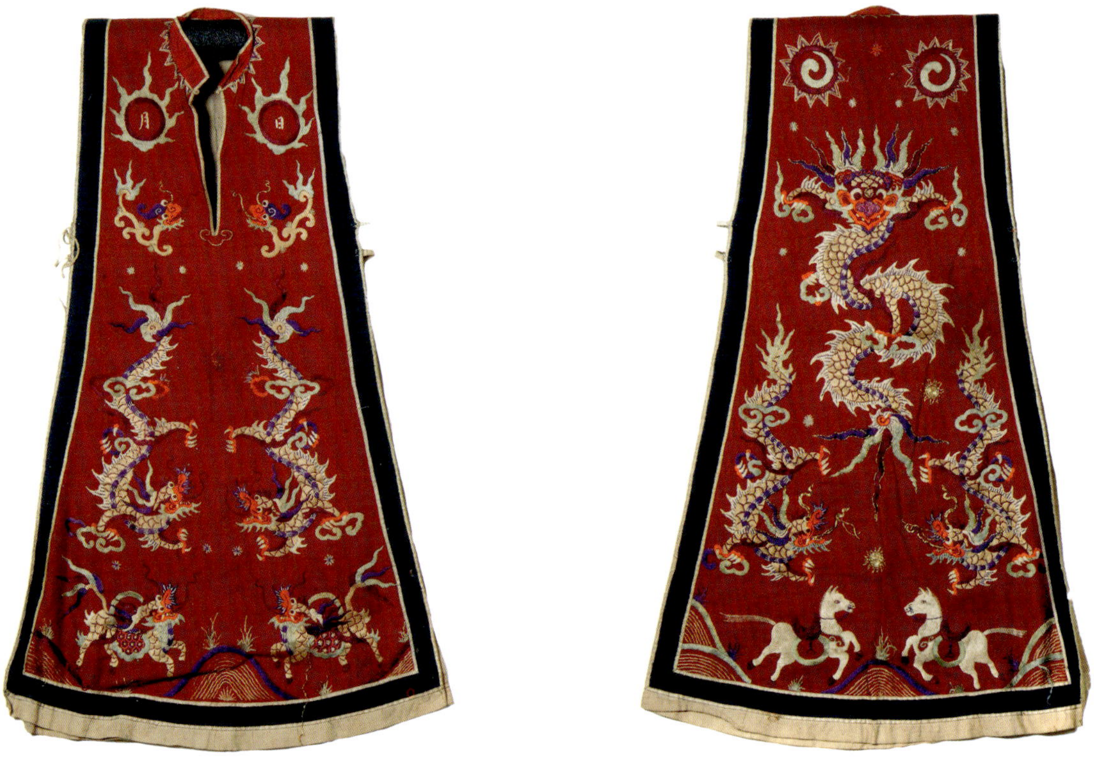

Fig. 161 (front and rear)

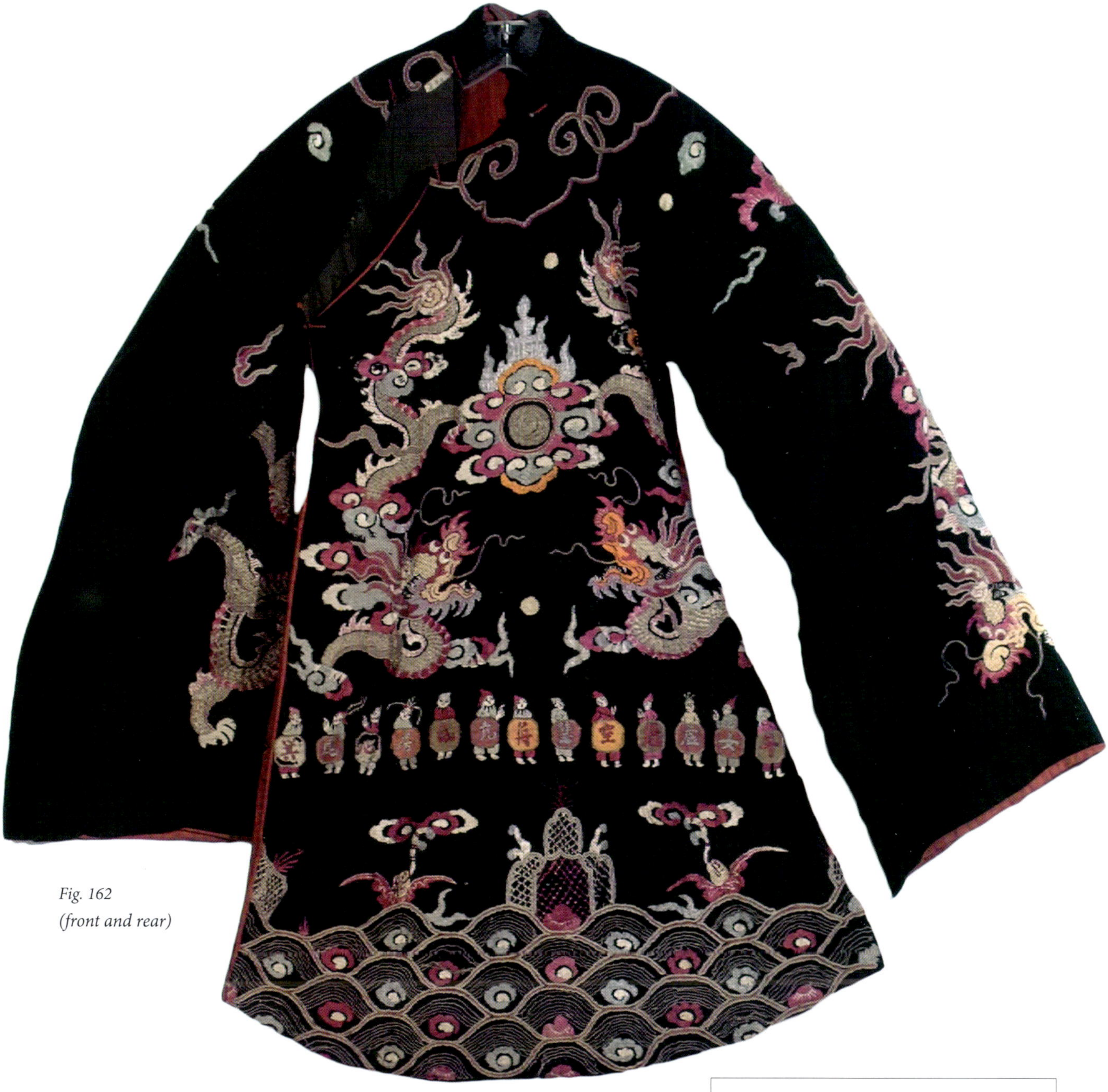

Fig. 162
(front and rear)

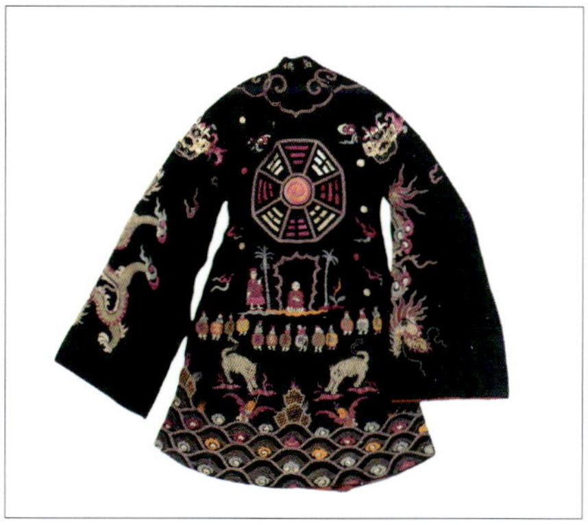

Fig. 159
Ritual robe, c. late 19th century
Sán Dìu, Vietnam

Fig. 160
Ritual robe, c. late 19th century
Tày or Nùng, Vietnam

Fig. 161
Sleeveless robe, c. early 20th century
Tight Trouser (Quần Chẹt) Yao, Vietnam

Fig. 162
Ritual robe, c. late 19th–early 20th century
Tày, Vietnam

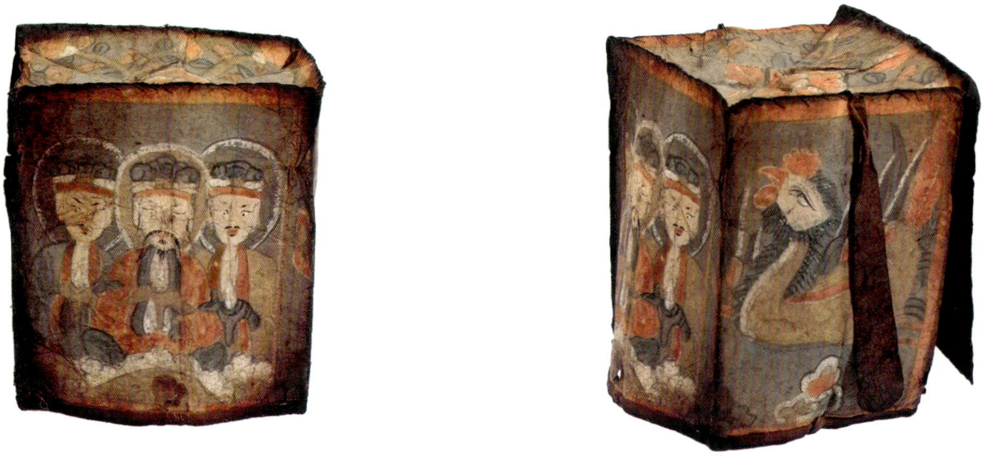

Fig. 163 (two views)

Fig. 163
Ritual Crown, c. late 19th century
Tight Trouser (Quần Chẹt) Yao, Vietnam

ethnic groups. Crowns of shaman priests or priestesses from the Tày, the Nùng, the Sán Chay, and the Sán Dìu are decorated with two phoenixes facing the sun, two flying dragons, the yin-yang symbol, or the Four Heavenly Messengers.[17]

The boxlike paper crown of the Tight Trouser Yao subgroup is painted with the Three Pure Ones in front, and a phoenix and crane on the sides (Fig. 163). This type of square crown, made of a special paper, reinforced with glue and joined together with thread, is only worn by the high shaman priest. It features two pieces of cloth, called "ears," on the left and right sides.[18] Another of their crowns, made of paper and cloth, is painted with the Three Pure Ones seated at the center, each holding a tablet (Fig. 164); the back depicts two underworld messengers (with animal heads) accompanied by the Lord of Death, whose face is often seen on decorative doors of Hindu and Buddhist monuments in central Java, Indonesia, and at the Dazu caves in Sichuan Province, China.

A Tày crown, made of paper and textile with seven folded parts, is embroidered with the seven Daoist stellar deities[19] on the front and the seven Buddhas of the Past on the back (Fig. 165).[20] Other crowns from the Tày and the Nùng are bedecked with two flying phoenixes facing the sun, or the yin-yang symbol (Figs. 166, 167). Sometimes the Three Pure Ones are indicated with the three Chinese characters 玉 上 太. Ethnic cultures other than the Yao integrated many Buddhist elements into their religious practices and had female priestesses, called *then* in Vietnamese. These crowns belonged to Tày and Nùng female shamans.

Headgear, Headdresses, Head Ties, and Turbans

The top part of the Tày crown seen in Fig. 69 and Fig. 70 is similar to other Tày crowns, which are usually decorated with auspicious animals. On the front, there are two dragons facing the sun and two flying phoenixes looking at each other as if they are dancing (Fig. 69). In the middle, rows of Chinese characters indicating the sun, moon, the four directions, the Three Jewels—Buddha, Dharma, and Sangha—the four seasons, and the twelve Chinese zodiac animals surround the dragons and phoenixes. The back is decorated with the sun at the top, two dancing peacocks, two unicorns facing each other, and Chinese characters indicating the five elements, the Eight Trigrams, the ten Celestial Stems (see p. 173) and the twelve zodiacal animals (Fig.

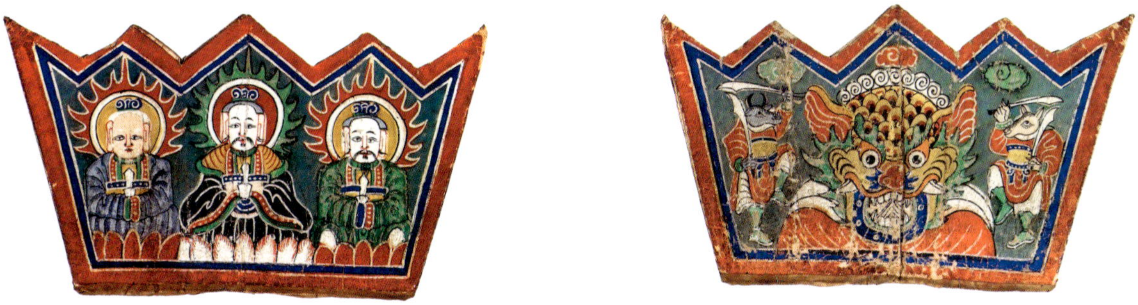

Fig. 164 (front and rear)

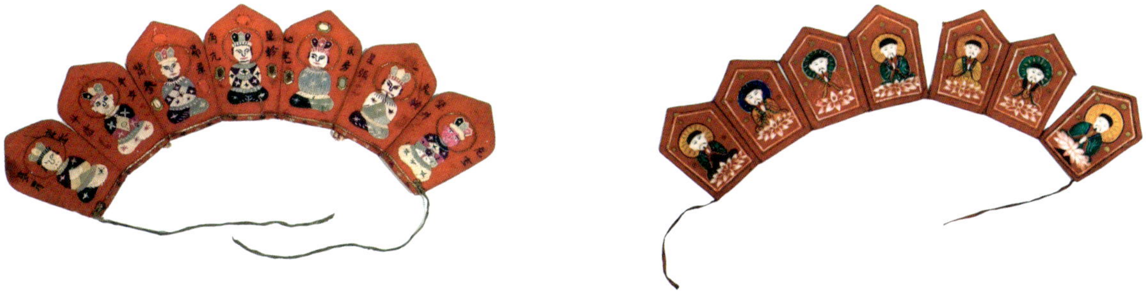

Fig. 165 (front and rear)

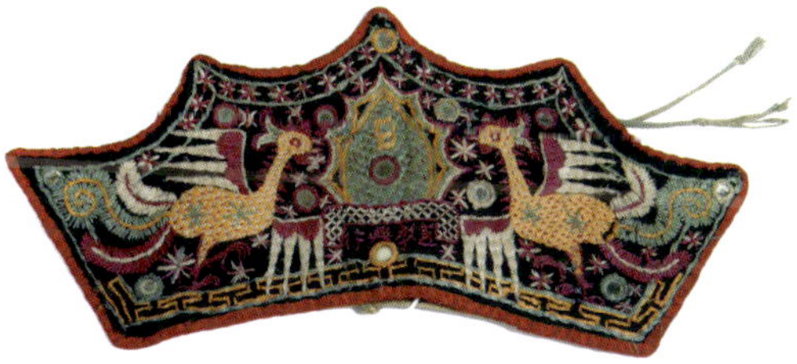

Fig. 166

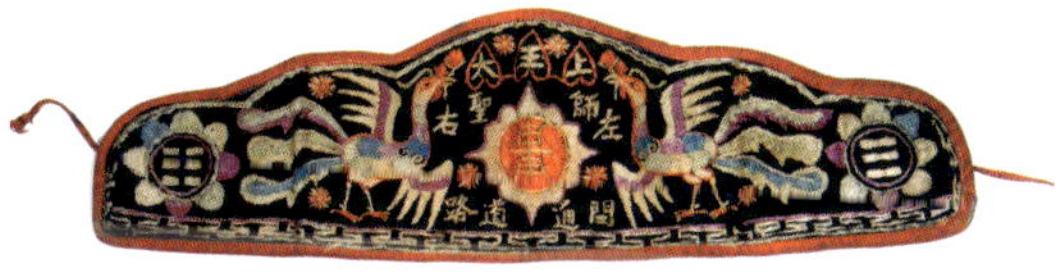

Fig. 167

Fig. 164
Ritual crown, c. mid-20th century
Tight Trouser (Quần Chẹt) Yao, Vietnam

Fig. 165
Ritual crown, c. early to mid-20th century
Tày, Vietnam

Fig. 166
Ritual hat, c. early–mid-20th century
Nùng, Vietnam

Fig. 167
Ritual hat, c. early–mid-20th century
Nùng, Vietnam

70). Below the crown hang long colorful bands of fabric divided into five levels, each being one of the five auspicious colors—blue, red, yellow, white, and black—in the Chinese tradition. Some crowns are square in shape and decorated with a stylized lotus flower at the center, with propitious symbols on the rims (Figs. 71–74) and colorful streamers embroidered with various stylized flowers.

In the Coin subgroup of the Yao, the shaman wears around his neck a pair of triangular pendants with numerous fabric streamers joined to the crown (Figs. 168, 169). Other headbands for this group are made of various cotton streamers. Long banners and streamers have been popular in Chinese Buddhist tradition dating back to the Tang dynasty. They were often employed in the ritual of guiding the souls of the recent dead into Buddha Amitābha's Pure Land.[21]

Skirts, Belts, and Leggings

Before wearing a dragon robe outside for a formal ritual, the high shaman priest must don leggings (Figs. 172, 173), a female skirt (Fig. 171), and a long robe (Fig. 170). These outfits are simple, either plain (Fig. 170), or with a modest amount of embroidery along the bottom (Fig. 171). The tunic is for daily wear and resembles a woman's garment, with extensive embroidery of traditional patterns and symbols on the lower parts of the front, back, and the ends of the sleeves. According to Lý Hành Sơn's *The Main Ceremonies and Rituals in the Life of the Coin Yao in Ba Bể, Bắc Kạn*, the female skirt must be made by the postulant's mother when he receives the ritual initiation, or by women who are beyond childbearing age. Women who still menstruate must not make the skirt, or it could cause serious problems during the ritual.[22]

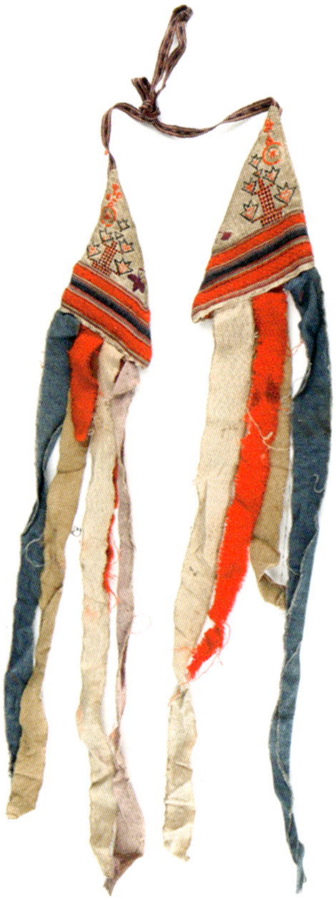

Fig. 168

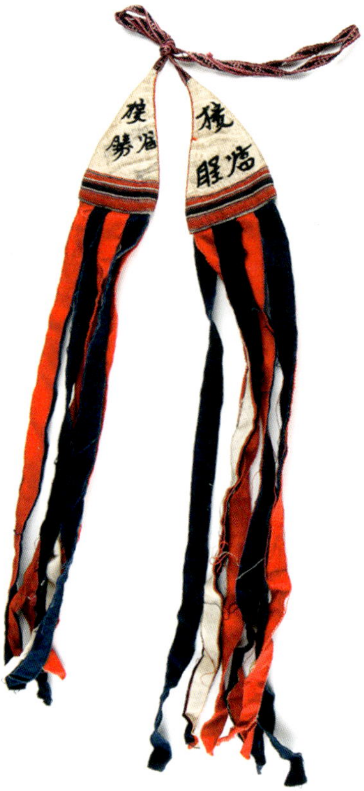

Fig. 169

Figs. 168, 169
Head ties, c. early–mid-20th century
Coin (Tiền) Yao, Vietnam

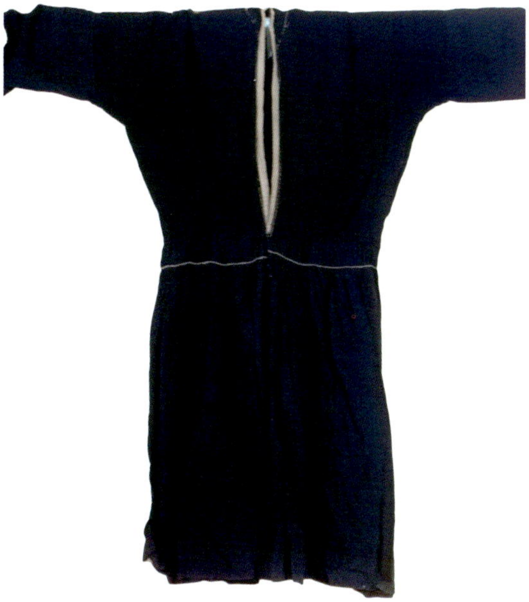

Fig. 170

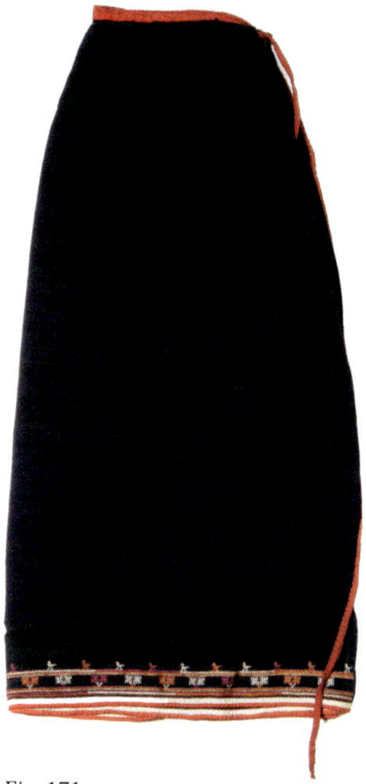

Fig. 171

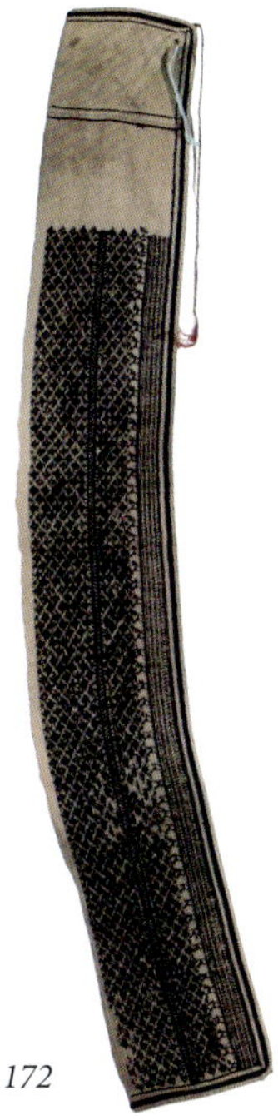

Fig. 172

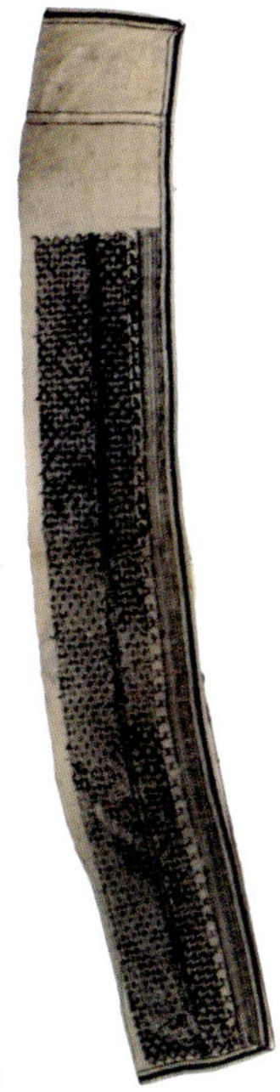

Fig. 173

Buddhist Items Adopted by Shamans

As previously noted, Tày shaman priests and priestesses adopted many Buddhist items for ritual and ceremonial use. Besides paintings depicting the Buddha, bodhisattvas, and the Ten Kings of the Underworld, they also appropriated a number of items required for the fully ordained Buddhist monk. Some outstanding objects in the collection are the following:

A Shaman's Stole

This is a priest's rectangular stole, made of various pieces of cloth sewn together in a patchwork fashion (Fig. 66). Worn outside a formal robe and wrapped over one shoulder, it is usually fastened with a cord and a ring on the left side of the chest, or with two long strings. This garment was closely modeled after the formal robe or cassock worn by a fully ordained monk in Mahayana Buddhist countries (China, Korea, Japan, and Vietnam). The Sanskrit word for this kind of a robe is *kaṣāya*, meaning it is decayed, impure in color, or dyed from primary colors. In Buddhism, the traditional *kaṣāya* usually has twenty-five pieces of cloth patched together with a large hem. A high-ranking monk's robe is sometimes adorned with Buddhist deities or auspicious symbols.[23] In Buddhist tradition, these prominent patterns are reminiscent of an Asian rice field, which symbolizes the monks' virtues.

Fig. 170
Robe, c. mid-20th century
Coin (Tiền) Yao, Vietnam

Fig. 171
Skirt, c. early–mid-20th century
Tight Trouser (Quần Chẹt) Yao, Vietnam

Fig. 172
Legging, c. early 20th century
Coin (Tiền) Yao, Vietnam

Fig. 173
Legging, c. early 20th century
Coin (Tiền) Yao, Vietnam

This rare textile comes from the Sán Chay community of Simacai district, Lào Cai province, Vietnam. This mountainous region is located near the southern border of Yunnan province in China, and is dominated by several ethnic minority peoples: the Tày, Nùng, Hmong, and Yao. The stole has six rows of horizontal and vertical patchwork, for a total of thirty-six square pieces. Each piece is embroidered with a stylized image of a Buddha or a bodhisattva seated on a lotus. The stole remains artistically and spiritually interesting for its mixture of Buddhist and Daoist elements; particularly the two central squares in the second row, which feature the image of Mañjuśrī, the bodhisattva of transcendent wisdom, riding on a blue lion; and the image of Samantabhadra, the Mahayana bodhisattva, who symbolizes practice and action, riding a white elephant. To make it a true Daoist priest's stole, two long patches of triangular cloth adorned with flying dragons facing the center, similar to those on the dragon robes, were added between the two outer columns on each side. Note the Eight Trigrams sewn along the bottom row. Since the Yao priests did not employ Buddhist deities or symbols in their ritual items, this stole is from the Sán Chay ethnic group.

Sitting Cloth or Ritual Cape

Another Buddhist item adopted by Tày shamans for ceremonial purposes is a large square embroidered textile (Fig. 174). For the fully ordained Buddhist monk, the ritual cape (坐 具), one of six required items, is used for sitting meditation or for spreading prostrate in front of Buddhist stupas or statues of the Buddha. For a Tày shaman, it is used as a cape, with two long strings tied around the shoulders.

This ritual sitting cloth or cape is a sacred item for a high priest. To integrate Daoist elements, the designer embroidered Daoist auspicious animals, symbols, and phrases. Pairs of dragons and phoenixes circle the sun in the center. The two upper corners are embellished with flying cranes, while the two lower corners portray turtles carrying sacred swords and boxes with the auspicious swastika. Symmetrically

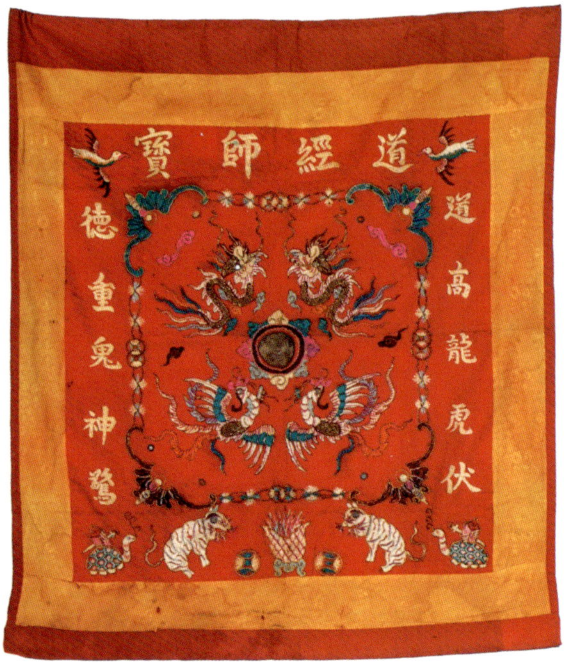

Fig. 174

at the bottom are two white-striped tigers facing an incense burner and two ancient coins. These four providential animals—azure dragon, white tiger, vermilion phoenix, and black turtle—are often used as emblems on Daoist sacred items. Around the four central animals is a square-shaped ring with four stylized bats at the corners joined by ancient coins and flowers. In the Chinese word for bat (蝙蝠, *biển bức*), the second character is pronounced the same as the word *fu* (福), which means "good fortune and happiness." Therefore, the bat frequently appears in Chinese traditional designs as a symbol for these. The red color, which signifies happiness and good fortune, provides the backdrop for the auspicious animals that decorate the cloth.

The fabric is inscribed with four Chinese characters at the top, 道 經 師 寶 (*Đạo kinh sư bảo*), which can be interpreted in two ways. One is to read the characters using the fourth one as a common suffix. In this case, they symbolize the Three Jewels: 道 寶 (Đạo Bảo), the Jewel of the Dao, referring to Daoism; 經 寶 (Kinh Bảo), the Jewel of Teaching, referring to the Daoist scripture; and 師 寶 (Sư Bảo),

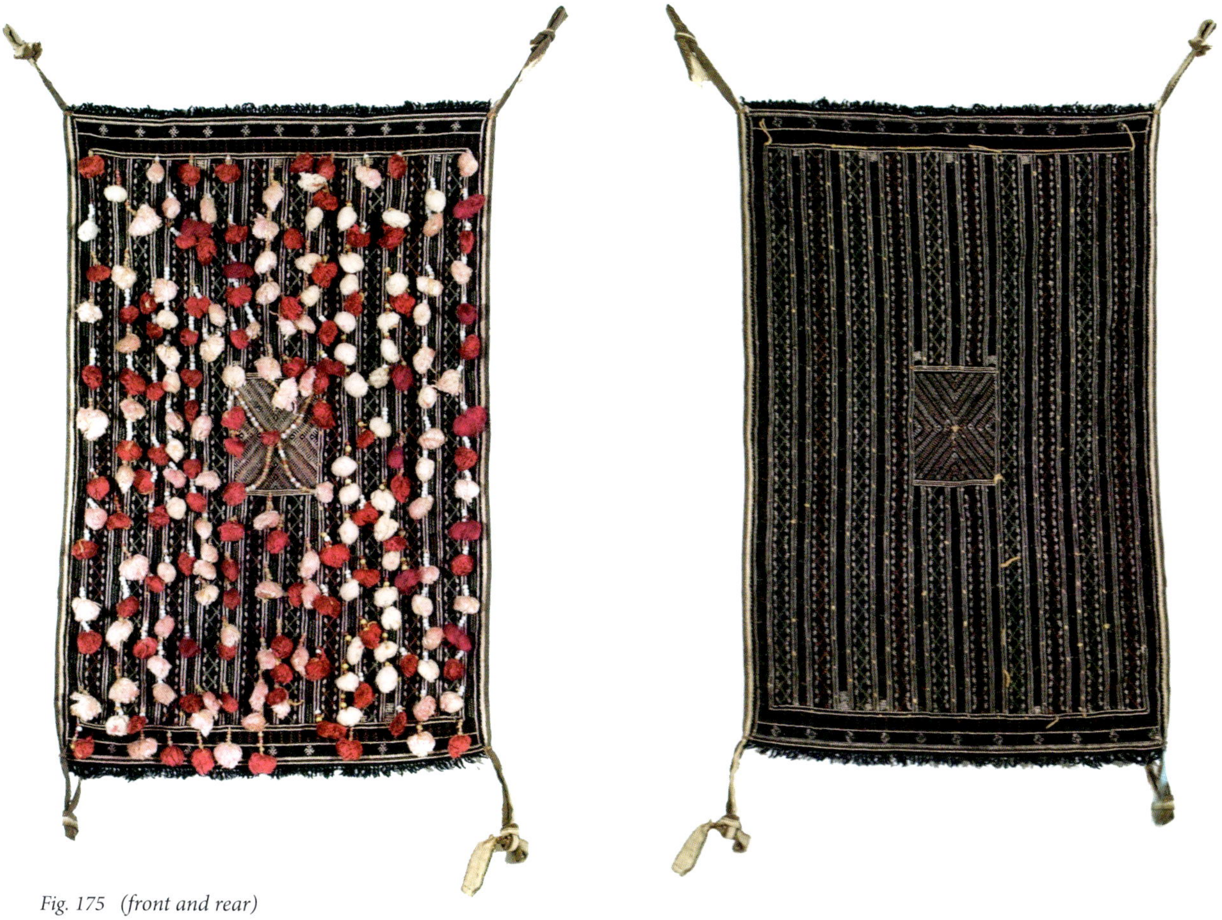

Fig. 175 (front and rear)

the Jewel of the Master, referring to Daoist priests. (Clearly, this was modeled after the Buddhist Three Jewels). In the second interpretation, it signifies that this is the sacred platform for the high Daoist master to perform the ritual.

The high priest's greatness is implied in the two inscribed phrases along the sides. First, he should have great magic powers to subdue the tiger and dragon, as stated in the five characters embroidered on the right: 道 高 龍 虎 伏 (*Đạo cao long hổ phục*). Second, he must be endowed with great virtues that enable him to frighten evil spirits and demons away, as indicated by the five characters embroidered on the left: 德 重 鬼 神 驚 (*Đức trọng quỷ thần kinh*). These two phrases often refer to powerful, virtuous Daoist shaman priests, but they can also be applied to highly venerable Buddhist monks in the Chinese and Vietnamese traditions.

Embroidered Headcloth (*Pa*) or Ritual Cape

Another type of ritual cape in the collection is a headcloth. This example (Fig. 175) is a beautifully embroidered *pa*, a type of headgear used only on the occasion of a Yao bride's wedding. On the wedding day the bride must put a wooden frame, called a *gong*, on her head. Then a mature woman must help her cover the *gong* with a red cloth. Finally, a *pa* is laid on top of the *gong*.[24] The *pa* is usually rectangular in shape and has a rectangle or square at the center decorated with a star motif, symbolized by an X form, and is also bordered by rows of similar motifs, known in the Yao language as *diem muoi*, seen

Fig. 174
Cape and banner, c. late 19th–early 20th century
Tày, Vietnam

Fig. 175
Headcloth, c. mid-20th century
Tight Trouser (Quần Chẹt) Yao, Vietnam

on the front side. This schematized design is derived from the dragon robe. On the back side, the woven patterns are skillfully tied together, forming red and white knots like beads or tufts of cloth. Because it is a bride's special outfit, it is adorned with auspicious motifs signifying stars and constellations. Later, the embroidered headdress might be used as a part of ritual outfit. For example, the *pa* is used in case the shaman priest does not possess an outfit similar to the ritual cape.

According to Phan Ngọc Khuê, these two shamanic ritual garments, the stole and the cape, are used during ceremonies such as praying for the well-being of others, safe journeys, funeral services, and exorcising bad spirits.[25] Although they have been adapted from the outfits of Buddhist monks, they have been thoroughly transformed into Daoist ritual costumes.

Conclusion

The concepts of the Daoist cosmos are manifested clearly in the imagery embroidered on dragon robes in particular, and present on other ritual items in general. The whole decorative program, including Daoist cosmic symbols—the sun and moon, the Great Net Heaven, stars, sacred animals and mountains, the Eight Trigrams, the Daoist yin-yang symbol—and the important members of the Daoist pantheon—the Three Pure Ones, the Two Celestial Masters, the Four Celestial Marshals, and the immortals—all are saturated with religious significance. In addition, they draw influence from imperial court costumes and the Chinese graphic design tradition.

Besides the Yao, the ritual outfits from the Tày, Nùng, Sán Dìu, and Sán Chay peoples also display cultural richness and colorful religious diversity. Not being bound to Daoist ritual principles, the priests and priestesses from other groups openly adopt the traditional Buddhist outfits used by monks and liberally incorporate important members of the Buddhist pantheon, as well as Buddhist symbols such as the swastika and the lotus flower, to decorate their outfits.

When the shamans wear these outfits, they meditate on the unification of the physical and the spiritual into a being that is sacred, endowed with magical powers, and able to command universal forces. When wearing these ritual outfits and equipped with other ceremonial instruments, they are believed to be the representatives of the Jade Emperor on earth, able to call upon the supreme deities and utilize their own spiritual forces in order to carry out their spiritual work. As true shamans, they are thought to possess the ability to cure the sick, pray for the well-being of others, and guide the souls of the dead to heaven. Mottoes embroidered on robes and other ritual items remind them to cultivate virtues and observe religious principles so that their work can successfully be actualized.

NOTES

1. Lý Sài Văn, a member of the Red Yao of Ta Phin, in Sapa, Lào Cai, a province of the mountainous northwest region of Vietnam that borders Yunnan, China, tells the legend. I have revised it with information from other sources. See Võ Mai Phương and Clair Burkert, *Our Craft Traditions: A Yao Community in Sapa, Vietnam* (Hanoi: Vietnam Museum of Ethnology, 2001), p. 64. See also Lý Hành Sơn, pp. 108–109. In this work the author also gives several reasons why the shaman priests must wear women's garments.

2. There are three stories told by three different Yao men from Ta Phin, Sapa. See Võ Mai Phương and Clair Burkert, pp. 64–65.

3. Stephen Little, *Taoism and the Arts of China*, p. 195.

4. For a brief discussion about the legend and symbolic meaning of "Carp Leap over Dragon Gate," see Anne Birell, *Chinese Mythology: An Introduction* (Baltimore: Johns Hopkins University Press, 1993), p. 242.

5. Jean C. Cooper, *An Illustrated Introduction to Taoism: The Wisdom of the Sages* (Bloomington, Indiana: World Wisdom, 2010), pp. 97–98.

6. Some dyeing techniques were observed and remarked on by Barry Kitnick, owner of the Kitnick Collection.

7. For discussion of Yao costumes and ritual garments, see Nguyễn Khắc Tụng and Nguyễn Anh Cường, *Trang phục cổ truyền của người Dao ở Việt Nam* [The Yao Traditional Costumes in Vietnam] (Hanoi: Social Sciences Publishing House, 2004). For some good examples of the ritual garments of Yao shamans, see pictures 13, 14, 15, 17, 27, 56, 57, and 142.

8. Stephen Little, *Taoism and the Arts of China*, p. 249. See also cat. 79 on the same page, and cat. 12 and 13, which illustrate and describe the names and functions of the gods of the Twenty-Eight Lunar Mansions, pp. 132–137.

9. Ibid., 137.

10. Ibid., 147.

11. Shih-Shan Susan Huang, *Picturing the True Form: Daoist Visual Culture in Traditional China* (Cambridge: Harvard University Asia Center, 2012), p. 133.

12. Mount Wudang (武 當 山,Wudang Shan), located in the northwestern part of Hubei province. Mount Wudang is known for its many famous Daoist monasteries and has been established as an academic center for learning and practicing meditation, Daoist Chinese martial arts (Taiji), traditional Chinese medicine, and other related arts of Daoism. It is additionally one of the earliest cradles of Daoism, established in the Eastern Han Dynasty (25–220 CE), was strongly supported by subsequent emperors, and is still very active today.

13. Mount Heming, or the Crane Chirping Mountain (鶴 鳴 山), located in Dayi County, Sichuan province. According to legend, the immortal Master Zhang Daoling ascended to heaven riding a crane from this mountain. Because of this, Mount Heming is considered one of the first ancestral sites of the Daoist Celestial Master.

14. Mount Dragon Tiger (龍 虎 山, Longhu Shan), located in Jiangxi province. This mountain is known as one of the birthplaces of Daoism. The Daoist movement known as the Way of Orthodox Unity emerged during the Tang Dynasty, with its leader, known as the Celestial Master (and often associated with Celestial Master Zhang), being closely tied to this mountain. Moreover, the mountain and its surrounding landscape were the backdrop of the well-known Chinese novel *Water Margin* (水 滸 傳), considered one of the Four Great Classical Novels in Chinese literature.

15. Mount Yujing (玉 京 山, Yujing Shan) is one of the three lofty peaks of Mount Sanqingshan (三 清 山), or the Three Pure Ones Mountain, located in the north of Yushan County, Jiangxi province. Because of its marvelous landscape, beautiful lakes, magnificent waterfalls, rare plants and animals, and natural phenomena that seem beyond the earthly world, it is considered a dwelling place of the Daoist immortals and an ideal place to practice Daoism.

16. The Kunlun Mountains (崑 崙 山), one of the longest mountain chains in Asia, is the fourth sacred place. Many mountain peaks of the Kunlun are considered sacred and mythical locations, connected with numerous Chinese legends and myths, and believed to be a Daoist paradise. According to the legend, King Mu (976–922 BCE) of the Zhou dynasty discovered the Jade Palace of Huang-Di (the Jade Emperor) here. Other myths say that the Yellow Emperor, originator of Chinese culture, and Xi

Wang Mu, Queen Mother of the West and subject of an ancient religious cult that reached its peak in the Han dynasty, dwelled in these mountains.

17. For further examples, see Nguyễn Khắc Tụng and Nguyễn Anh Cường, pp. 193, 201, and 231. See also Jess G. Pourret, plates 554 and 555.

18. See Jess G. Pourret, plate 554, p. 202, for a good example; see also a similar example illustrated in Nguyễn Khắc Tụng and Nguyễn Anh Cường, pp. 180, 193, and 231.

19. The stellar deities include the five planets, the sun, and the moon. According to the Daoist astrological system, the five planets are the Year Star (Jupiter), the Sparkling Deluder (Mars), the Grand White Star (Venus), the Chronographic Star (Mercury), and the Quelling Star (Saturn). Daoism worships the deities of the seven stars as the Stellar Sovereigns.

20. The Seven Buddhas of the Past are: Vipasyin, Sikhin, Visvabhu, Krakucchanda, Kanakamuni, Kasyapa, and Sakyamuni. According to the Buddhist sutras, there are six Buddhas who lived prior to the historical Buddha Sakyamuni. See William Edward Soothill and Lewis Hodous, *A Dictionary of Chinese Buddhist Terms* (Delhi: Motilal Banarsidass, 1977), p. 10.

21. For discussion of the origins and use of the Buddhist banners, see Money L. Hickman, "Notes on Buddhist Banners," in *Boston Museum Bulletin* 71, no. 363 (1973), pp. 4–20. For illustrations, see Zhang Webin, ed., *Dunhuang: A Centennial Commemoration of the Discovery of the Cave Library* (Beijing: Morning Glory, 2000), pp. 73, 110, 116, 134, and 135.

22. Lý Hành Sơn, p. 109.

23. For discussion of Buddhist robes, and two illustrated examples from the fourteenth century, see Helmut Brinker and Hiroshi Kanazawa, *Zen: Masters of Meditation in Images and Writings* (Zurich: Artibus Asiae, 1996), pp. 268–269. For paintings of monks wearing robes, see Brinker, pp. 258–259. See also Robert Fisher, *Buddhist Art and Architecture* (New York: Thames and Hudson, 1993), plate 108, p. 122, for one of the best paintings, dating to the thirteenth century, depicting a high-ranking Chan monk wearing the formal robe embellished with auspicious motifs.

24. For further discussion and examples of the *pa* used in the Yao wedding ceremony, see Võ Mai Phương and Clair Burkert, pp. 40–45. See also Vũ Quốc Khanh, pp. 148, 152, 156, 158, and 160–161.

25. Author interview with Phan Ngọc Khuê in Hanoi, June 2013.

Fig. 176
Ritual Hat, c. early 20th century
Tày, Vietnam

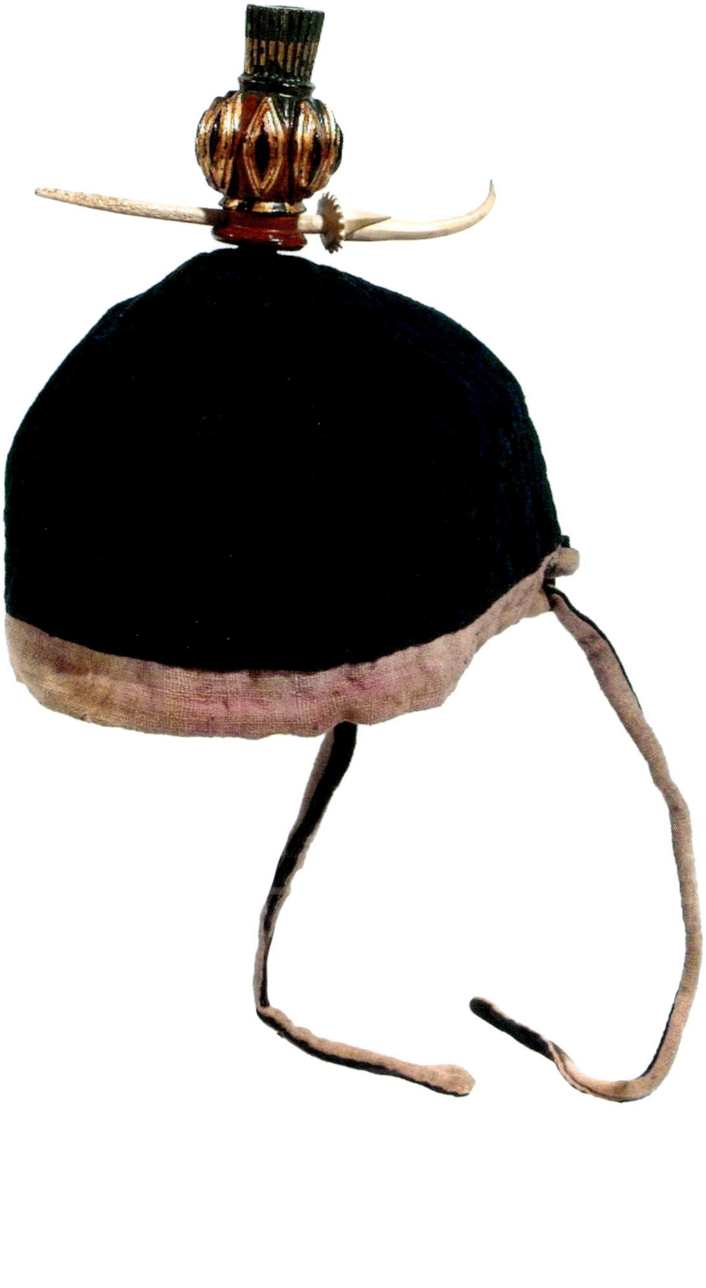

Fig. 176

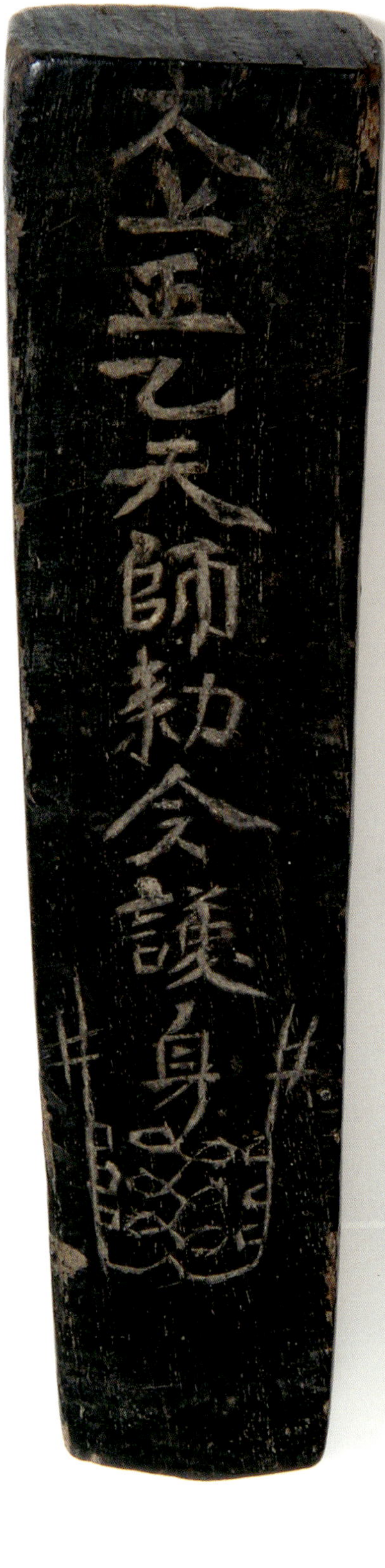

Fig. 177

RITUAL INSTRUMENTS:
Sealed Approval of the Heavenly Work on Earth

To conduct rituals and ceremonies, shaman priests and priestesses must possess a large number of ritual objects. Generally speaking, Daoist priests among the Yao, Tày, and Sán Dìu in southern China and the mountainous regions of northern Vietnam possess their own ritual instruments, including court tablets, ritual swords and daggers, rattles, seals, printing and yin-yang divination blocks, masks, and musical instruments.[1]

These items are used to summon spirit soldiers, to ward off evil forces, and to stamp inscriptions on memorials and petitions. They are often inscribed with the priests' names, but also embody a close relationship with the Daoist gods. Some are carved with the names of supreme deities such as the Jade Emperor or the Five Thunder Deities. Others, such as musical instruments, are employed for both religious services and cultural festivals. Ritual objects made for a shaman priest to use during his lifetime are supposed to be burned or desacralized on the shaman's death, so that spirits and magical powers cannot dwell within them.

Court Scepters and Power Sticks

A ceremonial scepter, known as a *kuei* (珪) in Chinese, is a decorated item symbolizing high authority and supreme power (Figs. 177–179, 180–182). Thus in Yao ritual paintings, the Jade Emperor, the Master of the Saints, the Officials of the Four Realms, the Ten Kings of the Underworld, and many other deities associated with authority are all depicted holding court scepters.

In practice Daoist high priests, among the Yao and other ethnic peoples, often possess several of them. These objects represent the powers of various divinities that have bestowed their magical authority upon the priests when they were ordained into the Daoist path. Many objects in the collection exemplify this concept. Several tablets are inscribed with the words "Commanding order by the Jade Emperor," or "Commanding authority given by the Five Thunder Deities." The commanding order confers power to the priests who, on the behalf of a deity, can destroy evil spirits and exorcise demons. Thus, when a Daoist priest or priestess holds the ceremonial tablet, they represent the deity and its authority. They can issue orders, invoke the gods, and command their spirit soldiers to fend off evil spirits and protect the altar.

Court scepters are always made of high-quality wood, finely carved and inscribed with Chinese characters. The Kitnick Collection has more than a dozen examples; some are hand-carved pieces that are inscribed with names of the Daoist deities and the commanding orders. For example, a four-sided Tày court scepter (Fig. 178) is engraved with divine commands. The two main sides state that "By the order of the Jade Emperor a person who holds this scepter has the authority to kill and destroy evil

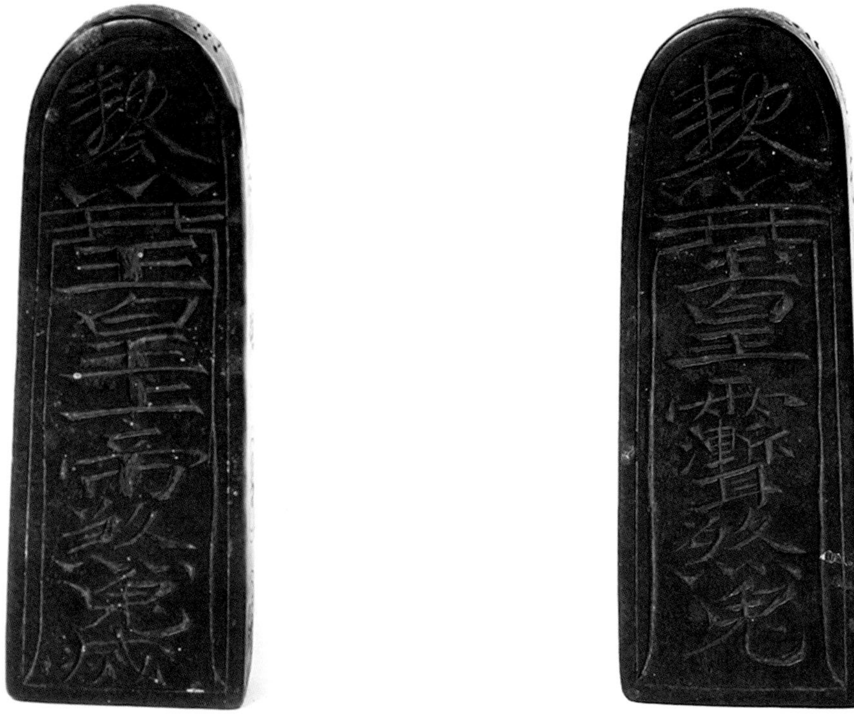

Fig. 178 (front and back)

(勅 玉 皇 上 帝 煞 鬼 威, Fig. 178), (勅 玉 皇 斬 煞 鬼). One small side states that this is the Origin's Talisman (元 始 符 令; the Origin is the title of the Jade Pure One, discussed in the chapter on the three basic scrolls), empowered with the authority of the Four Celestial Marshals—Deng, Zhao, Ma, and Guan (鄧 趙 馬 關)—for the shaman priest to use in ceremonial ritual. Note that in this rare case, the name of Celestial Marshal Guan appears with the other three popular marshals. Briefly, Marshal Guan is Guan Yu (d. 220 CE), a historical figure, a famous general serving under the warlord Liu Bei of the late Eastern Han Dynasty in the Three Kingdoms period. Guan was deified in the early Sui dynasty, and is regarded as the God of War and leading subduer of demons in Daoism. He was popularized by the Chinese masterpiece of historical literature *Romance of the Three Kingdoms*.

Another Tày scepter (Fig. 177) is a modest piece of wood, painted black and inscribed with ten characters, 太 上 正 乙 天 師 勅 令 護 身, meaning the Supreme Heavenly Master empowered this court tablet as a self-protection talisman. One Yao *kuei* scepter (Fig. 179) is beautifully carved with a dragon and a tiger in the middle section of the main sides and sacred symbols in the middle of the smaller sides. These two animals symbolize yin and yang respectively, the two cosmic forces and vital energies that make up and transform all things, representing fire and water, the most powerful ingredients in Daoist inner alchemy tradition.[2] One side is carved with the characters 五 雷 號 令, meaning by "the order of the Five Thunder Deities." The other side is engraved with seven Chinese characters, 玉 皇 上 帝 玄 門 令, meaning that this scepter is empowered with "the Jade Emperor's mysterious power." Several ceremonial scepters are engraved with the

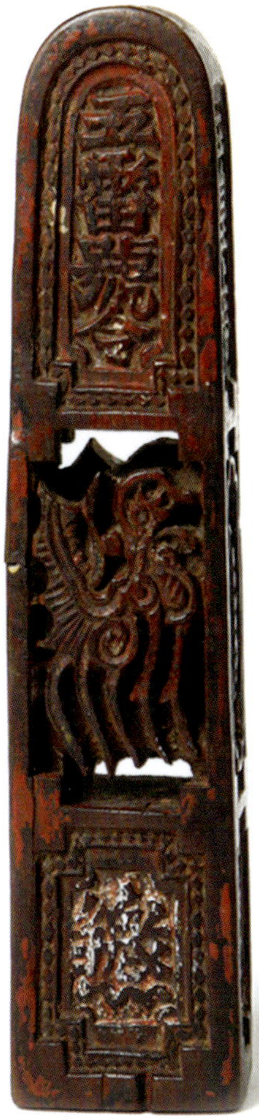

Fig. 179

Fig. 177
Ritual scepter, c. late 19th–early 20th century
Wood, 7 5/8 in.
Tày, Vietnam

Fig. 178
Ritual scepter, c. late 19th century
Tày, Vietnam

Fig. 179
Ritual scepter, c. late 19th century
Yao, China or Vietnam

ten Celestial Stems (干支, *tiengan*; 甲 乙 丙 丁 戊 己 庚 辛 壬 癸, *jia yi bing ding wu ji geng xin ren gui*) on the left edge, and the Earthly Branches, represented by the twelve-animal zodiac (子 丑 寅 卯 辰 巳 午 未 申 酉 戌 亥, rat, ox, tiger, rabbit, dragon, snake, horse, goat, monkey, rooster, dog, and pig), on the right. (The Celestial Stems and Earthly Branches are astronomically based numbering systems that combine to produce a sixty-year calendar cycle.) The top is inscribed with the characters of the Three Pure Ones (太 玉 上 清), and the bottom with the Chinese character 心 (*xin*) (Figs. 180, 181). This character represents the source of all mental activity, that which controls all thinking and calculating. In Chinese astrology, it is believed that a person reflects the characteristics of their zodiacal animal.[3] However, fateful aspects can be changed through mental determination, signified by this character. In addition, a high Daoist shaman with endowed magic powers can pray to the Three Pure Ones to change a person's fate.

Special scepters (Figs. 182, 183), as used by high Tày shaman priests, present different functions. The main engravings on these scepters are talismans (符 籙, or *fulu*), which are thought to be endowed with supreme magic powers, including curing illnesses, reversing curses, subduing negative forces, and absorbing universal energy for the practitioner.[4] As Shawn Eichman writes: "Talismans were believed to be sacred images that mirrored the forms of the primordial energies at the inception of the world."[5] These talismans are used to summon or give instructions to Daoist deities and other spirits, and act as magical devices for exorcisms. In addition to the various kinds of talismans, these scepters are also engraved with characters of the sun, the moon, and the five elements (metal, wood, water, fire, and earth), which are part of Daoist astrology. The high

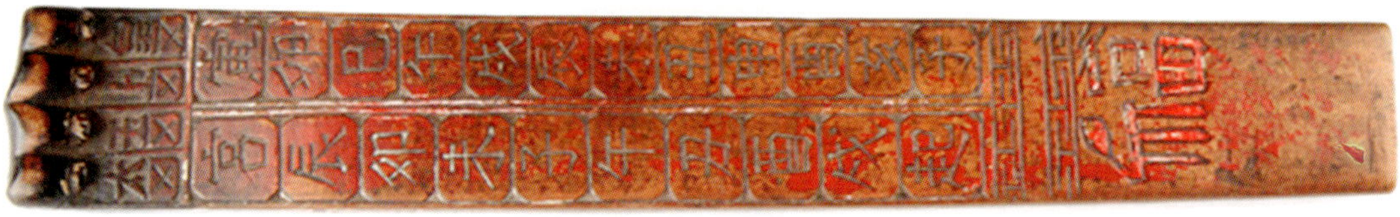

Fig. 180

Fig. 181

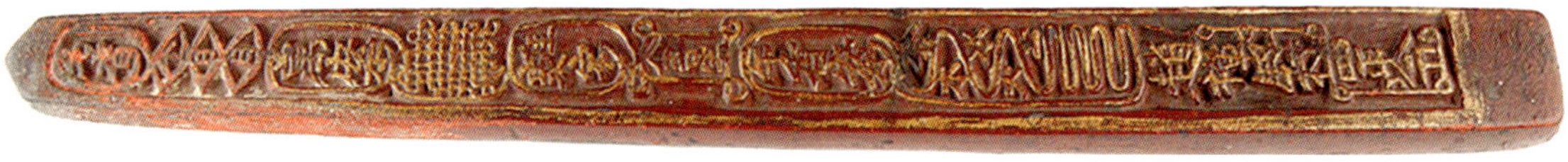

Fig. 182

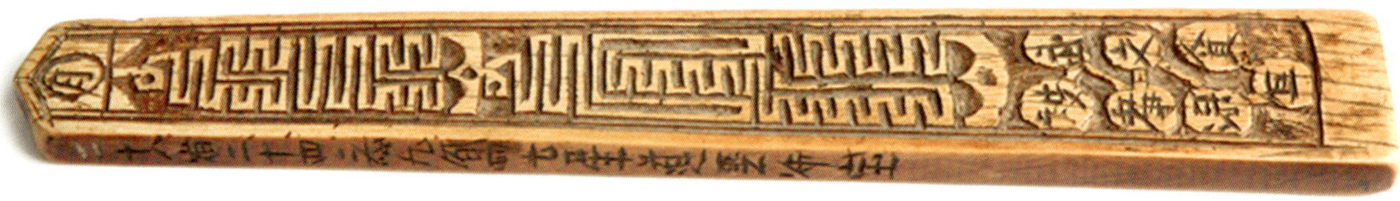

Fig. 183

priests are able to draw these talismans either in the air with holy water or on the ground with their scepters. Since these scepters once belonged to high shaman priests, they are inscribed with their names. One Tày scepter (Fig. 183) bears an inscription on both narrow sides saying that shaman Triệu Pháp Tiến (趙 法 進) had it made when he was twenty-eight years old, the year he was ordained with the Seven-Star Hanging Light Ritual.

The Kitnick Collection has three Yao power sticks made from polychromed wood (Figs. 89, 90). All three feature a major Daoist deity painted beautifully at the center, wearing formal court clothing and holding a court scepter in his hands. The lower section is painted with a dragon whose tail encircles the tablet from the back to the front side. Compared with ritual scepters, power sticks are slender and without any inscriptional carving. At an important point during Hanging Light Rituals, the high shaman holds a power stick to help the initiate visit Daoist heaven during his cataleptic trance.

Though the court scepters and power sticks are only a small part of the collection, they represent creative and spiritually important aspects of the Daoist shaman culture in Vietnam. Artistically, they vary from simple, unadorned scepters inscribed with commanding orders and religious functions to intricately carved ones that include auspicious animals, supernatural talismans, and beautifully painted Daoist deities. Significant deities are also inscribed on the scepters, along with their spiritual powers, which are bestowed upon the priests for self-protection, exorcism of evil forces, the protection of the altar, and the promotion of people's well-being and improved fates.

Ritual Weapons—Swords, Daggers, and Staffs

Ritual swords, daggers with rattles, and staffs are essential items for Daoist shaman priests. They are used during rituals to purify and protect the sacred altar and fend off evil spirits.

Ritual Swords[6]

The Cao Làn ritual sword seen in Fig. 92 is constructed and balanced in the same way as a combat sword; however, it is a symbolic weapon that has most likely never been sharpened. It has a short wooden handle and a double-edged blade with a relatively sharp point. The lower part of the handle is laminated in bronze and bears a Chinese inscription. The top of the blade is inscribed with the names of the Three Pure Ones. Beneath this, circled with three lines, is the most important inscription, which reads, 玉 皇 敕 釼, meaning, "The sword is bestowed by the Jade Emperor."[7] In the Yao Seven-Star Hanging Light Ritual, the chief priest uses this kind of ritual sword, along with power sticks, in helping the postulant undergo a process similar to being physically dead, in order to transform his soul and body.

The attached rattle contains four bronze coins that are joined to the tip of the handle. It is believed that when a shaman priest dances with the sword, the sound of the rattle drives away demons and creates healing powers. The magic sword is the signature weapon of the Two Celestial Masters, Li and Zhang, and it is always seen in their painted scrolls.

Fig. 180
***Kuei* scepter**, c. early 20th century
Sán Dìu, Vietnam

Fig. 181
***Kuei* scepter**, c. early 20th century
Sán Dìu, Vietnam

Fig. 182
***Kuei* scepter**, c. early 20th century
Tày or Sán Chay, Vietnam

Fig. 183
***Kuei* scepter**, c. late 19th–early 20th century
Tày, Vietnam

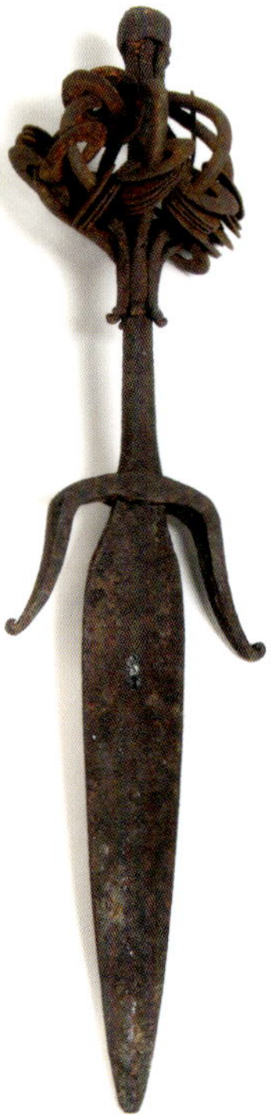

Fig. 184

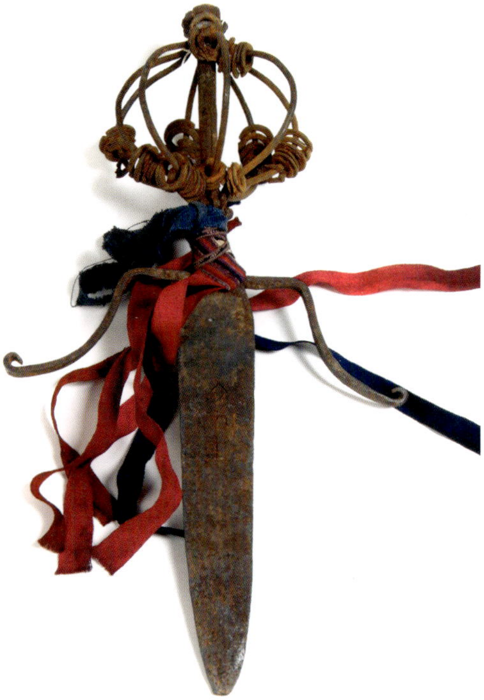

Fig. 185

Daggers with Rattles

Daggers with rattles (Figs. 184, 185) are the most common ritual weapon used by the shaman priest. They have the same religious function as swords: to fend off evil spirits when they are shaken. Each has a similar double-edged blade, but the handles vary. Some have short handles with one simple ring; others have large rings containing ancient coins or small metal circles. Several blades are engraved with Chinese characters. For example a Yao shaman's rattle (Fig. 185), a dagger bestowed by the ruler, is inscribed with three characters, 令 刀 王 (*lịnh đao vương*), meaning "The royal commanding dagger." Others have inscriptions providing the owner's name and auspicious wishes. Red and blue ribbons were tied to the handles of many of the daggers as propitious symbols to attract cosmic energy.

Staffs

In ancient China, the staff was regarded as a symbol of royal authority or military power. It was also utilized as an instrument to torture and punish criminals. In Yao Daoist rituals, staffs are used for different purposes (Figs. 80, 81).[8] When a temporary Daoist chapel is set up for an important ceremony, a Hanging Lamp Ritual for example, the chief shaman uses a *sanyuan* staff to open the main door leading to the room in the house where the ceremony is being held.[9] During the ceremony, when the postulants enter a cataleptic state, two priests hold staffs under their armpits to help them back on their feet.[10]

These staffs, made of solid wood or old bamboo, range from thirty-eight to forty-two inches long.[11] The heads are mounted with some kind of weapon—a crescent knife, a sword, or a spear—while the tips are spiked, so that they can easily penetrate the ground. The best staffs are usually made of strong bamboo, with seven or nine segments. On some the weapon on the head has been replaced with segments mounted on a round and square knob, representing heaven and earth (Fig. 81), since in ancient China it was believed that heaven was round and the earth was square.

Money Tree

The Sán Dìu ethnic minority in Vietnam often includes money trees in their funeral services. This practice is deeply rooted in ancient China, where money trees were important funeral items and were buried in the tombs of the elite during the Eastern Han dynasty (25–220 CE).[12]

The basic money tree consists of three levels formed by branches, with "leaves" that imitate ancient Chinese coins (Figs. 188, 189). The levels represent mountains that the souls of the dead must climb to reach the summit of immortality.[13] The money tree is also a symbol of rebirth and eternal life for the dead.[14] This meaning is connected with the demigod Yao, who had in his garden the miraculous Portent Plant, on which each leaf grows for fifteen days, before being shed for another to grow; thus, it was called a "calendar petal."[15] Deeply embedded with many profound meanings, the money tree is an integral component of the shaman's ritual tools.

Seals, Stamps, Printing and Divination Blocks

Seals, stamps, and printing and divination blocks are also required ritual objects that a high shaman priest must possess for religious services. These are usually made of wood, simply or intricately carved, and bear important inscriptions.

Seals Bearing Inscriptions and Talismans

The kind of seal called *yin* (印, *ấn*) usually has a square or rectangular shape. Although some are ivory or metal, most are made of wood. The upper section is sometimes plain, but most are carved with

Fig. 184
Dagger with rattle, c. early 20th century
Yao, Vietnam

Fig. 185
Dagger with rattle, c. early 20th century
Red Yao, Vietnam

Fig. 186
Jade Emperor Seal, c. late 19th–early 20th century
Sán Dìu, Vietnam

Fig. 187
Seal (Five Thunder Gods stamp), c. late 19th century or earlier
Tày, Vietnam

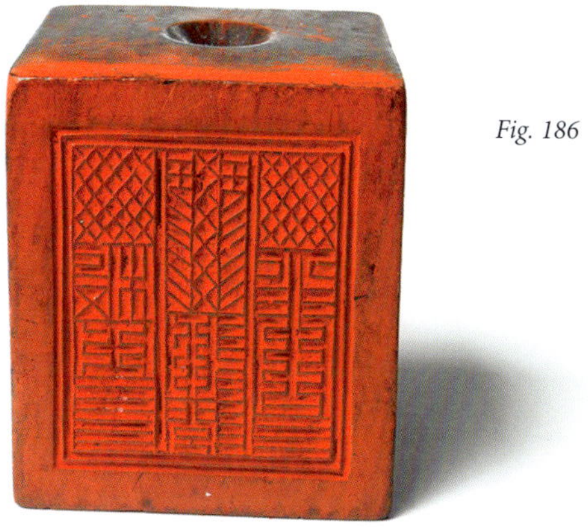

Fig. 186

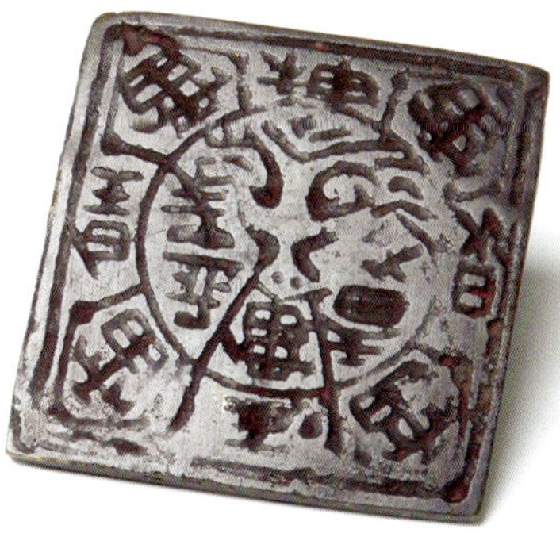

Fig. 187

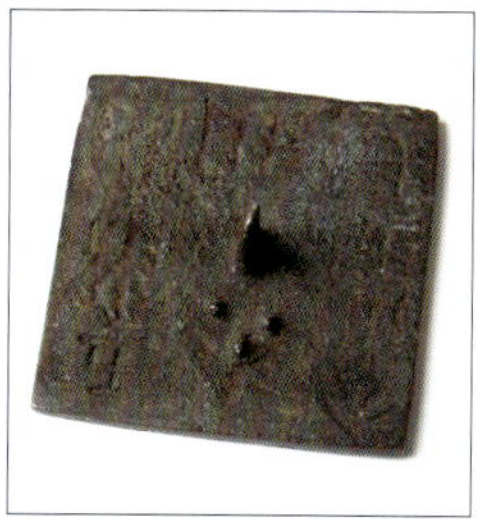

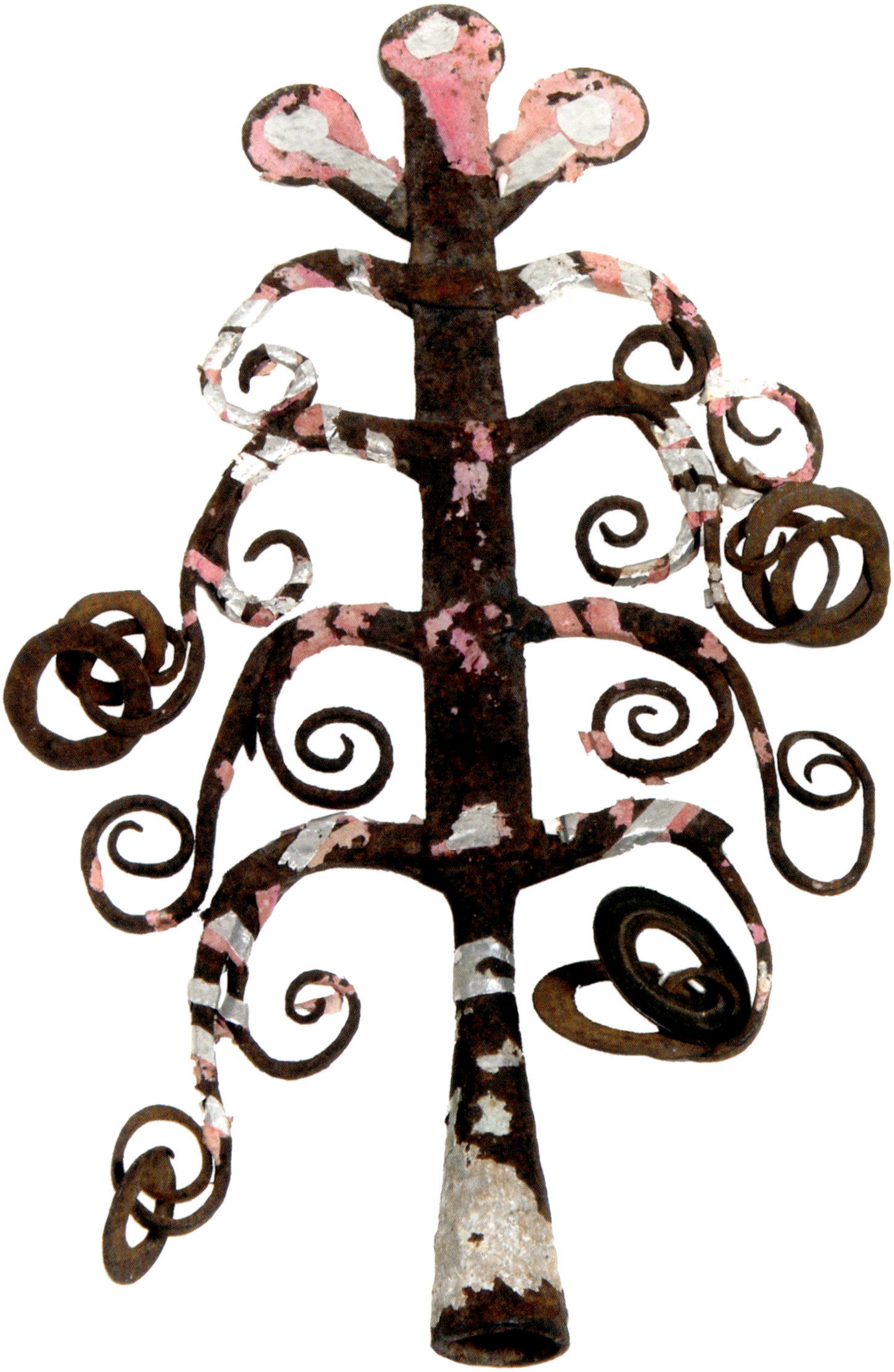

Fig. 188

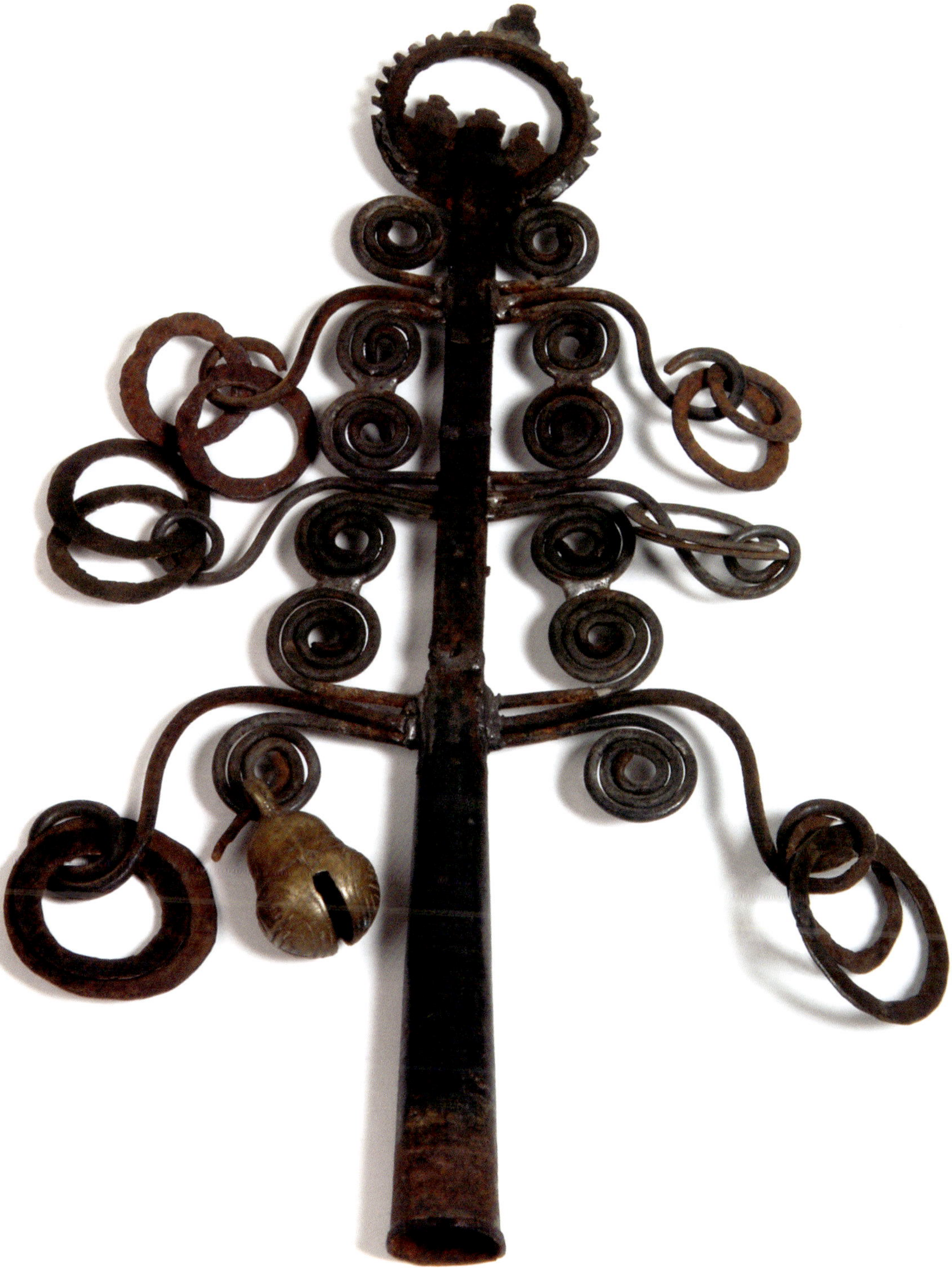

Fig. 189

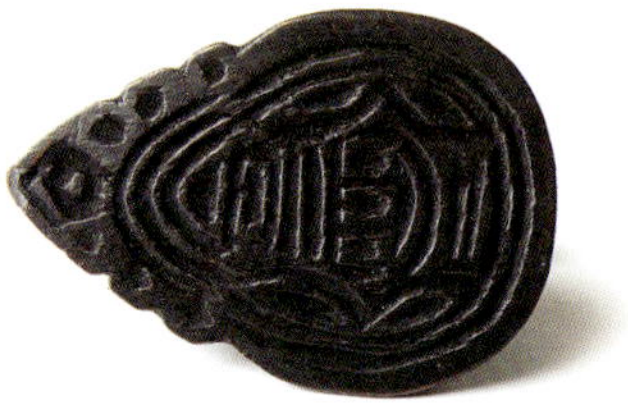

Fig. 190

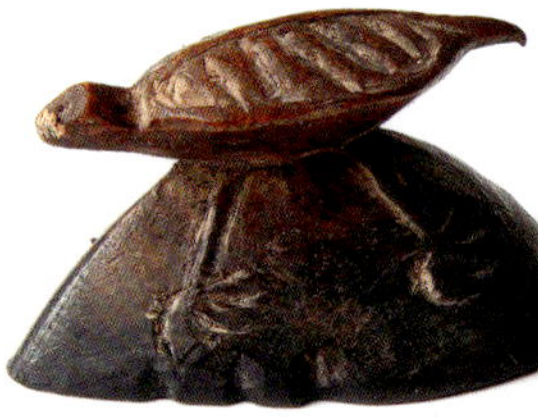

Fig. 191

Fig. 188
Money tree, c. early 20th century
Sán Dìu, Vietnam

Fig. 189
Money tree,
c. late 19th–early 20th century
Sán Dìu, Vietnam

Fig. 190
Seal, c. late 19th century
Yao, China or Vietnam

Fig. 191
Printing block, c. early–mid-20th century
Red Yao, Vietnam

Fig. 192
Pan Hu stamp,
c. late 19th–early 20th century
Nùng, Vietnam

Fig. 193
Printing block, c. early–mid-20th century
Red Yao, Vietnam

animals—a monkey, dog, or turtle—or human figures. Some are roughly carved in a stylized fashion, while others are dynamic and animated.[16]

Though the messages carved on the bases vary, the seals almost always have Daoist talismans carved on the entire surface (Figs. 46, 49, 186, 187). However, there are some seals engraved with the Chinese characters of the sun and the moon at the top, and five or six characters inscribed on the center, usually the title and names of the shaman. For example, Fig. 49 is a seal inscribed 太 上 老 君 急 勅, meaning, "By the expedited order of the Grand Supreme Elder Lord." Fig. 87 is engraved with six Chinese characters, 太 上 老 君 氣 合, connoting "The amalgamated energy of the Grand Supreme Elder Lord," which is another title of the Grand Pure One, a manifestation of Laozi, the founder of Daoism in China. Other seals are entirely engraved with the names of deities and their functions (Figs. 47, 48).

These seals are given by the high shaman masters to newly ordained postulants after their entry into the Daoist spiritual path. They keep the seals along with the paper copy of their ordination certificates, the latter being burned with them when they pass away. If the Three-Lamp Hanging Ritual postulants want to spiritually advance later through the Seven-Star Hanging Light Ritual, they stamp these seals on their petition papers to expedite messages to the gods. In practice, the high priests presiding over the rituals stamp the ordination certificates using a specific type of red ink.

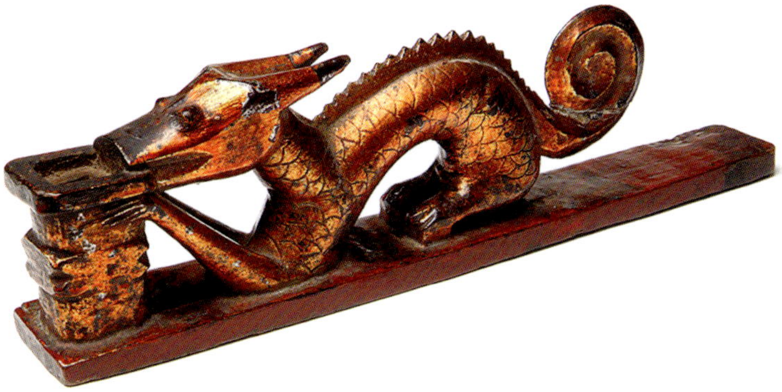

Fig. 192

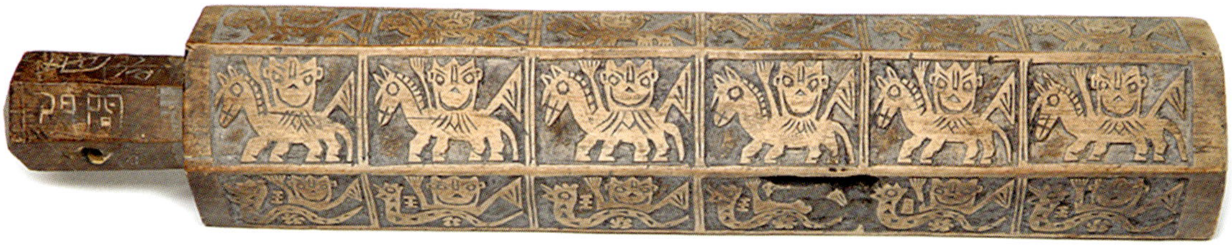

Fig. 193

Some of these seals belonged to Sán Dìu shaman priestesses (Fig. 216), or to the wives of the high shaman priests of the Yao (Fig. 190). In the latter case, the wives would receive a few seals and a small number of spirit soldiers (half as many as her husband) when their husbands underwent the Seven-Star Hanging Light Ritual.

Pan Hu Stamps

Another kind of stamp comes in the shape of an elongated rectangular panel with a thinner bottom block (Fig. 192). These seals are easy to recognize because they have a carved dragon-dog called Pan Hu (潘 護, Bàn Hộ), the first ancestor of the Yao, mounted on top. According Yao myth, the deity Pangu (盤 古) created the world, which was subsequently ruled by King Ping. King Ping had a vendetta with the king in a neighboring region. He announced that whoever could eliminate his enemy would be awarded his daughter and some land. Pan Hu then offered his assistance by turning into a dragon-dog, after which he killed the enemy king and returned with his head. Pan Hu was given the princess as his wife, and a new kingdom. She bore twelve children, and with this the twelve Yao clans were established.[17]

On some seals, the dragon-dog is roughly suggested. On others, its curving body is pronounced, as evident in the rendering of the front feet, and its mouth holds a large scroll. Its long tail curls into its body, making the legendary animal look more like a dragon than a dragon-dog. The underside of these wooden stamps is blank, with no engraving. Pan Hu stamps are used as a spiritual seal of approval; as Daoist priests recite magic formulas, they pass the seals over ritual manuals and spirit money (see next section) and spiritually "stamp" them. Most importantly, this is done at the end of the Hanging Lamp Rituals, when the legends of Pan Hu and the exodus of the Yao are sung, as an offering to the ancestors of the host family.

Printing Blocks

The priests' printing blocks, used to make spirit money, are an important part of ritual ceremonies (Figs. 191,193–195). Their main purpose is to stamp a kind of paper money in order to pay debts to the gods. Priests and their assistants spend days printing the spirit money for the upcoming ritual. It is habitually bundled, stacked, arranged in front of the altar, and, finally, burned during the ritual to dispatch messages to the gods. For example, as depicted in the scroll *Guiding the Soul*, the shaman priest must pay the Jade Emperor's treasurer when he prays to him, guiding the soul of a recently deceased person into heaven. In the complete set of paintings, images of the Local Officers (Fig. 115) and the Lords of the Four Realms (Figs. 111, 112) include a clerk carrying a big bag of money that has been submitted by a shaman.

The general term for spirit money is 進 馬 *(jinma, tiến mã)*, which literally means "tribute horse." All money-printing blocks are engraved with figures of horses, since long ago they provided the best means of transporting money. These printing blocks, made of wood, are usually from five to fifteen inches long and carved on four or six sides. The short stamps (Fig. 191) are engraved with two figures of a horse and rider on the sides. One of the smaller sides is carved with the name of the owner, Triệu, 趙 生 潙 适, the shaman priest. Another block (Fig. 194) is carved with four horses without riders on one side, and six horses on the opposite side. The Red Yao block (Fig. 195) is engraved with the Four Heavenly Messengers riding on a crane, a tiger, a horse, and a dragon, who will deliver the spirit money to the deities. The printing block of the Coin Yao subgroup (Fig. 193) is perhaps the finest among the whole

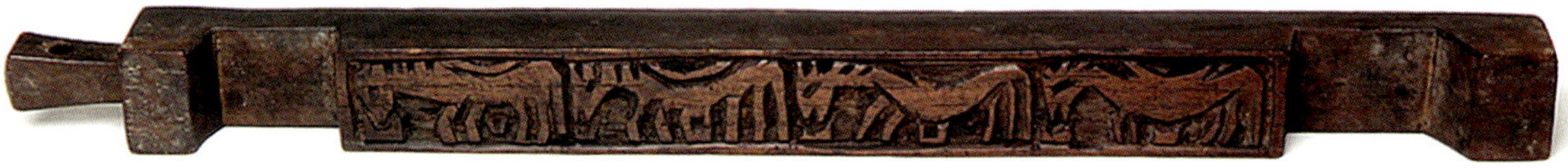

Fig. 194

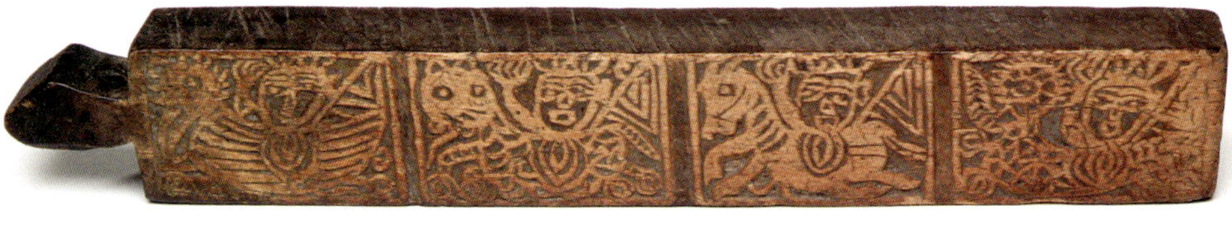

Fig. 195

group. It has six sides, three of which are engraved with a messenger riding a horse. The other sides exhibit messengers riding a crane, a tiger, and a dragon. The small handle is inscribed with Chinese characters stating that these animals are the messengers of the four realms: the messenger on a dragon belongs to the water worlds, 水 府; and the messenger riding a tiger belongs to the earthly realm, 地 府.

The carving of horses on the blocks is connected to a Yao legend recounting that the Jade Emperor came to earth on his heavenly horse in order to find his daughter, who had been kidnapped by a Yao man for his wife. The Yao patriarch honored the heavenly ruler with a big banquet but tricked him into drinking too much. When they hid his heavenly horse in the jungle, he could not return to his palace. He consequently stayed on earth to teach the Yao people, who later returned the horse. From then on, whenever the Yao make any offering to the Jade Emperor, they include spirit money with images of horses.[18]

Yin-Yang Divination Blocks

These pairs of blocks are used by priests to get answers to questions and requests (Figs. 77–79). They are carved into a rough crescent shape and made of bamboo, wood, or animal horn. Each block is round on the yin side and flat on the yang side. Before using them, the priest must purify them by holding the pair in his hand and circling them around the incense burners three times. After making a prayer or

Fig. 194
Printing block, c. early–mid-20th century
Coin (Tiền), Vietnam

Fig. 195
Printing block, c. early–mid-20th century
Red Yao, Vietnam

Fig. 196
Mask (from a set of 27), dated 1936
Yao (Mun), Vietnam

Fig. 197
Mask (from a set of 27), dated 1936
Yao (Mun), Vietnam

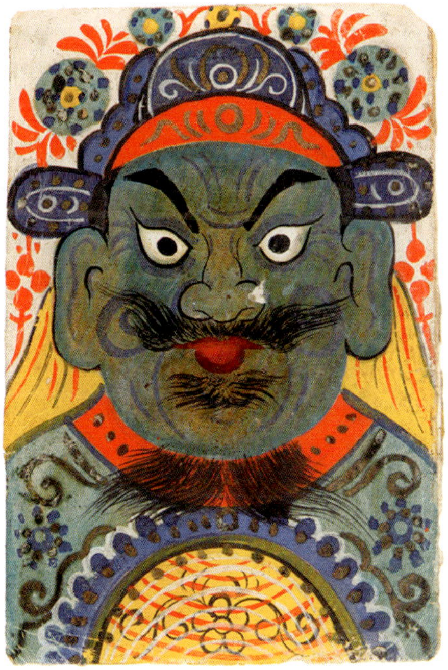

Fig. 196

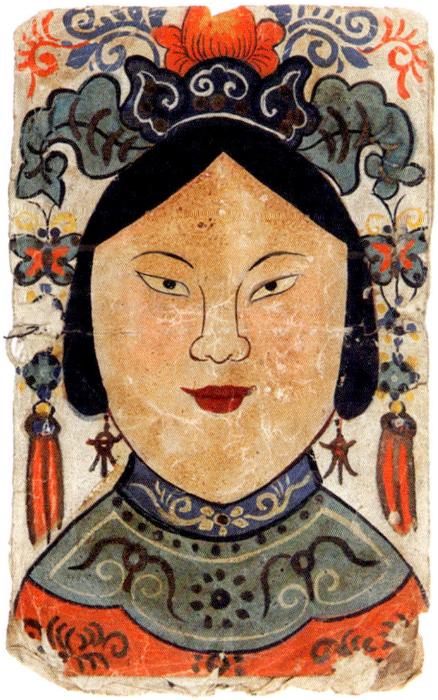

Fig. 197

asking for an answer he throws them on the ground in front of the altar and reads the position of each block. When they land with one yin and one yang side facing up, the answer is yes. When both sides are same, the answer is no.

Masks

Masks are also required possessions for high shaman priests, and are worn during certain rituals to impersonate particular deities. There are two major types: paper and wooden. After the Seven-Star Hanging Light Ritual a shaman must acquire paper masks along with the full set of painting scrolls and the long scroll of the *Dragon Bridge of the Great Dao*. Depending on his rank, a shaman may possess many paper masks.[19] In the Kitnick Collection there is one set of twenty-seven.

Wooden masks were often used in older times at outdoor ceremonies, but have become rare and are seldom seen among shaman priests in Vietnam today. Many of them are now in public and private collections.[20]

Paper Masks

Paper masks are square, each with a deity's face painted in the center. They are often made of several layers of paper glued together and are stitched with thread around the edges. The sides are held together with two thin sticks of bamboo, which are pierced so the priest can tie the mask around his head with string. Many masks are inscribed with the name of the deity on the left or right, and some bear the names of the shaman and the deity on the back. In some rituals, the shaman wears several masks on top of each other.[21] Yao female shamans may don paper masks of female deities during certain ceremonies.[22]

Paper masks in the collection represent both male and female deities. Here is a short list of popular and important deities depicted in the male masks: the Jade Emperor, the Three Pure Ones, the Three Generals, the God of the Year, the God of Thunder, the General of the Three Realms, the Four Heavenly Messengers, the local God of the Earth, the Five Wounded Deities, the God of Carpenters, and the God of Mountains. Popular female masks are Guanyin, the emperor's mother, the Dragon Phoenix Ladies, the Mother Goddess, and the children's patroness deity.

The set of twenty-seven paper masks in the exhibition is painted by an amateur artist, Mỹ Đình (美 亭), and dated May 1936. They are rendered in an unrefined manner, and the Chinese calligraphy on the back is roughly done as well. The back of a Guanyin mask provides an example of one inscription written in Chinese (觀 音, 丙 子 年 閏 三 月 上 旬 吉, 恭 奉 香 燈 第 壹 位, 美 亭 筆), which states the name of the deity, the date of creation, and that the mask is used when offering candles and incense to the altar and must be worn as the first mask layer.

Wooden Masks

Wooden masks are made of carved hardwood, finished with a plain polish, and covered with colored paper pasted to the surface (Figs. 198, 199, 202). On some masks animal fur, usually from buffalo tails, is glued on as eyebrows, beards, or mustaches. Metal nails are attached to the mouth to form teeth. Generally these added features create a more humanlike appearance. A few masks have a central finial with spiraling grooves and a crownlike protrusion, round and circling clockwise, on top of the head.

Shaman priests use wooden masks in ceremonies to seek a safe and happy return of villagers who have journeyed far away for long periods, or gone hunting in the jungle. Wooden masks covered with pink or white strips of paper, used in certain rituals by female shamans, represent, as observed by Jess Pourret, "one of those female deities who protect the souls of small children and oversee fertility in women."[23] Two examples are the Flower Mother Deity and the Holy Mother Queen of Flowers.[24] Although these masks are used by priestesses to impersonate female deities, they are also decorated with tufts of beards (Figs. 199, 203).

Musical Instruments

The ethnic groups discussed in this book employ a variety of musical instruments to enhance their ceremonies and rituals, punctuating the rhythm of recitations and building momentum for religious trances.

The water-buffalo horn, a signature of the Yao shaman priests in Vietnam, is used to summon the Jade Emperor and other spirits to preside over the service. The buffalo horn is probably the first musical instrument that a shaman would possess, since they are abundantly available among farmers, and it was traditionally used to announce the tribal or village meeting, or in case of emergency. The horn is usually polished and carved at the small end, so it is easy to play (Fig. 204). The painting scrolls of the Major Hoi Fan always include a detail of the chief priest blowing a buffalo horn, calling the Jade Emperor (Figs. 84, 85)

Drums are popular instruments, as they provide a primal rhythm of steady, hypnotic beats, inviting people to dance and enter into trances. The Kitnick Collection has three indigenous drums made from local materials. The first is a small two-headed terracotta hand drum from the Cao Làn people (Fig. 205). It is made by sewing the heads with rattan laces onto an hourglass-shaped body. The drumheads are made from calfskin or deerskin. In the house of the Yao clan head, where many rites and ceremonies are carried out, there are often drums, both small and large, representing that branch of the clan. Drums also symbolize the power of the shaman among the clan.[25] The second drum, which once belonged to the Nùng, is a hand drum (Fig. 206). Its skin surface is glued and nailed into place with old bamboo sticks and it has two strings for holding it pierced into

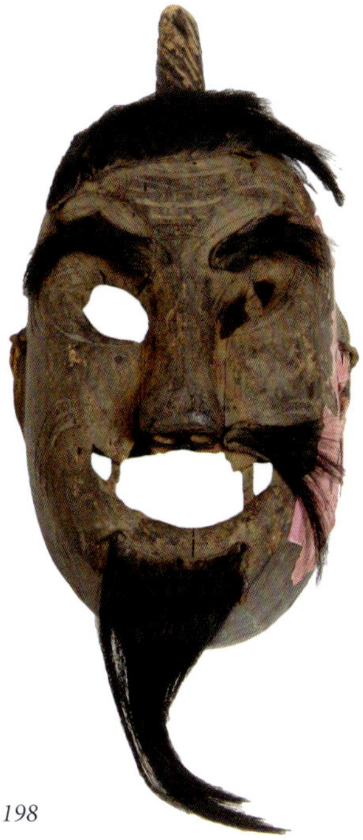

Fig. 198

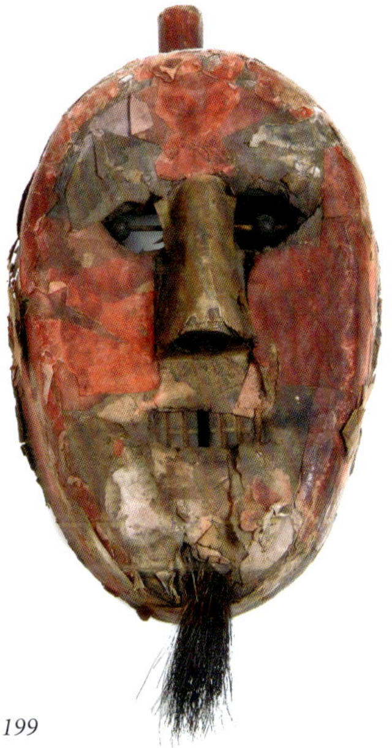

Fig. 199

Fig. 198
Mask, c. late 19th century
Coin (Tiền) Yao, China or Vietnam

Fig. 199
Mask, c. late 19th–early 20th century
Yao, Vietnam

Fig. 200
Mask, c. early 20th century
Yao, China or Vietnam

Fig. 201
Mask, c. late 19th–early 20th century
Yao, Vietnam

Fig. 202
Mask, c. late 19th–early 20th century
Yao, China

Fig. 203
Mask, c. early–mid-20th century
Yao, Vietnam

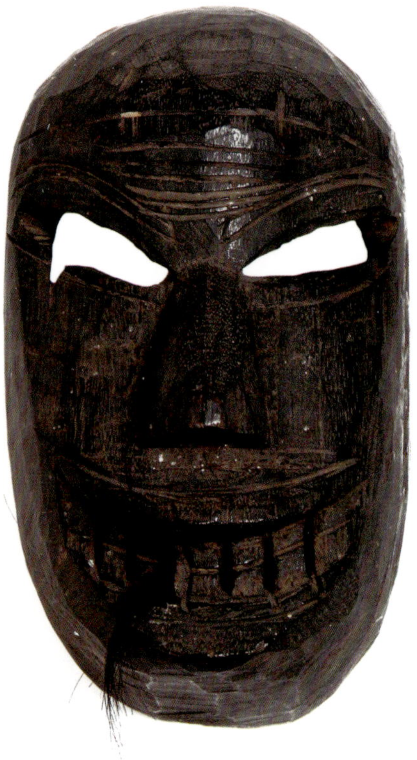

Fig. 200

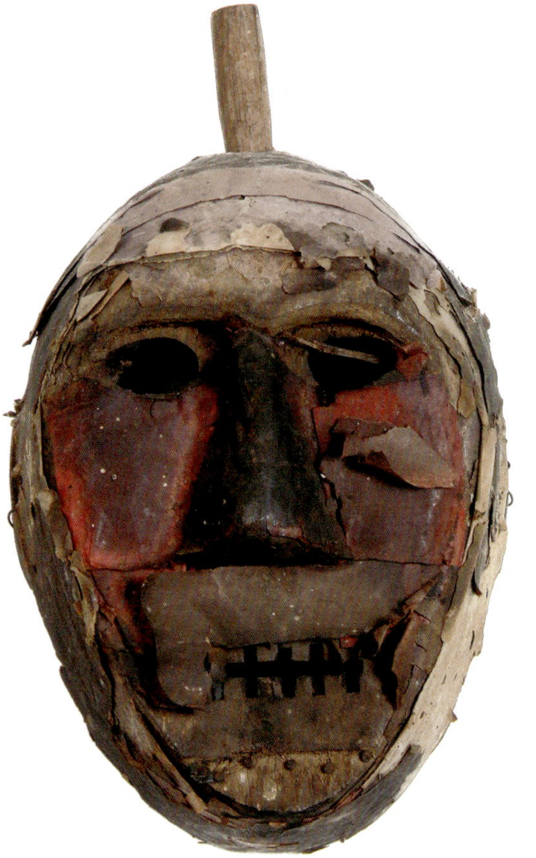

Fig. 201

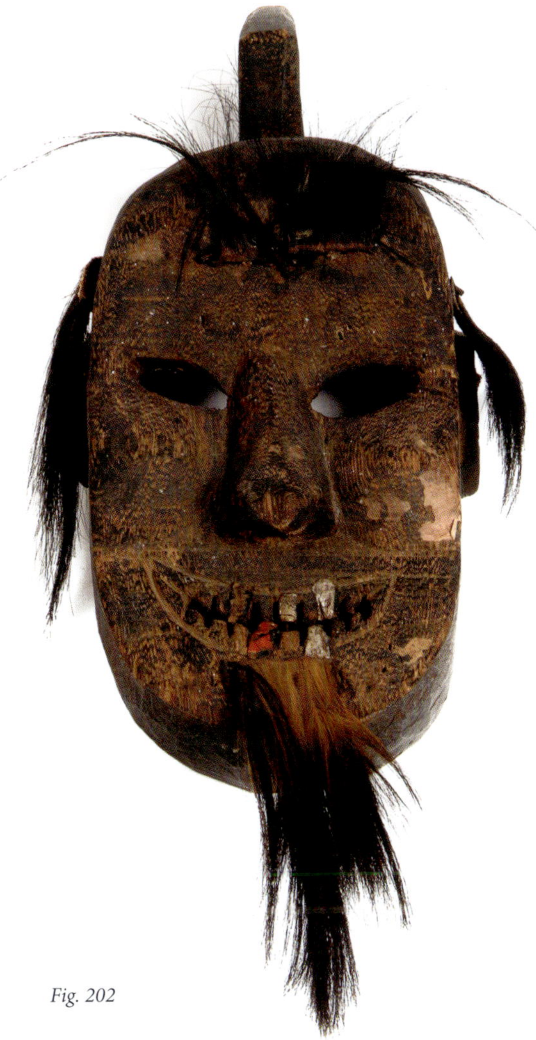

Fig. 202

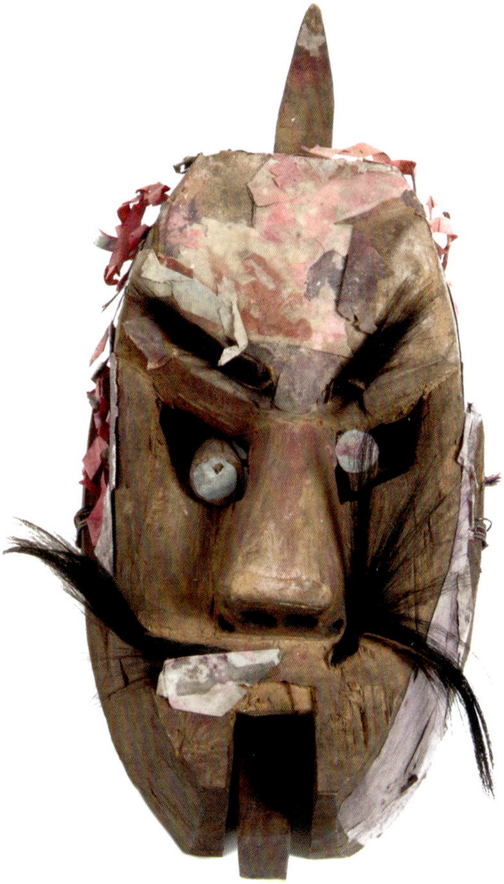

Fig. 203

its body. The third, from the Sán Chảy people, is a larger drum tied with rattan laces and pierced with pieces of young bamboo (Fig. 208). The two hand drums are double-sided, beautifully crafted using native wooden hoops and covered on both sides by calfskin. In practice, they are employed not only during religious services, such as funeral processions and weddings, but also during events like the New Year Festival.

The *tính* lute (Vietnamese *đàn tính*) is a two- or three-stringed instrument with a sound box made from a gourd (Fig. 65). Its cover is made of soft wood and its handle of mulberry. The *tính* is a signature musical instrument of the Tày people and is always played by female musicians. It is required for a shaman priestess during chanting or reciting ritual hymns and epic ballads. The *tính* lute produces a sweet, warm tone and balanced harmony, and can maintain the rhythm for both solemn ceremonies and joyous events.

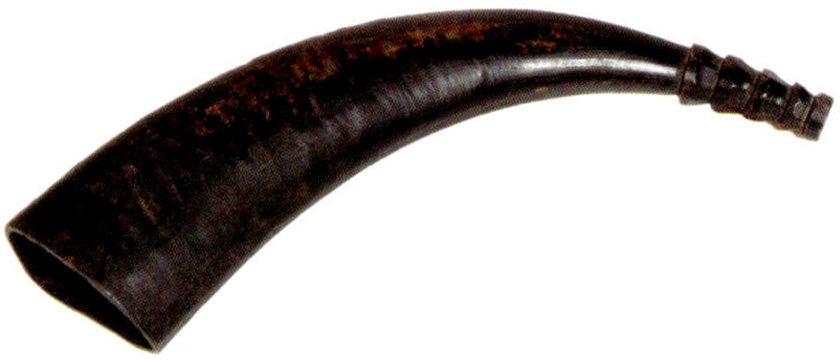

Fig. 204

Fig. 204
Horn, c. early–mid-20th century
Red Yao, Vietnam

Fig. 205
Small hand drum (two-headed), c. late 19th–early 20th century
Cao Làn–Sán Chi (Sán Chay), Vietnam

A pair of large metal cymbals is also part of the ensemble (Fig. 207). They are always depicted in the scroll of the Major Hoi Fan (Fig. 84) or as part of the grand funeral procession in the long scroll of *The Dragon Bridge of the Great Dao* (Fig. 143). Each cymbal has a large knob with a soft cloth cord strung through a hole in the center. They are made of thick bronze alloy to produce harmonic overtones, and provide rhythmic articulation and impetus in ritual chants.

Gongs also play a notable role in Yao rituals. They have a flat form with a large nipple at the center, which is hit by a mallet (Fig. 209). At the beginning of the ritual, the shaman priest usually strikes the gong three times to announce the service. The priest will occasionally hit it during the ritual to punctuate a long recitation or reading. Like the cymbal, a gong is often illustrated in the Major Hoi Fan and the *Dragon Bridge of the Great Dao* scrolls. This Sán Chảy gong was perhaps hung next to the main altar of the high shaman priest's family; the blackening would have been from incense smoke. The string that would have been tied onto the gong in order to hold it is missing.

There are five beautiful handbells in the collection (Figs. 210–214). This type of bell is very commonly used in religious rituals throughout China, Japan, and Vietnam, and was introduced into the religious services of the Tày and Nùng under the influence of Buddhism. However, it is not used by Yao priests. A close examination all the Yao painted scrolls reveals no examples.

The five bells range from the very simplest molding to slightly more complex casting. For example, the bell in Fig. 210 is very modest and plain; the one in Fig. 211 is covered with attached textile strips; and while the bell in Fig. 213 has not been decorated on the base, the handle is embellished with human figures. The bell in Fig. 212 has a three-pronged handle, like a trident. The most elaborate of them is seen in Fig. 214, with a six-pronged handle emerging from the crowned head of a Buddha. The body

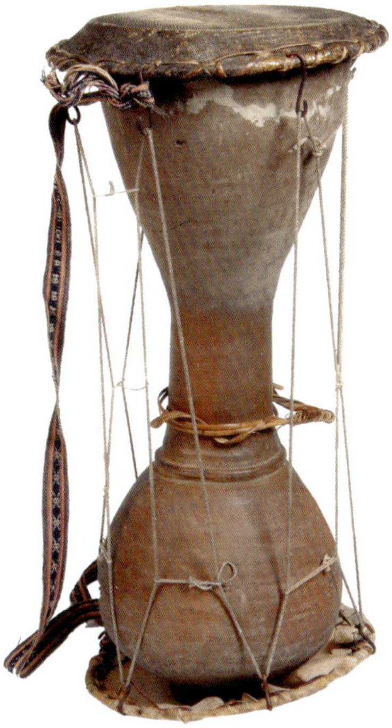

Fig. 205

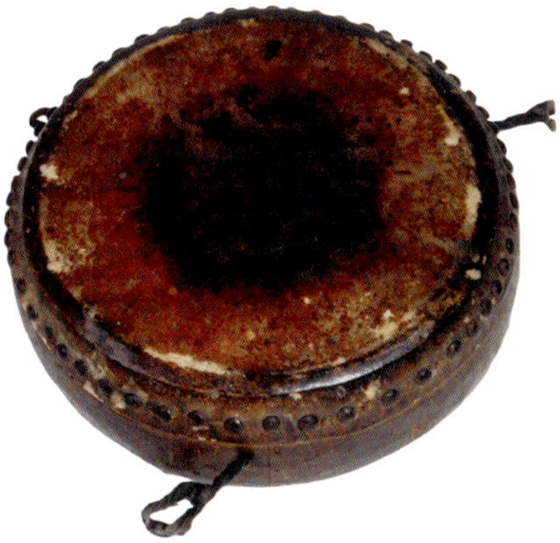

Fig. 206

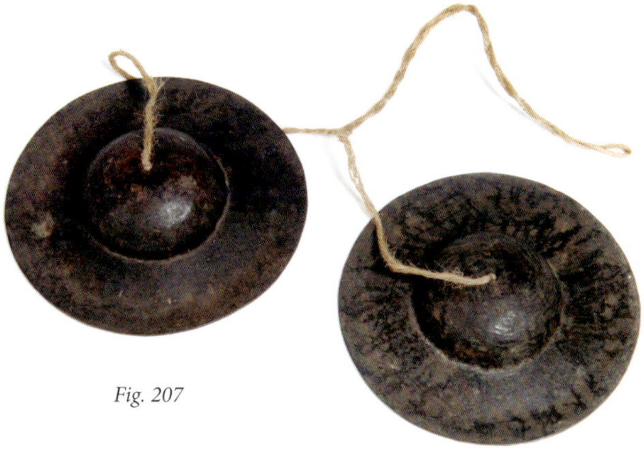

Fig. 207

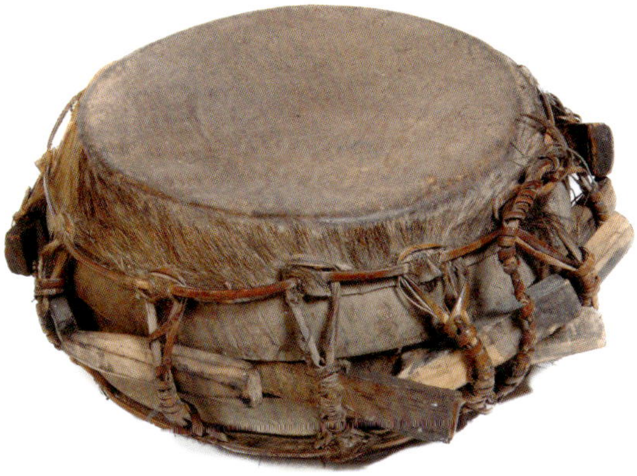

Fig. 208

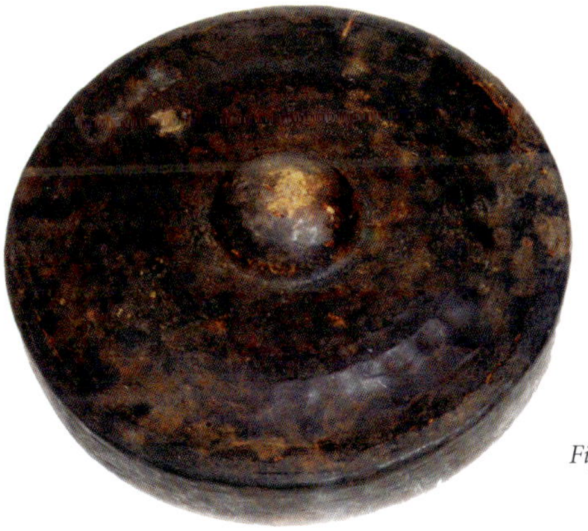

Fig. 209

Fig. 206
Small hand drum, c. early 20th century
Nùng, Vietnam

Fig. 207
Pair of cymbals, c. early 20th century
Cao Làn–Sán Chỉ (Sán Chay), Vietnam

Fig. 208
Drum (double-sided),
c. early–mid-20th century
Cao Làn–Sán Chỉ (Sán Chay), Vietnam

Fig. 209
Gong, c. early 20th century
Cao Làn–Sán Chỉ (Sán Chay), Vietnam

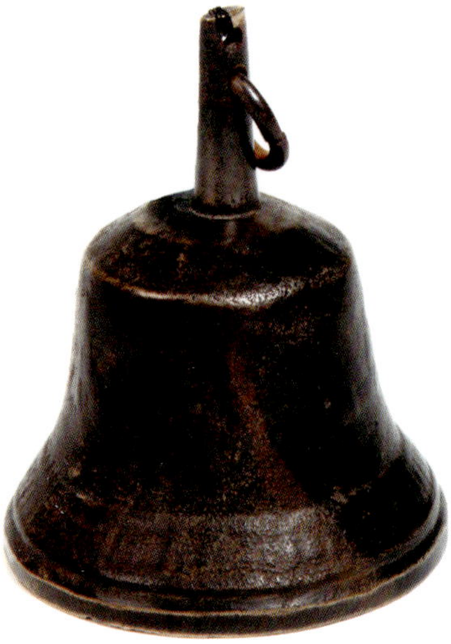

Fig. 210

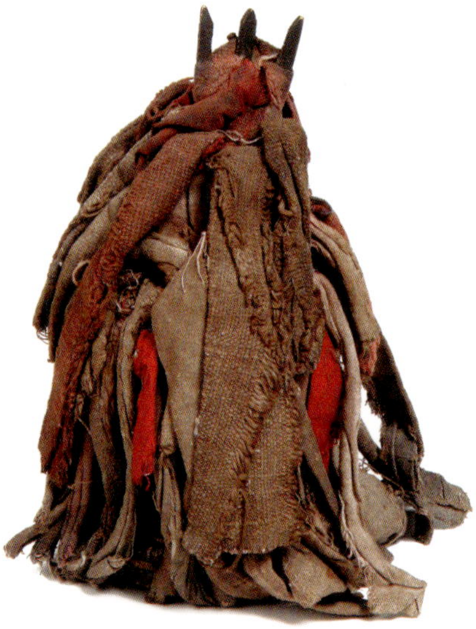

Fig. 211

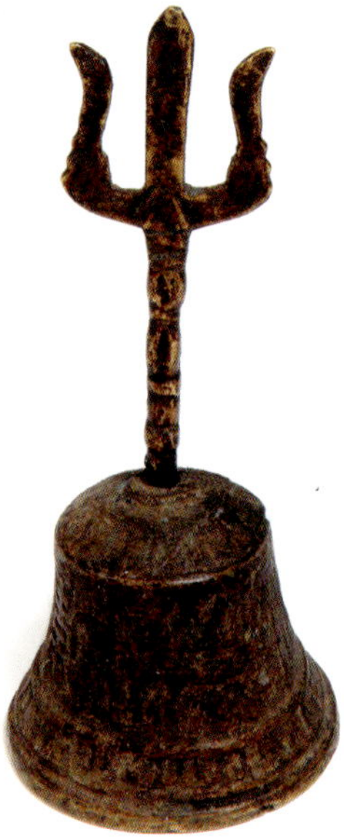

Fig. 212

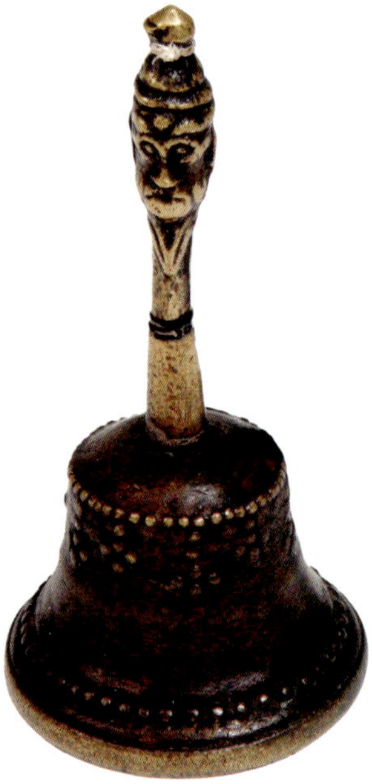

Fig. 213

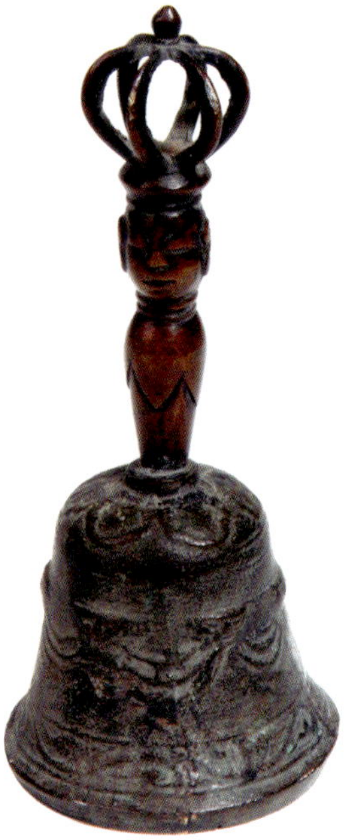

Fig. 214

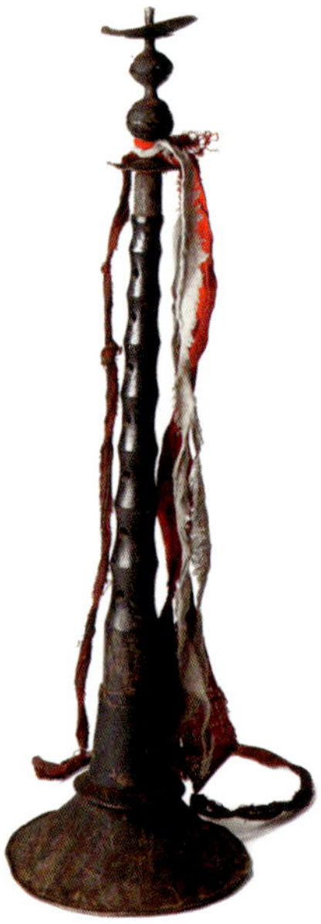

Fig. 215

features eight lotus petals, with stylized waves or cloud patterns below. The lower rim is decorated with schematized leaves. In general, this type of handbell produces a clear, deep sound, which blends harmoniously with other instruments. In a Buddhist context, its sound is meant to evoke protective deities and dispel evil spirits. They are the main ritual instrument used during repetitive chanting or incantations of the mantras.

Finally, the oboe has an important position within ensembles among the Yao and the Sán Chây, and is very popular among the Chinese and neighboring countries in Southeast Asia. Similar to the buffalo horn, bronze gong, Chinese cymbal, and small hand drum, the oboe is often included in Yao orchestras when alluding to Major Hoi Fan and in funeral processions. In fact, it forms an essential element of the music that accompanies the shaman priests' ritual performances of both auspicious and inauspicious rites, i.e., those for the living and the dead. The oboe produces a high melodious pitch, which the player can change through mouth and hand alterations. The collection has three old oboes, worn by time, made completely of bronze. Two are from the Yao (see Fig. 215) and one from the Sán Chây people. The latter has a conical wooden body connected to a tubular brass mouthpiece, to which a small double reed is affixed. One of them is still in mint condition, with a small double reed and a detachable metal bell at its end.

Overall, the musical equipment—buffalo horn, drum, lute, cymbals, handbell, and oboe—that has been explored in this section makes up a diverse selection of instruments that are used in the traditional music of the Yao and other ethnic groups in northern Vietnam, for ritual ceremonies and village festivals.

Conclusion

The ritual objects discussed in this chapter represent the religious functions as well as the dynamic cultural life of shaman priests, whether of the Yao or other ethnic peoples in northern Vietnam. These objects not only are deeply rooted in the Chinese Daoist and Buddhist traditions, but were also used in the Chinese imperial court. Certain objects have a clearly defined ritual function and are often closely associated with Daoist deities. Others, such as ritual weapons, court tablets, and magic seals, used to subdue evil forces, were originally related to the dynastic court. In some cases, especially musical instruments, the objects are meant to aid the shaman priests and priestesses in their ritual chanting and recitations. Despite the diverse array of ritual objects, each serves the same goal: to help the living and provide salvation for the dead.

The rich cultural and religious character of the artifacts in the Kitnick Collection provides a wealth of information, saturated with valuable social and artistic history, enhancing the study of these little-known cultures from a tiny corner of the world in southern China and northern Vietnam.

Fig. 210
Handbell, c. late 19th–early 20th century
Tày, Vietnam

Fig. 211
Handbell, c. late 19th–early 20th century
Nùng, Vietnam

Fig. 212
Handbell, c. late 19th century
Nùng, Vietnam

Fig. 213
Handbell, c. late 19th century
Tày, Vietnam

Fig. 214
Handbell, c. late 19th century
Tày, Vietnam

Fig. 215
Oboe, c. late 19th–early 20th century
Red Yao, Vietnam

NOTES

1. For example, a typical Tày shaman priest possesses several seals, a court scepter, a handheld bell, a small wooden gong, a pair of bronze cymbals, a magic staff, two printing blocks, etc. See Vũ Khánh, pp. 134–135.

2. Stephen Little, *Taoism and the Arts of China*, p. 130.

3. The topic of Chinese cosmology, astrology, calendars, and divination is complicated and beyond discussion here. The Kitnick Collection has a small group of manuscripts, texts, and manuals from the five ethnic groups mentioned in this book; at least half of them are related to this topic. For some discussion on this subject, see Thomas F. Aylward, *The Imperial Guide to Feng Shui and Chinese Astrology*. See also Ho Peng Yoke, *Chinese Mathematical Astrology: Reaching Out to the Stars* (London: Routlege Curzon, 2003).

4. *Taoism and the Arts of China*, pp. 201–202.

5. Ibid.

6. For excellent illustrations of early Chinese Daoist ritual swords, with full description and functions, see ibid., cat. 58–61, pp. 214–216.

7. Ibid.

8. Jean Cormerais's book *Les Chemises des Dieux* provides some good illustrations of staffs and their functions, pp. 117–118.

9. For example, in *Ceremony of the Hanging Lamps*, Phan Ngọc Khuê has diagrams of two different Yao houses where the Hanging Lamp rituals took place. He also notes where certain rites happened before, during, and after the whole ritual program, pp. 51–53.

10. For an illustration, see Phan Ngọc Khuê, *Taoist Paintings*, p. 197; see also Jess Pourret, plate 78, p. 50.

11. In Vietnam, China, and other Asian countries, there are many kinds and species of bamboo, including male and female types. The male is usually small, solid (without a hollow inside), and strong. The female is bigger, smooth, and hollow.

12. Wu Hung, "Mapping Early Taoist Art: The Visual Culture of Wudoumi," in Steven Little, *Taoism and the Arts of China*, pp. 84–5.

13. Ibid.

14. Steven Little, *Taoism and the Arts of China*, p. 155.

15. Anne Birell, pp. 238–239.

16. See Jess Pourret, pp. 206–207, for many different samples of Yao priests' chops and seals (*yen*) from his own collection, with a brief explanation. See also Jean Cormerais, pp. 118–119, for a short explanation and religious functions.

17. For brief discussion of the myth of Pan Hu, see Jess Pourret, p. 18. See also Jacques Lemoine for more extensive discussion of the myth and the immigration of the Yao, pp. 11–20.

18. See Doãn Thanh and Lê Trung Vũ, *Truyện Cổ Người Dao* [The Legendary Stories of the Yao] (Hanoi: Ethnic Culture Publishing House, 1978).

19. Jess Pourret, p. 244.

20. See Phạm Đức Sĩ, pp. 162–163.

21. The topic of paper masks used in the Yao ritual is very rich and interesting. Jacques Lemoine has a brief chapter discussing their functions, iconographic features, and material use, pp. 153–155; Pourret also has a good selection of samples illustrated in his book with some insightful knowledge, pp. 244–245. Jean Cormerais briefly covers the subject without much in-depth discussion, but has a few good illustrations, pp. 209–213.

22. Jess Pourret, p. 244.

23. Ibid., p. 246.

24. Hoàng Quý Quyển, in his paper "Tìm hiểu sơ bộ về những mặt nạ của người Dao [The initial step of understanding the Yao's Mask"], in *The Culture and Social Development of the Yao,* identifies the wooden masks of these two female deities as Hoa Căn Phụ and Hoa Căn Mẫu, pp. 364–365. These two deities are better explained and illustrated in Phan Ngọc Khuê, *Taoist Painting*, plates 95 and 96, pp. 182–184.

25. Võ Mai Phương and Clair Burkert, p. 78.

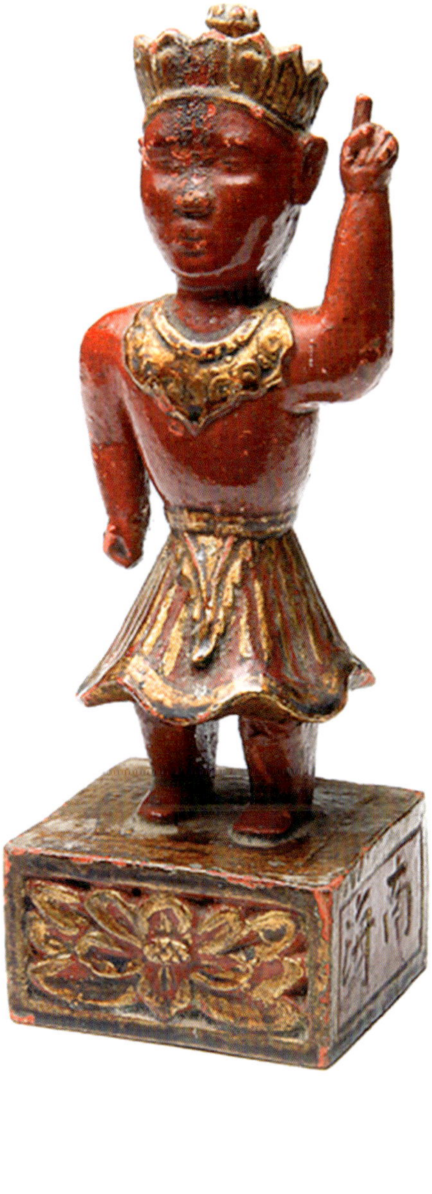

Fig. 216
Statuette of Baby Buddha, c. early 20th century
Sán Dìu, Vietnam

CATALOGUE CHECKLIST

Kitnick Collection numbers are in parentheses.

Fig. 1
Palace of the Grand Pure One, c. early to mid-20th century
Handmade paper, bamboo sticks, string, 32½ x 13 in.
Cao Làn–Sán Chi (Sán Chay), Vietnam (80)

Fig. 2
Palace of the Supreme Pure One, c. early to mid-20th century
Handmade paper, bamboo sticks, string, 25½ x 12½ in.
Cao Làn–Sán Chi (Sán Chay), Vietnam (81)

Fig. 3
Palace of the Jade Pure One, c. early to mid-20th century
Handmade paper, bamboo sticks, string, 25½ x 12½ in.
Cao Làn–Sán Chi (Sán Chay), Vietnam (82)

Fig. 4
Pan Hu's Five Banners of Knights, c. late 19th–early 20th century
Handmade paper, bamboo sticks, 15½ x 8½ in. each.
Red Yao, China (57)

Fig. 5
The Family Forebears, c. early to mid-20th century
Handmade paper, bamboo sticks, string, 26¾ x 12¼ in.
Cao Làn–Sán Chi (Sán Chay), Vietnam (91)

Fig. 6
Enforcers of Fasting and Charity, c. late 19th–early 20th century
Handmade paper, bamboo sticks, 15½ x 8½ in. each.
Red Yao, China (56)

Fig. 7
Ten Kings of the Underworld, 1829–30
Handmade paper, bamboo sticks, string, 44¾ x 18¼ in.
Red Yao, China (62)

Fig. 8
Ritual scepter, c. late 19th–early 20th century
Wood, 7 5/8 in.
Tày, Vietnam (193)

Fig. 9
Ritual scepter, c. late 19th century
Wood, 11 5/8 in.
Yao, China or Vietnam (0026)

Fig. 10
Ritual scepter, c. late 19th century
Wood, 5 7/8 in.
Tày, Vietnam (0023, rear of 0021)

Fig. 11
Avalokiteśvara (Bồ Tát Quán Thế Âm),
c. late 19th–early 20th century
Handmade paper, bamboo sticks, string, 18¼ x 10¾ in.
Sán Dìu, Vietnam (19)

Fig. 12
Samantabhadra (Bồ Tát Phổ Hiền), c. late 19th–early 20th century
Handmade paper, bamboo sticks, string, 18¾ x 10¾ in.
Sán Dìu, Vietnam (20)

Fig. 13
Mañjuśrī (Bồ Tát Văn Thù), c. late 19th–early 20th century
Handmade paper, bamboo sticks, string, 19¾ x 10¾ in.
Sán Dìu, Vietnam (21)

Fig. 14
The Ancestors/Heavenly Host, 1819
Handmade paper, bamboo sticks, string, 45 x 18¼ in.
Red Yao, China (40)

Fig. 15
The Buddha Jewel (The Buddha of the Present),
c. early to mid-20th century
Handmade paper, bamboo sticks, string, 39½ X 17¼ in.
Sán Dìu, Vietnam (100)

Fig. 16
The Shangha Jewel (The Buddha of the Past),
c. early to mid-20th century
Handmade paper, bamboo sticks, string, 40½ X 17¼ in.
Sán Dìu, Vietnam (101)

Fig. 17
The Dharma Jewel (The Buddha of the Future),
c. early to mid-20th century
Handmade paper, bamboo sticks, string, 40½ X 17¼ in.
Sán Dìu, Vietnam (102)

Fig. 18
Buddhas and bodhisattvas, portable scrolls (5), c. mid-20th century
Paper, bamboo sticks, c. 13½ in. (with sticks)
Cao Làn–Sán Chi (Sán Chay), Vietnam (271)

Fig. 19
Five Kings of the Underworld, portable scrolls (5),
c. mid-20th century
Paper, bamboo sticks, c. 13½ in. (with sticks)
Cao Làn–Sán Chi (Sán Chay), Vietnam (272)

Fig. 20
Buddhist and Daoist deities, portable scrolls (4),
c. early to mid-20th century
Paper, bamboo sticks, c. 13 in. (with sticks)
Tày, Vietnam (274)

Fig. 21
Buddhist and Daoist deities, portable scrolls (5),
c. early to mid-20th century
Paper, bamboo sticks, c. 13 in. (with sticks)
Tày, Vietnam (275)

Fig. 22
Celestial Master Zhang, 1819
Handmade paper, bamboo sticks, string, 45¾ x 18¼ in.
Red Yao, China (32)

Fig. 23
Celestial Master Li, 1819
Handmade paper, bamboo sticks, string, 45 x 18¼ in.
Red Yao, China (33)

Fig. 24
The Dragon Bridge of the Great Dao (part 1),
c. late 19th–early 20th century
Handmade paper, bamboo sticks, 92 x 8 in.
Red Yao, China (52)

Fig. 25
Feng shui manual, dated 1908
Handmade rice paper, 8½ in.
Cao Làn–Sán Chi (Sán Chay), Vietnam (282)

Fig. 26
Guiding the Soul, c. early to mid-20th century
Cotton, wood sticks, string, 121½ x 14¼ in.
Tày, Vietnam (316)

Fig. 27
Feng shui compass with lid, c. late 19th–early 20th century
Wood, paper, lacquer, metal, 7¼ in.
Cao Làn–Sán Chi (Sán Chay), Vietnam (206)

Fig. 28
Feng shui diagram, c. mid-20th century
Handmade paper, 28¾ in. diameter.
Cao Làn–Sán Chi (Sán Chay), Vietnam (60)

Fig. 29
Buddhist-Daoist manual, dated 1910
Handmade paper, 7⅞ in.
Tày, Vietnam (215)

Fig. 30
Manual of Daoist ritual and astrology, dated 1936
Handmade paper, 10⅝ in.
Yao, China or Vietnam (213)

Fig. 31
Book, c. late 19th century
Handmade rice paper, 8¼ in.
Cao Làn–Sán Chi (Sán Chay), Vietnam (283)

Fig. 32
Astrology manual, dated 1952 and 1956
Handmade rice paper, 8¾ in.
Tày, Vietnam (280)

Fig. 33
Four Heavenly Messengers, c. early to mid-20th century
Handmade paper, bamboo sticks, 22¼ x 10¼ in.
Tày, Vietnam (115)

Fig. 34
Four Heavenly Messengers, c. early to mid-20th century
Handmade paper, bamboo sticks, 19½ x 14¾ in.
Indigo Clad (Thanh-y) Yao, Vietnam (119)

Fig. 35
Roaring Tiger, c. late 19th–early 20th century
Handmade paper, bamboo sticks, string, 30 x 11¾ in
Tày, Vietnam (141)

Fig. 36
Humming Dragon, c. late 19th–early 20th century
Handmade paper, bamboo sticks, string, 30½ x 11¾ in.
Tày, Vietnam (142)

Fig. 37
Four Heavenly Messengers, c. late 19th–early 20th century
Handmade paper, bamboo sticks, string,
Vietnamese writing on rear, 30 ½ x 12 in.
Tày, Vietnam (143)

Fig. 38
The Grand Pure One, 1829–30
Handmade paper, bamboo sticks, string,
with rice paper attachments, 43½ x 18½ in.
Red Yao, China (70)

Fig. 39
The Jade Pure One, dated 1939
Handmade paper, bamboo sticks, string, 43½ x 18¼ in.
Red Yao, China/Vietnam (73)

Fig. 40
The Jade Pure One, dated 1819
Handmade paper, bamboo sticks, string, 45 x 18¼ in.
Red Yao, China (28)

Fig. 41
Rear of 40 (29, rear of 28)

Fig. 42
Ancestors/Heavenly Host, dated 1829–30
Handmade paper, bamboo sticks, string, 44¾ x 18½ in.
Red Yao, China (65)

Fig. 43
Rear of 42 (66)

Fig. 44
Ceremonial robe, c. late 19th century
Textile, embroidery, text, 47½ in.
Tày or Nùng, Vietnam (0126)

Fig. 45
Ceremonial robe, c. late 19th century
Textile, embroidery, text, 47½ in.
Tày or Nùng, Vietnam (0126)

Fig. 46
Seal, c. late 19th century
Wood, 1¾ in.
Tight Trouser (Quần Chẹt) Yao, Vietnam (0068)

Fig. 47
Seal (Five Thunder Gods stamp), c. late 19th century or earlier
Metal, 2¼ in.
Tày, Vietnam (0063)

Fig. 48
Seal, c. late 19th–early 20th century
Wood, 4⅜ in.
Nùng, Vietnam (0066)

CHECKLIST CONTINUED

Fig. 49
Seal, c. late 19th–early 20th century
Wood, 2¾ in.
Yao, Vietnam (0057)

Fig. 50
Mask (from a set of 27), dated 1936
Paper, bamboo sticks, string, 7⅝ in.
Yao (Mun), Vietnam (0129)

Fig. 51
Mask (from a set of 27), dated 1936
Paper, bamboo sticks, string, 7⅝ in.
Yao (Mun), Vietnam (0147)

Fig. 52
Mask (from a set of 27), dated 1936
Paper, bamboo sticks, string, 7⅝ in.
Yao (Mun), Vietnam (0133)

Fig. 53
Mask (from a set of 27), dated 1936
Paper, bamboo sticks, string, 7⅝ in.
Yao (Mun), Vietnam (0149)

Fig. 54
Celestial Marshals Ma and Deng, c. late 19th century
Handmade paper, bamboo sticks, string, 25½ x 11½ in.
Cao Làn–Sán Chi (Sán Chay), Vietnam (127)

Fig. 55
Celestial Master Li, c. late 19th century
Handmade paper, bamboo sticks, string, 25¾ x 11½ in.
Cao Làn–Sán Chi (Sán Chay), Vietnam (130)

Fig. 56
The Dharma Jewel, c. late 19th century
Handmade paper, bamboo sticks, string, 30½ x 11¾ in.
Cao Làn–Sán Chi (Sán Chay), Vietnam (123)

Fig. 57
The Buddha Jewel, c. late 19th century
Handmade paper, bamboo sticks, string, 29½ x11¾ in.
Cao Làn–Sán Chi (Sán Chay), Vietnam (124)

Fig. 58
The Sangha Jewel, c. late 19th century
Handmade paper, bamboo sticks, string, 31 x 11¾ in.
Cao Làn–Sán Chi (Sán Chay), Vietnam (125)

Fig. 59
Celestial Master Zhang, c. late 19th century
Handmade paper, bamboo sticks, string, 25¼ x 11¾ in.
Cao Làn–Sán Chi (Sán Chay), Vietnam (129)

Fig. 60
Celestial Marshals Zhao and Zhang, c. late 19th century
Handmade paper, bamboo sticks, string, 25¾ 11½ in.
Cao Làn–Sán Chi (Sán Chay), Vietnam (128)

Fig. 61
Four Heavenly Messengers, c. late 19th century
Handmade paper, bamboo sticks, string, 25½ x 11½ in.
Cao Làn–Sán Chi (Sán Chay), Vietnam (126)

Fig. 62
Belt, c. early 20th century
Textile, 16 in.
Tight Trouser (Quần Chẹt) Yao, Vietnam (324)

Fig. 63
Ritual robe, c. early 20th century
Handmade textile, embroidery, metal buttons, 43½ x 33 in.
Sán Chay, Vietnam (175, rear of 174)

Fig. 64
The God of Medicine, c. early 20th century
Handmade paper (repaired), bamboo sticks,
string, red fabric, 34¾ x 15¼ in.
Sán Dìu, Vietnam (8)

Fig. 65
Lute (*đàn tính*), c. early 20th century
Wood, metal, textile, mirror, bells, string, 40 in.
Tày, Vietnam (304)

Fig. 66
Formal robe, c. early to mid-20th century
Handmade textile, embroidery, string, 42½ x 67 in.
Cao Làn–Sán Chi (Sán Chay), Vietnam (177)

Fig. 67
Ritual hat, c. early to mid-20th century
Textile, 6¾ in.
Nùng, Vietnam (242)

Fig. 68
Small spherical bells (4 attached), c. early 20th century
Bronze, c. 1¾ in. each
Tày, Vietnam (0116)

Fig. 69
Ritual headdress, c. late 19th–early 20th century
Colored fabric, beads, metal, small mirrors,
silver and other thread, 55 x 16½ in.
Tày, Vietnam (149b)

Fig. 70
Front of 69 (149a)

Fig. 71
Ritual headdress, c. early 20th century
Colored fabric, metal, various threads. 51¾ x 19¾ in.
Tày, Vietnam (152)

Fig. 72
Front of 71 (153)

Fig. 73
Ritual headdress with banners, c. early 20th century
Textile, various threads, 54¼ in.
Tày, Vietnam (313)

Fig. 74
Front of 73 (314)

Fig. 75
Ritual robe, c. early 20th century
Handmade textile, embroidery, 42¼ x 30 in.
Tày, Vietnam (155, rear of 154)

Fig. 76
Ritual robe, c. early 20th century
Handmade textile and embroidery, 44¼ x 35½ in.
Cao Làn–San Chi (Sán Chay), Vietnam (320, rear of 319)

Fig. 77
Yin-yang divination blocks (2 sets), c. early 20th century
Water buffalo horn, 5 to 5¼ in.
Hmong, China or Vietnam (0101)

Fig. 78
Yin-yang divination blocks, c. early 20th century
Bamboo, 3¾ in.
Nùng, Vietnam (0103)

Fig. 79
Yin-yang divination blocks, c. early 20th century
Bamboo and red lacquer, 3 in.
Coin (Tiền) Yao, Vietnam (0102)

Fig. 80
Ceremonial staffs, c. early 20th century
Wood, metal, lead, textile, animal horn, 38 to 42 in.
Yao, Vietnam (305)

Fig. 81
Ceremonial staffs, c. early 20th century
Wood, metal, lead, 34 to 42 in.
Coin (Tiền) Yao, Vietnam (306)

Fig. 82
Scroll tubes (2), c. mid-20th century
Wood, 19 ½ and 14 ½ in. high
Coin (Tiền) Yao, Vietnam (0019)

Fig. 83
High priest's hat, c. early 20th century
Woven human hair, 3½ in.
Yao, China or Vietnam (0007)

Fig. 84
Major Hoi Fan, 1819
Handmade paper, bamboo sticks, string, 44¾ x 18 in.
Red Yao, China (41)

Fig. 85
Major Hoi Fan, 1829–30
Handmade paper, bamboo sticks, string, 44½ x 18½ in.
Red Yao, China (76)

Fig. 86
Seal, c. late 19th–early 20th century
Wood, 2¾ in.
Yao, China or Vietnam (0057)

Fig. 87
Turtle seal and box, c. late 19th–early 20th century
Wood, 2½ in.
Yao, China or Vietnam (0070)

Fig. 88
Seal, c. late 19th–early 20th century
Wood, red ink, 2⅝ in.
Sán Dìu, Vietnam (0074)

Fig. 89
Power sticks (3), c. mid-20th century
Wood, 9⅝ to 12 in.
Red Yao, China or Vietnam (0114)

Fig. 90
Rear of 94 (0115)

Fig. 91
Ceremonial shoes, c. late 19th–early 20th century
Textile, embroidery, paper soles, 15 in.
Yao, China or Vietnam (0011)

Fig. 92
Ritual sword with rattle, c. late 19th–early 20th century
Metal, bone, silver, coins, 16⅞ in.
Cao Làn–Sán Chi (Sán Chay), Vietnam (230)

Fig. 93
Ritual instruments, c. late 19th–early 20th century
Wood, lacquer, metal, coins, 5 in.
Sán Dìu, Vietnam (0094)

Fig. 94
Ritual headdress, c. late 19th–early 20th century
Textile, various threads, 18½ in.
Tày, Vietnam (308)

Fig. 95
The High Constable, dated 1899
Handmade mulberry paper, pigments, rice paper attachments, bamboo sticks, string, 45¼ x 17 in.
Red Yao, Vietnam (1)

Fig. 96
The Ancestors/Heavenly Host, dated 1899
Handmade mulberry paper, pigments, rice paper attachments, bamboo sticks, string, 45¼ x 17 in.
Red Yao, Vietnam (5)

Fig. 97
Minor Hoi Fan, dated 1899
Handmade mulberry paper, pigments, rice paper attachments, bamboo sticks, string, 45¼ x 17 in.
Red Yao, Vietnam (7)

CHECKLIST CONTINUED

Fig. 98
The Jade Emperor, 1819
Handmade paper, bamboo sticks, string, 45¼ x 18½ in.
Red Yao, China (44)

Fig. 99
The Grand Pure One, 1819
Handmade paper, bamboo sticks, string, 44½ 18¼ in.
Red Yao, China (30)

Fig. 100
The Jade Pure One, 1819
Handmade paper, bamboo sticks, string, 45 x 18¼ in.
Red Yao, China (28)

Fig. 101
The Supreme Pure One, 1819
Handmade paper, bamboo sticks, string, 45 x 18¼ in.
Red Yao, China (27)

Fig. 102
Master of the Saints, 1819
Handmade paper, bamboo sticks, string, 45½ x 18¼ in.
Red Yao, China (45)

Fig. 103
Celestial Master Li, 1819
Handmade paper, bamboo sticks, string, 45 x 18¼ in.
Red Yao, China (33)

Fig. 104
Celestial Master Zhang, 1819
Handmade paper, bamboo sticks, string, 45¾ x 18¼ in.
Red Yao, China (32)

Fig. 105
The Ten Kings of the Underworld, 1819
Handmade paper, bamboo sticks, string, 45 x 18½ in.
Red Yao, China (38)

Fig. 106
The Ancestors/Heavenly Host, 1819
Handmade paper, bamboo sticks, string, 45 x 18¼ in.
Red Yao, China (40)

Fig. 107
Minor Hoi Fan, 1819
Handmade paper, bamboo sticks, string, 44½ x 18½ in.
Red Yao, China (37)

Fig. 108
Major Hoi Fan, 1819
Handmade paper, bamboo sticks, string, 44¾ x 18 in.
Red Yao, China (41)

Fig. 109
The High Constable, 1819
Handmade paper, bamboo sticks, string, 44½ x 18½ in.
Red Yao, China (39)

Fig. 110
The Three Generals, 1819
Handmade paper, bamboo sticks, string, 45¼ x 18 in.
Red Yao, China (36)

Fig. 111
The Officials of Earth and Water, 1819
Handmade paper, bamboo sticks, string, 44¾ x 18½ in.
Red Yao, China (42)

Fig. 112
The Officials of Heaven and the Underworld, 1819
Handmade paper, bamboo sticks, string, 45¼ x 18½ in.
Red Yao, China (43)

Fig. 113
Celestial Marshal Deng, 1819
Handmade paper, bamboo sticks, string, 45¾ x 18 in.
Red Yao, China (34)

Fig. 114
Celestial Marshal Zhao, 1819
Handmade paper, bamboo sticks, string, 45½ x 18 in.
Red Yao, China (35)

Fig. 115
The Officials, 1819
Handmade paper, bamboo sticks, string, 45¼ x 18¼ in.
Red Yao, China (31)

Fig. 116
The Official of Heaven and the Official of Earth,
c. early 20th century
Handmade paper, bamboo sticks, string, red fabric, 36 x 15½ in.
Sán Dìu, Vietnam (14)

Fig. 117
Lord of the Three Caves, c. early 20th century
Handmade paper, bamboo sticks, string, red fabric, 37 x 15½ in.
Sán Dìu, Vietnam (17)

Fig. 118
The Twelve Divinities, c. early 20th century
Handmade paper (repaired), bamboo sticks,
string, red fabric, 34¾ x 15¼ in.
Sán Dìu, Vietnam (16)

Fig. 119
The Diety of Early Chinese Writing, c. early 20th century
Handmade paper (repaired), bamboo sticks,
string, red fabric, 34¾ x 15¼ in.
Sán Dìu, Vietnam (9)

Fig. 120
Celestial Master Li, c. early 20th century
Handmade paper (repaired), bamboo sticks,
string, red fabric, 34¾ x 15¼ in.
Sán Dìu, Vietnam (10)

Fig. 121
Governor of the Earth Soldiers, c. early 20th century
Handmade paper (repaired), bamboo sticks,
string, red fabric, 34¾ x 15¼ in.
Sán Dìu, Vietnam (12)

Fig. 122
Buddha's Soldiers, c. early 20th century
Handmade paper (repaired), bamboo sticks,
string, red fabric, 34¾ x 15¼ in.
Sán Dìu, Vietnam (13)

Fig. 123
The God of Medicine, c. early 20th century
Handmade paper (repaired), bamboo sticks,
string, red fabric, 34¾ x 15¼ in.
Sán Dìu, Vietnam (8)

Fig. 124
Brahma and Indra, c. early 20th century
Handmade paper (repaired), bamboo sticks,
string, red fabric, 34¾ x 15¼ in.
Sán Dìu, Vietnam (11)

Fig. 125
The Guardian Deity of the Left, c. early 20th century
Handmade paper (repaired), bamboo sticks,
string, red fabric, 34¾ x 15¼ in.
Sán Dìu, Vietnam (15)

Fig. 126
The Guardian Deity of the Right, c. early 20th century
Handmade paper, bamboo sticks, string, red fabric, 32¼ x 15½ in.
Sán Dìu, Vietnam (18)

Fig. 127
Four Heavenly Messengers, c. early to mid-20th century
Handmade paper, bamboo sticks, 22¼ x 10¼ in.
Tày, Vietnam (115)

Fig. 128
Four Heavenly Messengers, c. early to mid-20th century
Handmade paper, bamboo sticks, 22¾ x 11 in.
Sán Dìu, Vietnam (117)

Fig. 129
Four Heavenly Messengers, c. early to mid-20th century
Handmade paper, bamboo sticks, 23½ x 12½ in.
Sán Dìu, Vietnam (118)

Fig. 130
Four Heavenly Messengers, c. early to mid-20th century,
paper, bamboo sticks, string, 25¾ x 12¼ in.
Cao Làn–Sán Chi (Sán Chay), Vietnam (94)

Fig. 131
Four Heavenly Messengers, c. early to mid-20th century
Handmade paper, bamboo sticks, 24 x 10½ in.
White Trouser (Quần Trắng) Yao, Vietnam (116)

Fig. 132
Four Heavenly Messengers, c. early to mid-20th century
Handmade paper, bamboo sticks, 19½ x 14¾ in.
Indigo Clad (Thanh-y) Yao, Vietnam (119)

Fig. 133
Four Heavenly Messengers, c. early to mid-20th century
Handmade paper, bamboo sticks, 30½ x 12¾ in.
White Trouser (Quần Trắng) Yao, Vietnam (120)

Fig. 134
Four Heavenly Messengers, c. early to mid-20th century
Handmade paper, bamboo sticks, 30¼ x 14¾ in.
Indigo Clad (Thanh-y) Yao, Vietnam (122)

Fig. 135
Four Heavenly Messengers, c. early to mid-20th century
Handmade paper, bamboo sticks, 24½ x 14¼ in.
Indigo Clad (Thanh-y) Yao, Vietnam (121)

Fig. 136
The Dragon Bridge of the Great Dao (part 1), c. late 19th–early
20th century. Handmade paper, bamboo sticks, 92 x 8 in.
Red Yao, China (52)

Fig. 137
The Dragon Bridge of the Great Dao (part 2), c. late 19th–early
20th century. Handmade paper, bamboo sticks, 92 x 8 in.
Red Yao, China (53)

Fig. 138
The Dragon Bridge of the Great Dao (part 3),
c. late 19th–early 20th century
Handmade paper, bamboo sticks, 92 x 8 in.
Red Yao, China (54)

Fig. 139
The Dragon Bridge of the Great Dao (part 4),
c. late 19th–early 20th century
Handmade paper, bamboo sticks, 92 x 8 in.
Red Yao, China (55)

Fig. 140
The Dragon Bridge of the Great Dao (left side), c. early 20th
century
Handmade mulberry paper, bamboo sticks, string, 105½ x 8½ in.
Red Yao, Vietnam (108) (107)

Fig. 141
Praying for Salvation for the Dead, c. mid-20th century
Handmade paper, c. 8⅝ x 417½ in.
Tày, Vietnam (0228a–q)

Fig. 142
Guiding the Soul, c. early to mid-20th century
Cotton, wood sticks, string, 121½ x 14¼ in.
Tày, Vietnam (316)

CHECKLIST CONTINUED

Fig. 143
Dragon Bridge of the Great Dao (detail), c. late 19th century
Handmade mulberry paper, bamboo sticks, string (repairs on rear), 14¼ x 121½ in.
Yao, China (317)

Fig. 144
Respectfully Welcoming the Saints, c. mid-20th century
Paper, wood sticks, string, copper wire, 137¾ x 9 7/8 in.
Sán Dìu, Vietnam (111) (112)

Fig. 145
Respectfully Welcoming the Buddha, c. mid-20th century
Paper, wood sticks, string, copper wire, 137¾ x 9 7/8 in.
Sán Dìu, Vietnam (114) (113)

Fig. 146
The First King of the Underworld, c. late 19th–early 20th century
Handmade paper, bamboo sticks, string, 30¼ x 12¼ in.
Tày, Vietnam (131)

Fig. 147
The Second King of the Underworld, c. late 19th–early 20th century
Handmade paper, bamboo sticks, string, 30¼ x 12¼ in.
Tày, Vietnam (132)

Fig. 148
The Third King of the Underworld, c. late 19th–early 20th century
Handmade paper, bamboo sticks, string, 30¼ x 12¼ in.
Tày, Vietnam (133)

Fig. 149
The Fourth King of the Underworld, c. late 19th–early 20th century
Handmade paper, bamboo sticks, string, 30¼ x 12¼ in.
Tày, Vietnam (134)

Fig. 150
The Fifth King of the Underworld, c. late 19th–early 20th century
Handmade paper, bamboo sticks, string, 30¼ x 12¼ in.
Tày, Vietnam (135)

Fig. 151
The Sixth King of the Underworld, c. late 19th–early 20th century
Handmade paper, bamboo sticks, string, 30¼ x 12¼ in.
Tày, Vietnam (136)

Fig. 152
The Seventh King of the Underworld, c. late 19th–early 20th century
Handmade paper, bamboo sticks, string, 30¼ x 12¼ in.
Tày, Vietnam (137)

Fig. 153
The Eigth King of the Underworld, c. late 19th–early 20th century
Handmade paper, bamboo sticks, string, 30¼ x 12¼ in.
Tày, Vietnam (138)

Fig. 154
The Ninth King of the Underworld, c. late 19th–early 20th century
Handmade paper, bamboo sticks, string, 30¼ x 12¼ in.
Tày, Vietnam (139)

Fig. 155
The Tenth King of the Underworld, c. late 19th–early 20th century
Handmade paper, bamboo sticks, string, 30¼ x 12¼ in.
Tày, Vietnam (140)

Fig. 156
Ritual robe, c. early 20th century
Handmade textile, embroidery, metal buttons, 43½ x 33 in.
Sán Chay, Vietnam (174)

Fig. 157
Ritual robe, c. early 20th century
Handmade textile and embroidery, 44 ¼ x 35 ½ in.
Cao Làn–San Chi (Sán Chay), Vietnam (319–320)

Fig. 158
Ritual robe, c. early 20th century
Handmade textile, embroidery, 42 x ¼ 30 in.
Tày, Vietnam (154–155)

Fig. 159
Ritual robe, c. late 19th century
Handmade textile, embroidery, 48 x 37½ in.
Sán Dìu, Vietnam (166–167)

Fig. 160
Ritual robe, c. late 19th century
Textile, embroidery, text, 47½ in.
Tày or Nùng, Vietnam (0126, 0128)

Fig. 161
Sleeveless robe, c. early 20th century
Textile, embroidery, 39 x 24 in.
Tight Trouser (Quần Chẹt) Yao, Vietnam (321)

Fig. 162
Ritual robe, c. late 19th–early 20th century
Handmade textile, embroidery, 45½ x 29 ¼ in.
Tày, Vietnam (156, 158)

Fig. 163
Ritual crown, c. late 19th century
Handmade paper, 8 x 7¼ in.
Tight Trouser (Quần Chẹt) Yao, Vietnam (163–164)

Fig. 164
Ritual crown, c. mid-20th century
Handmade paper, textile, 15½ x 9¼ in.
Tight Trouser (Quần Chẹt) Yao, Vietnam (189–190)

Fig. 165
Ritual crown, c. early to mid-20th century
Paper, textile, embroidery, string, 25¼ x 6½ in.
Tày, Vietnam (159–160)

Fig. 166
Ritual hat, c. early to mid-20th century
Textile, 6½ in
Nùng, Vietnam (244–245)

Fig. 167
Ritual hat, c. early to mid-20th century
Textile, 5¾ in.
Nùng, Vietnam (246)

Fig. 168
Head tie, c. early to mid-20th century
Textile, embroidery, c. 22 in.
Coin (Tiền) Yao, Vietnam (0119)

Fig. 169
Head tie, c. early to mid-20th century
Textile, embroidery, c. 22 in.
Coin (Tiền) Yao, Vietnam (0120)

Fig. 170
Robe, c. mid-20th century
Handmade textile, 49¾ x 58 in.
Coin (Tiền) Yao, Vietnam (178)

Fig. 171
Skirt, c. early to mid-20th century
Textile, 26 x 88 in.
Tight Trouser (Quần Chẹt) Yao, Vietnam (325)

Fig. 172
Legging, c. early 20th century
Handmade textile, embroidery, 40½ x 6 in.
Coin (Tiền) Yao, Vietnam (179)

Fig. 173
Legging, c. early 20th century
Handmade textile, embroidery, 40½ x 6 in.
Coin (Tiền) Yao, Vietnam (180)

Fig. 174
Cape and banner, c. late 19th–early 20th century
Colored fabric, beads, metal, silver and other thread, 38¼ x 32¾ in.
Tày, Vietnam (150)

Fig. 175
Headcloth, c. mid-20th century
Cotton textile, beads, threads, 15¼ x 23¼ in.
Tight Trouser (Quần Chẹt) Yao, Vietnam (186–187)

Fig. 176
Ritual hat, c. early 20th century
Tày, Vietnam (162)

Fig. 177
Ritual scepter, c. late 19th–early 20th century
Wood, 7⅝ in.
Tày, Vietnam (193)

Fig. 178
Ritual scepter, c. late 19th century
Wood, 5⅞ in.
Tày, Vietnam (0021–0023)

Fig. 179
Ritual scepter, c. late 19th century
Wood, 11⅝ in.
Yao, China or Vietnam (0026)

Fig. 180
Kuei scepter, c. early 20th century
Wood, 11½ in.
Sán Dìu, Vietnam (0106)

Fig. 181
Kuei scepter, c. early 20th century
Wood, 15⅝ in.
Sán Dìu, Vietnam (0109, rear of 0108)

Fig. 182
Kuei scepter, c. early 20th century
Wood, 16 in.
Tày or Sán Chay, Vietnam (0110)

Fig. 183
Kuei scepter, c. late 19th–early 20th century
Bone, 9⅝ in.
Tày, Vietnam (0112)

Fig. 184
Dagger with rattle, c. early 20th century
Metal, 20½ in.
Yao, Vietnam (227)

Fig. 185
Dagger with rattle, c. early 20th century
Metal, textile ribbons, 18¼ in.
Red Yao, Vietnam (233)

Fig. 186
Jade Emperor seal, c. late 19th–early 20th century
Wood, 3 in.
Sán Dìu, Vietnam (0065)

Fig. 187
Seal (Five Thunder Gods stamp), c. late 19th century or earlier
Metal, 2¼ in.
Tày, Vietnam (0063–0064)

Fig. 188
Money tree, c. early 20th century
Metal, paper residue, 14¼ in.
Sán Dìu, Vietnam (236)

Fig. 189
Money tree, c. late 19th–early 20th century
Metal, bronze bell, stick, 11¼ in. (finial), 42⅞ in. (with stick)
Sán Dìu, Vietnam (237)

CHECKLIST CONTINUED

Fig. 190
Seal, c. late 19th century
Wood, 1 ⅞ in.
Yao, China or Vietnam (0075)

Fig. 191
Printing block, c. early to mid-20th century
Wood, 5¾ in.
Red Yao, Vietnam (0045)

Fig. 192
Pan Hu stamp, c. late 19th–early 20th century
Wood and lacquer, 13⅞ in.
Nùng, Vietnam (0099)

Fig. 193
Printing block, c. early to mid-20th century
Wood, 14⅛ in.
Yao, China or Vietnam (0031)

Fig. 194
Printing block, c. early to mid-20th century
Wood, 15¾ in.
Coin (Tiền), Vietnam (0042)

Fig. 195
Printing block, c. early–mid-20th century
Wood, 14½ in.
Red Yao, Vietnam (0044)

Fig. 196
Mask (from a set of 27), dated 1936
Paper, bamboo sticks, string, 7⅝ in.
Yao (Mun), Vietnam (0169)

Fig. 197
Mask (from a set of 27), dated 1936
Paper, bamboo sticks, string, 7⅝ in.
Yao (Mun), Vietnam (0147)

Fig. 198
Mask, c. late 19th century
Wood, fur, red paper, 16½ in.
Coin (Tiền) Yao, China or Vietnam (226)

Fig. 199
Mask, c. late 19th–early 20th century
Wood, fur, bamboo, red paper, 13 in.
Yao, Vietnam (221)

Fig. 200
Mask, c. early 20th century
Wood, fur, 10½ in.
Yao, China or Vietnam (219)

Fig. 201
Mask, c. late 19th–early 20th century
Wood, fur, bamboo, nails, red paper, 13 in.
Yao, Vietnam (220)

Fig. 202
Mask, c. late 19th–early 20th century
Wood, fur, paper residue, string, 13½ in.
Yao, China (238)

Fig. 203
Mask, c. early to mid-20th century
Wood, fur, metal, string, paper, 14½ in.
Yao, Vietnam (224)

Fig. 204
Horn, c. early to mid-20th century
Water buffalo horn, 17 in.
Red Yao, Vietnam (289)

Fig. 205
Small hand drum (two-headed), c. late 19th–early 20th century
Terracotta, hide, textile, string, 22 in.
Cao Làn–Sán Chi (Sán Chay), Vietnam (287)

Fig. 206
Small hand drum, c. early 20th century
Wood, hide, metal tacks, fiber, 8¼ in.
Nùng, Vietnam (288)

Fig. 207
Pair of cymbals, c. early 20th century
Bronze, 5¾ in.
Cao Làn–Sán Chi (Sán Chay), Vietnam (300)

Fig. 208
Drum (double-sided), c. early to mid-20th century
Wood, wicker, hide, 14½ in.
Cao Làn–Sán Chi (Sán Chay), Vietnam (303)

Fig. 209
Gong, c. early 20th century
Bronze, 10⅜ in.
Cao Làn–Sán Chi (Sán Chay), Vietnam (302)

Fig. 210
Handbell, c. late 19th–early 20th century
Bronze, 4⅛ in.
Tày, Vietnam (293)

Fig. 211
Handbell, c. late 19th–early 20th century
Bronze with textile, 6⅜ in.
Nùng, Vietnam (294)

Fig. 212
Handbell, c. late 19th century
Bronze, 6⅛ in.
Nùng, Vietnam (291)

Fig. 213
Handbell, c. late 19th century
Bronze, 5¾ in.
Tày, Vietnam (290)

Fig. 214
Handbell, c. late 19th century
Bronze, 6⅞ in.
Tày, Vietnam (292)

Fig. 215
Oboe, c. late 19th–early 20th century
Wood, bronze, textile, 16¼ in.
Red Yao, Vietnam (0003)

Fig. 216
Statuette of Baby Buddha, c. early 20th century
Wood, 5¾ in
Sán Dìu, Vietnam (0095)

SELECTED BIBLIOGRAPHY

Alberts, Eli. *A History of Daoism and the Yao People of South China*. Youngstown, N.Y.: Cambria, 2006.

Aylward, Thomas F. *The Imperial Guide to Feng Shui and Chinese Astrology*. London: Watkins, 2007.

Bế Viết Đẳng, Nguyễn Khắc Tùng, et al. *Người Dao ở Việt Nam* [The Yao in Vietnam]. Hanoi: Social Science Publishers, 1971.

Birell, Anne. *Chinese Mythology: An Introduction*. Baltimore: Johns Hopkins University Press, 1993.

Brinker, Helmut, and Hiroshi Kanazawa. *Zen: Masters of Meditation in Images and Writings*. Zurich: Artibus Asiae, 1996.

Bokenkamp, Stephen. *Early Daoist Scriptures*. Berkeley: University of California Press, 1997.

Ceremonial Paintings of Northern Ethnic Minorities in Vietnam. Hanoi: Qũy Đông Sơn ngày nay, 2006.

Chu Thái Sơn and Hoàng Hoa Toàn. *Người Nùng* [The Nùng People]. Ho Chi Minh City: Youth Publications, 2006.

Chu Thái Sơn and Võ Mai Phương. *Người Dao* [The Yao People]. Ho Chi Minh City: Youth Publications, 2006.

Cleary, Thomas, trans. and ed. *Alchemists, Mediums, and Magicians: Stories of Taoist Mystics*. Boston: Shambhala, 2009.

Cooper, Jean C. *An Illustrated Introduction to Taoism: The Wisdom of the Sages*. Bloomington, Indiana: World Wisdom, 2010.

Cormerais, Jean-Pierre. *Les Chemises des Dieux: l'Univers Magique de la Peinture Yao*. Paris: Tribal héritage, 2011.

Cuevas, Bryan J. *Travels in the Netherworld*. Oxford: Oxford University Press, 2008.

Doãn Thanh and Lê Trung Vũ. *Truyện Cổ Người Dao* [The Legendary Stories of the Yao]. Hanoi: Ethnic Culture Publishing House, 1978.

Doan, Tuyen Thi. "The Reemergence of Spirit Mediums: Then Practice among the Tay in Contemporary Vietnam." Ph.D. diss., University of Washington, 2011.

Đặng Nghiêm Vạn. "Vai trò tôn giáo tộc người trong việc thống nhất ý thức cộng đồng người Dao" [The religious functions in unifying all the Yao communities], in Phan Hữu Dật et al., *The Culture and Social Development of the Yao*, pp. 126–134.

Đỗ Đức Lợi, ed. *Tập tục trong chu kỳ đời người của các tộc người ngôn ngữ Mông-Dao ở Việt Nam* [The Life Passes Ceremonies of the Hmong and Yao People in Vietnam]. Hanoi: Ethnic Culture Publishing House, 2002.

Dudbridge, Glen. *The Legend of Miao-shan*. London: Oxford University Press, 1978.

Fisher, Robert. *Buddhist Art and Architecture*. New York: Thames and Hudson, 1993.

Hanks, Jane Richardson, and Lucien Mason Hanks. *Tribes of the North Thailand Frontier*. New Haven: Yale University Southeast Asia Studies, 2001.

Hickman, Money L. "Notes on Buddhist Banners." *Boston Museum Bulletin* 71, no. 363 (1973), pp. 4–20.

Hoàng Bé, Hoàng Hữu Bình, et al. *Các Dân Tộc Tày Nùng ở Việt Nam* [The Tày and Nùng Nationalities in Vietnam]. Hanoi: Institute of Ethnography, 1992.

Hoàng Hựu. "Đôi nét liên quan đến tôn giáo của dân tộc Tày-Nùng, vai trò của thầy trò Tào trong ma chay, cúng bái" [Some major religious features of the Tày-Nùng: Roles of the Daoist Shaman priest and his acolytes in funeral rites]. *Tạp Chí Hán Nôm* [Journal of Han-Nom Study], no. 5 (96), 2009, pp. 54–57.

Hoàng Quý Quyền. "Tìm hiểu sơ bộ về những mặt nạ của người Dao" [The initial step of understanding the Yao's mask], in Phan Hữu Dật et al., *The Culture and Social Development of the Yao*, pp. 364–365.

Hoàng Quyết. *Từ Điển Văn Hóa Cổ Truyền Dân Tộc Tày* [Dictionary of Tày Tradition and Culture]. Ho Chi Minh City: Nxb Thanh Niên, 2012.

Huang, Shih-Shan Susan. *Picturing the True Form: Daoist Visual Culture in Traditional China*. Cambridge: Harvard University Press, 2012.

Institute of Anthropology. *The Yao People in Vietnam*. Hanoi: VNA Publishing House, 2007.

Katz, Paul R. *Images of the Immortal: The Cult of Lü Dongbin at the Palace of Eternal Joy*. Honolulu: University of Hawaii Press, 1999.

Kohn, Livia, ed. *Daoism Handbook*. Leiden: Brill, 2000.

Lã Văn Lô and Hà Văn Thư. *Văn hóa Tày Nùng* [Tày and Nùng Cultures]. Hanoi: Nxb Văn Hóa, 1984.

Lemoine, Jacques. *Yao Ceremonial Paintings*. Bangkok: White Lotus, 1982.

———. "Yao Religion and Society," in *Highlanders of Thailand*, ed. John McKinnon and Wanat Bhruksasri. Kuala Lumpur: Oxford University Press, 1983, 195–212.

———. "Yao Taoist Paintings." *Arts of Asia* (Jan–Feb, 1981): 61–71.

Lewis, Paul, and Elaine Lewis. *Peoples of the Golden Triangle: Six Tribes in Thailand*. New York: Thames and Hudson, 1984.

Little, Stephen. *Taoism and the Arts of China*. Berkeley: University of California Press, 2000.

Lý Hành Sơn. *Các nghi lễ chủ yếu trong chu kỳ đời người của nhóm Dao Tiền ở Ba Bể, Bắc Kạn* [The Main Ceremonies and Rituals in the Life of the Yao People in Ba Bể, Bắc Kạn]. Hanoi: Social Science Publishers, 2003.

Manson, Penelope. *History of Japanese Art*. 2nd ed. Upper Saddle River, NJ: Pearson Prentice Hall, 2005.

Nguyễn Khắc Tụng and Nguyễn Anh Cường. *Trang phục cổ truyền của người Dao ở Việt Nam* [The Yao Traditional Costumes in Vietnam] Hanoi: Social Sciences Publishing House, 2004.

Nguyễn Thị Yên. *Then Tày* [The Tày Shaman *Then*]. Hanoi: Social Sciences Publishing House, 2006.

Nguyen. "Images of Anatapindika and Ananda in Vietnamese Buddhist Tradition." *Arts of Asia* 36, no. 6 (Nov.–Dec, 2006): 114–125.

Nguyen, Van Huy, and Laurel Kendall, eds. *Vietnam: Journeys of Body, Mind, and Spirit*. Berkeley: University of California Press, 1997.

Phạm Đức Sĩ. *Vietnamese Ceremonial Paintings: Pham Duc Si's Collection, 2001–2009*. Hanoi: Icon Communications, 2009.

Phan Cẩm Thượng, Lê Quốc Việt, and Cung Khắc Lược. *Graphic Art of Vietnam*. Hanoi: Fine Arts Publishing House, 1999.

Phan Hữu Dật et al., eds. *Sự phát triển văn hóa, xã hội của người Dao hiện tại và tương lai: kỷ yếu hội thảo do Trung tâm khoa học xã hội và nhân văn quốc gia, phố hợp tổ chức tại Thành phố Thái Nguyên từ 12–15 tháng 12 năm 1995* [The Culture and Social Development of the Yao: The Present and the Future; Proceedings of the International Symposium, Thai Nguyen, December 1995]. Hanoi: Social Sciences Publications, 1998.

Phan Ngọc Khuê. *Lễ cấp sắc của người Dao Lô Giang ở Lạng Sơn* [The Ceremony of the Hanging Lamps of the Yao in Lô Giang, Lạng Sơn]. Hanoi: Culture and Information Publishing House, 2003.

———. *Taoist Paintings of North Vietnam*. Hanoi: Vietnam Fine Arts Publishing House, 2008.

———. "Tranh thờ của dân tộc Dao ở Bắc Bộ Việt Nam [The religious paintings of the Yao in northern Vietnam]," in Phan Hữu Dật et al. eds., *The Culture and Social Development of the Yao*, pp. 136–137.

Phillips, Quitman E. "Narrating the Salvation of the Elite: The Jōfukuji Paintings of the Ten Kings." *Ars Orientalis* 33 (2003), pp. 120–145.

Pourret, Jess G. *The Yao: The Mien and Mun Yao in China, North Vietnam, Laos, and Thailand.* Chicago: Art Media Resources, 2002.

Quang Huy, ed. *Ancient and Traditional Paintings of Vietnam*. Hanoi: Culture and Information Publishing House, 1995.

Schipper, Kristofer. *The Taoist Body*. Berkeley: University of California Press, 1993.

Soothill, William Edward and Lewis Hodous. *A Dictionary of Chinese Buddhist Terms*. Delhi: Motilal Banarsidass, 1977.

Teiser, Stephen F. *The Scripture on the Ten Kings and the Making of Purgatory in Medieval Chinese Buddhism*. Honolulu: University of Hawaii Press, 1994.

Thorp, Robert L., and Richard Ellis Vinograd. *Chinese Art and Culture*. New York: Harry N. Abrams, 2001.

Trần Bình, Ngọc Bích, et al., eds. *Fifty-Four Ethnic Groups in Vietnam*. Hanoi: VNA Publishing House, 2011.

Trần Hữu Sơn. *Sách Cổ Của Người Dao* [The Traditional Books of the Yao], vols. 1 and 2. Hanoi: Nxb Văn Hóa Dân Tộc, 2011.

———. "Sách cổ của người Dao ở Lào Cai—Di sản văn hóa có giá trị [The traditional books of the yao: the valuable cultural heritage]," in Phan Hữu Dật et al., eds. *The Culture and Social Development of the Yao*, pp. 173–174.

Triệu Thị Mai. *Hành trình đi tìm vía của pụt Ngạn* [The Journey of Searching the Shaman's Pụt Spirits]. Hanoi: Nxb Từ Điển Bách Khoa, 2008.

Võ, Mai Phương, and Clair Burkert. *Our Craft Traditions: A Yao Community in Sapa, Vietnam.* Hanoi: Vietnam Museum of Ethnology, 2001.

Vũ Khánh. *The Tày in Vietnam*. Hanoi: Vietnam News Agency Publishing House, 2009.

Vũ, Quốc Khanh, ed. *The Yao People in Vietnam*. Hanoi: VNA Publishing House, 2006.

Walters, Derek. *The Chinese Astrology Bible*. New York: Sterling, 2008.

Wu Hung. "Mapping Early Taoist Art: The Visual Culture of Wodoumi Dao," in Stephen Little, *Taoism and the Arts of China*, pp. 77–94.

Yang, Lihui, and Deming An. *Handbook of Chinese Mythology*. Santa Barbara: ABC-CLIO, 2005.

Yoke, Ho Peng. *Chinese Mathematical Astrology: Reaching Out to the Stars.* London: Routlege Curzon, 2003.

Yu, Anthony C., trans. and ed. *The Journey to the West*. 5 vols. Chicago: University of Chicago Press, 2012.

Yu, Chun-fang. "Guanyin: The Chinese Transformation of Avalokitesvara," in *Latter Days of the Law: Images of Chinese Buddhism, 850–1850.* Ed. Marsha Weidner. Honolulu: University of Hawaii Press, 1994, pp. 151–181.

Zhang, Webin, ed. *Dunhuang: A Centennial Commemoration of the Discovery of the Cave Library.* Beijing: Morning Glory, 2000.

Websites

四值功曹 [Si zhi gong cao]. http://baike.baidu.com/view/302166.htm (7/15/2013).

Tìm Hiểu Về Tứ Trực Công Tào [Helping Understand the Four Heavenly Messengers] http://huyenthuat.com/index.php/vi/dien-dan/48-d-o-giao/242-tim-hi-u-v-t-tr-c-cong-tao (7/15/2013).

God of Wealth. http://taiwanpedia.culture.tw/en/content?ID=4429 (6/4/2014).

APPENDIX SEQUENTIAL ARRANGEMENT OF AN EIGHTEEN-PAINTING SET

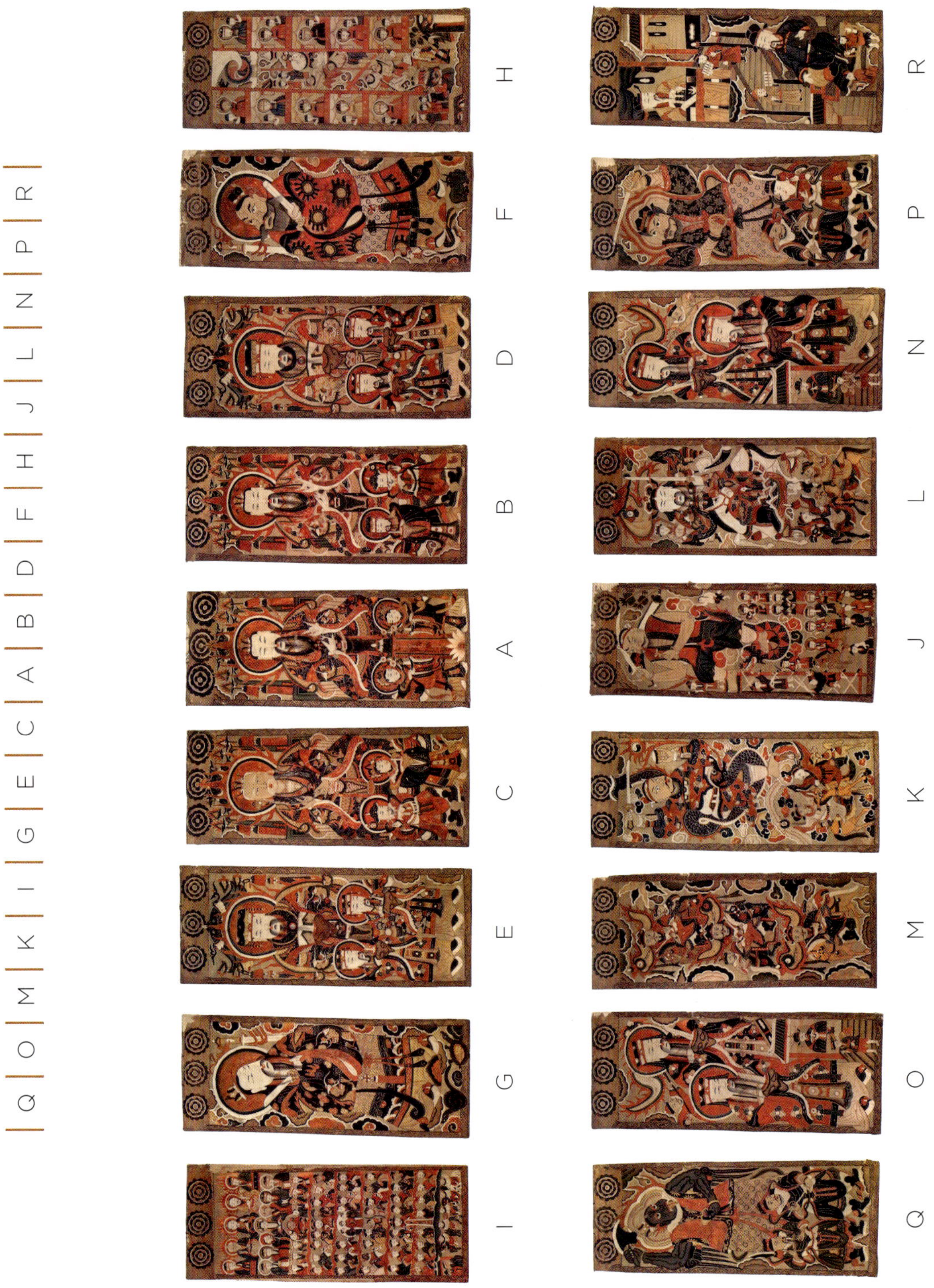